Katie McClymont , Bristol, 2014

THE COMMON GOOD AND
THE GLOBAL EMERGENCY

God and the Built Environment

Planning and architecture have to be understood in relation to climate change and peak oil, and the concept of the common good is key to understanding how important this is. Leading on from his previous book, *A Theology of the Built Environment*, T. J. Gorringe provides a theoretical and political framework of the common good, applying this to the built environment. This framework is used to discuss and highlight issues regarding place, transport, food and farming, and, as such, explains the relation of Christianity to the built world in which we live. Exploring new themes in the context of the concern about climate change and resource depletion, Gorringe provides an innovative account, covering a wide range of source matter and illustrating the connections between modern theology and ethics.

T. J. GORRINGE is Professor of Theological Studies at the University of Exeter. *A Theology of the Built Environment* (2002), his previous book with Cambridge University Press, was the first to reflect theologically on the built environment as a whole. He is also the author of *God's Just Vengeance: Crime, Violence and the Rhetoric of Salvation* (Cambridge, 1996).

THE COMMON GOOD AND THE GLOBAL EMERGENCY

God and the Built Environment

T. J. GORRINGE

CAMBRIDGE
UNIVERSITY PRESS

CAMBRIDGE UNIVERSITY PRESS
Cambridge, New York, Melbourne, Madrid, Cape Town, Singapore,
São Paulo, Delhi, Dubai, Tokyo, Mexico City

Cambridge University Press
The Edinburgh Building, Cambridge CB2 8RU, UK

Published in the United States of America by Cambridge University Press, New York

www.cambridge.org
Information on this title: www.cambridge.org/9781107002012

First published 2011

Printed in the United Kingdom at the University Press, Cambridge

A catalog record for this publication is available from the British Library

Library of Congress Cataloging in Publication data
Gorringe, T. J. (Timothy J.), 1946–
The Common Good and the Global Emergency : God and the Built Environment / T. J. Gorringe.
p.   cm.
Includes bibliographical references and index.
ISBN 978-1-107-00201-2 (hardback)
1. Common good – Religious aspects – Christianity.   2. Cities and towns – Religious aspects –
Christianity.   3. Human ecology – Religious aspects – Christianity.   I. Title.
BR115.P7G687   2011
261 – dc22   2010051437

ISBN 978-1-107-00201-2 Hardback

For Gill

A new politics of the common good has something to do with the project of building a common life, of shared citizenship. A lot of our public institutions – public libraries, public transportation, public parks and recreation centres . . . are also traditionally sites for the cultivation of a common citizenship, so that people from different walks of life encounter one another and so acquire enough of a sense of a shared life that we can meaningfully think of one another as citizens in a common venture.

Michael Sandel

Contents

vii

Figures

Preface

When *A Theology of the Built Environment* appeared in 2002 it was claimed that it was the first attempt to think theologically about the built environment as a whole. One reviewer challenged this claim, though without telling me where to look for rivals. Since then a number of books have appeared, most particularly Eric Jacobsen's excellent *Sidewalks in the Kingdom*, a most promising study by a young scholar. I am grateful to him for the parcel of second-hand books, which included J. H. Kunstler and Daniel Kemmis: he will see how much I have learned from them. Philip Sheldrake has beautifully explored the theological significance of space, and John Inge and David Brown of place, largely in relation to sacred space and building. Some of the essays in Sigurd Bergmann's *Architecture, Aesth/ethics, Religion* explore secular themes, though it too mostly deals with the sacred. Many articles on the theology of the built environment are now beginning to appear in learned journals, some in planning as well as theology. In general, however, the sacred–secular divide continues to appear self-evident: people are not convinced that 'the earth is the Lord's'. Although people take for granted the fact that the church has something to say about war and sexuality, and perhaps even economics (though this is more contentious), the idea that one can reflect theologically about the everyday built environment, and not about churches or temples, seems perplexing. It is worthwhile, therefore, once again to try and make the point.

After the book appeared I got to know Simon Fairlie and the Tinker's Bubble community. Simon did not like the book ('academic'), but every time we met he asked me if I had read Christopher Alexander. I knew only the article 'A City is not a Tree', which did not seem to me sufficiently revelatory to prompt further reading. However, the possibilities of prevarication are not endless, and I duly read Alexander's oeuvre: the results will be obvious. By and large Alexander is a prophet without honour. Some eco-architects say he does not respect the ecological imperative sufficiently.

I am sure, however, that the insights of the Pattern Language are indispensable towards the emergence of cultures in common (which are not
homogenised cultures) around the world. Following up footnotes also led
me to the Egyptian architect Hassan Fathy. Reading his work, so full of
humour, humility and wisdom, is to get a glimpse of that earlier world,
in twelfth-century Europe, where, while the military classes engaged in
power games, the intellectuals and artisans learned from each other and
largely agreed on fundamentals. So-called 'inter-faith dialogue' is as nothing
alongside sitting at the feet of such a great souled human being.

It was only after the book appeared that I started to teach a course on
theology and the built environment. The course has been taught from the
back of a lorry: visiting cities, towns and villages, talking to planners, and
sitting afterwards in churches, pubs and cafés to reflect on what we have
seen. I am immensely grateful to all the planning departments who have
given up time to talk to us when most of them are worked off their feet.
The material in this book on Plymouth, Milton Keynes, Poundbury and
Sherford all comes from these visits. In Milton Keynes Michael Synnot was
an inspirational guide. I am also grateful to the students, who all began
with perplexity and sometimes ended with it, but many of whom produced
brilliant work in reflecting on their home streets, towns and cities.

A number of universities and departments of theology and of planning
have responded to the first book. I am grateful to John de Gruchy in Cape
Town; to Charles Marsh and the University of Virginia; to Rob Furbey at
Sheffield; to Bob Scott and Mark Richardson at the Trinity Institute, New
York; and to Mark van der Schaaf in Minneapolis for arranging seminars
and conferences which utilised the work. Some of the material in Chapter 5
appeared in an earlier draft in the *International Journal of Public Theology*
and in *The Land*; in Chapter 6, *Theology* published an earlier draft of
material on public houses.

I had no intention of writing a second book on the theme. In 2004 I had
begun writing a book on the body, a topic which I have taught for many
years, when the death of my first wife intervened. I started to take this
up again in 2008, but after a few weeks a word from the Lord instructed
me with absolute clarity that I needed to return to the built environment.
Such a statement will be a gift to critical reviewers: I simply record it as
a fact. Demythologisers can translate it in terms of involvement with the
Transition Town movement and an increasing sense that climate change,
food and energy issues are going to be the key ethical issues of the coming
century. I have said something about the differences of emphasis between
this book and the first in the first chapter. Here I want only further to record

my debt to my daughter Iona, an inexhaustibly enthusiastic companion in walking streets, examining buildings and places and thinking about the issues.

The book is dedicated to Gill, with whom I am once again seeking to learn how to share a journey.

Epiphany 2010   TIM GORRINGE

CHAPTER I

The common good and the built environment

A TALE OF TWO CITIES

Siena is an ancient city but as we know it today it is largely the result of building undertaken over a sixty-year period, from 1287 onwards, by a group of nine magistrates, 'The Nine', from whom the nobility, judges and notaries were excluded. We know something about their ideology from the paintings which they commissioned for the room in which they met to deliberate, the 'Sala dei Nove': Lorenzetti's famous allegories of good and bad government, painted between 1338 and 1340 (Figure 1).

The room is rectangular, with windows to the south, and the fresco runs round the other three walls. The window thus functions to include the real world of Siena within the painting.

By means of this simple leap, practical politics (the actual 'good' government of 'The Nine' that takes place daily in the room) ideally merges with the painted allegorical Virtues (the figures surrounding the good Governor) and the sacred realm (in the form of the Mater Misericordia frescoed in the preceding room and embodied in the shape of the piazza outside) in a complex sequence of scenes that iconographically convey many symbolic readings simultaneously, while their novel realism speaks directly to the humblest petitioner.[1]

The north wall, facing the window, begins in the top left with a picture of Divine Wisdom hovering over Justice. In her left hand she holds a copy of Scripture; in her right the scales of distributive and commutative justice, the first dealing with the relation of parts and whole, the second with relations between persons. Cords from the scales of justice come down to

---

[1] D. Mayernik, *Timeless Cities: An Architect's Reflections on Renaissance Italy* (Oxford: Westview, 2003), p. 186. Twenty-five years before Lorenzetti, Simone Martini had painted the *Maesta* in the General Council Chamber, a painting of the Virgin Mary which likewise emphasised both Justice and subordination of the will of the individual to the common good. The inscription on the steps which lead to her throne read, 'The roses and lilies which spangle the fields of heaven do not delight me more than wise decisions.'

Figure 1. *The Allegory of Good Government,* 1338–40 (fresco) by Ambrogio Lorenzetti (1285–c.1348)

the figure of Concord, who twines them together and holds a carpenter's plane – a metaphor for the need to see that no one pursued their ambitions at the expense of others.[2] Sienese government took extraordinary steps to overcome the factionalism of big family loyalties, appointing yearly ombudsmen from outside the city to facilitate the task of government and making it illegal for them either to dine with, or receive gifts from, citizens.[3] Twenty-four elders – the elders of the book of Revelation transposed to fourteenth-century Siena to show that it anticipates the Heavenly City – pass the cords to Ben Commun, the Common Good, in whose right hand the cord ends. Common Good sits like a judge on a long bench flanked on one side by Peace, Fortitude and Prudence and on the other by Magnanimity, Temperance and Justice. The theological virtues of Faith, Charity

---

[2] D. Norman, 'The Paintings of the Sala dei Nove', in D. Norman (ed.), *Siena, Florence and Padua: Art, Society and Religion 1280–1400*, vol. II (New Haven: Yale University Press, 1995), p. 157.

[3] The podestà, or powerful one, had to reside in a different *terzo* from his predecessor and was not allowed to receive gifts from citizens or to eat with them. He was not to move more than one day's journey from the city. He was normally chosen from a cadre of men from Lombardy and Emilia. When his term of office came to an end he had to stay in the city for at least a week while his financial affairs were investigated, and this was no mere formality. Sometimes pay was withheld or docked if conditions had not been properly fulfilled or damage had been done to communal property. D. Waley, *Siena and the Sienese in the Thirteenth Century* (Cambridge University Press, 1991), p. 44.

and Hope hover above.[4] At the bottom of the painting an inscription runs, 'Wherever this holy virtue – Justice – rules, she leads many souls to unity, and these, so united, make up the Common Good.'

On the east wall is a depiction of good government. Good government provides security: within the city walls people get married, build, go to school, weave, make shoes, bring in food and drive in sheep. A group of girls perform a dance to a tambourine.[5] Outside the walls, presided over by Securitas, who hangs an offender, people farm and grow the crops with which the city will be fed, hunt and carry goods in peace. The text below the picture celebrates Justice, the chief of the virtues, rendering to everyone their due and securing peace.

The opposite wall depicts the effects of bad government. A scroll over the painting says, 'Where justice is bound nobody struggles for the Common Good or fights for law, but rather permits the rise of tyranny, which has no desire to do anything against the base nature of the vices which are here united with it, in order to give fuller rein to evil.' Tyranny here is flanked by the vices – Cruelty, Treason, Fraud, Fury, Division and War, while Pride, Avarice and Vainglory take the place of the theological virtues. Justice is bound and there are looting, rape and destruction. Fear replaces Security. Under bad government the land is uncultivated and then, of course, the people starve.[6] The text below the painting notes that where Justice is bound the common good is lost.

The painting has been called 'a distillation of Augustinian and Thomist thought'.[7] Thomist thought, it is probably fair to say, was the leading ideology in Italy, and even Europe, at the time, and it was especially dominant in Siena. The vast Dominican church of San Domenico had been begun in 1226, not long after the founding of the Dominican order, and guarded the entrance to the city from the east. Siena's most famous preacher, San Bernadino, who preached in the Campo to huge audiences, was a Dominican. Its most famous saint, Catherine, was a third-order Dominican and is buried in the Dominican church. This did not mean that Siena was a theocracy. On the contrary, thirteenth- and fourteenth-century Siena blurred the distinction between sacred and secular. 'Just as the ostensibly secular Palazzo Pubblico in the central Piazza del Campo embodied sacred messages', comments David Mayernik, 'the Dominicans in their house were conversely entrusted with secular responsibility.'[8] Thomism had a

---

[4] J. Hook, *Siena: A City and its History* (London: Hamish Hamilton, 1979), p. 86.
[5] Norman thinks they are young men, or more precisely itinerant professional entertainers. 'The Paintings of the Sala dei Nove', p. 161.
[6] Hook, *Siena*, p. 90.   [7] Ibid., p. 82.   [8] Mayernik, *Timeless Cities*, p. 190.

sophisticated political theology, at the heart of which lay the idea of the
common good. Dominican theologians had learned from Aristotle that
the good life is a life in common. 'Even if the good is the same for the
individual and the city', Aristotle had written, 'the good of the city is the
greater and more perfect thing to attain and to safeguard. The attainment
of the good for one person alone is, to be sure, a source of satisfaction; yet
to secure it for a nation and for cities is nobler and more divine.'[9] Aquinas
glossed this in Christian terms by arguing that God is the common good
of all things and all reality, even stone, 'loves the common good of the
whole more than its own particular good'.[10] An intense discussion about
the nature of the common good ran throughout the thirteenth century,
in the course of which Aristotle's insights were amplified by those of
Augustine and of Scripture. Aquinas, for example, understood the common
good of human society partly in terms of the unity of order, through
which the mutual relation of individuals in peace and harmony gives the
means of securing their ultimate goal and partly in terms of the unity of
goodness so that the happiness of the life of virtue is the goal of every
individual's activity.[11] When 'The Nine' were re-ordering the city Remigio
de Girolami was writing about the common good in nearby Florence,
arguing that the common good of political community must be defined
as peace and harmony.[12] The emphasis on security in Lorenzetti's painting
shows that he has learned this lesson: his vision of the common good is
informed by an Augustinian sensibility only too aware of the evil that
men do.

As Lorenzetti suggests, the re-ordering of Siena by 'The Nine' took
the common good as a central theme. 'The Nine' of course constituted an
oligarchy, and 'the common good' had no implication, either for them or for
Aquinas and the Dominican theologians, of equality. It did, however, mean
that everyone was *included* in the community. Octavio Paz has argued that
hierarchical societies do better than egalitarian ones at including culturally
different groups in a common moral order because they can give and accept
moral meaning to different levels of wealth and power. Some are poor and
weak but all are included in a common social body where the strong and

---

[9] Aristotle, *Nicomachean Ethics*, 1094b, in *Complete Works*, ed. J. Barnes (Cambridge University Press, 1984), vol. II, p. 1728.

[10] Aquinas, *Summa theologiae*, 60 vols. (London: Blackfriars in association with Eyre and Spottiswoode, 1964–81), 2a2ae 26.3, vol. XXXIV, p. 127.

[11] M. S. Kempshall, *The Common Good in Late Medieval Political Thought* (Oxford University Press, 1999), p. 127.

[12] Ibid., p. 338.

rich have special obligations to look out for others.[13] Equal justice before the law was insisted on. The city was divided into thirds, and each *terzo* had a magistrate whose job it was to defend the poor. These Advocates were paid for by the commune. There was also an energetic effort to see both that inexpensive food was available and that the city had adequate water (though there was not adequate sanitation – Alberti commented that the city stank throughout the year!). In other words, the common good meant making sure that the grounds for an adequate life together were established.

But second, the common good included the beautification of the city. No less a person than San Bernadino noted 'how vital to the city are the arts and crafts and how useful it is when they are legitimately exercised . . . This is our foundation, and we shall see that it is impossible to live well, if the arts and crafts are not properly exercised.'[14]

'The Nine' undertook a huge public building enterprise, including parks and the extension of the Cathedral, 'for the honour of the commune of Siena, and for the beauty of the city'.[15] Because there was no rigid distinction between secular and sacred the Cathedral was understood as 'the mirror of all citizens'. 'All the iconographic and decorative schemes of the Duomo are civic in inspiration.'[16] 'In no area of civic government . . . did the Sienese mania for corporate decision-making manifest itself so consistently and so regularly over so long a period as it did in the building of the cathedral. And such corporate decision-making was bound to have artistic and cultural consequences.'[17]

Siena is, of course, most famous not for its cathedral but for the great market place, formed where the three hills on which the city is built converge (Figure 2). The Campo, says Judith Hook, 'is one of the most successful uses of space in any city, with an articulation which is unique'.

Both an autonomous and a total work of art, every element is essential to the whole, and no one part has any artistic value without the rest. It is a perfect example of urbanisation, created at a time when shape and proportion were determined neither by a surviving classical model . . . nor by the rationalizing, linear demands of renaissance architecture which it was early enough to escape. It was rather an intuitive, intentional adaptation to the needs of the medieval town. Reflecting the corporate organization of Siena, the Campo was the deliberately designed centre

---

[13] Quoted in R. Bellah, R. Madsen, W. Sullivan, A. Swidler and S. Tipton, *Habits of the Heart: Individualism and Commitment in American Life* (Berkeley: University of California Press, 2008), p. 206.
[14] Hook, *Siena*, p. 88. [15] Ibid., p. 36. [16] Ibid., p. 60. [17] Ibid., p. 59.

Figure 2. Piazzo del Campo, Siena

of the secular and administrative life of the city, distinct from, but always related to, its religious heart which lay in the area around the cathedral.[18]

In terms of Thomist theology, with its belief that grace perfects nature, grounded in the analogy of being, we have to think not of a circle with one centre, but of an ellipse with two foci – the Cathedral and the Campo. Certainly the meaning of the common good is enunciated by the Cathedral: there we learn what the wisdom and justice which inform the common good are; but they are instantiated in the Campo and the Palazzo Pubblico. There is no sacred and secular divide of the type familiar since the eighteenth century. Indeed, because the common good is grounded in God, the origin and end of all things, it embraces all creation.

The Campo was large enough for the whole citizen body to meet, whether to hear a sermon, celebrate a feast or witness an execution. It was the place where food was distributed during famines. No one was allowed to bear arms in it. It was 'a physical expression of the ideal of good government, of substitution of love for city in place of loyalty to faction'.[19] Building regulations ensured harmony without uniformity. The private palaces which bordered the Campo were completed by the Palazzo

---

[18] Ibid., p. 72.   [19] Ibid., p. 79.

Pubblico, which had the highest tower, thus symbolising the priority of the common good over any individual fortune. The tower's bell marked the curfew, summoned councils and signalled the lunch break. The very built form of the Palazzo Pubblico was supposed to represent the themes of good government, with the ombudsman or podestà in one wing, 'The Nine' in another and the Treasury and the General Council in between. At the same time, 'from the beginning the Palazzo was conceived of as an aesthetic object, as a work of art, expressing the aspirations of the Sienese people'.[20] The paintings by Martini and Lorenzetti which adorned it were thought of not as decoration but as a proper part of the common good.

Contrast this with the rebuilding of another small and ancient city five hundred years later, the city of Exeter in which I live. In his catalogue of the buildings of England Nicolas Pevsner comments on the charm of pre-war Exeter, which had a jumble of medieval streets such as York has preserved. This was changed with one of the 'Baedeker raids' in 1942. The bombs fortunately missed the Cathedral, but they destroyed almost the whole of the heart of the old city. Thomas Sharp, the author of one of the two best-known books on town planning of the day, was brought in to advise on rebuilding. Throughout Britain rebuilding was poorly done, partly because of lack of money but even more because architects lacked any confident and beautiful vernacular to appeal to (I shall say more about this in Chapter 10). However, Sharp was responsible for one of the first pedestrian precincts to be built in Britain, 'Princesshay', so called because it was opened by the future Queen Elizabeth II.[21] The development was small-scale and fairly charmless, used mostly by local shops. The precinct gave out on to Bedford Square, where the largest building was the Post Office, an important place in welfare state Britain, the place where people went to collect their pensions, often to bank their savings and to obtain dog licences and TV licences, as well as to post letters and parcels and to send telegrams. The Square, in the very heart of town, was a significant public space. Demonstrators gathered there, people sang carols at Christmas, charities set up their stalls, and when farmers' markets came into fashion this was where they were held.

Some time in the next fifty years this complex was acquired by 'Land Securities', a company which was founded in 1944 and made its money, initially, in developing bomb-damaged cities and now gets its return from

---

[20] Ibid., p. 86.
[21] 'Hay' is Devon dialect for 'hedge' or 'boundary'. So there are a Southernhay, a Northernhay and a Friernhay in Exeter. The name was a compliment to the future monarch.

rents in inner-city areas, and which actively redevelops them to increase this income. The rental value of the post-war scheme could not have been great, and, as the Millennium approached, a complete redevelopment was proposed. The plan was displayed in Bedford Square and attracted much local interest and even greater opposition. The first plan was seen off, but a second was at once put forward, the main difference being that the new plan was now, according to the best Jane Jacobs orthodoxy, mixed-use. The same display, the same request for comment – which was as far as 'consultation' went – the same opposition, but this time the proposal was accepted, the bulldozers moved in and in due course the new Princesshay was opened. Visually the new development is an improvement on the old. The architects have opened up some powerful views of the Cathedral, their line is varied and not dominated by the right angle, and there is variety of finish. However, what has been lost is public space. Princesshay is now discreetly policed by private security guards. It is not possible for homeless people to sell *The Big Issue* there. There are no small shops, and the precinct is dominated by chain stores. The farmers' market was turfed out to a location at the edge of town where it cannot survive. The Post Office was moved from its previous central position to somewhere where it can be accessed only by an escalator. Its previously busy shop has already been shut down. There seems to be an assumption that a café culture, a culture of affluence, constitutes the public realm.[22] The year after the development opened the New Economics Foundation judged Exeter to be the 'clone town' of Britain – the city centre with the fewest independent shops.

The obvious difference between these two redevelopments is that in the latter there is an assumption that consumption replaces the common good. Whereas the city of Siena owned the Campo and built it 'for the honour of the commune of Siena, and for the beauty of the city', Land Securities redeveloped Exeter, like hundreds of thousands of redevelopments over the past forty years, to make sure its shareholders got the best return on their investment.

Is there a connection between commitment to the common good and the beauty of cities like Siena? David Mayernik thinks there is. 'What Florence and Siena most deeply share', he writes, 'is that they saw their urban forms, and especially their skylines, as directly representing the hierarchy of their collective civic values.'

---

[22] When I asked a taxi driver what he thought of the new development he replied robustly that he had never been there. 'It's not for the likes of us' was his comment. He and his family shop and take their refreshment in the old and still working-class area of St Thomas.

This is truly remarkable to us – who have effectively surrendered our cities' skylines to chance and developers for the last hundred years and more, surrendering thereby any opportunity to make them speak in other than economic terms . . . Cities that speak must be designed, and . . . their forms can speak eloquently, like an accomplished orator, both in plan (walls, streets and squares) and in profiles or skyline. But the job of the orator, as Cicero and Plato would have it, was as much concerned with what to say as with how to say it; what our cities have to say is all of our responsibility to decide, or else it will be decided by default.[23]

Loss of meaning is at the heart of his diagnosis of what is wrong with our own cities.

Forms that arise without meaning are arbitrary and therefore at best meaningless. At worst they are bearers of meanings we may not endorse (consider the cynical message of the Manhattan skyline, where the city's hierarchy of values, if it matches the heights of the buildings, is solely economic in scale). In noble cities redolent with meaning we find the best of our human capacity to intervene in the world and leave behind a legacy that allows our children to most fully live the good life.[24]

Mayernik is arguing that we cannot build our towns and cities, or indeed even our houses, well without an idea of 'common civic values'. I want to elaborate that suggestion in terms of the idea of the common good and I want to begin by asking whether the language of the common good any longer makes sense.

THE COMMON GOOD IN A MULTICULTURAL SOCIETY

In their reflections on the common good the Dominican theologians drew on a long tradition which they debated, refined and amended. In particular they drew on Aristotle, who taught that human beings are by nature communal animals, and that they 'by nature' seek the good life together. The polis was a fact of nature because human beings were not self-sufficient and the political community was understood as a common project. What they meant by the common good was the question of how to identify the true human end, something which Aristotle identified above all with the practice of justice. We have seen how Lorenzetti interpreted it. The common good ultimately derives from the Divine Wisdom, or the Holy Spirit, which inspires that justice which 'brings many souls to unity'. This understanding of the common good, as we have seen, lay behind the rebuilding of Siena. It expressed a 'culture in common', to use Raymond

---

[23] Mayernik, *Timeless Cities*, p. 194.   [24] Ibid., p. 234.

Williams' term, which found architectural expression in both city and Cathedral.

There are a number of questions to put to the idea of the common good, and in this chapter I begin by asking whether such a vision is of any relevance in a multicultural situation where different ethnicities, religions and views of the world have to learn to live together cheek by jowl. Can we agree on the 'true human end' which ought to shape our collective endeavour? The violent rhetoric of the 'clash of civilisations' and of radical Islamism would suggest we cannot. Is not the best we can hope for in that situation the ability to live together with tolerance? Bhikhu Parekh has argued that multicultural societies throw up problems that have no parallel in history. 'They need to find ways of reconciling the legitimate demands of unity and diversity, achieving political unity without cultural uniformity, being inclusive without being assimilationist, cultivating among their citizens a common sense of belonging while respecting their legitimate cultural differences, and cherishing plural cultural identities without weakening the shared and precious identity of shared citizenship.'[25] Wherever there have been great cities, of course, there has been a plurality of cultures. The difference today, we could argue, is that in Western polities at least, there is both a legal and a cultural obligation to respect the rights of the other. In this situation is 'shared citizenship' all that we have? By the latter I take it that we mean such things as governance, the economy and transport, but even here some suggest that very little can be agreed in practice. To such scepticism the economist Albino Barrera suggests three minimum conditions for specifying the common good: the maintenance of justice, the nurturing of interpersonal relationships and a conscious effort towards a fair division of shared resources.[26] He thinks of the common good in terms of the instantiation of a society of due order in which not simply criminal justice but the justice of exchange and the justice which respects fundamental needs of all people are honoured.[27] A working democracy, we could say, is a society which, whilst far from perfect, is a society where these issues are at least acknowledged and where attempts to realise them are consistently made. In his 2009 Reith Lectures Michael Sandel argued for 'a new politics of the common good' which would prioritise 'the infrastructure

---

[25] B. Parekh, *Rethinking Multiculturalism: Cultural Diversity and Political Theory* (Basingstoke: Palgrave, 2000), p. 343.

[26] A. Barrera, *Economic Compulsion and Christian Ethics* (Cambridge University Press, 2005), p. 152.

[27] These are the Aristotelian ideas of justice taken up by Aquinas: commutative justice (equivalence in exchange) and distributive justice (maintaining the rights of every member of the community).

of civic life'.[28] Beyond due order and such infrastructure, I would argue, we should not underestimate the possibility and the power of the emergence of 'cultures in common'. In the first place we have examples of the way in which sub-cultural integrity may be preserved whilst sharing the aesthetics of a larger culture: think of Sephardic and Ashkenazi Judaism, ways of life which preserved religious integrity but both shared with and contributed to the larger culture. Second, and anecdotally, my own experience of being part of a family which is both Hindu and Christian, British and Sri Lankan (an experience which I note is, mutatis mutandis, very widely shared), suggests that cultures in common run much deeper than merely shared citizenship, and includes many aspects of taste, including food, fashion, film, music and views about architecture. I therefore want to suggest that the mixture of ethics, aesthetics and applied technology which is planning largely cuts across cultural divides. Thus in Cape Town, Jews, Christians, Hindus and Muslims, black and white, can agree on those aspects of the city which need change (townships), and on what adequate and gracious provision for everyone might look like. The disagreement is about the political process needed to realise that. In broad terms, I believe, what we call a multicultural society is capable of a shared view of the good which can take form in the built environment, and I shall be giving examples of this throughout the book and in particular in Chapter 6, on public space. In this sense I believe that the Thomistic idea of the common good, in terms of shared vision, is still possible. I turn now, however, to sketch the way in which theology may develop the idea of the common good in relation to the built environment.

THEOLOGY, THE COMMON GOOD AND THE BUILT ENVIRONMENT

'The extent to which architecture was anathematized by Christianity', writes John Onians, 'has seldom been appreciated by historians... The Scriptures are clear: building is bad; even erecting a house for God is difficult to justify.'[29] The Scriptures are clear only, we have to respond, given a particular way of reading them. I hope to show not only that is architecture not anathematised, but that there are clear theological imperatives as to how we should build. Why, then, is there such a silence about the built environment in the Christian tradition? In *A Theology of the Built*

---

[28] M. Sandel, 'A New Politics of the Common Good', BBC Radio 4, 30 June 2009.
[29] J. Onians, *Bearers of Meaning: The Classical Orders in the Middle Ages and the Renaissance* (Cambridge University Press, 1988), p. 113.

Environment I proposed a number of reasons for this. These might include the influence of a Platonising metaphysic in the church, which valorised eternal verities over mere material things; the use of religion as an opiate; and the growth of the sacred–secular divide, which included ideas of sacred and secular space and reserved theological comment for the former. Disneyworld's Tomorrowland, says Howard Kunstler, represents a denatured life of endless leisure, where the only purpose of existence is the eventual permanent escape from planet Earth to colonize other worlds. 'It is, of course', he adds, 'another version of evangelical Protestantism's dull preoccupation with the hereafter, as well as its cultivated hatred for the things of this world (such as the dignity of work) – otherwise why be so anxious to leave the planet?'[30] In addition we can note that even in the homes of the rich standards of comfort were never very high, as we know from Erasmus' complaints about his stay with Thomas More, or Parson Woodforde's diary, and so perhaps there was a kind of Stoicism at best, or fatalism at worst, about the built environment. Yet what eighteenth-century builders like Nash were doing, or what critics like Cobbett were saying about the homes of the poor, seems to contradict this. The silence remains puzzling.

The silence is all the more strange because concern with the built environment springs from the most central core of Christian faith. Thus we have theological arguments around the use of icons which insist that 'matter matters'. Where would that apply more profoundly than in the houses in which we live and the settlements we shape? We have the centrality of the everyday to our Scriptures, so memorably emphasised by Auerbach and more recently by liberation theology, so that all life, in all its aspects, is a sacred realm. This is sacramentally set out in the eucharist, which lies at the heart of our liturgy. We have the recognition by the Priestly Writer that artistic and indeed architectural creativity is the gift of the Creator Spirit (Exod. 31). From the incarnation comes our concern with human equality, the fact that every person is made in Christ's image. That this had implications in law was early recognised, but not its implications in the built environment. We have the Calvinist insistence on the lordship of Christ over all life, reiterated at Barmen, which of course includes the built environment. And if eschatology is fundamentally about hope then this applies to the built environment as to all other areas of human existence. Again, if we open any book on architecture or town planning we find anthropological assumptions, and therefore ethical assumptions, immediately.

[30] J. H. Kunstler, *The Geography of Nowhere* (New York: Simon & Schuster, 1993), p. 226.

To talk of values is to talk of a culture's account of its priorities. What does it value and why? The built environment is a peculiarly sensitive barometer of the values of a culture, as Lewis Mumford illustrates again and again in *The City in History*. For example, the early Mesopotamian city, 'with its buttressed walls, its ramparts and moats, stood as an outstanding display of ever-threatening aggression, which achieved lethal concentrations of suspicion and vengeful hatred and non-cooperation in the proclamation of kings'.[31] In fifth-century Athens noble poverty was more esteemed than ignoble wealth, and the houses of rich and poor could hardly be distinguished. What made the brilliance of Athens possible eluded analysis and turned into 'a concentration in stone'. What took its place was the Hellenistic city, 'sanitary, orderly, well organized, aesthetically unified; but grossly inferior in its capacity for fostering creative activity. From the fourth century on buildings began to displace men.'[32] Such value judgements accompany the entire history of the city but the problem today is that, as John Tomlinson notes, echoing MacIntyre, the failure of modernity is a specifically cultural one, namely the inability to decide what people should value, what they should believe in and what sense they ought to make of their everyday lives.[33] If that analysis is right, then it is impossible to build well in such a situation. Conversely, good building will emerge as part of ethical regeneration, finding our feet again. Ethics I take to be the conversation of the human race about its common project, about where it is going and how it is going to get there. Theological ethics, in all of its diversity, is part of that conversation.

A Theology of the Built Environment was an attempt to energise what was at best a very partial conversation. Could there perhaps be, as with so-called 'Just War' theory, a set of guidelines which Christians brought with them to the discussion of the built environment? In that book I concentrated on the vernacular and community empowerment as the direction in which Christian theology seemed to lead. I continue to believe that these emphases are essential, and I have reiterated them, especially in Chapter 10. I have not repeated the material about the ownership of land, not because I think it is no longer important, but because I have nothing to add: I take the earlier discussion for granted. However, there were other areas in the earlier book which were either not sufficiently explored or not explored at all: these include pedigreed architecture, town planning, transport, place and public space. In the chapter on housing I paid little attention to slums, and

[31] L. Mumford, *The City in History* (Harmondsworth: Penguin, 1991), p. 57.   [32] Ibid., p. 200.
[33] J. Tomlinson, *Cultural Imperialism* (London: Continuum, 1991), p. 169.

in relation to the vernacular I had not come across Hassan Fathy, whose work ought to be required reading for any aspiring architect. Sustainability was a key concern of the earlier book but involvement with the Transition Town movement and the debate around climate change have sharpened my concerns here. It has accordingly moved from the final chapters to the second, and informs the entire argument. The themes of grace and the common good emerged as the leading themes in the reflection sessions in the built environment classes that I began after the publication of that book, as we tried to make sense of what we had seen, and I have tried to structure the argument around them. The earlier book was largely written in Dundee. The move to Devon meant a much closer engagement with the farming community and eventually taking on a smallholding. This led to an increasing interest in the production of food, reflected in an earlier small book on food and farming and taken up here. The issue of how we are going to feed eight or nine billion is certainly one of the key questions of the next century and in my view an ethical and social question before it is a technological one. But in what sense is the concern properly theological?

For Christians, as the Dominican theologians make clear, the idea of the common good springs out of and returns to the doctrine of God: this is its 'circular flow'. In the light of the story of Christ, and in the light of the stories that story presupposes (i.e the Tenakh), we understand by the word 'God' the creativity which is love, or the love which is creativity, which stands at the beginning and end of all things. Christianity has classically articulated this in terms of the doctrine of the Trinity. Reflecting on a threefold narrative of revelation, in Israel, in Jesus and at Pentecost, four centuries of intense argument and discussion came to the view that 'God' was to be understood as a pattern of relationships. The claim that 'God is love' was to be construed as saying that God was relationship in Godself, a relationship in which, as the sixth-century Athanasian creed put it, 'there is none afore and none after, but one perfect equality'. This has immense consequences if, as is further claimed, human beings are made in the image of God. It means in the first instance that radical individualism is not a possibility for Christians, for to be in the image of God is to be constituted by relationship. There are good reasons to be sceptical of community, but such reasons are overridden, for Christians, by revelation, according to which we cannot be properly human outside community. This challenges the idea, taken for granted since Adam Smith, that human beings are primarily rational utility maximisers, and that altruism is in short supply. Not so, Christian theology claims. In fact, we truly flourish only in community (though the possibility and the need to withdraw from time to time are recognised). But second, as the nineteenth-century Christian socialists pointed out, we are created in the image of God, in whom there is 'one perfect equality'. This constitutes an out-and-out challenge to all hierarchical views, or to neo-Darwinian celebrations of the relation of the strong and the weak. The doctrine of God, therefore, has obvious implications for the environment we build. To the extent that the built environment instantiates injustice (and it does at every turn), then what this understanding of God leads to is a liberation theology, a theology which understands the petitions of the Lord's Prayer to be about the strong sense of the common good. As Leonardo Boff has argued, a theology of liberation is also a theology of grace, for there can be no freedom outside the divine self-gifting. A clearer understanding of that has resulted in the emphasis of the present book.

A further implication of Trinitarian theology for the built environment was spelled out by Karl Barth, who, as long ago as 1937, already initiated a 'spatial turn' in theology. The origin of all space, according to him, is to be found in the Trinitarian relations. It is the fact that God is present to Godself, that there is a divine proximity and remoteness, which is the basis and presupposition of created proximity and remoteness.[34] God's omnipresence is to be understood primarily as a determination of God's love, in so far as God is not only one, unique and simple, but as such is present to Godself and therefore present to everything which by God is outside God.[35]

Drawing on the biblical language which talks of God's own place, Barth outlined a theology of divine spatiality which offers a theological grounding for all forms of created space, and therefore for the built environment. Barth argues that it is God's 'eminent spatiality' which grounds our own created spatiality. Space, in other words, is not something contingent, something which will one day be annihilated and 'be no more', because it has its true and intrinsic ground in God. God is present to other things, and is able to create and give them space, because God in Godself possesses space apart from everything else.[36] What truth, Barth asks, could correspond to phrases like 'in Christ', 'in God' and 'in the Spirit' if God were not genuinely and primordially spatial? 'If it is not an incidental or superfluous belief that we can obtain space from God and find space in him, but a truth which is decisive for the actuality of creation, reconciliation and redemption and the trustworthiness of the Word of God, we cannot evade the recognition

---

[34] K. Barth, *Church Dogmatics*, vol. II/1 (Edinburgh: T. & T. Clark, 1957), p. 463.
[35] Ibid., p. 464.   [36] Ibid., p. 474.

Table 1 *A Trinitarian theology of the built environment*

	God the Creator	God the Reconciler	God the Redeemer
Known in	Order	Embodiment	Creativity
Built environment correlate	Planning	Structuring community	Utopian vision
Theological/ethical reflection	Values which underlie planning	Priority of life together	Nature of the human home
Realisation	Common good Human scale	'Breaking barriers': race – ghettoes class – social housing gender – patriarchal space	Gracious building and planning
Core concept	Ecology	Place	Empowerment

that God himself is spatial.'[37] Equally, we could not think of our own space being redeemed or reconciled if there were not space in God.

Christian reflection on the Trinity in the fourth and fifth centuries appealed to two basic rules, or grammar. First, it is obvious that the doctrine of the Trinity does not mean that there are 'three Gods'. God is God, and cannot be divided. However, Christians argued that it might be 'appropriate' to speak of one or other person of the Trinity in relation to different aspects of the divine work. In relation to the built environment these appropriations might be mapped as in Table 1.

God the Creator brings order out of chaos, and is therefore the origin of all constructive planning; from creation springs the strong sense of the common good which grounds the common treasury and the idea of the Commons, which I shall outline in the next chapter. God the Reconciler is concerned with all efforts to structure life-giving community; here we are concerned with the way in which justice leads to the common good, as the Dominican theologians insisted. God the Redeemer is the origin of all utopian visions, the unquiet promise which cannot be complacent with the world we have fashioned and the situations human beings find themselves in. The values which we seek in the built environment emerge from this understanding of God: in the light of them we both evaluate what has been done and envision what we want to do further. At the same time the second rule qualifies the first: *opera Trinitatis ad extra indivisa sunt* (the works of the Trinity outside Godself are undivided). In terms of

[37] Ibid., p. 475.

the structure of this book this means that it cannot be organised according to the appropriations, as I once thought, but these need to be reflected under each locus. The structure of the book is therefore as follows. In the next chapter I continue with the theme of the common good, arguing that there was another tradition alongside the Thomist one, which we need to refer to when thinking how to respond to what I shall call the 'global emergency'. I then turn to the second main theological theme, that of grace, and examine the place of order and beauty in the built environment, drawing especially on the work of Christopher Alexander. Following that I take up the fashionable discussion of place, and in particular its relation to bioregionalism and the political vision which follows from that. This leads on to planning, in which I consider the relation of democracy to the common good. I turn then to the nature of public space, and in the following chapter to the function of human settlements within what Lessing called 'the education of the human race'. I then take up the ancient theme of the relation of town and country, thinking especially of the role of farming, before turning to a consideration of connections – the roads, railways, rivers, harbours and airports which connect human beings to one another. In the final two chapters I take up Bernard Rudofsky's distinction between pedigreed and non-pedigreed architecture to think about housing, 'the challenge of slums' and the great architectural tradition. I have tried to point up how the chapters dovetail, but the argument is not conceived in terms of logical progression, but more in terms of the loci which seem to me important in thinking about this theme. Throughout I shall argue that the built environment as a whole has to function in terms of the common good if it is to embody values which teach us, as Ruskin put it, to desire and labour for the things which lead to life, and which teach us to scorn and destroy the things that lead to destruction. As such it is in its own way a contribution to a theology of liberation, a theology committed to justice, empowerment and the fullness of life.

CHAPTER 2

The common good and the global emergency

In the previous chapter I outlined the Thomistic idea of the common good, which, it seems, was one of the main contributory factors in the building of cities as fine as Siena.

This idea rests on the assumption that all things 'by nature' seek the common good, but its understanding of justice included no idea of equality. Justice was 'to render each their due', which, married to a hierarchical view of reality, was consistent not simply with huge inequalities of wealth and outcome, but with an ontological understanding of such difference. God really did make them 'high and lowly / and ordered their estate'. There is, however, another sense, derived not from Aristotle but from Stoicism and Scripture, which has much more radical social and political outcomes, and it is this idea I want to explore in this chapter.

THE COMMON GOOD AND THE COMMON TREASURY

Stoicism was a pantheistic system which believed that all things shared in the cause of all things, the *Koinos Logos*, or Universal Reason. For Stoicism,

All human beings are interrelated, all have the same origin and destiny, all stand under the same law and are citizens of one state, for all share in the same Logos. Consequently, all should act in accordance with the *Koinos Logos* – that is, in *koinonia*. The world itself is a *koinonia*, of human beings and all other beings, and the necessity of unconditional submission to the laws and requirements of this *koinonia* must be respected.[1]

Doubtless influenced by Stoic thought, the term *koinonia* (fellowship, communion, sharing) was important for the early Christians. In Acts we learn how the early community devoted itself to *koinonia* and because of that had all things in common (*koinos*). Paul speaks of the Christian

---

[1] C. Avila, *Ownership: Early Christian Teaching* (Maryknoll: Orbis, 1983), p. 39.

community as a *koinonia*, a fellowship, and demands therefore that a better-off part must share its goods with a poorer part in an act of *koinonia* (2 Cor. 8.4, 9.13). For Paul *koinonia* was life in Christ, the mutual fellowship of believers.

This idea of *koinonia* already implied that the universe had to be under-stood as a totality. It is in the profoundest sense an ecological idea. The interconnectedness of all things is already implicit in the Priestly account of creation (Gen. 1) with its carefully integrated steps leading up to the creation of human beings and the institution of the Sabbath. It is equally implicit in Paul's summary of his argument in Romans 8, where the resur-rection of Christ is a promise not just to human beings but to the whole creation, groaning in bondage.

The Church Fathers developed from this idea of what was common a strong teaching of social justice. Thus Clement of Alexandria (c.150–216 AD) writes in his book *The Teacher*:

It is God himself who has brought our race to a *koinonia*, by sharing Himself, first of all, and then by sending His Word to all alike, and by making all things for all. Therefore everything is common, and the rich should not grasp a greater share. The expression, then, 'I own something and I have more than enough; why should I not enjoy it?' is not worthy of a human nor does it indicate any community feeling (*koinonikon*).[2]

In his great treatise on Naboth's vineyard, Ambrose (b. 333) declares that 'The earth was made in common for all' and derives this truth from the fact that we are born and die with nothing.[3] In his commentary on 1 Corinthians, John Chrysostom (b. 344) likewise notes that 'all this about "mine" and "thine" is mere verbiage, and does not stand for reality. For if you say the house is yours, it is a word without reality: since the very air, earth, matter, are the Creator's; and so are you too yourself who have framed it; and all other things also.'[4] Such quotations can be multiplied copiously.[5] It is true, of course, that this teaching existed side by side with a strongly hierarchical vision of reality, particularly after Dionysius the Areopagite, and, though the sentiment was picked up by populist preachers like John Ball and by Langland, it was subordinate to this other tradition. Thus Aquinas allowed that any person had a right to take those things they

[handwritten margin note: denial of ownership as all owned]

---

[2] Quoted in ibid., p. 37.   [3] In ibid., p. 66.   [4] Ibid., p. 97.
[5] So, for example, Basil of Caesarea: 'Let us who are rational not seem more savage than those without reason . . . Flocks of sheep pasture on the same mountain . . . but we lock up what is common; we keep for ourselves the things that belong to everyone'; and Gregory of Nyssa: 'All belongs to God, our common father. And we are all brothers of the same race.' Quoted in S. R. Holman, *The Poor are Dying: Beggars and Bishops in Roman Cappadocia* (Oxford University Press, 2001), pp. 191, 197.

needed to survive, in virtue of their sharing in the gifts of all creation, but he also believed that distributive justice meant that some should have much and others very little. The radical potential of the teaching of the common good, however, never entirely disappeared, and it resurfaces in a most surprising way in the work of the Digger leader Gerrard Winstanley in the middle of the seventeenth century, in his notion of 'the common treasury':

> The Earth (which was made to be a Common Treasury of relief for all, both Beasts and Men) was hedged in to In-Closures by the teachers and rulers, and the others were made Servants and Slaves: And that Earth that is within this Creation made a Common Store-house for all, is bought and sold, and kept in the hands of a few, whereby the great Creator is mightily dishonoured, as if he were a respector of persons, delighting in the comfortable Livelihood of some, and rejoycing in the miserable povertie and straits of others. From the beginning it was not so.[6]

Unlike the Dominican theologians, therefore, both the Church Fathers and the seventeenth-century radicals read strongly egalitarian implications from the idea that the world was created to be held in common. This generated a strong and politically radical idea of the common good which, in Britain at least, held out for 'the Commons', land which was not appropriated by any individual but which was there for the whole community. This still has echoes today. In Britain 'The Land is Ours' campaigns for land for homes, space for low-cost and self-designed housing in cities; places for travellers and low-impact settlers in the countryside. It seeks protection and reclamation of common space; reform of planning and public inquiries; mandatory land registration; community ground rents; a right to roam. It wants land for livelihoods, and farm subsidies and planning directed to small-scale, high-employment, low-consumption land uses.[7] Economists, says its manifesto, 'The Land', define wealth and justice in terms of access to the market. 'Politicians echo the economists because the more dependent that people become upon the market, the more securely they can be roped into the fiscal and political hierarchy. Access to land is not simply a threat to landowning elites – it is a threat to the religion of unlimited economic growth and the power structure that depends upon it.'[8]

In assuming that 'all things seek the common good' the Thomistic idea thinks that the common good can be reached without struggle. But as the example of the Diggers shows, the very idea leads to struggle, as vested

[6] G. Winstanley, 'The True Levellers Standard Advanced', in *The Works of Gerrard Winstanley*, ed. G. Sabine (New York: Cornell University Press, 1941), p. 252.
[7] www.tlio.org.uk (last accessed 23 November 2009).   [8] *The Land*, 8 (Winter 2009–10), 2.

interests have to be overcome. It assumes that the common good is something which has to be argued for and contested, and cannot simply be taken for granted. In the language of liberation theology, it involves the 'preferential option for the poor'. As the movement The Land is Ours shows, this is not simply a Third World issue. The movement sees itself as standing in solidarity with the Via Campesina and other peasant movements in the global South, but it understands the question of access to land, and the planning which would enable that, as a truly radical step in the direction of a new economy.

THE DECLINE OF THE COMMON GOOD

The reason for the decline of the idea of both senses of the common good, but especially this second one, is without doubt what Karl Polanyi called 'the great transformation' from an agricultural, semi-feudal society to an industrialised capitalist one. Under the old system, land, labour and capital were all understood as part of a common patrimony. Writing at the beginning of what was a new world order, John Locke acknowledges that the world was given to men in common, but goes on to say that this signifies little if it is not appropriated. The one thing which is truly ours and to which no one else has a right is our body and thus also its labour. It follows then that what we produce through our labour we own, and this is not held in common.

Thus the Grass my horse has bit; the Turfs my servant has cut; and the Ore I have digged in any place where I have a right to them in common with others, become my Property, without the assignation or consent of anybody. The labour that was mine, removing them out of that common state they were in, hath fix'd my Property in them.[9]

So far so good, but what disrupts the scale of such appropriation is the introduction of money which allows people to own more property than their labour can actually work. Money is a device which allows property to accrue to the industrious and the rational. In Locke's view it is plain

that Men have agreed to disproportionate and unequal Possession of the Earth, they having by a tacit and voluntary consent found out a way, how a man may fairly possess more land than he himself can use the product of, by receiving in exchange for the overplus, Gold and Silver, which may be hoarded up without injury to anyone, these metals not spoiling or decaying in the hands of the Possessor.[10]

[9] J. Locke, *Two Treatises of Government*, ed. P. Laslett (Cambridge University Press, 1960), p. 288.
[10] Ibid., p. 302.

This argument now overturns the common treasury. In the state of nature all things were common, but not all people were rational and industrious. Some (like the North American Indians, according to Locke) were quarrelsome and contentious, and did not make a proper use of their land. The earth belongs, then, not to all, but to those whose wit and industry allow them to exploit it. This idea was to have a long history, being the father of the neo-liberal argument that capitalism rests on people (entrepreneurs) using their wit and intelligence ('caput').

Another part of the great transformation was the change from an ethic of conservation to a view of the world based on extraction, which Mumford believed happened some time in the sixteenth century. The fundamental metaphor for the world ceased to be that of a garden or a farm, and became that of a mine, which you exploited until its resources ran out before moving on. The idea that resources might some day run out simply did not occur. Given the likely world population in, say, 1550, and given the technology available, that was not so stupid an assumption, but as technology became more successful, and as population rose exponentially, it became more and more dangerous.

Likewise part of the great transformation is the rise of individualism, a term coined by Alexis de Tocqueville in the second volume of *Democracy in America*, published in 1840. 'Individualism', he said, 'is a calm and considered feeling which disposes each citizen to isolate himself from the mass of his fellows and withdraw into the circle of family and friends; with this little society formed to his taste he gladly leaves the greater society to look after itself'.[11] Robert Bellah and his fellow authors, musing on de Tocqueville's work, distinguish between utilitarian individualism, for which the model is Benjamin Franklin, and expressive individualism, the model for which is Walt Whitman. The two traditions of individualism, they argue, 'offer us only the cost benefit analysis of external success and the intuition of feeling inwardly more or less free, comfortable and authentic on which to ground our self approval. Ideas of the self's inner expansion reveal nothing of the shape moral character should take, the limits it should respect and the community it should serve.'[12] Alasdair MacIntyre demonstrates that already in the early eighteenth century the idea of a

---

[11] A. de Tocqueville, *Democracy in America* (London: Everyman's Library, 1994), p. 98.

[12] Bellah *et al.*, *Habits of the Heart*, p. 79. We might also think that the rise of individualism represented, as Mumford suggested, the democratisation of the baroque conception of the despotic prince: 'now every enterprising man sought to be a despot in his own right: emotional despots like the romantic poets: practical despots like the businessmen'. L. Mumford, *The City in History* (Harmondsworth: Penguin, 1991), p. 510.

shared conception of the community's good had been lost and with it the understanding of how one might contribute to the achievement of that good.[13] The appearance of Homo economicus at the end of the eighteenth century institutionalises that loss.

What happens to others does not affect Homo economicus unless he or she has caused it through a gift. Even external relations to others, such as relative standing in the community, make no difference. In addition, only scarce commodities, those that are exchanged in the market, are of interest. The gifts of nature are of no importance, nor is the morale of the community of which Homo economicus is a part.[14]

The loss of the idea of the common good was accompanied by loss of the idea of a shared value system, the situation which MacIntyre describes as living 'after virtue'.[15] There are at least two ways in which this can be stated. We can say that the very idea that there were ever societies bound together by a vision of the common good is wishful thinking. Thus, it is obvious that what was said to be common by Aristotle was in fact very partial: women, immigrants and slaves were all excluded from it. Siena, like every medieval city, was class-divided and patriarchal. The very idea of the common good, we could say, is obfuscatory, drawing our attention away from the realities of unequal power. We could gloss this by saying that supposedly universal moral standards are in fact always historically and socially specific and subject to change. States of affairs which are justified 'by nature', or on which 'all people agree', or which are justified as 'the ways in which this culture does things', turn out to be defences of the power of particular groups, very often those of powerful men. Today, when we at least pay lip service to egalitarianism, we can argue with Rawls that the differences in our plural society are so great that we cannot imagine a common good on which we could all agree.[16]

Responding to these objections, we might say that arguments such as Rawls' rest on a highly individualistic account of the human which does not stand up to inspection. Human infants are the most helpless of mammals, and survive only through the care and attention of others for their first three or four years. That level of dependence does not decrease in complex society but increases. The person who insists on the right to difference is

[13] A. MacIntyre, *After Virtue*, 2nd edn (London: Duckworth, 1985), p. 232.
[14] H. Daly and J. Cobb, *For the Common Good* (London: Green Print, 1919), p. 87.
[15] MacIntyre, *After Virtue*. op.cit. Schweitzer had already made this point. A. Schweitzer, *Civilization and Ethics* (London: A. & C. Black, 1947), p. xiv.
[16] J. Rawls, *Political Liberalism* (New York: Columbia University Press, 1993), p. 201.

nevertheless dependent upon thousands of other human beings for his or her food, warmth, clothing and health care. At the heart of the individualist vision is freedom, but this turns out to be impossible without community: freedom is always freedom in community.

> To possess this freedom is not simply to be left alone. Rather it comes into being when a person participates in interactive life with other persons . . . human freedom is never a solitary possession. Securing and sustaining this freedom demands more than keeping disconnected individuals from interfering with each other. To eliminate interaction entirely would not protect personality but dissolve it.[17]

To argue for the common good, then, begins with the assumption that human beings are constituted by relationships. The common good also, in fact, includes all those areas articulated by the UN declaration of human rights: housing, food, health, education, work. 'Food, housing and public safety', writes Hollenbach, 'are intrinsic parts of a shared life together, not simply means to the well being of individuals. By sharing in these goods, people share a common life that no hungry, homeless or crime threatened individual can know.'[18] In the same way the welfare state, where it emerged, 'institutionalized commonality of fate: its provisions were meant for every participant (every citizen) in equal measure, thus balancing everybody's privations with everybody's gain . . . [It] makes tangible the bond between public and private – community and individual, and casts the community as the pledge of the individual's security.'[19] The idea of the common good, then, is a recognition of our necessary interdependence, and individualist arguments represent illegitimate abstractions from that.

Second, if there are 'common bads', as I shall argue there are, then their remedies represent common goods. At the most obvious level, broken pavements or poor sewage arrangements in a town affect everyone, rich or poor: their remedy benefits everyone. What is meant by the common good here is the good of all, the good in which everyone has a share. Because it is these things it is at the same time the good to be pursued in common.[20] One way in which Christianity modified Stoic teaching was in reading the whole story of creation in the light of a particular life and death, that of Jesus of Nazareth. A key thing it took from that story was an account of the significance of human sin, an understanding of a

[17] D. Hollenbach, SJ, *The Common Good and Christian Ethics* (Cambridge University Press, 2002), p. 77.
[18] Ibid., p. 83.   [19] Z. Bauman, *Postmodern Ethics* (Oxford: Blackwell, 1993), p. 243.
[20] These are among definitions of the common good in P. Miller and D. McCann (eds.), *In Search of the Common Good* (London: T. & T. Clark, 2005).

common bad. In Paul's writings sin appears a 'power' under which we are 'bound'. The question is not primarily of the extraordinary viciousness, wickedness or even selfishness of particular human beings, but of the way in which we all collectively get trapped in life-denying forms of behaviour, though there is a recognition that some (as we shall see in Chapter 10) bear a disproportionate brunt of such behaviour. A good example of this is the way in which human beings can destroy the complex ecological balance which sustains them. The economist E. F. Schumacher argued that 'Nature always . . . knows when to stop. Greater even than the mystery of natural growth is the mystery of the natural cessation of growth . . . the system of nature, of which man is part, tends to be self-balancing, self-adjusting, self-cleansing.'[21] Human beings, unfortunately, do not know when to stop – a prime complaint of ancient moralists, including the Church Fathers already cited. On the individual level this is the stuff of tragedy, but it has a collective dimension as well. All over the ancient Near East civilisations eliminated themselves by overcropping and overgrazing, and turning their hinterlands into desert. Humans are themselves part of nature but modify natural processes in uniquely constructive or destructive ways. Constructive intervention has found ways to grow more and better vegetables, grains and fruit, to use animals which can process cellulose to produce the huge range of dairy products, to irrigate in ways which sustain populations over millennia, as in Egypt. Destructive intervention, on the other hand, can produce terminator seeds, put fertile land under tarmac, over-irrigate so that salinisation makes land unproductive, fell trees so that desert takes over – in short, destroy a host ecological system as in ancient Sumeria, and as may be happening in contemporary Egypt. Once full-scale industrialisation was in place it became a rule that the wheels must never cease turning: it was 'inefficient' for them to do so. The world's economy was predicated not on a rhythm of production and rest, but on endless production and consumption.

This possibility has been theorised by the American ethicist Garret Hardin in terms of the 'tragedy of the Commons', an idea anticipated by the eighteenth-century poet John Dyer in his poem *The Fleece*:

> Inclose, inclose, ye swains!
> Why will you joy in common field . . . ?
> . . . In fields
> Promiscuous held all culture languishes.

---

[21] E. F. Schumacher, *Small is Beautiful* (London: Sphere, 1974), p. 122.

Just so, Hardin argued, given a common grazing area and a number of farmers, each farmer will be led by self-interest to overgraze, and the result will be the destruction of the Commons. 'Each man is locked into a system that compels him to increase his herd without limit – in a world that is limited. Ruin is the destination toward which all men rush, each pursuing his own best interest in a society that believes in the freedom of the Commons. Freedom in a commons brings ruin to all.'[22] The ruin of the Commons followed, Hardin argued, from Adam Smith's assumption that the result of everyone following their self-interest will be mutual benefit. In fact, he argued, it is quite the contrary. We need by law, therefore, to make quite clear that some things are not 'common'. The privatisation of land, in his view, was what saved it from destruction, and looking at the North American National Parks he foresaw the need to restrict visitors in some way if their beauty was to be retained.

Although there are clear examples of the tragedy of the Commons, as we shall see, Hardin's original example was not best chosen to make his point. The old English Commons were not overgrazed because each person with a right to them zealously policed his neighbour. It was bonds of community, the need to survive in a community with a strong common ethos, which prevented overgrazing.[23] Hardin's selfish commoner would have been literally or metaphorically pilloried. Rather than the inefficacy of conscience being the root of the problem, as Hardin suggested, it is the absence of real community which leads to the tragedy he outlined. The question, then, is what 'real community' might mean in the global village.

The 'tragedy of the Commons' is about a common bad. If it could be constructively addressed we would have a common good. The theme of that restitution, as it applies to the built environment, is the central theme of this book. First, however, I shall outline my understanding of the current 'tragedy of the Commons', which I shall call 'the global emergency'.

THE GLOBAL EMERGENCY

What I am calling the global emergency rests on three facts. The first is world population, which has more than doubled in the past forty years, and currently increases by between 75 and 80 million per year, so that the United Nations predicts world population will reach 9 billion by 2050. This rise in

---

[22] G. Hardin, 'The Tragedy of the Commons', *Science*, 162 (1968), 1243–8.
[23] A. McEvoy, 'Towards an Interactive Theory of Nature and Culture', *Environmental Review*, 11 (1987), p. 299. Hardin later conceded this point. 'The Tragedy of the "Unmanaged" Commons', in R. V. Andelson (ed.), *Commons without Tragedy* (London: Shepheard Walwyn, 1991), pp. 162–85.

population is enormously problematic for a number of reasons. First, as the United Nations report *The Challenge of Slums* very graphically illustrates, and as I shall document in Chapter 10, one-sixth of humanity lives not simply in sub-standard conditions but in conditions of what Mike Davis calls 'Kurtzian horror'. If the reports of the Intergovernmental Panel on Climate Change (IPCC) represent an unprecedented scientific consensus on the dangers of global warming, he says, then *The Challenge of Slums* sounds an equally authoritative warning about the worldwide catastrophe of global poverty.[24]

The other side of this coin is that huge numbers mean huge impacts. The Indian firm Tata is now manufacturing a car for £1,300 with the aim of offering it to 'the Indian masses'. It is planning to market it in Latin America, south-east Asia and Africa. 'The sheer numbers likely to appear on the roads will certainly result in large-scale environmental consequences.'[25] China, which in 2004 was predicted to pass United States emissions in 2030, actually passed them in 2006.[26]

As I shall explore in Chapter 8, there are urgent issues about feeding and watering this population. Water is not evenly spread around the world. Some 60 per cent of fresh water is found in just nine countries.[27] It is estimated that within twenty years almost half the world's population will experience water scarcity. Each of the world's nearly 7 billion people needs about five litres of water a day for drinking and cooking and another twenty-five to forty-five litres a day for hygiene and health. Global consumption of water is doubling every twenty years, more than twice the rate of human population growth. Domestic use, however, accounts for only 10 per cent of water use. The biggest user is agriculture, accounting for about 65 per cent of world water use. Most of this is used for irrigation on which 45 per cent of world food supply now depends. Industry claims the rest. Since water is a finite resource there is competition between agriculture and industry for supply. One ton of wheat requires 1,000 tons of water. If you measure the price of wheat against the price, say, of computers, computers will be far more cost-effective. China has made just this calculation and there has been an increasing shift of water use in China from agriculture to industry to power China's 'economic miracle'. It generates huge foreign

[24] M. Davis, *Planet of Slums* (London: Verso, 2006), p. 21.
[25] A. Giddens, *The Politics of Climate Change* (Cambridge: Polity, 2009), p. 47.
[26] L. Starke (ed.), *State of the World 2009: Confronting Climate Change* (London: Earthscan, 2009), p. 7.
[27] Water-sufficient countries are those which have more than 1,700 cubic metres per person. Between 1,000 and 1,700 cubic metres there is water stress, and below 1,000 cubic metres there is water scarcity.

exchange earnings, but the question is how far China's water budget can be stretched, a problem currently being addressed by vast and megalomaniac river diversion schemes.

The second key aspect of the global emergency is the problem of climate change. The biosphere is the most fundamental aspect of the Commons, a fact recognised by organisations like the Global Commons Institute, which campaigns to reduce carbon dioxide emissions. The biosphere is a cycle in which 'every plant yielding seed', as Genesis puts it, transforms carbon dioxide, produces oxygen during photosynthesis and in turn uses up oxygen and releases carbon dioxide. This cycle has been disrupted in the past 200 years by colossal man-made discharges of carbon dioxide, as well as the other greenhouse gases – methane, nitrous oxide and CFCs. According to the IPCC, the present carbon dioxide concentration has not been exceeded during the past 420,000 years and probably not during the past 20 million years. Currently we are adding 6 billion tons of carbon to the atmosphere each year. The result is a hotter planet. We are already seeing damaging results from global warming, but even more fundamentally all life on earth, and not just human life, thrives within a relatively narrow temperature band. The addition of just one degree may dramatically raise the level of species extinction, and a few degrees could lead to irreversible damage. The mass extinction of the end of the Permian age was associated with a rise of 6°C, which is within the range of what the IPCC considers possible.[28] In 2001 the IPCC considered that global warming had to be limited to 2°C to avoid catastrophic effects. Scientists at NASA's Goddard Institute for Space Studies suggest that the tipping point, beyond which feedback mechanisms could cause global warming to simply run away, may already have been reached.[29] Such a tipping point would bring about change not gradually but very suddenly.[30] The Tyndall Centre, in Britain, considers 4–5°C of warming probable. Therefore there is a genuine fear that the world may cross tipping points which make accelerated warming inevitable – such as the death of the rainforests and melting of the permafrost (both of which

[28] M. Lynas, *Six Degrees* (London: Fourth Estate, 2007), p. 244.

[29] J. Hansen, M. Sato, P. Kharecha, G. Russell, D. W. Lea and M. Siddall, 'Climate Change and Trace Gases', *Philosophical Transactions of the Royal Society A*, 365 (2007), 1925–54, quoted by G. Monbiot, 'A Sudden Change of State', *The Guardian*, 3 July 2007. Above about 3°C the world's vegetation will become a net source of carbon. This is just one of the climate feedbacks triggered by a high level of warming. G. Monbiot, 'If We Act as if it's Too Late, Then it Will Be', *The Guardian Weekly*, 27 March 2009.

[30] F. Pearce, quoted in Giddens, *Politics*, p. 25.

would then become sources of carbon emissions), the loss of almost all glaciers and the melting of the polar ice caps.[31]

Global warming is largely driven by human economic activity. 'An irresistible economy seems to be on a collision course with an immoveable ecosphere.'[32] The built environment is a key part in this story. For very good reasons many nations aspire to the lifestyle of the affluent North. Indian entrepreneurs are copying the model of budget airlines and hoping to make air travel available to the mass of the Indian population. Most aspects of the global economy are committed to constant growth. A globally competitive economy means that every firm and every country has to grow in relation to its competitor or it will lose out. China, currently the world's most populous country, is growing at 10 per cent per annum. The inevitable consequence of such growth is that ever greater demands are put upon resources. We know that already we are exceeding the earth's carrying capacity, living in bio-deficit. For every one to live like a Londoner we need three planets; like a citizen of Los Angeles, five planets; like a citizen of Dubai, ten planets. The United States and the European Union, with only 10 per cent of the world's population, are responsible for 45 per cent of all carbon dioxide emissions. Texas emits more than France, and California more than Brazil. The United Kingdom's per capita emissions total 9.6 tonnes of carbon dioxide a year, where a sustainable person's is 2.45 tonnes. In their celebrated working-out of the ecological footprint Wackernagel and Rees calculate the 'earthshare' that each human being has, the amount of land needed to provide all the things we need in a sustainable way. Today, with 7 billion people on earth, this is 1.89 global hectares (gha) per person. Unfortunately, the United States average is 9.5 gha, and the British average 5.9. Given the amount of poverty in both these countries, this means that some are over-consuming to a huge extent. Urgent issues of equity are raised by this disparity. 'Barring manna from heaven', writes Charles Landry, reflecting on these facts, 'it is safe to say that civilization will not survive in its present form. This is not to make an ideological point. There's just not enough planet to maintain culture as we now know it.'[33] Ted Trainer of the University of New South Wales writes:

[31] Oxfam, *Suffering the Science*, www.oxfam.org.uk/resources/policy/climate_change/suffering-science-climate-change.html, July 2009. p. 9 (last accessed 30 July 2009).

[32] M. Wackernagel and W. Rees, *Our Ecological Footprint* (Gabriola Island: New Society, 1996), p. 13. Although fertility rates show a slight falling-off, the base population rate is so large that very extensive increases are inevitable.

[33] C. Landry, *The Art of City-Making* (London: Earthscan, 2006), p. 93.

There is a widespread assumption that a consumer-capitalist society, based on the determination to increase production, sales, trade investment, 'living standards' and the GDP as fast as possible and indefinitely, can be run on renewable energy . . . But if this assumption is wrong, we are in for catastrophic problems in the very near future and we should be exploring radical social alternatives urgently.[34]

The tragedy of the Commons is apparent in the reactions this evokes, summed up in the failure of the Copenhagen summit in December 2009. No cap for carbon dioxide concentrations was agreed, no target date for peaking emissions was fixed; there was no concrete deal on reducing emissions from deforestation and forest degradation. The issue of resource depletion did not seem to be on the agenda at all. 'Politics is being weighed in the balance and found wanting', commented Polly Toynbee. 'The writing is on the wall. The leadership required within and between each nation is heavier lifting than the machinery of governmental power can manage.'[35] 'The nation states', wrote George Monbiot, 'pursuing their own interests, have each been passing the parcel of responsibility since 1992. Corporate profits and political expediency have proved more urgent considerations than either the natural world or human civilisation.'[36] Copenhagen is the tragedy of the Commons writ large.

The tragedy follows from insisting that it is possible to have one's cake and eat it. A favourite ploy is to deal with climate change through offsets. There are many problems with these schemes, especially the idea that in some simple way planting trees is the solution. As Heidi Bachram notes, scientific understanding of the complex interactions between the biosphere (trees, oceans, etc.) and the troposphere (the lowermost part of the atmosphere) is limited. She comments: 'There is no scientific credibility for the practice of soaking up pollution using tree plantations.'[37] In Britain the House of Commons Environmental Audit Committee noted that the focus on climate science and technology 'is creating the appearance of activity . . . whilst evading the harder national and international political decisions which must be made if there is to be a solution'.[38] The Global Commons Institute is of the view that these ploys tackle neither rising

---

[34] T. Trainer, *Renewable Energy cannot Sustain a Consumer Society* (Berlin: Springer Verlag, 2007), p. 9.

[35] P. Toynbee, 'Gutless, Yes. But the Planet's Future is no Priority of Ours', *The Guardian*, 19 December 2009, p. 35.

[36] G. Monbiot, 'Bickering and Filibustering while the Biosphere Burns', *The Guardian*, 19 December 2009.

[37] H. Bachram *et al.*, *Hoodwinked in the Hothouse* (Amsterdam: Transnational Institute, 2005).

[38] House of Commons Environmental Audit Committee, 'Carbon Capture and Storage', Ninth Report of Session 2007–8, HC 654 (London: Stationery Office Ltd, 2008).

emissions nor atmospheric greenhouse gas concentrations. They fail to recognise that climate change is a justice issue, in that the richest 20 per cent of the world's population uses nearly 60 per cent of all energy.

Given that the market is the metaphysic of our world it is hardly surprising that schemes such as trading in emissions quotas between economies or between greater and less sensitive ecological areas are suggested. The Durban Declaration on Carbon Trading notes that the attempt to trade in carbon follows the reduction of everything else to a commodity and that the Earth's ability and capacity to support a climate conducive to life and human societies are now passing into the same corporate hands that are destroying the climate. 'It presupposes that choices can be reduced to questions of monetary value.'[39]

The third dimension of the global emergency is resource depletion. All sorts of resources, like copper, phosphorus and uranium, are becoming scarce, but the most pressing problem is that of oil. A growing body of independent oil experts and oil geologists have calculated that oil production either has peaked or is about to do so. They argue that technological advances in oil extraction and prospecting will have only a minor effect on depletion rates. Oil field depletion goes together with declining discovery rates of new oil fields and increasing demand. A 50 per cent drop in conventional oil production is predicted with immediate effect.[40] Peak oil does not mean that the world is suddenly going to run out of oil, as your car runs out of petrol if you do not fill it up. What it does mean is that we shall reach the point where cheap, easy-to-get oil is exhausted. When that happens, then every successive year will see an ever-diminishing flow of oil, as well as an increasing risk of interruptions to supply. Since our society is built on cheap energy, this spells the end of the world as we know it.[41] The consequences are particularly crucial for agriculture, because the feeding of 7 billion or more is dependent on oil. One of the best-known analysts of peak oil, Richard Heinberg, has suggested three possible scenarios as oil shortages bite.[42] The first is fascism, designed to protect the property of the rich, including rich nations. The second is what Susan George calls

---

[39] www.carbontradewatch.org/durban/durbandec.html (last accessed 3 November 2009).

[40] Global Witness, *Heads in the Sand: Governments Ignore the Oil Supply and Threaten the Climate*, October 2009, www.globalwitness.org/heads_in_the_sand.pdf, pp. 30, 36 (last accessed 30 October 2009). The report shows that the International Energy Authority has consistently understated the size of the problem.

[41] 95 per cent of all global transportation relies on oil; 95 per cent of all products in shops are delivered using oil; 99 per cent of food production uses oil or gas at some stage in its production.

[42] R. Heinberg, 'As the World Burns', Museletter 186, October 2007, www.richardheinberg.com/museletter/186 (last accessed 11 December 2007).

'Environmental Keynsianism'. Here the government undertakes economic redistribution, re-organises agriculture and promotes conservation rather than consumerism.[43] Currently, the only government which is prepared for such steps is Cuba, which was forced to take them following the collapse of Soviet oil supplies. The third option involves power being taken at the local level, an option I shall explore in Chapter 4. Local communities, in this scenario, will have to find ways of providing food, structuring employment and dealing with emergencies. However, Heinberg notes that 'it would be unwise to give up prematurely on efforts at the national and international levels, even if the long-term goal is a society organized according to bioregional principles'. In any event, 'two things are absolutely clear: business as usual is not one of the options; and the more we do now to prepare at every level, the better off we all will be'.[44] Commenting on Copenhagen, he remarks that the idea that every nation can reach the level of the rich countries is impossible because there simply are not enough fossil fuels for that to happen. The Copenhagen talks, he writes, 'took place in a conceptual fantasy world in which climate change is the only global crisis that matters much:

in which rapid economic growth is still an option; in which fossil fuels are practically limitless; in which western middle class staring at the prospect of penury can be persuaded voluntarily to transfer a significant portion of its rapidly evaporating wealth to other nations; in which subsistence farmers in poor nations should all aspire to become middle class urbanites; and in which the subject of human overpopulation can barely be mentioned.[45]

Even the cautious IPCC considers that resource-based wars will mark the present century and that mass destitution and mass migration are probable.[46]

Is it right to describe these three issues of rising population and poverty, global warming and peak oil as a global emergency? David Harvey, for one, is highly sceptical. He disallows any talk of either collapse or limits and 'insists' (his word) that the problems facing us are soluble. 'The postulation of a planetary ecological crisis', he writes, 'the very idea that the planet is somehow vulnerable to human action or that we can destroy the

---

[43] www.globalnetwork4justice.org/story.php?c_id=313 (last accessed 10 December 2009).

[44] Heinberg, 'As the World Burns'.

[45] R. Heinberg, 'The Meaning of Copenhagen', Museletter 212, January 2010, www.richardheinberg.com (last accessed 28 January 2010).

[46] Intergovernmental Panel on Climate Change, *Climate Change 2007: Synthesis Report* (Geneva: IPCC, 2007).

earth, repeats in negative form the hubristic claims of those who aspire to planetary domination . . .'

it is crucial to understand that it is materially impossible for us to destroy the planet earth, that the worst we can do is to engage in material transformations of our environments so as to make life less rather than more comfortable for our own species being, while recognising that what we do also has ramifications (both positive and negative) for other living species . . .

Millenarian and apocalyptic proclamation that ecocide is imminent . . . is not a good basis for left politics and it is very vulnerable to the arguments that . . . the doomsday scenario is far fetched and improbable.[47]

In this insistence he puts himself in some very odd company. Responding to Frederick Soddy in the 1930s, Robert Millikan argued that one may sleep in peace 'with the consciousness that the Creator has put some foolproof elements into his handiwork and that man is powerless to do it any titanic physical damage'.[48] But this is the merest superstition. It may well be that debates about ecoscarcity are also debates about the preservation of a particular social order, as Harvey argues, but they are not simply about this. He is on much firmer ground in citing Barry Commoner to the effect that the environmental crisis can be addressed only in terms of social justice.[49] Heinberg notes that 'We have no agreements in place to prevent the death of the oceans. There is no global policy to avert economic impacts from fossil fuel depletion. There is no worldwide protocol to protect the precious layer of living topsoil that is all that separates us from famine. There is no effective convention on fresh water conservation.'[50] We face a genuine emergency, 'an emergency with long term risks comparable to world war but requiring the surrender of no one and the cooperation of all'.[51] This was recognised by the Earth Charter, drawn up by people from more than fifty countries in 2003, the preamble of which ran:

We stand at a critical moment in Earth's history, a time when humanity must choose its future. As the world becomes increasingly interdependent and fragile, the future at once holds great peril and great promise. To move forward we must recognize that in the midst of a magnificent diversity of cultures and life forms we are one human family and one Earth community with a common destiny. We must join together to bring forth a sustainable global society founded on respect for nature, universal human rights, economic justice, and a culture of peace. Towards

[47] D. Harvey, *Justice, Nature and the Geography of Difference* (Oxford: Blackwell, 1996), p. 195.
[48] Quoted in Daly, *Beyond Growth*, p. 174.   [49] Harvey, *Justice*, p. 397.
[50] Heinberg, 'The Meaning of Copenhagen'.
[51] R. Engelman, 'Sealing the Deal to Save the Climate', in Starke (ed.), *State of the World 2009*, p. 169.

this end, it is imperative that we, the peoples of Earth, declare our responsibility to one another, to the greater community of life, and to future generations.[52]

This is, in effect, a recognition of the need for the idea of the common good. Note that the idea of the common good as the Dominican theologians understood it precisely embraces the whole created earth, because 'God' is the ground of all being. For them the problem is in dealing with the fact that humans mistake the nature of the good, identifying it with consumption or power rather than with God. Their response to the tragedy of the Commons, therefore, is that what is required is that human beings identify the true nature of the good. At Copenhagen it seems that the world community could not do that. The pressures of a market economy, ironically led by Communist China, made it impossible. If we are to survive, however, some such agreement on the true nature of the good will have to be reached.

ECONOMICS AND THE COMMON GOOD

In 1989 the (at that time) World Bank economist Herman Daly and the Process theologian John Cobb published a celebrated book, *For the Common Good*, which made it plain that we cannot think about economics without thinking of the common good, and vice versa. That this is not generally recognised is because, since the late eighteenth century, classical and then neo-classical economics has usurped the place the idea of the common good held in medieval society, providing both our metaphysics and our morals. According to the economic orthodoxy of the past century or more I do good by increasing the Gross National Product, by extending the pie so that there is more to go round. What does it mean to be virtuous? It means, first, to be industrious, to use one's creative powers to produce more goods, to invent, to trade. Later, as industrial capitalism emigrates to Asia and finance capital takes over in the West, to be virtuous is to consume, for without consumption the system does not work: it falters, people lose their jobs, and the whole system is threatened. Hence the extraordinary scale of the bank bail-outs during 2009.

In relation to the built environment it is clear that our understanding of the economy shapes our cities, the relation of town and country and, to a large extent, in the West at least, our housing. The question of economics comes up at every juncture. The economics in question takes rise only

---

[52] www.earthcharter.org (last accessed 30 October 2009).

in the eighteenth century. There is a very different and ancient tradition, linked to thinking about the common good, which goes back to the reforms of Solon and to Aristotle in Greece, and to the reflections of the authors of Leviticus in Scripture. Like the idea of the common good, this tradition was never forgotten and appears, for example, in John Ruskin in the nineteenth century. This tradition points out that the word 'economics' comes from *oikonomia*, household management. In Luke 16 Jesus tells a parable about an unjust *oikonomos*, a household manager or steward. This Greek term is the origin of our word 'economist'. To be an economist is to manage our affairs in such a way as to further what we perceive to be good ends. As the parable says, some of us do that well, others not. Whichever way, we do so as economists. We have come to think of economists as specialists but on this older definition we are all involved, although we must distinguish levels of involvement. The initial level implied in the Greek word is that of the *domestic economy*: the level which is of concern to all of us for all of our lives and with which we are most familiar: how to balance expenditure, roughly, against income. That activity draws on the *local economy*: the shops where I buy my food and the local establishments I patronise. The local economy in turn relates to the *regional*, and that to the *national*. National budgets have to address the myriad demands of a population as allowed by the productive activity of the citizenry. Beyond that, however, comes what we have become increasingly familiar with over the past thirty years – the *global economy* – the intermeshing of the regional and national economies of the whole world, so that in some remote fashion my shopping is dependent upon the labour of unknown millions in the remotest parts of the world.[53] As the thirteenth- and fourteenth-century Dominican theologians realised, economics is a fundamental part of Christian responsibility. Wendell Berry puts it most forcefully:

To be uninterested in economy is to be uninterested in the practice of religion; it is to be uninterested in culture and in character. Probably the most urgent question now faced by people who would adhere to the Bible is this: What sort of economy would be responsible to the holiness of life? What, for Christians, would be the economy, the practices and restraints, of 'right livelihood'? I do not believe that organized Christianity now has any idea. I think its idea of a Christian economy is no more or less than the industrial economy – which is an economy firmly founded on the seven deadly sins and the breaking of all ten of the Commandments. Obviously, if Christianity is going to survive as more than a

---

[53] Anyone who ever uses a supermarket knows this reality: beans from Kenya, flowers from all over Asia, apples from South Africa, butter from New Zealand, citrus fruit from Israel, avocados from Chile, and so on and so forth.

respecter and comforter of profitable iniquities, then Christians, regardless of their organizations, are going to have to interest themselves in economy – which is to say, in nature and work.[54]

All the levels of the economy I have so far mentioned are absolutely familiar. What most professional economists omit to observe, however, is that all of these levels of economic activity are dependent upon what Berry calls '*the great economy*', which he proposes as a way of talking about the kingdom of God.[55] The great economy is the giftedness of all reality, our ultimate dependence on photosynthesis, the fact that we do not, and cannot – not even with the most advanced genetic science – create the raw materials of life out of nothing. The great economy, theologically God's creation of all things, or grace, sustains all that is. We are part of it, bound up in the bundle of life with all that is. In that sense it is quite wrong to speak, as people sometimes still do, of an 'environmental problem'. We are part of the whole. Our peculiarity as humans is in our capacity for creative management on the one hand, and our capacity for damage on the other.

This layering of economic activity means that 'economics' is a far bigger thing than is represented in the 'economics' or 'financial' pages of the newspapers. It is far bigger than what is dealt with by the Chancellor of the Exchequer or the Secretary of State for the Treasury. Economics is the management of the whole *oikoumene*, to use another, and related, Greek word, the whole inhabited earth, in the interests of fullness of life (Jn 10.10). To evaluate our economic activity is to evaluate what we are doing in relation to that goal. In the American Book of Common Prayer there is a prayer which asks that we should be delivered 'in our several callings, from the service of mammon'. As Berry notes, it has become a relic.

The industrial nations are now divided almost entirely into a professional or executive class that has not the least intention of working in truth, beauty and righteousness, as God's servants, or to the benefit of their fellow men, and an underclass that has no choice in the matter. Truth, beauty and righteousness now have, and can have, nothing to do with the economic life of most people.[56]

In other words, the common good is excluded from economics.

The standard paradigm of economics thinks in terms of the circular flow of goods and services from households to industry and commerce to government to public services and so back to households. Critically, it

[54] W. Berry, 'Christianity and the Survival of Creation', in *Sex, Economy, Freedom and Community* (New York: Pantheon, 1992), p. 100.
[55] W. Berry, 'Two Economies', in *Home Economics* (New York: North Point, 1987), pp. 54–75.
[56] W. Berry, 'God and Country', in *What are People For?* (San Francisco: North Point, 1990), p. 101.

denies that there may be limits. It is predicated on an anthropology which valorises competition and is essentially individualist. Behaviour which was self-centred, private, separate and concerned only with self-interest rather than the public or common good was what, in classical Greek, characterized an 'idiot'.[57]

It assumes an unlimited thirst for consumption. Mumford understood it as a democratisation of courtly life so that the meaning of life is understood in terms of 'conspicuous expenditure, extravagant waste, a glut of novelties and sensations, organized into a carnival of triviality for the sole purpose of keeping an expanding economy in operation'.[58] Today the moral basis of all this is the belief that a rising tide raises all boats. Somewhere down the line adequate healthcare, education and work will be available for all.

The alternative paradigm begins with the recognition of limits. It recognises that the ecosystem, the Great Economy, is finite, non-growing and materially closed. It is bound by the second law of thermo-dynamics: all energy degrades. Since this is the case, as the economy grows it becomes larger in relation to the ecosystem. For this reason the alternative paradigm takes account of the question of scale: how many persons simultaneously living at what level of per capita resource use are best for community, where community includes concern for the future and nonhuman species as well as presently living humans?[59] The standard paradigm carefully excludes land from economics (despite Adam Smith's attention to the question). 'Nothing is forever in history, except geography.'[60] In factoring in land, the alternative factors in limits.

Because it insists on limits it insists, therefore, that doing something about poverty is primarily about redistribution rather than growth. Because this is the case it has to distinguish between needs and wants and to recognise that consumption has to be limited by justice. It puts co-operation in place of competition. For the standard paradigm competition is bracing: it is what energises the search for new inventions and for better standards of production. The alternative paradigm, on the other hand, puts a different set of virtues in its place. As Berry puts it,

Rats and roaches live by competition under the laws of supply and demand; it is the privilege of human beings to live under the laws of justice and mercy. It is impossible not to notice how little the proponents of the ideal of competition have to say about honesty, which is the fundamental economic virtue, and how very little they have to say about community, compassion and mutual help.[61]

---

[57] Landry, *Art of City-Making*, p. 196.   [58] Mumford, *City*, p. 41.
[59] Daly and Cobb, *Common Good*, p. 241.   [60] *The Land*, 8 (Winter 2009–10), 2.
[61] W. Berry, 'Economy and Pleasure', in *What are People For?*, p. 135.

Moreover, since we all live within the great economy, competitiveness makes no sense. It fails to recognise our mutual indebtedness. The moral principles of this paradigm are 'some concept of enoughness, stewardship, humility and holism'.[62] Politically, at some stage accepting these principles will entail common ownership of the means of production, including land. This idea was dropped in Britain by 'new' (i.e. market-driven) Labour, but the great emergency makes the adoption of this as a political programme, and as part of the practical way of addressing global warming, more imperative than ever.

In the standard paradigm virtues are understood as individual preferences, admirable perhaps, but having nothing to do with the shape of the real world. In fact 'a growing body of research shows that the more people value money, image, status and personal achievement, the less they care about other living species and the less likely they are to recycle, to turn off lights in unused rooms, and to walk or bicycle to work'. Conversely, 'the pursuit of intrinsic values has been empirically associated with more sustainable and climate friendly ecological activities'.[63] What we believe, in other words, profoundly influences the human future. Many studies have also shown that happiness has very little correlation with prosperity.[64]

The standard paradigm builds on, and is comfortable with, huge differences of reward. The alternative, by contrast, thinks in terms of limited inequality. Unlimited inequality, Herman Daly argues, is inconsistent with community, no matter how well off the poorest are. 'Even relative poverty breeds resentment, and riches insulate and harden the heart. Conviviality, solidarity and brotherhood weaken with economic distance.'[65] The principle of limited inequality he finds, very plausibly, implied in the Jubilee legislation which deconstructed debt either every seven or every fifty years.[66] As a rule of thumb, he believes, a factor of one to ten is about the limit within which a society can thrive. From a Thomist perspective Albion Barrera adds to his account of the common good as due order the notion of 'due proportion', which likewise recognises that 'beyond a certain limit, even legitimate inequalities erode the bonds that tie people together in solidarity'.[67]

---

[62] Daly and Cobb, *Common Good*, p. 47.
[63] T. Kasser, 'Shifting Values in Response to Climate Change', in Starke (ed.), *State of the World 2009*, pp. 122–3.
[64] For example, R. Layard, *Happiness: Lessons from a New Science* (Harmondsworth: Penguin, 2005).
[65] H. Daly, *Beyond Growth* (Boston: Beacon, 1996), p. 214.
[66] Daly and Cobb, *Common Good*, p. 331.   [67] Barrera, *Economic Compulsion*, p. 170.

The standard paradigm worships at the altar of free trade, though everyone knows, and has always known, that there is no such thing. Today it chiefly benefits the great corporations. Following Keynes, Daly and others propose making capital less global and more national.[68]

At the roots of both paradigms is a religious conviction. Classical economics represented the Deism of the eighteenth century with its infallible providence and its eternal laws. The alternative paradigm requires, in Daly's words, 'a change of heart, a renewal of the mind, and a healthy dose of repentance. These are all religious terms, and that is no coincidence, because a change in the fundamental principles we live by is a change so deep that it is essentially religious whether we call it that or not.'[69] To turn to this paradigm is, as Daly and Cobb argue, to return to the idea of the common good. It is also, as I shall argue in the next chapter, to take up the idea of grace, and it is to this that I now turn.

[68] Daly, *Beyond Growth*, p. 93.   [69] Ibid., p. 201.

CHAPTER 3

Grace and the built environment

Following David Mayernik, I have argued that some version of the common good is necessary for the shaping of what he calls 'timeless cities'. I made a distinction between the Thomistic idea, drawing on Aristotle, which thought of the common good in terms of a common vision of the human end, and another tradition, drawing on Stoicism and Scripture, which understood the earth as a common treasury to be equally shared. I argued that any sense of the common good whatever is threatened by the global emergency and that answering that would be the most fundamental establishment of the common good. In this chapter I want to take these arguments further by developing a theology of grace. Another way of understanding Mayernik would be to say that his 'timeless cities' were shaped by an understanding of grace. I shall try to show how this was the case and to show how grace and the common good belong together.

THE MEANING OF 'GRACE'

In the Hebrew Bible we find a cluster of words which characterise human conduct: *hen*, meaning gracious address to another; *hesed*, meaning loyalty, faithfulness, loving kindness, solidarity; *emeth*, meaning truth or reliability; *tsedeq* and *tsedequah*, meaning righteousness; and *racham*, meaning compassion. These words characterise the kind of relationships God wills, and sometimes depict relationships in which God is disclosed, as in the meeting of Jacob and Esau (Gen. 33). These words, which originated in perceptions of human conduct, were later transferred eminently to God. The meaning of the words then change: they are now vested with a transcendent sense so that they judge and norm human conduct. They apply primarily to God and only derivatively to human beings. They describe God's attitude towards the whole of creation and indeed characterise God in God's self, as in Exodus 34.6: 'The Lord passed before his face and proclaimed,

40

"The Lord, the Lord, a God merciful [*rahum*] and gracious [*chanun*], slow to anger, and abounding in steadfast love [*hesed*] and faithfulness [*emeth*]."'

The people who translated the Hebrew Bible into Greek translated two of these words, *hen* principally, but also *hesed*, by *charis*, which was then in turn translated by the Latin word *gratia*, so giving us the term 'grace'.

All translation is falsification, and perhaps *charis* was an odd choice for these Hebrew words. Words formed from the Greek root *char* indicate things which produce well-being.[1] *Charis* is, in classical Greek, 'that which causes favourable regard – gracefulness, loveliness of form, graciousness of speech'.[2] In fact the semantic range of the word is quite wide: meanings including favour, beauty, thankfulness, gratitude, delight, kindness, expression of favour, good turn and benefit are recorded. To use this word in place of *hen* and *hesed* already implied a broad redefinition of the meaning of the word, but an even more radical redefinition stems from the apostle Paul.[3] Like all original thinkers Paul is a wordsmith who mints terms anew in the fire of his genius or, better (bearing Kierkegaard in mind), in the light of his experience of Christ. For Paul the word becomes a kind of *koan* for Christ.[4]

Paul draws on the gospel stories which speak of the quality of mercy, as in the story of the Good Samaritan; of God's initiative in seeking the lost, and of joy in heaven at finding them; of great celebrations to which the outcast are bidden. They speak of grace in the sense that they are never moralising. The word expresses or points towards the wellsprings of human joy. Perhaps this is the reason why Paul uses it in greeting. He amends the ordinary greeting, 'Shalom shalom', to 'grace and peace', where 'grace' perhaps means 'goodwill' but a goodwill stemming from the new era established by God. To say 'grace' to someone seems to mean something like 'the joy of the new order be with you'. The grace known in Christ calls forth gratitude: reciting what God has done leads Paul to say 'thanks be to God' (*charis de to Theo*: Rom. 6.17).

For Paul, over and over again, grace has the character of excess: 'If, because of the one man's trespass, death exercised dominion through that

---

[1] H.-H. Esser, in C. Brown (ed.), *Dictionary of New Testament Theology* (Exeter: Paternoster, 1976), p. 115.

[2] G. Abbot-Smith, *A Manual Greek Lexicon of the New Testament* (Edinburgh: T. & T. Clark, 1936), p. 479.

[3] The word *charis* does not appear at all in Mark and Matthew; it appears some twenty times in Luke-Acts and four times in John, but one hundred times in Paul.

[4] For the full exegetical basis for this claim see T. J. Gorringe, *Redeeming Time* (London: Darton, Longman and Todd, 1986), p. 114.

one, much more surely will those who receive the abundance of grace [*parisseain tes charitos*] and the free gift of righteousness exercise dominion in life through the one man Jesus Christ' (Rom. 5.17). Grace is always fullness, and from the fullness of Christ human beings receive 'grace upon grace' as John puts it (Jn 1.16), gifts for the realisation of God's kingdom which are, in Jesus' words, 'pressed down, shaken together, running over' (Luke 6.38). Later theologians concluded that God is excess in Godself, always more than we can possibly grasp. Since grace characterises the action of God, there is then about this the mark of excess, of superfluity, of superabundance.

In his Prologue John makes a connection which has been fundamental to Christian discussion of grace. Christ, he says, was full of 'grace and truth' (Jn 1.14, 17). This grace and truth has a radiance which John characterises as 'glory' (*doxa*) (Jn 1.14). It is from here that we derive the connection between grace and beauty. Paul makes the same connection, speaking of Christians beholding with 'unveiled face' 'the light of the knowledge of the glory of God in the face of Christ' (2 Cor. 4.6) which shines through the ecclesia so that 'as grace extends to more and more people it may increase thanksgiving' (4.15).

The word 'grace', then, is basically the summary of a narrative. When Christians speak of 'God' they are speaking of the origin and end of all things as this is made known in Christ. The biblical narratives give us a way of making sense of our experience, a way of responding to the seeming chaos and injustice of human history, a belief that creation is not the outworking of a neo-Darwinian narrative and a hope that love will be the end of all things. As Paul insists, this is a matter of faith (2 Cor. 5.7), and faith is our response to the narratives, liturgies and so forth which the community receives and lives by (Rom. 10.17). The word 'God' therefore is the sum of a *credimus* – we believe. For Christians it represents the belief that the clue to the meaning of all things is revealed in Jesus, and therefore in the stories and communities which gave rise to him. At the heart of these stories is the conviction that God is living and active, that God 'listens', 'speaks', 'acts', 'illuminates', but that God does all these things graciously. The quotation marks indicate the analogical nature of all language about God, but they do not mean the language is nonsense. *Charis*, then, and the Hebrew words it translates are abstract nouns which function adverbially or adjectivally. They characterise the quality and the nature of the divine action, and therefore also of the divine being. Joseph Sittler spoke beautifully of 'the ancient, steady reality of the hilaritas of a gracious God'.[5] The formal way of putting this is to think of 'grace' as one of the divine attributes. The medieval theologians spoke of God as 'uncreated grace', grace in Godself. If God is grace, then grace characterises the heart of all reality: grace has a metaphysical dimension. As we shall see, for the medieval cathedral builders, and perhaps also for the Renaissance theorists, this had enormous implications for their understanding of the built environment.

This way of using the words translated 'grace' changed early on. T. F. Torrance argued that already by the time of the Apostolic Fathers grace reverts to the idea of spiritual energy, 'a ghostly potency not very different from the deifying *charis* of the mystery religions'.[6] For Augustine, the *doctor gratiae*, grace is 'an internal and secret power, wonderful and ineffable' by which God operates in human hearts.[7] This power anticipates us (it is 'prevenient'), it works with us, but it is irresistible and carries all before it. 'Grace in Augustinian terminology means primarily the salvific will of God, operating partly by way of the providential arrangement of exterior circumstances, partly by secret inspiration of good thoughts and the communication of interior spiritual vitality: by a natural metonymy, it comes to mean the good thoughts and the spiritual vitality so imparted.'[8] To say that we are saved 'by grace' now means not so much that we are saved because God is merciful and loving but that we are given 'grace' to help us be good. Grace, received in the sacraments, is divorced from God in Godself. As J. H. Newman put it:

> O, that a higher gift than grace
> Should flesh and blood refine:
> God's presence, and God's very self,
> And Essence all divine.

'Grace' ceases to be primarily a qualitative word and becomes a reference to something God gives, almost a form of spiritual glucose. This change in meaning at the same time changed the opposition of sin and grace. If 'grace' primarily means the quality of relationships – relationships marked by mercy, love, forgiveness and so forth – then sin is the opposite of those relationships. 'Sin' is closed in, arrogant, egocentric, unforgiving

[5] J. Sittler, *Evocations of Grace* (Grand Rapids: Eerdmans, 2000), p. 148.
[6] T. F. Torrance, *Grace in the Apostolic Fathers* (Edinburgh: Oliver and Boyd, 1948), p. 140.
[7] Augustine, 'On the Grace of Christ and Original Sin', 1.25, in P. Schaff (ed.), *Nicene and Post Nicene Fathers* (Grand Rapids: Eerdmans, 1971), vol. V, p. 227.
[8] N. P. Williams, *The Grace of God* (London: Hodder and Stoughton, 1930), p. 26.

behaviour. If grace is a ghostly potency, however, then sin is the mysterious and ultimately unintelligible opposition to that power, and it becomes more difficult to spell out precisely what we mean by it and certainly to apply it to the built environment. If, however, with Karl Barth, we understand sin through its opposition to the graciousness of God, and therefore as (in the Doctrine of Reconciliation) pride, sloth and lying, then it is at once apparent that all three of these forms of sin are everywhere exemplified in the built environment: buildings which owe their existence to the Viagra of power; buildings which are the product of lazy or slothful thought; and buildings which lie about their durability, fitness for purpose and social philosophy.

Christian reflection on grace has not, fortunately, been wholly identified with the ghostly potency idea. In particular, that God is grace in Godself has been seen to have radical implications for our understanding of the created order. It was, we can say, the basis for the rejection of Manicheanism both in the second century and in the thirteenth century. That neither creation nor history matches God's will as that is discerned in Christ is what gives us the doctrine of the 'fall'. Only occasionally, however, within orthodox circles, has this been taken to imply that creation in itself is warped, a second-best. By and large the metaphor of the fall has been applied to the will of free creatures, whether angels or humans, as a way of trying to understand the nature of evil. To accept that creation is the product of the divine self-gifting means, in Barth's words, that there is 'nothing which does not point to grace and therefore come from grace; nothing which can enjoy independent life or exercise independent dominion'.[9] For Barth, one of his most insightful commentators claims, creation is 'one vast symbol of grace'.[10] It is not simply that creation is a gift for which we have to be thankful. Created reality also expresses the God who creates: it is the product of the kind of divine self-giving which we glimpse in Christ. It is 'created grace', 'the grace that inheres in the world by virtue of a gracious God'.[11] The world in which and with which we build, therefore, is marked by grace. We could say that there is an inbuilt potential for grace within it.

Aquinas' understanding of grace helps us further to see how grace and the built environment come together. For Aquinas grace is a way of talking about the illumination of the Spirit (he calls God the 'intelligible sun').[12]

---

[9] K. Barth, *Church Dogmatics*, vol. III/1 (Edinburgh: T. & T. Clark, 1958), p. 62.
[10] H. U. von Balthasar, *The Theology of Karl Barth* (San Francisco: Ignatius, 1992), p. 124.
[11] Sittler, *Evocations of Grace*, p. 83.
[12] Aquinas, *Summa theologiae*, 1a2ae.109.1, vol. XXX, p. 73.

One can see how this could be construed as a form of 'ghostly potency', but it is more profound. God is the source of all intelligibility, of everything that makes sense. This is the reason why light metaphors are used of God. In John's language God is the 'light which lightens every person' (Jn 1.9), but, more than that, all reality. Aquinas argues that the soul gives form to the body, but God, the intelligible sun, forms the soul. Grace (God, the intelligible sun) acts on the soul as a formal cause, shaping it.[13] Indirectly, grace shapes what the soul shapes. The point of this in relation to the built environment is obvious: grace is the free, creative, self-gifting of God which transforms the creature, but which thereby transforms the creature's creations. Grace can be manifest in what the creature creates. By the same token, sin, which is the refusal of grace, is manifest in these creations. As Sittler (a Lutheran!) puts it, 'abuse is use without grace'.[14]

GRACE AND BEAUTY

As we have seen, beauty was implicit in the original idea of the word 'grace'. The re-thinking of the word in terms of Christ meant that grace could no longer be identified *tout court* with charm or beauty. If grace is christically defined, then 'the loveliness which causes favourable regard' stems from the one 'in whom there is no form or comeliness' (Is. 53.2). What we understand by loveliness is radically redefined. At the same time it has not proved possible to get away from the connection between grace and beauty which is still implicit in everyday language. The inner radiance of the good implied in John's yoking of grace and glory found theological expression in the idea that God was the most beautiful object of human contemplation. God is beautiful precisely because God is grace in Godself. Another way of putting that is to say that what we mean by 'God' is the ultimate source of meaning, value and goodness. The tendency to equate beauty and goodness stems from the fact that true beauty seems to need meaning, value and goodness. 'Beauty itself is a form of knowledge', argues Carroll Westfall, 'and a beautiful building teaches. While people take delight, that is, pleasure, in beauty, beauty is more than pleasure and is based on more than mere attractiveness.'[15] To say this is to insist that the judgement that something is beautiful is not simply a matter of sense experience.

---

[13] Ibid., 1a2ae.110.2, vol. XXX, p. 115.   [14] Sittler, *Evocations of Grace*, p. 57.

[15] C. Westfall and J. van Pelt, *Architectural Principles in an Age of Historicism* (New Haven: Yale University Press, 1991), p. 247.

To be an object of reason it must be a form of speech; to be a beautiful object, it must be eloquent speech. To put it another way: For a building to be beautiful, it must be visible and open to the inquiry of reason. Its purpose must be just and noble, and its form must be and must appear to be, appropriate to its purpose.[16]

This is what David Mayernik was arguing in respect of Siena and other medieval Italian cities: their plans and their skylines are not haphazard but instantiate meaning and purpose, a coherent view of the world. Roger Scruton agrees, arguing that the cultivation of aesthetic taste is part of phronesis, or practical wisdom. He appeals to Alberti, for whom beauty is 'the harmony and concord of all the parts achieved in such a manner that nothing could be added or taken away or altered except for the worse'. 'Beauty is something lovely which is proper and innate and diffused throughout the whole.'[17] Building on these definitions, Scruton argues that the sense of what is appropriate is central to the aesthetic judgement. It is clear from Alberti's definition of beauty, he says, that what was appropriate interested him more than beauty. It is the notion of the appropriate that sums up the process of reasoned fitting together which is the primary intellectual gesture in any decorative art. The notion of appropriateness is in fact a way of linking aesthetics and ethics, for we speak of what is appropriate in every sphere of rational conduct.[18] Anselm would agree with him, for the aesthetic character of the work of redemption is central to the argument of *Cur deus homo*, which constantly appeals to what is 'fitting' and appropriate.[19] It is a great mistake, remarks Westfall, to think that beauty is to be found in the senses. Because the senses quickly become sated 'the architect must reach into extremes . . . if he is to produce something thought to be beautiful; it puts beauty in a category of experience that is incompatible with reason and it removes beauty from being in the thing perceived and makes it instead a property possessed by the person doing the perceiving.'[20]

Aquinas does not identify the good and the beautiful but nevertheless argues that 'A good thing is also in fact a beautiful thing, for both epithets have the same basis in reality, namely, the possession of form.' Aristotle had argued that beauty rested on right proportion in that violent colours

[16] Ibid., p. 274.

[17] L. Alberti, *The Ten Books of Architecture*, Leonie edn (New York: Dover, 1986), bk VI, ch. 2, p. 113.

[18] R. Scruton, *The Aesthetics of Architecture* (Princeton University Press, 1979), pp. 225–7.

[19] Anselm argues that objectors should consider how fitly (*convenientur*) human redemption is procured; it was fitting (*oportebat*) that human sin should be addressed in this way. Because God's acts are fitting they have an 'indescribable beauty' (bk I.3). Sin is a disturbance of the order and beauty of the universe, and redemption the restoration of that (bk I.15).

[20] Westfall and van Pelt, *Architectural Principles*, p. 274.

or sounds upset proportion and therefore disturb us. Aquinas picks this up: 'beauty is a matter of right proportion, for the senses delight in rightly proportioned things as similar to themselves, the sense-faculty being a sort of proportion itself like all the knowing faculties'.[21] Later he defines beauty in terms of the conjunction of integrity or perfection (*integritas*), due proportion or harmony (*consonantia*), and brightness or radiance (*claritas*).[22] Compare this with Alberti's account of beauty as consisting in a 'harmony [*concinnitas*] of parts, fitted together with just reflection, in such a way that nothing could be added, diminished or altered but for the worse'. In some ways, argues Scruton, this is a bad definition because we often need to make alterations, but the key thing is 'to see an adequate correspondence of part to part, a harmony of detail, a visual completion that is felt as intrinsically correct... There is no appreciation of the beauty of a building that does not involve an awareness and understanding of its parts.'[23] Perhaps this is what Aquinas means by 'due proportion and harmony'.

There are obvious objections to Aquinas' definition of beauty. It seems, for instance, to imply that beauty cannot be known in dissonance – say, in Beethoven's late quartets or in Grunewald's *Crucifixion*. Furthermore, the connection of beauty and morality is not self-evident. Not only is beauty neither truth nor goodness, says Nicholas Wolterstorff, roundly, but 'Truth and goodness do not determine beauty.'[24] Many aesthetes may be immoral people and aestheticism may act as a surrogate religion. We seek beauty in the built environment but it is not our overriding end.[25]

This may be true but we can still argue, with John de Gruchy, that truth and beauty need one another: 'Truth without goodness and beauty degenerates into dogmatism, and lacks the power to attract and convince; goodness without truth is superficial, and without beauty – that is without graced form – it degenerates into moralism. Alternatively we could say that truth and goodness without beauty lack power to convince and therefore to save.'[26] 'Graced form' is what emerges from a culture which understands and honours the inner radiance of truth. It cannot do so, however, as

---

[21] Aquinas, *Summa theologiae*, 1a.5.4, vol. II, p. 73, citing *De anima*, III.2. 426b4.
[22] Aquinas, *Summa theologiae*, 1a.39.8, vol. VIII, p. 133.　　[23] Scruton, *Aesthetics*, p. 209.
[24] N. Wolterstorff, *Art in Action* (Carlisle: Solway, 1997), p. 173.
[25] W. H. Auden warned that 'A society which was really like a good poem, embodying the aesthetic virtues of beauty, order, economy and subordination of detail to the whole, would be a nightmare of horror for, given the historical reality of actual men, such a society could only come into being through selective breeding, extermination of the physically and mentally unfit, absolute obedience to its Director, and a large slave class kept out of sight in the cellars'. Quoted in Westfall and van Pelt, *Architectural Principles*, p. 347.
[26] J. de Gruchy, *Christianity, Art and Transformation: Theological Aesthetics in the Struggle for Justice* (Cambridge University Press, 2001), p. 107.

Lorenzetti's paintings in the Sala dei Nove implied, without respecting justice.

GRACE AND JUSTICE

In Scripture grace is bound to justice. The locus classicus is Micah 6.8:

> He has told you, O mortal, what is good;
> and what does the Lord require of you
> but to do justice, and to love kindness [*hesed*],
> and to walk humbly with your God.

Justice, we see, is given its distinctive content by being linked to *hesed*, steadfast love or loving kindness. This love is the key mark of the divine commitment to the covenant with Israel, and the measure of all human behaviour. As the opening oracles in Amos make clear, the claims of justice are grounded in the common humanity which all persons share in their relationship to God. Justice is never abstract. The practice of justice is equivalent to the knowledge of God:

> Did not your father eat and drink
> And do justice and righteousness?
> Then it was well with him.
> He judged the cause of the poor and needy;
> Then it was well.
> Is not this to know me?
> Says the Lord. (Jer. 22.15–16)

In the New Testament justice or righteousness is known in grace, which is to say in the death of Christ, understood both as God's faithfulness to the divine purpose and in terms of forgiveness. Quite apart from the law, says Paul, 'the righteousness [*dikaiosune* – also 'justice'] of God has been disclosed, and is attested by both Torah and Nebiim [law and prophets], the righteousness of God through faith in Jesus Christ for all who believe. For there is no distinction, since all have sinned and fall short of the glory of God; they are now justified by his grace as a gift, through the redemption that is in Christ Jesus' (Rom. 3.21–5). In other words, for Paul, justice is realised through grace, or gift, God's self-manifestation in Christ.

Three things for our theme may be taken from this connection between justice and grace. First, as Duncan Forrester has insisted, justice is more than fairness. In the most famous account of justice in recent times, John Rawls argues that justice must be understood in terms of three co-ordinated principles of fairness: equal liberty for all, equal opportunity and the difference principle: the higher expectations of those better situated are just if and only if they work as part of a scheme which improves the expectations of the least advantaged members of society. Forrester comments that the difference principle would ensure that in applying these principles to Jesus' parable of the rich man and Lazarus, Lazarus' interests would be taken into account but would do nothing to call upon the rich man to do anything to respond to his needy neighbour's condition unless he saw that it was in his self-interest. The inseparability of justice and grace, on the other hand, means that Christians are called to respond 'with sacrificial and spontaneous generosity to the needy neighbour. The idea of fairness does not go far enough.'[27] We need to add, in relation to the global emergency, that climate change is also a justice issue, as the Climate Justice summit in The Hague affirmed, both in the fact that it is caused mostly by the rich but affects principally the poor, and in its impacts on future generations.[28] Justice, Ruskin already realised, is an inter-generational issue. The idea of self-denial for the sake of posterity, he said, 'of practising present economy for the sake of debtors yet unborn, of planting forests that our descendants may live under their shade, or of raising cities for future nations to inhabit, never, I suppose, efficiently takes place among publicly recognised motives of exertion. Yet these are not less our duties.'

God has lent us the earth for life; it is a great entail. It belongs as much to those who are to come after us, and whose names are already written in the book of creation, as to us . . . men cannot benefit those that are with them as they can benefit those who come after them; and of all the pulpits from which human voice is ever sent forth, there is none from which it reaches so far as from the grave.[29]

Second, it is oriented towards the common good, the flourishing of all members of the community. Paul insists that grace is known concretely; *charis* manifests itself in *charismata*. Such gifts are given precisely 'for the common good' (as the RSV translates *pros to sumpheron*: 1 Cor. 12.7).[30] Paul argues that if grace is treated as something for my own advantage, or my own glorification, then I nullify it. The gifts are given to enhance fullness of life in the whole community. This gifting creates order in freedom and freedom in order. The charismata are articulated for the good of the whole.

---

[27] D. Forrester, *Christian Justice and Public Policy* (Cambridge University Press, 1997), p. 132.
[28] 'Climate Justice Summit Provides Alternative Vision', 21 November 2000, www.corpwatch. org (last accessed 3 March 2009).
[29] J. Ruskin, *The Seven Lamps of Architecture* (New York: Dover 1989), p. 186.
[30] The verb *sumphero* means 'to bring together'; the participle, here, means 'profitable' or 'to advantage'.

Grace, then, ultimately creates the common good, which is the justification of the RSV's rather over-free rendering.

Divine justice seeks the transformation of all forms of human society and culture. This means that justice is essentially social. Hayek's claim that there cannot be social justice because the results of the allocation of the market are not intended or foreseen and depend on a multitude of circumstances not known in their totality to anybody is an abrogation of responsibility. If, as Aristotle argued, justice is a virtue, this means that it has to do with obligations and responsibilities. Justice is constitutive of community. The reverse of this is what Judith Shklar, appealing to Cicero, calls passive injustice, the failure to get involved.

In our cities, a Ciceronian would see not only the injustices committed by officials, criminals, and cheats but also, emphatically, those of citizens who refuse to report crimes, to notify the police, to give evidence in court, and to come to the aid of victims... the typically passive citizen is... a free rider and little else. Typically, he does not vote, attend meetings, keep informed, or speak up.[31]

Such a citizen would not feel outrage about unfair planning decisions either, about the way in which smallholders are unable to get permission for low-impact dwellings, while volume builders buy up hundreds of acres and coin money with the building of boring and repetitive estates, or about the way in which middle-class nimbyism opposes the building of wind farms.

Third, justice is related to proportion. With a look back to Plato, for whom injustice is a disorder of soul, Aristotle considers the unjust person to be 'unequal' or, as we might say, 'out of kilter'. He or she has more than he or she needs. The just person, on the other hand, is a balanced person. Justice is, according to Aristotle, the disposition to give and receive neither too much nor too little. Balance, or equality, involves getting the proportions right. It involves a proper understanding of the merits and deserving of person and of the goods by which he or she is rewarded. The just, then, he says, is a species of the proportionate, and the unjust is what violates proportion. He derives the word for justice (*dichaion*) from *dicha*, meaning two parts, arguing that the role of the judge is to restore equality.[32] In response to this it can be argued that any understanding of justice which was adequate to the New Testament would demand the resignation of proportionate justice out of compassion for the needy and for the sake of the well-being of the community as a whole. There is a creativity about

[31] J. Shklar, *The Faces of Injustice* (New Haven: Yale University Press, 1990), p. 42.
[32] Aristotle, *Nicomachean Ethics*, Bk V. 1–3, in *Complete Works*, vol. II, pp. 1781–6.

justice which Aristotle misses.[33] At the same time the connection between justice, grace and proportion is not adventitious. Should it be applied to architecture, however? This might seem a step too far, just too tendentious, but a long tradition of thought wants to insist on the connection between grace and proportion, and then to go on and say that building which respects this connection at the same time both reflects and helps to build better human societies. In outlining this case I shall begin by considering the connection between grace and human scale.

GRACE AND HUMAN SCALE

Pythagoras is credited with having formalised the harmonic scales: the ratio 1:2 gives the octave; 3:2, the fifth; and 4:3, the fourth. Reportedly he considered these ratios an insight into the nature of the universe, and it was an insight adopted by Plato in the Timaeus. According to Plato the human soul mirrors the divine soul and is therefore primed to respond to these harmonies.[34] The divine *tektainomenos*, or architect of the universe, designs the world in his own image, and his children, the gods, make men and women after the same model. The human being is related to the cosmos as microcosm to macrocosm, and one consequence of this for architecture, which Vitruvius in the first century already appealed to as ancient wisdom, is that the human figure should be taken as the basis of architecture. Architecture, said Vitruvius, depends on order, arrangement, eurythmy, symmetry, propriety and economy. 'Symmetry is a proper agreement between the members of the work itself, and relation between the different parts and the whole general scheme, in accordance with a certain part selected as standard. Thus in the human body there is a kind of symmetrical harmony between forearm, foot, palm, finger, and other small parts; and so it is with perfect buildings.'[35] Proportion, or *analogia*, which is 'a correspondence among the measures of the members of an entire work, and the whole to a certain part selected as standard', is found in all reality. In the human body the human face is a tenth of average human height; the open hand from the wrist to the tip of the middle finger is the same;

[33] E. C. Gardner, *Justice and Christian Ethics* (Cambridge University Press, 1995), p. 69.
[34] Plato, Timaeus, 37, in *The Collected Dialogues*, ed. E. Hamilton and H. Cairns (Princeton University Press, 1961), p. 1116.
[35] Vitruvius, *The Ten Books of Architecture*, bk I.2; tr. M. Morgan (New York: Dover 1960), p. 14. The idea of the body as the microcosm which related to the macrocosm was taken up again by Le Corbusier in his idea of the Modulor. This includes a number of dimensions taken from the body of a 6-foot man in various positions, a measure which he preferred to the metre.

the head from the chin to the crown is an eighth; from the middle of the breast to the summit of the crown is a quarter; and so on. Furthermore, the well-built man, with extended hands and feet, fits into the most perfect geometrical figures, circles and squares:

Therefore, since nature has designed the human body so that its members are duly proportioned to the frame as a whole, it appears that the ancients had good reason for their rule. That in perfect buildings the different members must be in exact symmetrical relations to the whole general scheme . . . Further, it was from the members of the body that they derived the fundamental ideas of the measures which are obviously necessary in all works, as the finger, palm, foot, and cubit. These they apportioned so as to form the 'perfect number', called in Greek *teleion*, and as the perfect number the ancients fixed upon ten.[36]

The principle of empathy is central to the understanding of Greek architecture, argues Spiro Kostoff.

It comes about intangibly, through the proportional interlocking of the members, which evoke the proportional relationships of a standing human. Proportion, according to Vitruvius, 'is a correspondence among the members of an entire work and of the whole to a certain part selected as standard . . . as in the case of a well shaped man'. This implies an affinity between the user and the building so that, for example, the ratio of column to capital could not be too far removed from the ratio of the human frame to the head. It is this affinity that enables us to comprehend the scheme of the peristyle, and what the column is capable of, in terms of our own capabilities. In the end, this humanly inspired reasonableness is what distinguishes the experience of a Greek temple from the crushing gigantism of Egyptian structures.[37]

The Greek column has to be understood in relation to the human body, particularly in terms of balance. 'The column height and its thickness in relation to the mass of the superstructure are determined with a sense of visual justice, so that both look adequate to their task.' The human scale of Greek temples was underscored by the fact that their precincts were full of statues. This kind of teaching was picked up by Filarete, writing in the mid-fifteenth century, who followed Plato in arguing that human architects should imitate God by designing columns based on the perfect proportions of the first man, Adam.[38]

---

[36] Vitruvius, *Ten Books*, bk III.1, p. 72. Ten is perfect, he tells us, because it is the number of fingers on both hands but also because it is composed of monads (individual units).

[37] S. Kostoff, *A History of Architecture*, 2nd edn (New York: Oxford University Press, 1995), p. 126.

[38] Onians, *Bearers of Meaning*, p. 222.

Rather differently, Roger Scruton approaches the question of human scale appealing to a Hegelian idea of self-realisation. A significant correspondence between architecture and the human frame arises, he argues, because we can see inert materials as endowed with impulses which have their origin in us; in fulfilling those impulses in architecture we 'realise' a conception of ourselves, not as isolated subjectivities, but as self-conscious beings with an enduring identity in a public world.[39] It follows from this that we need to build in relation to human scale. There is a 'crushing gigantism' which has to be avoided.

On a practical level, human scale is everywhere in architecture since stairs reflect the human foot and pace (*scala*, meaning stairs, gives us 'scale'), doorknobs match the human hand, and so forth. 'These forms have been important to humankind, because they accommodated the initial human act of constructing a dwelling, the first tangible boundary beyond the body, they accommodated the act of inhabiting, and they called attention to the sources of human energy and to our place between heaven and earth.'[40] More subtly, implications for scale follow from the way the eye functions:

> The best way to view a building is in its entirety... If the maximum eye rotation above the horizon is 30°, and the optimum is 25°... then the ideal vertical viewing angle should be somewhere around 27°... this is exactly the angle established when you stand twice as far away from an object as it is tall, and the experience of centuries has confirmed that this is in fact a successful ratio for viewing both the details and the totality of any object. Thus to have a complete view of an ordinary two-story house at a single glance without moving your head, you would have to stand at a distance twice its height... a similar measurement may be made for horizontal viewing angles... that is why the most successful residential streets, those that satisfy in some indefinite way as you walk or drive along them, are those with houses set back from the street about 50 feet or so.[41]

The German architect H. Maertens calculated that 72 feet is the greatest distance at which people can recognise one another; 48 feet is the furthest at which facial expression can be discerned. Using the 27° formula, a street width of 72 feet gives a maximum building height of 42 feet, about three storeys, and a street 48 feet wide gives 30 feet, or two to three stories. He comments, 'these are the heights that even now we recognize as being the "normal" size for urban dwellings and shops except in the most built-up parts of our city centres, the size that feels most natural and comfortable... these are the heights that allow us to observe the tops of

[39] Scruton, *Aesthetics*, p. 252.
[40] K. Sale, *Human Scale* (New York: Coward, McCann & Geoghegan, 1980), p. 176.
[41] Ibid., p. 171, quoting work by Henry Dreyfuss.

trees over roofs'.[42] Such heights actually constitute the most satisfactory parts of cities, creating environments which are containable and knowable, and where people feel an organic part of a place. Similarly, the distance where general outlines, clothes, gait and colour can be distinguished, is 450 feet, which Maertens suggests is the best distance for parks, malls and plazas: this turns out to be the distance of the Acropolis, from the Propylaea to the farthest corner of the Parthenon, and the width of the oval in front of St Peter's, the Place Vendôme in Paris and the Piazza San Marco in Venice. The architect and city planner Hans Blumenfeld comments, 'There appears to be a definite upper limit to the size of a plaza, as to the length of a street, which can convey a strong spatial experience beyond which they can no longer be related to the human being: their scale is no longer "superhuman" but colossal and inhuman.'[43] If this were the case then, using the 27° rule, a building would have to be no higher than 225 feet, or fifteen to twenty storeys, for public monuments such as churches or civic centres. In fact a rule in place since the Renaissance suggests that building heights should be one-third of the longest dimension of the plaza.

In either case, one would avoid such urban design disasters as the Empire State Building, the World Trade Centre, the Sears Tower in Chicago . . . indeed one could almost say almost all contemporary skyscrapers – which are built so far in excess of the spaces they are set in that, incredible as it may seem, it is actually impossible to find any point from which they can be viewed whole.[44]

To stand in a personal relation to a building, argues Roger Scruton, I must comprehend it visually, without strain, and without feeling dwarfed or terrorised by its presence. 'If the cathedral does not frighten us, it is because it is an act of worship: an offering to God, and an attempt to reach up to him with incorruptible fingers of stone.' What thrills us in Manhattan also disturbs us as it speaks of human beings overreaching themselves.[45] This effectively makes the connection between grace and human scale, and is perhaps what Pythagoras and Plato were reaching for. Grace is what is beautiful, but what is beautiful includes, we saw, the question of what is appropriate, what is fitting. The story of the Tower of Babel is the story of human beings overreaching themselves, refusing to acknowledge limitations, putting themselves in the place of God, acting ungraciously. To act and to build graciously, by contrast, is to acknowledge human scale.

---

[42] Sale, *Human Scale*, p. 173.   [43] Quoted in ibid., p. 175.   [44] Ibid., p. 175.
[45] R. Scruton, *The Classical Vernacular: Architectural Principles in an Age of Nihilism* (London: Carcanet, 1994), p. 14.

GRACE AND PROPORTION

'The aim of classical architecture has always been to achieve a demonstrable harmony of parts', wrote John Summerson. 'Harmony in a structure is achieved by proportion, that is to say by ensuring that the ratios in a building are simple arithmetical functions and that the ratios of all parts of the building are either those same ratios or related to them in a direct way.'[46] In fact, this did not just apply to classical architecture.

Vitruvius appealed to music but did not pick up Pythagoras' idea that in it we have a clue to the nature of the universe. This was fundamental, however, to both Augustine and Boethius. Augustine baptised Pythagorean number mysticism and argued that through proportion and number we are led to contemplation of the divine.[47] Both music and architecture, being dependent on mathematics, have this anagogical function. 'As the icon is thought to partake of the sacred reality it represents, so, according to Augustinian aesthetics, the musical consonances in visual proportions created by man partake of a sacred concord that transcends them. Hence the contemplation of such harmonies can actually lead the soul to the experience of God.'[48] Musical harmony and geometrical proportion are created echoes of divine grace, the perfect harmony of God. Augustine was the most important teacher of the early Middle Ages, and reflection on his thought suggested the idea of God as an architect, 'composing and harmonizing the variety of created things by means of the "subtle chains" of musical consonance'.[49] Church building was carried out using the proportions which Augustine had suggested. For Abbot Suger, the true originator of Gothic, harmonic proportion was the source of all beauty. He believed that the successful builder had to be in a state of grace and that grace had to take possession of the architect's soul.[50] Chartres was built according to these beliefs, with an allegory of the four mathematical disciplines on the portal of the incarnation. It was geometry alone which was believed capable of conveying a vision of ultimate glory.[51] Villard de Honnecourt's model book records a Cistercian church where the architectural proportions are all derived from music.

[46] J. Summerson, *The Classical Language of Architecture* (London: Thames and Hudson, 1963), p. 8.

[47] Augustine, *De ordine*, II.39 ff., in J. P. Migne (ed.), *Patrologia latina*, vol. XXXII (Paris, 1844), pp. 1013–14.

[48] O. von Simson, *The Gothic Cathedral: Origins of Gothic Architecture and the Medieval Concept of Order* (Princeton University Press, 1988), p. 24.

[49] Ibid., p. 31.   [50] Ibid., p. 127.   [51] Ibid., p. 155.

Thus the length of the church is related to the transept as the ratio of the fifth (2:3). The octave ratio (1:2) determines the relations between side aisle and nave, length and width of the transept, and we may assume on the basis of Cistercian practice of the interior elevation as well. The 3:4 ratio of the choir evokes the musical fourth; the 4:5 ratio of nave and side aisles taken as a unit corresponds to the third; while the crossing, liturgically and aesthetically the centre of the church is based on the 1:1 ratio of unison, most perfect of consonances.[52]

Alberti, in the fifteenth century, also subscribed to these ideas. In his treatise on architecture he wrote,

I am every day more and more convinced of the truth of Pythagoras that Nature is sure to act consistently, and with a constant analogy in all her operations: from whence I conclude that the same numbers, by means of which the agreement of sounds affects our ears with delight, are the very same which please our eyes and our mind. We shall therefore borrow all our rules for the finishing our proportions, from the musicians, who are the greatest masters of this sort of numbers, and from those particular things wherein nature shows herself most excellent and complete.

It followed from this that discussion about beauty was not an arbitrary matter: 'the Judgement which you make that a thing is beautiful, does not proceed from mere opinion, but from a secret argument and discourse implanted in the mind'.[53] Here was a way to relate microcosm and macrocosm. The whole universe exemplified harmony and order, and this was evident in music; by following musical rules one could then translate this into architecture. By doing this one would increase one's chance of producing harmony and order in society. Beauty in a building, then, was a matter of 'maintaining a uniform system of proportion throughout all parts of the building'.[54] Palladio followed this consistently.[55] How this worked could not necessarily be said. Sir Henry Wotton described Santa Giustina in Padua as 'in truth a sound piece of good Art, where the Materials being but ordinary stone, without any garnishment of sculpture, doe yet ravish the Beholder, (and he knows not how), by a secret Harmony in the Proportions'.[56]

[52] Ibid., p. 199.

[53] Alberti, *Ten Books*, bk IX.5: 'Ut vero de pulchritudine iudices non opinion: verum animis innata quaedam ratio efficiet'.

[54] Rudolf Wittkower, *Architectural Principles in the Age of Humanism* (London: Tiranti, 1967), p. 33.

[55] In the Villa Emo there are rooms of 16×16, 12×16, 16×27 and 27×27 feet. The ratio 16:27 gives a fifth and a major second (2:3 and 8:9), and 12:27 gives an octave and a minor second (1:2 and 8:9). 'The whole building appears... like a spatial orchestration of the consonant terms 12, 16, 24, 27, 48.' Wittkower, *Architectural Principles*, p. 131.

[56] H. Wotton, *The Elements of Architecture* (London, 1643), p. 9, quoting Vitruvius, *Ten Books*, bk I.3.

These beliefs about ratio and proportion fell apart in the eighteenth century. Lord Kames, among others, pointed out that musical proportions are different from visual ones because, owing to perspective, apparent proportions change as we move about.[57] Far from being objectively grounded, beauty was now located in sentiment, and 'to seek the real beauty, or real deformity, is as fruitless an inquiry, as to pretend to ascertain the real sweet or the real bitter'. For Burke, 'nothing could be more unaccountably whimsical, than for an architect to model his performance by the human figure, since no two things can have less resemblance or analogy, than a man, and a house or temple'. 'Proportion became a matter of individual sensibility and in this respect the architect acquired complete freedom from the bondage of mathematical ratios.'[58] 'It was realised that proportion is a form of beauty,' wrote Geoffrey Scott.

It was realised that proportion is a mode of mathematics. But it was not realised that the word has a different bearing in the two cases.... Our aesthetic taste is partly physical; and while mathematical proportion belongs to the abstract intellect aesthetic proportion is a preference in bodily sensation... there can be no sure criticism of architecture till we have learnt the geometry of taste.[59]

For Roger Scruton the geometrical theory of proportion – the view that all harmony, acoustic or visual, can be encompassed and explained by mathematical relations – is 'One of the most disastrous fallacies of modernism'.

The residue of two millennia of airy speculation can be found in the modulor. If measures are arranged according to a particular mathematical pattern, Le Corbusier suggested, the overall composition will strike the eye as harmonious... But it is fruitless for a building to be based on measurement, if the measures cannot be perceived. And they can be perceived only if a building is divided into significant parts... Harmony can be achieved only where there is also composition.[60]

That mathematical proportions are no substitute for composition is surely right, but I want now to argue that what the Pythagorean tradition was about was a version of the design argument, which, as a product of a posteriori reflection, reflection on experience, had something important to say about how the built environment bears on the common good. I shall do this with reference to the work of the contemporary architect and theorist Christopher Alexander.

[57] P. H. Scholfield, *The Theory of Proportion in Architecture* (Cambridge University Press, 1957), p. 73.
[58] Wittkower, *Architectural Principles*, p. 153.
[59] Geoffrey Scott, *The Architecture of Humanism: A Study in the History of Taste*, 2nd edn (New York: Doubleday, 1956), p. 156.
[60] Scruton, *Classical Vernacular*, p. 20.

GRACE AND THE QUALITY WITHOUT A NAME

Alexander has been led to a metaphysical vision of order in the teeth of the empiricist prejudices that he acquired studying mathematics at Cambridge. Alexander began by trying to identify 'the quality without a name', a quality 'which is the root criterion of life and spirit in man, a town, a building, or a wilderness', which is 'objective and precise, but cannot be named'.[61] To illustrate it he instances a corner of an English country garden, where a peach tree grows against a wall.

The wall runs east to west; the peach tree grows flat against its southern side. The sun shines on the tree and as it warms the bricks behind the tree, the warm bricks themselves warm the peaches on the tree. It has a slightly dozy quality. The tree, carefully tied to grow flat against the wall; warming the bricks; the peaches growing in the sun; the wild grass growing around the roots of the tree, in the angle where the earth and roots and wall all meet. This quality is the most fundamental quality there is in anything.[62]

What Alexander is describing here is not, except very remotely, the result of intention, but it is the sense of rightness or fit which Henry Wotton was trying to describe in Padua. The quality is never the same because it is always shaped by a particular context – in one place calm and in another stormy, light or dark, soft or hard, etc. 'It is a subtle kind of freedom from inner contradictions.' As Wotton implies, this quality can be the result of design. In that case, Alexander thinks, it springs from an inner integrity which he believes speaks to us at the most primitive level.[63]

Although the quality cannot be defined we can illustrate it from experience. Something which has it is alive, has a self-maintaining fire; something which lacks it stifles life. For example, when courtyards are too tightly enclosed and have no view out, people feel uncomfortable and tend to stay away. By contrast,

When a courtyard has a view out to a larger space, has crossing paths from different rooms, and has a veranda or a porch, these forces can resolve themselves. The view out makes it comfortable, the crossing paths help generate a sense of habit there, the porch makes it easier to go out more often . . . and gradually the courtyard becomes a pleasant customary place to be.[64]

---

[61] C. Alexander, *The Timeless Way of Building* (New York: Oxford University Press, 1979), p. 19.
[62] Ibid., p. 26.   [63] Ibid., p. 26.
[64] Ibid., p. 109. This should be compared with Hassan Fathy's description of the courtyard in Chapter 9 below, where Alexander's arguments may not work.

Similarly, windows can bring to life or deaden. People are phototropic, tend towards the light, and if you are in a room for any length of time you want to sit down. In that case well-designed rooms have window seats or a place where you can draw up a chair. A room which has no window place, by contrast, in which the windows are just 'holes', sets up an irresolvable inner conflict.[65]

The quality without a name is also free, not calculated or perfect but with a freedom which is generated from the forces of the material or the situation. It is eternal precisely in its ordinariness:

We have a habit of thinking that the deepest insights, the most mystical, and spiritual insights, are somehow less ordinary than most things – that they are extraordinary. This is only the shallow refuge of the person who does not yet know what he is doing. In fact, the opposite is true: the most mystical, most religious, most wonderful – these are not less ordinary than most things – they are more ordinary than most things. It is because they are so ordinary, indeed, that they strike to the core.[66]

This is illustrated by 'the simple rule that every room must have daylight on at least two sides (unless the room is less than eight feet deep)'. 'Rooms which follow this rule are pleasant to be in; rooms which do not follow it, with a few exceptions, are unpleasant to be in.'[67]

Above all the secret of the quality without a name is that it is egoless. Only this allows a building to live. Most architecture of the past century does not have this quality, not even that of the so-called 'natural' architects like Frank Lloyd Wright, nor even funky hippy-style architecture. 'These places are not innocent, and cannot reach the quality without a name, because they are made with an outward glance ... Even when they are made to seem natural, even their naturalness is calculated; it is in the end a pose.'[68]

Alexander seems to be influenced by Taoism, but from a Christian perspective 'the quality without a name' has analogies with our understanding of 'grace'. Grace is God in action. The word, we said, was the summary of a narrative. We can note markers of grace such as beauty, justice, proportion and so on but we cannot define it. The 'excess' of grace insisted on by Paul means that it cannot be pinned down and summarised. To the extent that grace is God in Godself it is ineffable. At the same time, because creation is graced, there are echoes of this ineffable quality all around us. Alexander's comment on the spiritual quality of the ordinary captures precisely what

---

[65] Alexander, *Timeless Way*, p. 111.   [66] Ibid., p. 219.   [67] Ibid., p. 220.   [68] Ibid., p. 536.

Auerbach wanted to argue about the sacred everydayness of the gospel.[69] The language of sacraments was one way of trying to speak of this. Sacraments point to the sacredness of all things: they are windows through which we glimpse another dimension to the reality we take for granted. For Alexander the intuition of order in all reality plays this role. Reflecting on this, he was led to a form of natural theology emerging from the built environment.

THE PATTERN LANGUAGE

In attempting to see how we arrive at the quality without a name Alexander and his co-workers attempt to set out a grammar, a pattern language. The patterns (253 of them!) are arrived at phenomenologically, and they imply a space in which they are instantiated. For example, the patterns for a building are:

Intimacy gradient, indoor sunlight, common areas at the heart, entrance room, the flow through rooms, short passages, staircase as a stage, zen view, tapestry of light and dark, light on two sides of every room, couple's realm, children's realm, sleeping to the east, farmhouse kitchen, private terrace on the street, a room of one's own, sequence of sitting spaces, bed cluster, bathing room, bulk storage, flexible office space, communal eating, small work groups, reception welcomes you, a place to wait, small meeting rooms, half-private office, rooms to rent, teenager's cottage, old age cottage, settled work, home workshop, open stairs.[70]

Patterns combine to form languages, sets of symbols which allow their users to create buildings, gardens, towns, all of which can be understood as combinations of patterns.[71] There are languages for every aspect of the environment, from the layout of fields to that of public squares and buildings, for mending walls, for making stairs, for the arrangement of the shops and cafés along the street and so forth.[72] As we can see from the list above, what Alexander calls patterns are observations about what makes places culturally successful, enabling of family, community and individual life, and therefore more generally life-enhancing. Such observations are obviously culture-relative. Thus in Britain for some years now the 'farmhouse kitchen' has been fashionable. It reflects the greater gender equality of the Western middle-class home and the new-found emphasis on the virtues of

---

[69] Auerbach argued that in the Old Testament 'the sublime, tragic and problematic take shape *precisely in the domestic and commonplace* ... The sublime influence of God here reaches so deeply into the everyday that the two realms of the sublime and the everyday are not only unseparated but basically inseparable.' E. Auerbach, *Mimesis* (Princeton University Press, 1974), p. 22.
[70] Alexander, *Timeless Way*, pp. 331, 334.   [71] Ibid., p. 186.   [72] Ibid., p. 209.

home-prepared food. The kitchen is no longer, as it was fifty years ago, a tiny space where the woman of the house laboured to bring food into the dining room, where the messy business of the preparation of food went unnoticed. Many cultures would not appreciate this. In many cultures men and women still do not eat together. In the vast majority of Indian homes there is no separate 'kitchen'. A critic could object that Alexander's list presupposes a fairly affluent lifestyle, though the co-operative living patterns I illustrate in Chapter 10 might be a response to this. He could also respond that some patterns are believed to be archetypal, and key to any significant human flourishing, and that others are proposals which are up for discussion. At the same time he wants the patterns to be taken as a whole. 'The quality without a name occurs, not when an isolated pattern occurs, but when an entire system of patterns, interdependent, at many levels, is all stable and alive.'[73]

Alexander argues that the problem in the past century is that the pattern languages have broken down. They are no longer shared, and they have ceased to form part of our cultural depths. It is therefore, in his view, 'virtually impossible for anybody, in our time, to make a building live'.[74]

The time when a pattern language was a song, in which people could sing the whole of life, is gone. The pattern languages in society are dead. They are ashes and fragments in people's hands. As the pattern languages die, everyone can see the chaos which emerges in our towns and buildings. But the people do not know that it is the pattern languages which cause it. They know that buildings are less human than they used to be. They are willing to pay great prices for old buildings which were made at a time when people still knew how to make them human. They complain bitterly about the lack of life, the danger, the merciless inhuman quality of their environment. But they do not know what to do about it.[75]

This could be illustrated, as we shall see in Chapter 10, from the preference of Egyptian bureaucrats for modern row housing over the beautiful patterns which Hassan Fathy wanted to use. But we have to note that not all the pattern languages of the past were life-affirming. Alexander's 'quality without a name' is a criterion for choosing between them. In fact, there

---

[73] Ibid., p. 131. Brian Walker notes that *A Pattern Language* (for which see below) is 'an attempt to start a social dialogue and . . . a first stab at what [the authors] hope might be the correct patterns that people will choose within deliberation'. He understands the patterns as 'ways of defining land use so as to establish an equilibrium among the many different forces and requirements to which one might want to respond in a modern urban environment'. B. Walker, 'Another Kind of Science: Christopher Alexander on Democratic Theory and the Built Environment', *Canadian Journal of Political Science*, 36/5 (December 2003), 1058.

[74] Alexander, *Timeless Way*, p. 225.   [75] Ibid., p. 237.

have always been life-affirming and life-denying patterns, as any history of building and planning illustrates.

Alexander wants to downplay the role of imagination in architecture partly because he believes that really life-giving building has to be egoless, and therefore that the cult of the 'great architect' is mischievous, but also, more fundamentally, because he believes that buildings are generated by following rules. 'The simple fact is that the structure of the environment comes from the languages that the people who made it are using.' There is an analogy with Chomsky's universal grammar, which concerns the rules which generate sentences.[76] If Chomsky is right these generative rules are not a metaphor but actually exist. Alexander wants to say that the same is true of the built environment. Were we to allow this analogy we would have to insist on the enormous differences in the surface grammars of the three and a half thousand existing languages and therefore, by extension, to recognise greater differences in patterns than Alexander seems inclined to allow. It does not seem possible to map his patterns on to Inuit culture, for example, or to the yurt-dwelling culture of Mongolia.

ORDER AND DIVINE PRESENCE

The journey from *The Timeless Way* to explicit talk of God is bound up with the theory of centres, which is a development from Alexander's reflection on patterns. He begins from the need to think of wholeness. The success of a building comes from the fact that it works as a whole, and this whole includes its surroundings. Wholeness is, to start with, the structure defined by all the various coherent entities that exist in that part of space and the way these entities are nested in and overlap each other. Whatever we are considering, the wholeness is made of parts, the parts by the wholeness. We can recall the importance of *integritas* in Aquinas' definition of beauty, and the harmony of all parts such that nothing can be altered except for the worse of Alberti's definition.

The importance of wholeness has echoes not only in the older sources but also in some work in contemporary biology and physics in the sense that an ultimate metaphysical divide between mind and matter is disallowed. Thus George Wald, professor of biology at Harvard, argued in 1984 that mind, rather than emerging as a late outgrowth in the evolution of life, has existed always as the matrix, the source and condition of physical reality – that

---

[76] S. Grabow, *Christopher Alexander: The Search for a New Paradigm in Architecture* (Stocksfield: Oriel, 1983), p. 47, quoting Alexander.

the stuff of which physical reality is composed is mind stuff. Pauli, in 1955, argued that 'It would be most satisfactory of all if matter and mind could be seen as complementary aspects of the same reality.' Schrödinger, four years later, believed he had proved that there must be somewhere in our universe 'One mind' in which we are all participants. C. F. von Weissacker argued in 1980 that consciousness and matter are different aspects of the same reality, and the British physicist David Bohm, about the same time, argued that the universe is close to being made of a non-material ground, a plenum, and that both matter and consciousness arise from that ground.[77] 'Alexander is certainly not claiming that he is doing physics. But what he is saying is that the tone of the work, the level at which the statements are made, and the way that they fit together, is consistent with the deepest and most interesting things that are being said or done in physics.'[78]

Life, Alexander argues, arises from a wholeness which lies under the surface of every place, at every time, in buildings, meadows, streets and so forth, and which is the natural origin of life. To understand wholeness, however, we need to understand the theory of centres. A centre is 'a distinct set of points in space, which, because of its organization, because of its internal coherence, and because of its relation to context, exhibits centredness, forms a local zone of relative centredness with respect to the other parts of space'.[79] 'Life comes from the particular details of the ways the centres in the wholeness cohere to form a unity, the ways they interact, and interlock, and influence each other.'[80] That is the key to what is actually a metaphysical proposal: that life emerges through the interaction of parts. It is a wholly relational view of reality. Centres are always made of other centres. A centre is not a point, not a perceived centre of gravity. 'It is rather a field of organized force in an object or part of an object which makes that object or part exhibit centrality. This field, like centrality, is fundamental to the idea of wholeness.'[81] Alexander argues that what we call material reality is alive because of its structure, and because of its geometry. 'What is alive, is the earth, and rock, and space itself. The life includes the air, again inorganic. It is not life in space, not an inorganic mechanical substrate, filled with a few living organisms. It is one living thing, the space has come to life, it is nonsense to separate the two.'[82] Life is something which exists in every event and building, even in everyday functional life, as a

[77] C. Alexander, *The Luminous Ground* (Berkeley: Centre for Environmental Structure 2002), p. 323.
[78] Grabow, *Christopher Alexander*, p. 123.
[79] C. Alexander, *The Phenomenon of Order* (Berkeley: Centre for Environmental Structure, 2002), p. 84.
[80] Ibid., p. 106.   [81] Ibid., p. 118.   [82] Ibid., p. 430.

consequence of the structure of space. The actual substance out of which the environment is made consists of relations, or patterns, not things; and it is actually generated by the implicit, language-like system of rules which determines the structure.[83]

Reality, then, or 'nature', is a living structure, but life depends on the relation of centres. This is not an automatic thing. As Geoffrey Scott insisted, order is distinct from beauty. 'Many of the ugliest patterns and most joyless buildings – buildings from which no being can ever have derived delight – possess order in a high degree. Instances of this among the hideous flats, warehouses and other commercial buildings of our streets require no citation. Here is Order and no beauty, but, on the contrary, ugliness.'[84] There are living and dead places, and the artist and the architect are charged with helping structures come to life. 'The nature of space matter, being soul like, is such that the more whole it becomes . . . the more it realizes itself, releases its own inner reality.' Because this is the case, and because art is about building and shaping, 'it has an importance that goes to the very core of cosmology'. 'The task of building things and shaping things is fundamental to the spiritual condition of the world and to our own spiritual development. It is our closest approach, almost God like, to creating life, and to seeing and reaching the essential core of things.'[85]

This takes Alexander on to theological reflection.

To make living structure – really to make living structure – it seems almost as though somehow, we are charged, for our time, with finding a new form of god, a new way of understanding the deepest origins of our experience, of the matter in the universe so that we, too, when lucky, with devotion, might find it possible to reveal this 'something' and its blinding light.[86]

In his view – and I think there is an analogy with the Gothic builders here – when we encounter harmony in things or people 'then spirit is made real'. The underlying spirit of the world becomes visible. 'We are then face to face with God. This quality, when it appears in things, people, in a moment, in an event, is God. It is not an indication of God living behind all things, but it actually is God itself. That is spirit made manifest.'[87] There is a similarity here to the claim that God can be known in the experience of grace, whether in the eucharist, in a relationship, or in St Denis or Chartres. *Ubi caritas* (understood here as grace, rather than as love), *ibi Deus est*.

Like the fourteenth-century mystics, Alexander finds pure unity at the root of all things.

---

[83] Grabow, *Christopher Alexander*, p. 45.   [84] Scott, *Architecture*, p. 155.
[85] Alexander, *Luminous Ground*, p. 331.   [86] Ibid., p. 42.   [87] Ibid., p. 302.

I assert that this domain exists as a real thing; that it is parallel to the material world, but that it is inherently incapable of having structure, because it is pure 'one'. But it is occasionally visible. At least it is potentially visible, some of the time, under some special circumstances. It becomes visible when the structure of a strong field of centres gently raises the lid, lifts the veil, and through the partial opening, we see, or sense, the glow of the Blazing One beyond... When I see a beautiful tile, or walk into the beautiful building, it is as if I just lift up the corner of the flap and temporarily see into that blazing 'one'. It looks like heaven.[88]

As we understand that God lies behind all things so we recognise that a building, or a building detail, is to some degree or other, spirit.

When a thing is well made it is an actual realization of spirit, a physical appearance and creation, realization, of spirit in this world... The process by which a centre is made is the process by which spirit becomes manifest, becomes actual. Thus, the tawdry concrete blocks, plaster, and pieces of wood become in their substance, spirit itself, to some degree or other.[89]

Again one is reminded of the claim made by theologians like John of Damascus that icons, although 'tawdry pieces of wood', may mediate the presence of the divine. Alexander describes the state of mind which produces this in the language of grace. Each building, he says, has to be a gift to God. 'It belongs to God, it does not belong to you. Without this it is not possible to reach the priority of mind to create a living thing. It is the only process which reliably keeps me concentrated on what is, and keeps me away from, my own vain and foolish thoughts.'[90] Compare Suger's belief that a builder has to be in a state of grace to build well.

Alexander believes the old forms of religion cannot help us to do this.[91] 'I suspect', he writes, 'that the organized religions are unfortunately rather far from any connection with the ground, or with the facts about the universe which cause an inner connection between the realm of matter and the real, of God or I.'[92] The tradition to which he stands closest is that set out by Aldous Huxley in *The Perennial Tradition*. For him wholeness is the key.

The activity of building – what we call architecture, and with it also the disciplines we call planning, ecology, agriculture, forestry, road building, engineering – may reach deeper levels of value by increasing wholeness, or they may break down value by destroying wholeness. This is not a stylistic observation, or a culturally induced opinion, depending on a point of view... this is a matter of fact about the wholeness of the world. Life will increase, or it will degenerate, according to

---

[88] Ibid., p. 150.   [89] Ibid., p. 302.   [90] Ibid., p. 304.
[91] Alexander, *Phenomenon of Order*, p. 2.   [92] Alexander, *Luminous Ground*, p. 314.

the degree in which the wholeness of the world is upheld or damaged by human beings or human processes.[93]

This is, of course, close to the fundamental insight of ecology that 'everything is related to everything else', including the spiritual and moral states of individuals and societies.

Alexander is still left with the question why God is more visible in some events than in others. 'Why is it that this shining forth of God is visible more in some things than others; why is God visible more in some events and less in others? What causes life in things; what causes God to be more visible in one thing, more visible in one moment, less visible in another?'[94] He is puzzled, but he has already suggested an answer, which is that life-giving building has to be egoless. In Christian terms, what gets in the way of life-giving building is sin or, as Augustine calls it, the *libido dominandi*.

There is an analogy between Alexander's arguments and the understanding of grace which I have sketched, especially as this was set out in the Thomist tradition. Aquinas' 'intelligible sun', who grounds the intelligibility of all things, recalls Alexander's 'blazing one'. The key difference seems to be in Alexander's assumption that the way to wholeness is to get in touch with our inner selves, a process in which God is disclosed. Here Alexander is much closer to Sergei Bulgakov, and to many contemporary traditions of meditation, than to Aquinas. Most Christian traditions will want to object that 'failure to be comfortable with oneself' is a very weak account of the kind of inner contradictions and compulsions which they have called 'sin'. Alexander's is a natural theology for which revelation happens as we intuit wholeness and are honest about what makes us whole. Compare Calvin's argument that our very understanding is darkened and that we could not therefore be clear about what makes us whole without revelation, by which he means fundamentally the narrative of Christ. Alexander shares with the tradition an understanding that human brokenness is part of a vicious circle where brokenness creates brokenness. He differs in his understanding of *metanoia*, and of the source of wholeness or salvation.

His argument that the order in the universe, which we tap into in building, leads us to a sense of God, recalls the old Pythagoreanism but is not tied to mathematical formulae in the same way, though it is no less incapable of proof. What both theories share is a sense that the deepest forms of order are a miracle pointing beyond themselves to an order which grounds the universe. This surely is what Pythagoras was implying,

---

[93] Alexander, *Phenomenon of Order*, p. 295.   [94] Alexander, *Luminous Ground*, p. 146.

and what Augustine picked up in *De musica*. It is a hunch which, as Alexander notes, is shared by much contemporary biology and physics. It is a hunch which cries out to be translated into architectural forms because, as he correctly insists, there are buildings in which we are comfortable, and in which we feel enlivened and feel joy, and there are buildings which are quite the opposite. For the most part, he argues, we live surrounded by the latter, which are both a mark of our alienation and, to some extent, a cause of it. The Pythagorean tradition, which reads grace and order together, is one of the 'long rumours of wisdom' within Western culture. The arguments for proportion as a 'science' were confuted at the Enlightenment, but the hunch they represent does not go away so easily. There is an analogy with the argument from design. Kant was able to dispose of most of the classical 'proofs for the existence of God', but the design argument remained, not as a proof but as a persuasion. Just so with Alexander's arguments: they prove nothing but they are powerful stimulants to thought and in his case to better, which is to say more gracious, building.

GRACE, THE BUILT ENVIRONMENT AND THE COMMON GOOD

I have argued that 'God', the beginning and end of all things, that which holds all things in being, is grace – unceasing gift – and that because this is the case there are echoes and analogies of grace in that which is not God which inform and pattern every aspect of human experience. Of course they can be resisted (which is what Christians call 'sin'), and such resistance likewise informs and patterns all aspects of existence, not least the built environment. Echoes and analogies of the divine reality that is grace, I have argued, are encountered wherever we find beauty, justice and order, or proportion. Here we encounter another multicultural objection, because one of the deepest convictions of post-Enlightenment Western culture is that there is no disputing about taste, and one person's taste is as good as another's. If that were simply mapped on to the built environment we would have chaos. That this is not the case is due partly to the survival of vernaculars, partly to the rise of the dominance of the modernist idiom over the past century and partly to the role of local government and of volume builders in providing housing. The result, however, satisfies very few. Virtually everywhere, for different reasons, there seems to be agreement that the pattern language has been lost, that neither our settlements nor our dwellings nourish the soul. In response to that Christopher Alexander, like Raymond Williams, calls for the emergence of a culture in common; he is arguing for the prioritisation of beauty, justice and order, set within a democratic process, in our building and planning. In theological terms this is about the realisation of grace, but it is also about the realisation of the common good because human beings need justice, beauty and order to thrive. This is not an argument for architectural or stylistic uniformity, the adoption of something like Le Corbusier's modulor. On the contrary, I believe that the maintenance of vernaculars is crucial. It is an argument, rather, for much more reflection on just what it is we want to build and what kind of criteria we apply in doing so. Well-insulated, weatherproof, durable, certainly, but also buildings which respect human proportion, which seek to be beautiful and which respect the priority of the common treasury. Where we have buildings which are beautiful, and environments which are just, we have echoes and analogies of grace, and we also have the common good because it is in such environments that all humans thrive. In all forms of the built environment, whether in building or in planning, the dimensions of grace are what we should be looking for and seeking to create. Think for a moment of any town or city street that you know. If it is of any period, say, prior to World War I, then there are likely to be gracious buildings in it on which the eye rests with pleasure, but alongside them will be buildings put up without any regard to their neighbours, built cheaply and without thought – graceless. Grace and its opposite are everywhere. The one ministers to the common good, the other destroys it. Grace, as Paul insisted, liberates: it is the heart of any liberation theology, which is to say a theology which ministers to the whole social body and to the body of each person. In this sense it is a theology of grace, which is also an account of the common good, which I am seeking to explore in this book. In the next chapter I shall pursue the theme in relation to place, the basic setting of the built environment.

CHAPTER 4

Grace and place

The rambler who, for old association's sake, should trace the forsaken coach road running almost in a meridional line from Bristol to the south shore of England, would find himself during the latter half of his journey in the vicinity of some extensive woodlands, interspersed with apple-orchards. Here the trees, timber or fruit-bearing as the case may be, make the wayside hedges ragged by their drip and shade, their lower limbs stretching in level repose over the road, as though reclining on the insubstantial air. At one place, on the skirts of Blackmoor Vale, where the bold brow of High Stoy Hill is seen two or three miles ahead, the leaves lie so thick in autumn as to completely bury the track. The spot is lonely, and when the days are darkening the many gay charioteers now perished who have rolled along the way, the blistered soles that have trodden it, and the tears that have wetted it, return upon the mind of the loiterer.

The physiognomy of a deserted highway expresses solitude to a degree that is not reached by mere dales or downs, and bespeaks a tomb-like stillness more emphatic than that of glades and pools. The contrast of what is with what might be, probably accounts for this. To step, for instance, at the place under notice, from the edge of the plantation into the adjoining thoroughfare, and pause amid its emptiness for a moment, was to exchange by the act of a single stride the simple absence of human companionship for an incubus of the forlorn.[1]

So Thomas Hardy introduces *The Woodlanders*, a novel in which, as in many of his works, place is often as important a subject as the characters. This is what has been called 'anthropological place', 'the one occupied by the indigenous inhabitants who live in it, cultivate it, defend it, mark its strong points and keep its frontiers under surveillance, but who also detect in it the traces of chthonian or celestial powers, ancestors or spirits which populate and animate its private geography'.[2] Mircea Eliade argued that we should not regard 'the superstitions and metaphors of being born of the earth as meant only for children'.

[1] T. Hardy, *The Woodlanders* (London: Macmillan, 1906), p. 1.
[2] M. Augé, *Non Places: Introduction to an Anthropology of Supermodernity* (London: Verso, 1995), p. 42.

Reality is more complex. Until recently there persisted among Europeans the obscure awareness of a mystic solidarity with the land of one's birth. It was not a commonplace love of country or province; it was not admiration of a familiar landscape or veneration of ancestors buried, generation after generation, around the village church. It was something entirely different: the mystic experience of autochthony, of being indigenous, the profound sense of having emerged from the local ground, the sense that the earth had given birth to us, much as it had given birth, in its inexhaustible fertility, to rocks and streams and flowers... The obscure memory of a pre-existence in the womb of the earth has had significant consequences. It has produced among men and women a feeling of cosmic related-ness to the environment; one could even say that at one period men were less aware of belonging to the human species than of a kind of cosmic-biologic participation in the life of their landscape... This sort of experience produced a mystic link with place, whose intensity is still echoed in folklore and popular tradition. But this mystic solidarity was not without consequences. It prevented among men the feeling of being creators. In legitimizing his children who 'arrived' from some part of the Cosmos, the father did not have children of his own, properly speaking, only new members of the family, new implements for work.[3]

Although Hardy had a sense of ancient custom and belonging, his account is much less mystical and more deeply earthed than this, shaped by his prevailing pessimism and by his awareness of class tension. In the situation described in *The Woodlanders* place was destiny. 'Place severely circum-scribed vocation and community. Inseparable from such a strong sense of place is a lack of freedom. The rootedness of [such] existence was bought at a price few of us would or should be willing to pay.'[4] We need, Karsten Harries argues, to recognise technology's ability to liberate human beings and thus to allow them to become more truly themselves. The other side of this limitation, however, was an extraordinary depth of knowledge. So the hero and heroine of *The Woodlanders* had a profound knowledge of the woods in which they worked:

From the light lashing of the twigs upon their faces when brushing through them in the dark, either could pronounce upon the species of the tree whence they stretched; from the quality of the wind's murmur through a bough, either could in like manner name its sort afar off. They knew by a glance at a trunk if its heart were sound, or tainted with incipient decay; and by the state of its upper twigs the stratum that had been reached by its roots.[5]

[3] Quoted in J. B. Jackson, *Discovering the Vernacular Landscape* (New Haven: Yale University Press, 1984), p. 41.
[4] K. Harries, *The Ethical Function of Architecture* (Cambridge, Massachusetts: MIT Press, 1998), p. 163.
[5] Hardy, *The Woodlanders*, p. 415.

Some argue that Hardy was romanticising. Already by the middle of the nineteenth century, argues David Gross, 'the past lay in ruins', and traditions which had provided order and cohesion for societies for hundreds of years were reduced to a mosaic of fragments which the folklorists then had to pick up.[6] Perhaps, then, Hardy and Eliade describe a vanished world with no relevance to the twenty-first century, and such accounts of places are essentially atavistic. I want to argue, by contrast, that knowledge of place, and of the practices of care that it makes possible, is essential to a liberatory politics, which is to say a politics which is sustainable in the long run and which enables human flourishing, which underwrites a genuinely common good. It is part, I shall argue, of a practical politics of grace.

THE LOSS OF PLACE

The philosopher Edward Casey tells a story according to which the category of place, which had a central role in Aristotle, was slowly replaced by the more abstract category of space, a process in which Christian theology played a key role. In the sixth century the Christian philosopher Philoponus, challenging Aristotle, proposed an understanding of an absolute space that was more than a void, an idea which was developed in the Middle Ages, when God's omnipresence was understood as coextensive with the whole of space.[7] The priority of space over place increased in the seventeenth and eighteenth centuries with the rise of the new physics and the invention of the chronometer, which allowed safer long-distance navigation.

Doubtless this is part of the truth but it seems more likely that the loss of a sense of place so keenly felt in the past forty years has to do rather with the 'death of distance' which followed good roads, the petrol combustion engine and air travel. In *The Woodlanders* the tragic action turns upon the impossibility of walking seven or eight miles in the rain. Once car ownership becomes general it is hard to get under the skin of that sense: such a journey would take twenty minutes at maximum and getting drenched would not be an issue. I live twelve miles from my place of work. Had I to walk, over three steep hills and valleys, it would take me three hours each way. Matthew Arnold walked this distance each day – though over much less hilly country – to his work as an inspector of schools in east

---

[6] D. Gross, *The Past in Ruins* (Amherst: University of Massachusetts Press, 1992).
[7] E. Casey, *The Fate of Place: A Philosophical History* (Berkeley: University of California Press, 1998), p. xii.

London in the 1850s. In the village in which I live the time when journeys
to the nearest market town, seven miles distant, were an undertaking when
the ways were 'dirty' is still within living memory. The loss of place owes
much more to asphalt and oil than it does to the philosophers. Certainly
this is Howard Kunstler's view. The confusion that Americans feel about
place and the abstract quality of their thinking about it spring, he thinks,
from the fact that the car has destroyed the physical relationships between
things and thereby the places themselves. The car promised liberation
from the daily bondage of place but in fact it destroys the idea that people
and things exist in some sort of continuity, 'that we belong to the world
physically and chronologically, and that we know where we are'.[8]

There is more to the loss of place, however, than the death of distance.
'We are threatened by two kinds of environmental degradation', wrote
E. V. Walter in 1988, 'one is pollution – . . . the other is loss of meaning.
For the first time in human history, people are systematically building
meaningless places.'[9] This claim can be understood in at least five ways. A
large part of the problem is the impact of what George Ritzer has called the
'McDonaldization of culture'. Fast food shops, coffee shops, fashion shops
have spread around the globe. There is even a McDonald's in Mecca. The
corporations speak of diversity but what they actually give us is 'a One world
placelessness created by an ethnic food court approach'.[10] In a globalized
world, says Zygmunt Bauman, localities lose their meaning-generating and
meaning-negotiating capacity and are increasingly dependent on sense-
giving and interpreting actions which they do not control.[11] The locality
no longer belongs to the people who live there but to those who 'invest' in
it, people who are not bound to the place, and thus constitute a new class
of absentee landlords.[12] Standardisation and uniformity seem to be almost
inevitable outcomes of a globalised economy dominated by massive globe-
spanning corporations geared to mass production and marketing, remarks
David Korten. 'It is difficult to imagine a civilization moving more totally

---

[8] Kunstler, *Geography*, pp. 240, 86, 118.
[9] E. V. Walter, *Placeways: A Theory of the Human Environment* (Chapel Hill: University of North
Carolina Press, 1988), p. 2.
[10] M. Carr, *Bioregionalism and Civil Society: Democratic Challenges to Corporate Globalism* (Vancouver:
UBCP Press, 2004), p. 8.
[11] Z. Bauman, *Globalization: The Human Consequences* (Cambridge: Polity, 1998), p. 3.
[12] Ibid., p. 10. Wendell Berry agrees. The global economy 'operates on the superstition that the
deficiencies or needs or wishes of one place may safely be met by the ruination of another place.
To build houses here, we clear-cut the forests there. To have air conditioning here, we strip mine
the mountains there. To drive our cars here, we sink our oil wells there. It is an absentee economy.'
Berry, *Sex, Economy*, p. 37.

toward standardization and uniformity than one unified by Coca Cola and MTV.'[13] Echoing Marx, the manifesto of The Land is Ours notes that

The first and inevitable effect of the global market is to uproot and destroy land-based cultures. The final and inevitable achievement of a rootless global market will be to destroy itself: Rome fell; the Soviet Empire collapsed; the stars and stripes are fading in the West. Nothing is forever in history, except geography. Capitalism is a confidence trick, a dazzling edifice built on paper promises. It may stand longer than some of us anticipate, but when it crumbles, the land will remain.[14]

Seemingly much more harmless activities, like planting non-native trees, may also contribute to the loss of place. The botanist Oliver Rackham laments the loss of indigenous species, which he feels leads to loss of meaning.

The landscape is a record of our roots . . . Every oak or alder planted in Cambridge (traditionally a city of willows, ashes, elms and cherry-plums) erodes the difference between Cambridge and other places. Part of the value of the native lime tree lies in the meaning embodied in its mysterious natural distribution; it is devalued by being made into a universal tree.[15]

Here there is a call for respect for local distinctiveness known not just in cultural traditions but even in flora and fauna.

Second, tourism, a major industry almost everywhere, encourages Disneyfication, and fascination with travel as an end in itself. It begets a loss of authenticity. Anthony Smith fears that all that will be left of indigenous cultures will be museums for the tourists:

Beneath a modernist veneer we find a pastiche of cultural motifs and styles, underpinned by a universal scientific and technical discourse . . . Standardized, commercialised mass commodities will draw for their contents upon revivals of traditional, folk or national motifs and styles in fashions, furnishings, music and arts, lifted out of their original context and anaesthetized. A global culture would operate at several levels simultaneously: as a cornucopia of standardized commodities, as a patchwork of denationalised ethnic or folk motifs, as a series of generalized 'human values and interests', as a uniform 'scientific discourse of meaning' and finally as the interdependent system of communications which forms the material base for all other components and levels.[16]

---

[13] D. Korten, *When Corporations Rule the World* (West Hartford: Kumarian, 1995), p. 269.
[14] *The Land*, 8 (Winter 2009–10), 2.
[15] Quoted in A. McIntosh, *Soil and Soul: People versus Corporate Power* (London: Aurum, 2002), p. 39.
[16] A. Smith, 'Toward a Global Culture?', in M. Featherstone (ed.), *Global Culture* (London: Sage, 1990), p. 176.

It can be objected that travel has been a feature of all cultures and that they therefore need to be understood in terms of dwelling *and* travel, of roots *and* routes, and therefore as sites of constant cross-fertilisation.[17] Doreen Massey insists that place should not be romanticised and that it has always been subject to negotiation and open to influences from elsewhere.[18] Both these points are just, but what has changed is not only the scale of travel and therefore its impact, but also its nature. The package holiday to a 'foreign' resort equipped to make foreigners 'feel at home', the purpose of which is to 'get some sunshine', is very different from, say, Thomas Doughty's travels in Arabia. There is, of course, increasing tourism from Asia to Europe, but the weight of tourism of all kinds, including back-packing, still takes culturally dominant Western norms into other cultures, begetting, as for instance in Goa or in Kerala, local protest movements aimed at preserving local culture. To say that all localities are in some way networked to the global is an unhelpful obfuscation of the immense differences in the ways in which this is true, and in particular of the power imbalances between places.

In addition to tourism there are huge movements of peoples, displaced by war, poverty or climate change, which means that there are large cultural groups far from their place of origin – the United Nations reported that whereas in 1975 there were 2 million refugees, in 2008 there were 42 million, and the number was growing.[19] As the impact of climate change becomes more marked we can only expect this to continue. As we shall see in Chapter 7, migration may often be a good thing for a local culture. There are claims that it is crucial to the creativity of cities. It does, however, mean that the process of re-constituting what is meant by 'local', which goes on all the time, is immeasurably speeded up. For many critics of Westernisation the worry is that difference will increasingly be elided and that we will end up with a bland, homogenised world.

Third, the anthropologist Marc Augé speaks of the 'non places' of super-modernity. This is the world where we are born in the clinic and die in the hospital, in sterile unrooted places, where there are endless transit points, whether luxury hotels or refugee camps, 'a world surrendered to solitary individuality, to the fleeting, the temporary and the ephemeral'.[20]

---

[17] J. Clifford, 'Travelling Cultures', in Grossberg *et al.* (eds.), *Cultural Studies* (London: Routledge, 1992), pp. 96–116.
[18] D. Massey, *For Space* (London: Sage, 2005), p. 101.
[19] UNHCR report, June 2009, www.unhcr.org/4a375c426.html (last accessed 25 June 2009).
[20] Augé, *Non Places*, p. 78.

Motorways take us around historic places signifying them but avoiding them.

> The landscape keeps its distance, but its natural or architectural details give rise to a text, sometimes supplemented by a schematic plan when it appears that the passing traveller is not really in a position to see the remarkable feature drawn to his attention, and thus has to derive what pleasure he can from the mere knowledge of its proximity.[21]

Fourth, some attempts to deal with the loss of place do not themselves help. Tim Cresswell cites the building of Rancho Santa Margarita in the United States, where a phoney 'sense of the past' is cultivated by neo-traditional architecture and by the circulation of family history newsletters.[22] Kunstler instances an estate agent's office in Saratoga Springs built to look like an eighteenth-century American church, 'cheaply cute, out of scale, symbolically false, stuck in the middle of a parking lot, its mendacious symbolism cheapening the town a little more'.[23]

Lastly, we can point to the dominance of the international style which 'derived from working in every place but understanding no place'.[24] The most appalling buildings of our time, says Scruton, have been commissioned by those who live elsewhere and in another style.[25] In a quite different way suburbanisation likewise produces 'no place', with rows of identical houses which have lost all the traditional connections and continuities of community life, and replaced them with cars and television.[26] Roads run through landscapes littered with cartoon buildings and commercial messages, says Kunstler.

> We whiz by them at fifty-five miles an hour and forget them, because one convenience store looks like the next. They do not celebrate anything beyond their mechanistic ability to sell merchandise. We don't want to remember them. We did not savour the approach and we were not rewarded upon reaching the destination, and it will be the same next time, and every time. There is little sense of having arrived anywhere, because everyplace looks like noplace in particular.[27]

---

[21] Ibid., p. 97.   [22] T. Cresswell, *Place: A Short Introduction* (Oxford: Blackwell, 2004), p. 97.

[23] Kunstler, *Georgraphy*, p. 137.

[24] M. Hough, *Out of Place: Restoring Identity to the Regional Landscape* (New Haven: Yale University Press, 1990), p. 154. Hough points out, however, that pedigreed forms of architecture have denied regional identity for at least 2,000 years without the same impact (p. 18).

[25] Scruton, *Classical Vernacular*, p. 72. By contrast he cites Quinlan Terry, who argues that true style is always in the last analysis local, a response to place, climate, people and history. 'For that very reason it is universal, drawing on the deepest level of man's for home.'

[26] Kunstler, *Geography*, p. 105.   [27] Ibid., p. 131.

Taking all these together, we have the sense of homogenisation that Italo Calvino captures in his reprise of Marco Polo's travels:

If on arriving at Trude I had not read the city's name written in big letters I would have thought I was landing at the same airport from which I had taken off. This was the first time I had come to Trude, but I already knew the hotel where I happened to be lodged . . . Why come to Trude I asked myself. And I already wanted to leave. 'You can resume your flight whenever you like' they said to me, 'but you will arrive at another Trude, absolutely the same, detail by detail. The world is covered by a sole Trude, which does not begin and does not end. Only the name of the airport changes.'[28]

THE SIGNIFICANCE OF PLACE

Does the loss of place matter? Lots of people, including, curiously, many geographers, think it does not. Thus Karsten Harries argues that 'the desire to defeat the tyranny of place is as old as humanity; technology has simply provided us with far more effective means'.[29] 'To be genuinely at home in this world, we have to affirm our essential homelessness . . . every attempt to step into the true centre, to come home in this sense . . . denies the essential ec-centricity of human dwelling – an ec-centricity that needs to be thought in relation to a centre, but a centre that withdraws whenever we seek to seize it.'[30] David Harvey believes that to say that places are a fundamental aspect of human existence is to opt for an exclusionary parochialism. People have deserted the village over the past two centuries because it was so oppressive to the human spirit and so otiose as a form of socio-political organisation.[31] Leonie Sandercock argues that in multicultural societies there is no shared sense of place and the idea of place is not the best 'glue' for understanding and co-existence within them. We should not, therefore, be framing policy initiatives based on the assumption of an integrated community of mutuality and common interest.[32]

Some find hostility to, or at least ambivalence about, place in Christianity. Judaeo-Christian culture, comments Richard Sennett, is at its very roots about spiritual dislocation and homelessness.[33] He points to Abraham, a model of faith for the New Testament authors, who was called to leave his native place and go somewhere completely new. He could have cited

---

[28] I. Calvino, *Invisible Cities* (London: Vintage, 1997), p. 128.   [29] Harries, *Function*, p. 168.
[30] Ibid., p. 200.   [31] Harvey, *Justice*, pp. 320, 425.
[32] L. Sandercock, *Cosmopolis II: Mongrel Cities in the 21st Century* (London: Continuum, 2003), p. 104.
[33] R. Sennett, *The Conscience of the Eye: The Design and Social Life of Cities* (New York: Norton, 1990), p. 6.

the celebrated first-century text known as *The Epistle to Diognetus*, which describes Christians as living in fatherlands of their own, but as aliens, sharing all things as citizens and suffering all things as strangers. 'Every foreign land is their fatherland, and every fatherland a foreign land . . . They pass their days on earth, but they have their citizenship in heaven.'[34] This vision might seem to imply that physical place is not really important. It is group solidarity which matters, not where you live.

Theologically what is at issue is always what promotes life and what destroys it. John's 'I am come to give you life, life in all its fullness' (Jn 10.10) looks back to the great concluding sermon of Deuteronomy in which the author (or authors) urges a choice between a way of life and a way of death. The way of life, for this author (or authors), was tied to obeying Torah, and it included an absolute ban on moving the neighbour's boundary marker (Dt. 27.17). This is because the vision of the Deuteronomist is of a nation of smallholders, where everyone has a stake in the means of production (the land) and where expropriation is the first step towards debt slavery, which is identified as the primary cause of social and economic ruin. But could place be understood as essential to the things which make for life in the twenty-first century? Does place necessarily bind us to exclusionary practices? I shall propose four reasons for regarding place as important for the promotion of fullness of life.

First, there is an ethics of care for the environment which is tied to place. 'A culture capable of preserving land and people', argues Wendell Berry, 'can be made only within a relatively stable and enduring relationship between a local people and its place.'[35] Kindly use of a farm or a town – or a city, we may add – 'depends upon intimate knowledge, the most sensitive responsiveness and responsibility'.

One cannot live in the world; that is, one cannot become, in the easy, generalizing sense with which the phrase is commonly used, a 'world citizen'. There can be no such thing as a global village. No matter how much one may love the world as a whole, one can live fully in it only by living responsibly in some small part of it. Where we live and who we live there with define the terms of our relationship to the world and to humanity. We thus come again to the paradox that one can become whole only by the responsible acceptance of one's partiality.[36]

Profound attachment to place, we could say, is some version of the 'bondage which is freedom'. In Aristotelian terms, acceptance of limits is essential to

[34] Tr. from H. G. Meecham, *The Epistle to Diognetus* (Manchester University Press, 1935), p. 31.
[35] Berry, *Sex, Economy*, p. 171.
[36] W. Berry, 'The Body and the Earth', in *The Unsettling of America: Culture and Agriculture* (San Francisco: Sierra Club, 1996), p. 123.

our humanness and to proper care of the planet. A key way of talking about limits is to talk about place. Yi-Fu Tuan argues that if time is conceived as flow or movement then place is pause.[37] Place involves 'spatial limitation, usually enclosure and the invitation to linger rather than merely pass through'.[38] Thinking of place in terms of limits is perhaps what is meant by M. V. McGinnis' description of human beings as 'boundary creatures', which is to say creatures needing boundaries, disintegrating without them. Such boundaries are represented by all cultural fundamentals – language and cuisine, but also, contrary to the dogmas of modernism, building styles. These boundaries are not respected by the hybridised world of the global economy which is based on the development and homogenisation of space (as opposed to place).[39] 'Managed borders are essential to the very existence of life', argues David Korten. 'If we are to take economic democracy seriously, decisions regarding economic policies and choices must be firmly in the hands of a country's citizens.'[40]

The Old Testament scholar Walter Brueggemann speaks of place as 'a declaration that our humanness cannot be found in escape, detachment, absence of commitment and undefined freedom'.[41] Here again there is insistence on boundaries and limits. For him such limits are implicit in the stories which give meaning to places. Places have meaning because they have a history. Conversely stories have authority 'because they are located in a place'.[42] To be human is to have a story, and stories are located even if, as in Toni Morrison's *Beloved*, they are stories of slavery, captivity, uprooting and homelessness. In many twentieth-century accounts time became a more important category than place. This was even claimed to be a central mark of the Christian revelation. But place includes the category of time, precisely in being storied. To turn that around, time is always, for embodied beings, placed. There are other ways of thinking about this. The human longing for permanence, says Kunstler, represents a response to contingency, the fact that life is 'short, fraught with uncertainty, and sometimes tragic'. The sense of belonging answers this existential need.[43]

[37] Y.-F. Tuan, *Space and Place: The Perspective of Experience* (Minneapolis: University of Minnesota Press, 1977), p. 198.

[38] C. Day, *Spirit and Place* (London: Architectural Press, 2002), p. 162. Cresswell's remark that a ship can be a place and so location is not necessary or sufficient condition of place seems to miss the point. A ship is a bounded space at any given point, occupying a certain longitude and latitude.

[39] M. V. McGinnis, 'A Rehearsal to Bioregionalism', in M. V. McGinnis (ed.), *Bioregionalism* (London: Routledge, 1999), p. 5.

[40] D. Korten, *The Post Corporate World* (West Hartford: Kumarian, 1999), p. 193.

[41] W. Brueggemann, *The Land* (Philadelphia: Fortress, 1975), p. 185.   [42] Ibid., p. 185.

[43] Kunstler, *Geography*, p. 275.

Community cultures, Berry argues, necessarily differ, and sometimes radically so, because places differ. An authentic community is made in reference less to who we are than to where we are. This sounds counterintuitive, but there are ways in which we can understand it. For example, there is the interesting fact that there are no caste communities above 7,000 feet, presumably because there is simply not enough surplus at these altitudes to allow for caste distinction. We can likewise think of the impact of place on Bedouin or Inuit culture, and the disintegration of the latter as climate change begins to destroy the possibility of traditional ways of life. But do cities and towns around the world differ that much? Harvey believes that to attribute causal powers to places is 'the grossest of fetishisms' unless we 'confine ourselves' to the definition of place as social process.[44] This is a surprisingly undialectical position for a Marxist. Of course place cannot be understood without process. 'Place is what takes place ceaselessly, what contributes to history in a specific context through the creation and utilization of a physical setting.'[45] This 'taking place ceaselessly' involves ongoing power struggles between classes, races and genders over the possession and interpretation of place. All place is palimpsest, endlessly written over, something that the heritage industry easily denies. But to *reduce* place to social process is as falsifying as the attempt to understand community purely through place. It is, of course, essential to remember the dispossessed and the refugee: Deuteronomy insists on this as a condition of life. If process is all, however, then all difference and dialect are elided, which brings me to my second point.

In Peter Shaffer's play *Equus* the psychiatrist Dysart says, 'Look! Life is only comprehensible through a thousand local Gods. And not just the old dead ones with names like Zeus – no, but living Geniuses of Place and Person! And not just Greece but modern England! Spirits of certain trees, certain curves of brick wall, certain chip shops, if you like, and slate roofs.'[46] This echoes the remark of the Brazilian bishop Pedro Casadaliga that 'The universal word only speaks dialect.' According to the Jewish and Christian scriptures shalom – peace, justice and welfare, the common good – is impossible without attachment to place. In an article written in 1933, the year when the Nazis came to power in Germany, von Rad reflected on 'rest' in the Old Testament. 'Rest' is about security. Thus the narrative of Joshua concludes with it: 'Thus the Lord gave to Israel all the land that

---

[44] Harvey, *Justice*, p. 320.
[45] A. Pred, 'Place as Historically Contingent Process: Structuration and the Time-Geography of Becoming Places', *Annals of the Association of American Geographers*, 74:2 (1984), p. 279.
[46] Quoted in Walter, *Placeways*, p. 209.

he swore to their ancestors that he would give them; and having taken possession of it, they settled there. And the Lord gave them rest on every side just as he had sworn to their ancestors' (Josh. 21.43–4).

'Rest' and possession of the land are bound up with each other. As von Rad puts it:

> It is emphasised that redemption is a present reality and that all Israel is the chosen people; and it is evident that this notion of the land which Israel is to inhabit . . . is a theological concept of the highest order . . . We must not spiritualise any of this: this 'rest' is not peace of mind, but the altogether tangible peace granted to a nation plagued by enemies and weary of wandering. It is altogether a direct gift from the hand of God.[47]

We can think about this not only in relation to Zionism's quest for place, 'rest', somewhere where Judaism is not 'harried among the nations', but also now in relation to the Palestinians. How do you flourish without place? Following Jeremiah's advice, Judaism flourished in Poland, in Spain, in Germany, as it now flourishes in the United States, but in each of the first three places lack of a homeland spelled disaster, and in every case 'place' remained in the promise, rehearsed each year at Passover, that 'next year' would be in Jerusalem. Judaism was thus sustained by attachment to a place which was at the same time real, alienated and symbolic. Nomadic cultures are not a true counter-example because they operate within set boundaries. Their 'place' is more widely defined than that of other cultures but it is place nonetheless. Perhaps this also applies to the Roma, currently persecuted all over Europe, whose 'place' has been a large cultural area where language, music and cuisine have overlapped with the dominant culture.

The results of human flourishing are the thousands of different cultures world-wide, with their own languages, cuisines, arts, religions and ways of doing things. None of these things, and in particular language, would be possible without place, for geographical permanence is needed for vernaculars of all kinds to emerge. It is important to see things from the perspective of the immigrant or migrant, but when the migrant settles down, sooner or later a new culture emerges, modifying the vernacular (for example in Creole or Yiddish).

Brueggemann's argument that space becomes place through stories which 'envision destiny' is too grand as a general way of thinking about places. Certainly this is true of some places, but a place is no less a place

---

[47] G. von Rad, *The Problem of the Hexateuch and other Essays* (Edinburgh: Oliver & Boyd, 1966), p. 95.

because it is the site of nothing more than the routine maintenance at the heart of culture – hedging, ditching, planting, harvesting, caring for stock in the countryside, maintaining buildings, renewing, rebuilding, generating plans in the town. These unheroic activities likewise en-story the landscape – as for example in the hedges and banks of my area of Devon, which are more than 1,000 years old, or the terracing in Peru, which may be 4,000 years old. Sometimes names attach to these phenomena, but often they do not. They tell stories all the same. And as Berry argues, the people who did all the routine maintenance work were the 'earth keeping classes', whose destruction first by industrialisation and then by globalisation is a disaster.[48]

Third, Sue Clifford and Angela King argue that it is the fineness of grain of our knowledge of neighbourhoods which makes us at home in the world. Human beings, they argue, respond to mosaic. 'We need the nourishment of detail, in things as ordinary as rumples in a field, detail in doors and windows, dialect, local festival days, seasonal variation in the goods on sale in the market, to subtly stimulate our senses and sensibilities.'[49] Tuan speaks of 'topophilia', the affective bond between people and place. The word is anticipated by the much older category of topography, detailed studies of place paying attention to history, culture, flora, fauna and geology which came into fashion already in the eighteenth century and of which the many English county studies are outstanding examples. In his great study of Devon, W. G. Hoskins worked not just from the one-inch but from six-inch and twenty-five-inch maps. Every lane, he found, 'has its own history: it is not there by accident: and every twist it makes has some historical meaning, which we can sometimes decipher today, but not often'.[50]

The claim that humans need the nourishment of detail could be called an aesthetic argument but it is more about a sense of scale. It is an argument that to be truly human involves a kind of depth for which the 'absentee landlord' approach of globalisation is inadequate.

Fourth, Raymond Williams argued that place was essential for liberatory struggles in relation to footloose capital. He envisaged a 'militant particularism' as a way of pursuing the universal goals of socialism. Such a militant particularism might be represented in José Bové's struggle for the cultural integrity of French food, as opposed to the import of hormone-fed American beef; or it might involve the struggle against the Harris superquarry

[48] W. Berry, *The Gift of Good Land* (Berkeley: Counterpoint, 1981), p. 277.
[49] S. Clifford and A. King, *Local Distinctiveness* (London: Common Ground, 1993), p. 14.
[50] W. G. Hoskins, *Devon* (London: Collins, 1954), p. 4.

documented by Alastair McIntosh.[51] Such struggles involve telling stories about place. As Harvey puts it,

> The creation of symbolic places is not given in the stars but painstakingly nurtured and fought over precisely because of the hold that place can have over the imaginary... If places are the locus of collective memory, then social identity and the capacity to mobilize that identity into configurations of political solidarity are highly dependent upon processes of place construction and sustenance... Materiality, representation and imagination are not separate worlds.[52]

'Non place' is contested by struggles which recognise the significance of place. This may involve both ideas of place, as sacred and as healing.

SACRED PLACES

Minucius Felix, in the second century, made it a boast to his pagan contemporaries that Christians 'had no shrines or altars'. This was not on the grounds that sacred spaces were superstitious, but on the grounds that the whole earth was holy, both as created and as redeemed. Soon enough, however, both shrines and altars followed. We can argue that this is necessary. Thus David Harvey argues that the social preservation of religion as a major institution within secular societies has been in part won through the successful creation, protection and nurturing of symbolic places.[53] Lesslie Newbigin was defeated in his attempt to get Tamil villagers to do without church buildings and to revert to house churches, because the buildings provided a locus of identity. It will be interesting to see how long the charismatic movement, which meets in school halls, cinemas and so on, manages without permanent buildings. There are many advantages to such buildings, and once they are obtained it is odd to have them as just another space, without any markers of transcendence. Drawing on Heidegger, Norberg-Schulz argues that sacred buildings 'clarify' a place, set it within a cosmic context. The village church, or the cathedral, then, set the village or the city within another interpretive context in the same way

---

[51] J. Bové and F. Dufour, *The World is not for Sale* (London: Verso, 2001); McIntosh, *Soil and Soul*. Richard Sennett points out that contemporary capital is not as footloose as all that and that it has discovered that 'local social and cultural geographies count for a great deal in particular investment decisions'. *The Corrosion of Character* (New York: Norton, 1999), p. 136.

[52] Harvey, *Justice*, p. 322. From a rather different perspective Harries argues that it is the function of buildings to turn space into place: *Function*, pp. 154, 213.

[53] D. Harvey, 'From Space to Place and Back Again: Reflections on the Condition of Postmodernity', in I. Bird *et al.* (eds.), *Mapping the Futures: Local Cultures, Global Change* (London: Routledge, 1993), p. 23.

that the act of anamnesis in the eucharist sets our daily bread in another context.

The term 'context' here means a credo and a vision of the world that is expressed as a 'place par excellence'. In Europe for centuries the church has fulfilled this role, and its architecture clearly illustrates what is concealed by the word 'clarification'. The church above all has clarified the place and its life as a collective part of the order of the universe.[54]

Casey asks whether it is accidental that the obsession with space as something infinite and ubiquitous coincided with the spread of Christianity, a religion with universalist aspirations.[55] What he misses is the dialectical nature of the gospel from the very start, for the Bible is a book full of place names. Think of Jabbok, Dothan, Bethel, Gibeon, Ramah, Bethlehem, Jerusalem, Samaria, Nazareth, Corinth, Ephesus, Rome. All of these are richly storied, they attest to divine engagement and to redemption in particular places at particular times. In one way or another each place name reiterates the truth that the Word becomes flesh.

Belden Lane remarks that a theology of transcendence will never be fully comfortable with place, but although this seems logical, simply recalling the importance of place in Islam shows that it misses an important point.[56] In Islam sacred places speak either of God's revelation to Mohammed or to later messengers. In Christianity pilgrimage sites were sometimes storied – think of Assisi – though often the stories were invented for ideological reasons, as at Compostella or Cologne. Karl Barth returns us to Minucius Felix in his doctrine that God's omnipresence means that God can be present to all things in infinitely differentiated ways – one way in the eucharist, another in personal encounter, another in the natural world and so on.

How, then, should we understand the countless places which people do find 'holy' in contrast to others, in the way in which George Macleod found Iona to be a 'thin place', a place where the boundary between this world and the other world is easily broken through? Christopher Day suggests that wholeness and integrity depend upon the place's underlying invisible ecology. Spirit of place is influenced by human thought and action: how

[54] C. Norberg-Schulz, *Architecture: Presence, Language, Place* (Milan: Skira, 2000), p. 39.

[55] Casey, *The Fate of Place*. Cf. A. Escobar: 'Since Plato, Western philosophy – often times with the help of theology and physics – has enshrined space as the absolute, unlimited and universal, while banning place to the realm of the particular, the limited, the local and the bound.' 'Culture Sits in Places: Reflections on Globalism and Subaltern Strategies of Localization', *Political Geography*, 20/2 (2001), p. 143.

[56] Cited in J. Inge, *A Christian Theology of Place* (Aldershot: Ashgate, 2003), p. 41.

places are used, revered, un-valued or exploited affects them. The 'cultured landscape of Europe bears the marks of a thousand years of Christendom. As well as spiritual values and social patterns every settled or tended piece of land was permeated by the sound of church bells.'[57] For him any place that makes us aware of the presence of spiritual powers, changing our inner state and inducing reverence, is a holy place. This experience, both humbling and ennobling, transforms our relationship to the world around us. It is personally, socially and environmentally therapeutic.[58]

This account makes sense, though we need to think of the way in which places of horror, for example Dachau or Auschwitz, can become calls to repentance or to conversion, and how holy places can be taken over by pious tack. It does not change Barth's insight that so-called sacred places exist not in a different class from all other space but to signal the possibilities inherent in all place. Sacred places should be understood sacramentally so that 'holy' places point to the redemption of all places in Christ. A shrine, argues John Inge, is a permanent and much needed reminder that this is not a human-centred universe: it revolves around God and for God. 'The shrine should be a protest against every worldly presumption, against every political dictatorship, against every ideology that wishes to say everything regarding the human being, because the shrine reminds us that there is another dimension.'[59] Sacred places, then, are reminders of the truth that Minucius Felix wanted to adumbrate, but they are perilous reminders because there is always the danger that they work in the opposite way, as they did in so much of European history, and teach a fundamental divide between sacred and secular which prevents us from understanding 'the earth as the Lord's'.

The opposite of seeing the whole earth as sacred is seeing everything as profane. Objecting to that, Kunstler appeals to the concept of charm, which, as we have seen, is related to the idea of grace. The word 'charm', he says, may seem fussy, trivial and vague.

I use it to mean explicitly that which makes our physical surroundings worth caring about. It is not a trivial matter, for we are presently suffering on a massive scale the social consequences of living in places that are not worth caring about. Charm is dependent on connectedness, on continuities, on the relation of one thing to another, often expressed as tension, like the tension between private space and public space, or the sacred and workaday, or the interplay of a space that is easily comprehensible, such as a street, with the mystery of openings that beckon, such as a doorway set deeply in a building. Of course if the public space is degraded

---

[57] Day, *Spirit and Place*, p. 164.   [58] Ibid., p. 239.   [59] Inge, *Christian Theology*, p. 109.

by cars and their special needs . . . the equation is spoiled. If nothing is sacred, then everything is profane.[60]

Kunstler appeals to the sacred–secular distinction, among others, as something which introduces difference and helps us delight in, and therefore cherish, places. If we fail to do that, he argues, we end up by building places unworthy of love, precisely the 'no place' he thinks Americans have created over the past fifty years.[61] Profanity, then, lack of charm, lack of grace, gives us an ugly, utilitarian landscape. Some kind of recognition of grace is needed to endow the built environment with beauty and mystery. Without this we wither culturally.

HEALING PLACES

Kunstler's argument is put in another way by Christopher Alexander. As we saw in the last chapter he argues that the difference between a good and bad building or town is objective and makes the difference between health and sickness, wholeness and dividedness, self-maintenance and self-destruction. The language he uses has close affinities with the semantic range of *sozein* (to save) in the New Testament. 'In a world which is healthy, whole, alive and self maintaining, people themselves can be alive and self creating. In a world which is unwhole and self-destroying, people cannot be alive: they will inevitably themselves be self-destroying and miserable.'[62] Partly because of the model we absorb from the natural sciences, where the building blocks of reality are imaged as being identical, but also because the quality without a name cannot be pinned down, Alexander argues that people are not prepared to believe that there are objective factors which make a building or a place good or bad, life-creating or life-immiserating.

However, we all know that places and buildings affect us. We do not just have to think of slums and toxic chemical plants, nor even of sick building syndrome, but of the everyday environments that perhaps most of the world's population live in. Christopher Day points out that damaged places correlate with high rates of tuberculosis, schizophrenia, alcoholism, coronary disease, pregnancy complications, accidents and suicide.[63] There is abundant evidence, Alexander argued in 1977, to show that high buildings make people crazy.

High buildings have no genuine advantage, except in speculative gains for banks and land owners. They are not cheaper, they do not help create open space, they

---

[60] Kunstler, *Geography*, p. 168.   [61] Ibid., p. 173.   [62] Alexander, *Timeless Way*, p. 25.
[63] Day, *Spirit and Place*, p. 150.

destroy the townscape, they destroy social life, they promote crime, they make life difficult for children, they are expensive to maintain, they wreck the open spaces near them, and they damage light and air and view. But quite apart from all of this... empirical evidence shows that they can actually damage people's minds and feelings.[64]

Buildings communicate to us. 'Their messages stem from the underlying attitudes with which places are planned, made, used and maintained. Few of us consciously acknowledge these messages, but subliminally we all experience them, all are affected by them.'[65] At heart, this is about values, the spirit that underlies them, the subliminal language of place.

The obverse of this is both that places can be healed and also that there can be healing places. You do not have to go to Lourdes or the Ganges for healing. It is as an art of place, remarks Norberg-Schulz, that architecture can promote healing.[66] Much of Camillo Sitte's work on city planning should be understood as a way of making places more beautiful and therefore more wholesome. The way we design a square and the siting of a statue or a fountain are not trifling matters but can make all the difference between a life-giving or a life-denying place. 'Environment can heal as well as harm. Places of spirit-uplifting beauty, honest and unpretentious, with loving care manifest in every detail, nourish both individual and society. They encourage sensitivity to other's feelings, responsibility for actions, communal concert and honesty; provide soul-contentment without need for physical props, and build membership of community and of place: physical, ecological and spiritual.'[67] Places of transformative beauty – places which inspire, motivate, give meaning and fulfilment – are spirit-nurturing. 'This is about artistic commitment. Not ego assertive art but listening to situations so form condenses out of the needs of place, people and circumstance. Social participation and ecological appropriateness are part of this – so is loving commitment: inspiration, care, energy and will.'[68]

It is interesting that both Alexander and Day think of healing places as egoless. Both men, so far as one can judge, find inspiration in traditions other than Christianity, but their work chimes in with much Christian reflection over the centuries, and in particular with the observation that sin, as ego-assertion, the will to power which rides rough-shod over others and over place, is destructive and needs redemption. 'Salvation' of course derives from the word for healing. We have come rather late to the perception that healing is not just a matter of mind and body, but of the surroundings we

[64] Alexander *et al.*, *Pattern Language*, p. 115.   [65] Day, *Spirit and Place*, p. 155.
[66] Norberg-Schulz, *Architecture*, p. 11.   [67] Day, *Spirit and Place*, p. 117.   [68] Ibid., p. 184.

make for ourselves as well. I shall turn to the business of place-making in the next chapter, where I consider planning.

It was Patrick Geddes in Edinburgh who first insisted that a city should be considered together with its region. This insistence was taken up by Lewis Mumford, and already implemented in the work of the Regional Planning Association in America. From the 1970s onwards it has developed in terms of the movement we know as 'bioregionalism', the key insight of which is that present political boundaries map very crudely, if at all, on to boundaries represented by watersheds, soil, and the species differentiation which goes with them. 'A bioregion is literally and etymologically a life place – a unique region definable by natural (rather than by political) boundaries with a geographic, climatic, hydrological, and ecological character capable of supporting unique human and nonhuman living communities.'[69]

Borrowing a phrase from an Irish writer at the time of the Easter Rising, and ultimately from Scripture, Kirkpatrick Sale spoke of bioregionalism in terms of learning to become 'dwellers in the land'. Place was central to his understanding:

> The crucial and perhaps only and all-encompassing task is to understand place, the immediate specific place where we live. The kinds of soils and rocks under our feet; the source of the waters we drink; the meaning of the different kinds of winds; the common insects, birds, mammals, plants and trees; the particular cycles of the seasons; the times to plant and harvest and forage. The limits of its resources; the carrying capacities of its lands and waters; the places where it must not be stressed; the places where its bounties can best be developed; the treasures it holds and withholds. And the cultures of the people, of the populations native to the land and of those who have grown up with it, the human social and economic arrangements shaped by and adapted to the geomorphic ones, in both urban and rural settings . . . That, in essence, is bioregionalism.[70]

The need to be attentive to the conditions of flourishing in any given region if we are thinking of a world population of eight or ten billion ought to be self evident, but Sale's talk of 'populations native to the land' rings alarm bells. Some such appeal is made by right-wing parties throughout

---

[69] R. L. Thayer, *Life Place: Bioregional Thought and Practice* (Berkeley: University of California Press, 2003), p. 3.

[70] K. Sale, *Dwellers in the Land: The Bioregional Vision* (Athens: University of Georgia Press, 1991), p. 42.

Table 2 *The bioregional paradigm, from Sale,*
Dwellers in the Land

	Bioregional paradigm	Industrio-scientific paradigm
Scale	Region	State
	Community	Nation/world
Economy	Conservation	Exploitation
	Stability	Change/progress
	Self-sufficiency	World economy
	Co-operation	Competition
Polity	Decentralisation	Centralisation
	Complementarity	Hierarchy
	Diversity	Uniformity
Society	Symbiosis	Polarisation
	Evolution	Growth/violence
	Division	Monoculture

Europe, wanting immigrants to 'return home'; it was the ground of ethnic cleansing in the former Yugoslavia. Place has grounded some of the most reactionary politics. Many historical struggles over boundaries were over rivers, watersheds and ports, but equally colonialism and cease-fires left a world full of arbitrary boundaries which cannot easily be unpicked, as the present map of the Middle East, or of northern India, makes obvious. Could place ground a progressive rather than a reactionary politics? Could there be such a thing as a politics of grace? Is not politics inevitably a 'dirty game', the 'art of the possible'? Would not a politics of grace be the Kingdom of God, and is it not a theological axiom that this cannot be 'built' and will not be realised this side of eternity? These objections are cogent but at the same time, according to Scripture, human beings are charged with seeking to shape reality in conformance with God's will of justice, mercy and love. There can be approximations to these things, as well as wicked denials of them. Politics is not abandoned to the devil. The question, then, is whether place might play any part in such approximations. Sale mapped out the differences between bioregionalism and the reigning paradigm, which he called 'industrio-scientific', as shown in Table 2.[71] I shall follow Sale's main headings in asking whether place has a part in a redemptive politics, beginning with scale.

[71] Ibid., p. 50.

Scale

The organisation of the world into groups of nations is a relatively recent event, beginning in Europe in the fifteenth century and not completed even there until the nineteenth. The result of European colonialism and the North American hegemony which followed that has been the export of either parliamentary democracy or republican government on the American model to much of the rest of the world. This is what has counted for 'freedom' in the political rhetoric of the past sixty years. But in the first place it becomes increasingly clear that representative democracy in large-scale nation states is a very imperfect realisation of rule 'by the people, for the people'. Though these forms of government are doubtless better than what preceded them, the sheer scale of representative democracy, organised around great party machines, subject to manipulation by a media owned by a few immensely wealthy moguls, means that people feel disempowered. 'Voter apathy' represents not so much a disinterest in politics as a cynicism about a certain kind of politics, about career politicians and about the ability to shape the future by casting one's vote for a large-scale party every few years.

Second, over the past forty years globalisation has challenged the control of the nation state, with crucial economic decisions made in unelected boardrooms, while at the same time global institutions like the International Monetary Fund and the World Bank have assumed greater prominence. The nation state, Castells argues, has lost much of its sovereignty, having been undermined by the dynamics of global flows and trans-organisational networks of wealth, information and power.[72] These well-known trends are challenged by the environmental movement because, with regard to the environment, scale is crucial. Bioregionalism argues that in the face of the global emergency any politics worth the name has to care properly for the environment but that this can happen only when it is organised on a regional level. Of course a global emergency has to be addressed globally, but Sale argues that worthwhile environmental interventions can be made only 'where the forces of government and society are still recognizable and comprehensible'. It is a question not primarily of political principle but of pragmatism: what is it that actually works? When the effects of individual actions are visible 'people will do the environmentally correct thing not because it is thought to be moral *but rather*

---

[72] M. Castells, *The Power of Identity* (Oxford: Blackwell, 1997), p. 342.

the practical thing to do. That cannot be done on a global scale nor a continental nor even a national one because the human animal being small and limited has only a small view of the world and a limited comprehension of how to act within it.'[73] The democratic legitimacy of the institutions to which we yield power, argues Korten, derives, first, from their being duly constituted by and accountable to the sovereign people; second, from their conducting their operations according to an appropriate code of morals and ethics; and, third, from their producing desirable consequences for the whole. Currently, he argues, they are failing on all three counts because they are too big and too distant.[74] 'Scale', we could argue, would be an important part of a progressive politics in allowing for the proper engagement of the citizenry. We could read it as analogous to the proportion we saw instantiating grace in the previous chapter.

In a celebrated piece of analysis Hedley Bull canvassed the possibility of a 'new medievalism' with overlapping and segmented authorities. Such a development, he thought, might lead to a more peaceful world. In tying states together in a tight web of economic, cultural and social relations the resort to war might be inhibited. Any such development, he noted, depended on maintaining and extending a consensus about common interests and values that provide the foundations of common rules and institutions.[75] He was sceptical of the possibility of agreement on such values, and the present 'clash of civilisations' between Western capitalism and Muslim fundamentalism perhaps underlines that. On the other hand, there is growing evidence of awareness of the need to address the global emergency, which can rest only on common values – values which prioritise not the state or capital, but people and planet. Any such new regionalism would need a strong co-ordinating body such as the United Nations to ensure that problems were truly being addressed globally.

The argument in favour of regionalism is far from conclusive because one might have the bulk of a population, as seems to have been the case in Serbia, in favour of ethnic cleansing. The question of how one prevents such a community lapsing into a poisonous chauvinism was perhaps the question which exercised the Levitical writers, with their constant reiteration of the need to care for the migrant worker and the immigrant. For them an ethic of care was one of the defining marks of the community. This points to a vision of open place, but such a vision will always be threatened when resources become scarce.

---

[73] Sale, *Dwellers*, p. 53 (my italics).   [74] Korten, *Post Corporate World*, p. 294.
[75] H. Bull, *The Anarchical Society* (London: Macmillan, 1977), p. 315.

Antony Giddens challenges the view that the nation state has had its day. In his estimate it is crucial in addressing the global emergency. 'Bottom-up' initiatives cannot tackle the causes of climate change, and only a few big states have the capability to pioneer the relevant technological innovation.[76] Small-scale, local initiatives have their place but by themselves they are no solution to the problems we face. The argument is cogent to the extent that we have to envisage institutions which network regions and communities, and ultimately enforce commonly made decisions, but this could be a version of the United Nations rather than the nation state as we know it.

Does such a vision of a politics of place represent a romantic return to a pre-capitalist and communitarian world of non-scientific understandings with limited divisions of labour? Rather than that, Harvey argues that we must seek re-enchantment with the sensuous world through more sensitive science, social relations and material practices.[77] Part of what is at issue here is what the impact of the global emergency is likely to be. One of the most interesting responses to the global emergency, socially and politically, is the Transition Town movement.[78] This presupposes both that we are going to have to live without present levels of oil use very soon and that there is no substitute for oil on the horizon. It therefore looks to build local resilience by thinking about 'foodsheds' – areas which can provide food for a given town, city or region which is not dependent on being trucked or flown in. It also thinks about how this will be produced. This involves 'the great re-skilling' – learning the rudiments of the pre-oil technology which are necessary for the production of the means of life. Is this romanticism or realism? Richard Heinberg calls the view that 'something will turn up' 'waiting for the magic elixir', but we could equally call it the Micawber principle. Predicting the future is, of course, notoriously chancy, as any inspection of books on alternative economics from twenty years ago will verify. At the same time, refusing to think about the likely impacts of peak oil and climate change in the belief that something or other will turn up which will enable us to maintain our present way of life is irresponsible superstition. The Transition movement builds on the earlier work of bioregionalism. Thinking in terms of regions is one way of thinking, practically, about the likely response to the global emergency.

---

[76] Giddens, *Politics*, pp. 91, 220.   [77] Harvey, *Justice*, pp. 199, 200.
[78] For this see R. Hopkins, *The Transition Handbook* (Totnes: Green Books, 2008).

Economy

Because a community is by definition placed, argues Wendell Berry, 'its success cannot be divided from the success of its place, its natural setting and surroundings: its soils, forests, grasslands, plans and animals, water, light, and air. The two economies, the natural and the human, support each other; each is the other's hope of a durable and a liveable life.'[79] Berry is not thinking primarily about regions here, but an important influence on bioregional understanding has been Jane Jacobs, who argued that cities, rather than nations, were the principal generators of wealth and that cities had to be understood within their regions. As Sale put it,

> Every city is part of a region, after all, and depends on the surrounding countryside for many of its resources and much of its market, and every city is built upon a natural foundation. Knowing place for the urban dweller, then, means learning the details of the trade and resource dependency between city and country and the population limits appropriate to the region's carrying capacity. It also suggests exploring the natural potential of the land on which the city rests . . . one can discover and measure the possibilities for rooftop gardens, solar energy, recycling, urban silviculture and the like.[80]

Daniel Kemmis, sometime Mayor of Missoula in Montana, wants to argue that there is no such thing as 'rural America' or 'the rural economy'. These are misleading abstractions. Rather, there are real places like Louisville and the region surrounding it, and real economies like Missoula, whose long-term prosperity depends on learning to make the region operate as a natural economy.[81] Seattle has rejected plans for a suburb of 4,500 homes because it has begun to understand that its long-term viability can be secured only by acting like a city region or city state and therefore it has to begin to knit together the destinies of city, suburbs and surrounding countryside.[82]

For Jacobs the main motor of any economy is trade between cities which are just rising to prominence, and where import substitution takes place within the city region. One of the problems with this argument is that Jacobs paid no attention to corporate ownership. More than a decade ago *The Economist* reported that in the automotive, airline, aerospace, electronic components, electrical and electronics and steel industries the top five firms control more than half of the global market. Globalisation does not increase competition, argues David Korten, but strengthens global

---

[79] W. Berry, 'Does Community have a Value?', in *Home Economics*, p. 192.   [80] Sale, *Dwellers*, p. 45.
[81] D. Kemmis, *The Good City and the Good Life* (Boston: Houghton Mifflin, 1995), p. 119.
[82] Ibid., p. 120.

monopoly.[83] Already by 1993 the largest 300 global corporations owned around one-quarter of the world's productive assets. This means that at least a quarter of the assets on which the world's people and communities depend for their living are held under the most extreme form of absentee ownership delinked from concern or responsibility for their well-being.[84] One of the things that bioregional economics is concerned with, then, is the democratisation of the economic process. George Monbiot, with many others, argues that corporate power has to be restricted. In 1720, after corporations had exceeded their powers in Britain, the government introduced an act which provided that all commercial undertakings 'tending to the common grievance, prejudice and inconvenience of His Majesty's subjects' 'would be rendered void'. Big business, Monbiot argues, must once again be forced to apply for a licence to trade, which would be revoked as soon as its terms were breached.[85]

Taming the corporations is certainly an aspect of a progressive economy, but bioregionalists also envisage a network of regional economies around the globe focussed on local production, recycling, local taxes and currencies and the like.[86] Bioregional economics 'is by definition about trust, interdependence, mutual aid, and cooperative and compassionate relations among humans and between humans and all species'.[87] Local currencies have been taken up by the Transition Town movement, having been long tried in American cities such as Ithaca. As an Ithacan representative puts it,

We printed our own money because we watched federal dollars come to town, shake a few hands then leave to buy rain forest lumber and fight wars. Ithaca's HOURS stay in our region and help us to hire each other. While dollars make us increasingly dependent on multinational corporations and bankers, HOURS reinforce community trading and expand commerce that is more accountable to our concerns for ecology and justice.[88]

The question that sceptics have about this vision is whether it is not reintroducing subsistence economies in which the dynamism and creativity of the past 250 years, with all their real gains, are lost. How would research and development be funded? Even if we allow that many new inventions are not worthwhile there is an argument that the culture of creativity needs to be sustained, and that this requires the kind of money that both corporations and nation states can muster. Could the impoverishment which often attaches to restrictions on foreign trade be overcome? Are

---

[83] Korten, *Post Corporate World*, p. 223.   [84] Ibid., p. 167.
[85] G. Monbiot, *Captive State* (London: Macmillan, 2000), p. 354.   [86] Sale, *Dwellers*, p. 120.
[87] Carr, *Bioregionalism*, p. 105.   [88] Thayer, *Life Place*, p. 141.

welfare and health services envisaged, and if not, what follows them? If they are, how are they funded? Where do the funds for the present level of medical research come from? Not everyone is cheerful about replacing a National Health Service, however rickety, with a reliance on acupuncture and herbal medicine! Without the global stockmarket would there be the pensions which many Western citizens have come to take for granted? All these are serious questions but there are some very clear guiding principles. One is that the present, corporate-driven, model is unsustainable. The second is that a world economy run in the interests of the 1 per cent of the world's citizens who own any stocks and shares is self-evidently unjust and, if the principles of democracy are conceded, as I shall argue in the next chapter that they ought to be, then finding realistic ways for realising economic democracy is important.[89] Giddens, who, as we saw, does not put his faith in local initiatives, nevertheless believes that subsidiarity should come fully into play. 'Many policies will be best forged and delivered primarily in local communities. Local knowledge will be important in how best to proceed.'[90] He also believes that an important role remains for the United Nations and its many offshoots. What is important here is the replacement of the Bretton Woods Institutions with the democratic economic institutions that Keynes wanted. Noting that we cannot predict the impacts of the global emergency with regard to climate, water, food and so forth, Richard Heinberg argues that the only way forward is to build resilience throughout the system. 'Resilience implies dispersed control points and dispersed inventories, and hence regional self-sufficiency – the opposite of economic efficiency, the central rationale for globalization – and so it needs to be organized primarily at local level.'[91]

Polity

The processes of economic globalisation, David Korten argues, are not only spreading mass poverty, environmental devastation and social disintegration, they are also weakening our capacity for constructive social and cultural innovation at a time when such innovation is needed as never

[89] Harvey argues that we cannot 'reject the world of sociability which has been achieved by the interlinking of all people and places into a global economy and we should somehow build upon this achievement and seek to transform it and use it for progressive purposes'. *Justice*, p. 314. One wonders what world of sociability he is talking about. Would a world where most of the people most of the time were on the move be sustainable, or would it not, once again, be a dark ages?

[90] Giddens, *Politics*, p. 167.

[91] Richard Heinberg, 'The Meaning of Copenhagen', Museletter 212, January 2010, www.richardheinberg.com (last accessed 28 January 2010).

before.[92] He cites John Dillon to the effect that if one concedes that financial markets largely rule the world, then all that is left for governments and central banks is to try to please these markets by pursuing the policies the bond traders demand: low inflation enforced through monetarist policies of high real interest rates and high unemployment, and policies of fiscal austerity. 'In essence this means abandoning the most basic principles of democracy.'[93] The political vision of bioregionalism may be understood as a way of realising a form of participative democracy. It thinks in terms of the local community in the region, taking responsibility for its own affairs, which is exactly the understanding of the Transition movement. This is democracy not by two-thirds majority but by consensus, not by propaganda but by persuasion, grounded in practical ways to respond to the global emergency. It is political because it is about ordinary people taking their future into their own hands, shaping their own economies and their communities. Place is important because, as Daniel Kemmis argues, to inhabit a place is 'to dwell there in a practised way, in a way which relies upon certain regular, trusted, habits of behaviour'.

Our prevailing individualistic frame of mind has led us to forget this root sense of the concept of inhabitation. We take it for granted that the way we live in place is a matter of individual choice. We have largely lost the sense that our capacity to live well in place might depend upon our ability to relate to neighbours on the basis of shared habits of behaviour. In fact, no real public life is possible except among people who are engaged in the project of inhabiting a place.[94]

The political vision is gradualist. 'It suggests that the processes of change – first of organizing, educating, activating a constituency and then of reimagining, reshaping and recreating a continent are slow, steady, continuous and methodical, not revolutionary and cataclysmic.'[95] Sale suggested that not every bioregion would be signed up to democracy, equality, liberty, freedom and justice. 'Different cultures could be expected to have quite different views about what political forms could best accomplish their bioregional goals.'[96] This nod to difference, which alarms some critics as suggesting that authoritarian forms of government might be acceptable, and therefore raising the spectre of eco-fascism, is qualified by the observation that 'The task is to build power at the bottom, not to take it away at the top, to release the energies, the long hidden and systematically blunted energies,

---

[92] Korten, *When Corporations Rule the World*, p. 269.   [93] Korten, *Post Corporate World*, p. 163.
[94] D. Kemmis, *Community and the Politics of Place* (Norman: University of Oklahoma Press, 1990), p. 79.
[95] Sale, *Dwellers*, p. 176.   [96] Ibid., p. 108.

of people where they actually live and on the issues they regularly face.'[97] Of course, these issues might be understood as immigration or, as in the case of the Taliban, the rejection of Western views of the rights of women. It is clear that commitment to place is not in itself a guarantee of a progressive politics. Talk of the need for education and re-imagination would certainly be construed in some circles as yet another form of Western colonialism. Such an allegation would discern rightly that there are normative views of the human at stake here, which Sale does not quite own up to, but which we have no need to feel embarrassed about. As argued in Chapter 1, ethics is the conversation of the human race about its common project, and how it understands itself. Different understandings of what it means to be human, and therefore to live in community, are in contest. Christianity insists on the equal humanity of all, and on the political rights which follow from that. The polity that a proper respect for human equality leads to, one could argue, must be in some shape or form democratic.[98] Bioregionalism asks us to think about how our understanding of the human is affected by place. It does not deny the universal, but it notes that the universal is always known in and through particulars. In virtue of its doctrine of incarnation Christianity cannot but agree with this.

incarnate universalism

Many have suggested that the state must not be weakened as this would simply hand the palm to the corporations. Over-mighty subjects need to be policed by adequate power – a re-run of the emergence of the nation state in Europe. But would regionally organised participatory democracy lack power? That is surely a very questionable assumption, as a more regionally organised world would all the more need fora like the United Nations. One of the weaknesses of the present United Nations is that its assumptions, for example about human rights, rest on beliefs which some members reject. Once again we are brought back to the contest of moral opinions which underlie law. In arguing these out we explore the most fundamental bases of ethics. Given the need for concerted action in response to climate change, these debates, especially those between Christianity and Islam, take on an added urgency.

Society

As we see, arguments about economics and politics rest on a view of society and of the human. Such views may be either religious or secular. Certainly

---

[97] Ibid., p. 170.
[98] Karl Barth argued this in 'The Christian Community and the Civil Community', in *Against the Stream: Shorter Post-War Writings* (London: SCM, 1954), p. 44.

in the West, but perhaps more widely, the scientific world-view 'shapes the patterns of our psyches, the foundation of our various social systems, the sources and sustenance of our economy, the latticework of our political systems. In short it has become our god.'[99] In its place Sale wants to put a vision which emphasises the interdependence of human beings and the natural world. To do this, he believes, we need smaller-scale regions. 'As books are improved by division into chapters, houses into rooms, and ships into compartments, so human societies are improved by division into regions, a natural phenomenon found in all cultures – and regions into areas and cities into communities.'[100] Contrary to the reigning paradigm, Sale does not assume that the bigger the better but rather that there are scales beyond which it does not make sense to go, especially with regard to the size of cities.

Mike Carr argues that the Great Transformation rested on a change in the concept of the human being and that we need another great transformation 'away from an acquisitive, materialistic, alienated culture and toward a sustainable society rooted in qualitative relationships among whole individuals integrated or embedded in healthy families and communities'.[101] Western economies, as we have seen, are built on the idea of the 'rational utility maximiser' who meets his or her needs through consumption. By contrast, 'bioregionalists' experiences support a view of humans as genuine social beings quite capable of discovering the joy of sharing common identities with other beings of place and the spiritual empowerment of emotional, embodied connection with the community of all beings in a particular place'.[102] Co-operation has to take the place of competition if we are to survive, it is argued. Robert Thayer argues that the evolutionary survival of humanity 'has depended largely upon social cooperation in place' and that this has been true for the majority of the world's people until the past couple of decades.[103] In other words, prioritising the common good has been the way humanity has both survived and progressed.

Sale takes from natural phenomena a challenge to the Darwinist 'survival of the fittest' paradigm, speaking of symbiosis instead, by which he means the preparedness of forms of life to sacrifice life or good for others. In human relations he looks to the sacrifices involved in parenting, while at the regional level he looks at the relation of city and country. 'Following a symbiotic model, the goals would be to establish parity in the relationships between a city and its hinterlands, a mutual flow that recognizes the

---

[99] Sale, *Dwellers*, p. 21.   [100] Ibid., p. 128.   [101] Carr, *Bioregionalism*, p. 36.
[102] Ibid., p. 294.   [103] Quoted in Thayer, *Life Place*, p. 55.

dependence – a needful, mutually understood dependence – of one upon the other.'[104]

He discerns in nature, again, not novelty and rapidity but stability and adjustment. 'The overall character of a bioregional society, therefore, is directed by images of sustenance and maintenance, the slow healing and mending behaviour of all living things, rather than those of alteration and inconstancy, which are usually the signs of damage and disease.'[105] Morality would not be centred on protecting private property but on securing bioregional stasis and environmental equilibrium.

It would be 'wrong' in such a society to urinate in five gallons of water and flush it into a river, to use chemical fertilizers, to build a skyscraper or a mall or any energy wasteful building, to eat high on the food chain day after day, to devote a farm to a single crop, to burn or discard organic garbage, to be ignorant of the phrases 'carrying capacity' and 'biotic community'.[106]

The proposal is, then, that a place-based politics, rather than being exclusionary, chauvinist and parochial, could be a basis for a nurturing and co-operative society in which individual dignity is respected and the needs of eight or ten billion are met. Prophecies that the nation state is dead are probably premature, but that there are more creative ways of organising human community has to be true, and perhaps a proper attention to the physical features which sustain us is as promising a way to think about alternatives as any. In prioritising justice and compassion with regard both to the neighbour and to the natural world such a politics would be a politics of grace and would at the same time be a promotion of the common good in both the Thomist and the Patristic sense. Key to the whole argument is a vision of placed community. Community, I have argued, is unintelligible without rootedness even if these are the roots or routes of Roma or Bedouin migration. Christians are led by their faith to cherish place while at the same time recognising that the whole earth is the Lord's, and therefore celebrating difference. In an overcrowded world this is already a key ethical demand, and the requirement to celebrate both place and difference, to seek the common good in the place to which we are sent, in Jeremiah's terms, will be crucial to the maintenance of fully human values in the coming century.

---

[104] Sale, *Dwellers*, p. 114.   [105] Ibid., p. 119.   [106] Ibid., p. 120.

CHAPTER 5

Grace, politics and planning

Jesus tells his disciples to 'take no thought for the morrow', which is a warning against being so preoccupied with the cares of everyday life that the priorities of the kingdom are neglected. It is not, I suggest, a condemnation of planning. In the theological romance which concludes the book of Genesis the whole of salvation history turns on planning. Joseph deals with the pattern of uneven harvest, good years and bad years, by establishing vast grain silos where grain can be stored and then made available in time of need. It is this prescience, according to the narrator, that allows Israel to survive, and Joseph sets it down to God: 'God sent me before you to preserve life' (Gen. 45.7). Where there is no vision the people perish', said the Wisdom writer, thinking of the purposes which guide a community (Prov. 29.18). In the New Testament what happened in Christ is understood as God's plan (*oikonomia*) of salvation (Eph. 3.9). Jesus, according to Luke, was delivered up 'according to the definite plan [*boule*, counsel] and foreknowledge of God' (Acts 2.23). In the Church Fathers the idea of the divine *oikonomia* represented everything that God did for the salvation of the world from creation to the second coming. Such ideas led Karl Barth to speak of God as both 'the Planner and the Plan', a dangerous ploy in the era of Soviet Five Year Plans! He accordingly distanced himself from a totalitarianism which subordinated the individual to the good of the whole.[1] If we are to speak of a divine plan we must free the idea from all thoughts of predestination and understand it, instead, in terms of divine wisdom, as the word *boule* in Acts suggests. Wisdom is God's infinite creativity and grace in gifting freedom to the creature and preserving and accompanying creation in response to that freedom. 'Plan', in fact, is the wrong word: 'meaning, purpose and directedness' would be better, implying guidance by an infinite redemptive resourcefulness. That the wisdom of God is the ground of creation means that there is

---

[1] K. Barth, *Church Dogmatics*, vol. III/3 (Edinburgh: T. & T. Clark, 1960), p. 173.

a promise of sense in what otherwise appears senseless in historical and created process. Grace and wisdom, I suggest, are the ways in which we have to think theologically of planning. In the Trinitarian scheme set out in Chapter 1 I appropriate planning under God the Creator, the one who brings order out of chaos. All plans rest on values, as I shall illustrate in detail. 'What is the nature of man?' asked Raymond Unwin. 'What are we like? What do we aim at being? Do we want to become standardised men and women?'[2] These questions underlie every plan, whether stated overtly or not. Every plan has some response to the question of the common good, perhaps in dispensing with the idea. Every plan changes the ecology of an area, for good and ill, and therefore ecology, the understanding that 'everything relates to everything else', as Barry Commoner put it, is the core concept in planning and in turn expresses overarching values.

Town planning goes back at least to Hellenistic times and is implicit in any large-scale human enterprise. Considerable planning must have been involved in the construction of Stonehenge! I want to begin, however, with what Lewis Mumford, following Camillo Sitte, called 'organic planning'.

ORGANIC PLANNING

'Old planning was not conceived on a drafting board', wrote Camillo Sitte, thinking especially of Siena, 'but instead developed gradually *in natura*, allowing for all that the eye notices *in natura* and treating with indifference that which would be apparent only on paper.'[3] The growth of Siena, like that of many medieval cathedrals, took several hundred years, at each stage of which the city council deliberated in relation to what had gone before. The adaptations of organic planning, Mumford argued, 'become increasingly coherent and purposeful, so that they generate a complex, final design, hardly less unified than a pre-formed geometric pattern'. In organic planning one thing leads to another, and what began as the seizure of an accidental advantage may prompt a strong element in a design which an a priori plan could not anticipate, and in all probability would overlook or rule out. 'Those who dismiss organic plans as unworthy of the name of plan', he wrote, 'confuse mere formalism and regularity with purposefulness, and irregularity with intellectual confusion or technical incompetence. The towns of the Middle Ages confute this formalistic illusion. For all their variety, they embody a universal pattern; and their very

---

[2] Quoted in F. Jackson, *Sir Raymond Unwin: Architect, Planner and Visionary* (London: Zwemmer, 1985), p. 145.
[3] C. Sitte, *The Birth of Modern City Planning*, ed. G. and C. Collins (New York: Dover, 1986), p. 189.

departures and irregularities are usually not merely sound, but often subtle, in their blending of practical need and aesthetic insight.'[4] A gridiron plan on hilly sites, for example, puts a constant tax on the time and energy of inhabitants. In contrast the winding streets of medieval Siena respected the contours, but intersected them at intervals to open up a view, dropping steeply in flights of stairs to serve as pedestrian short cuts. 'This demonstrates admirably the aesthetic and engineering superiority of an organic plan, carried out with other ends in view than the maximum number of saleable lots and the minimum exercise of imagination.'[5] Mechanical and organic planning, Mumford argued, are quite different. One springs out of the total situation, the other simplifies the facts of life for the sake of an artful system of concepts. One works co-operatively with 'the materials of others', perhaps guiding them, but first acknowledging their existence and understanding their purpose; the other, that of the baroque despot – or of many modern planners – insists upon his law, his order, his society, and is imposed by a single professional authority, working under his command.[6]

It could be argued that the idea of organic planning is a chimaera, on the grounds that it dignifies a haphazard process which we happen to like with a sense of purpose. Sitte argued that the irregular places of the Middle Ages were definitely designed on sound, artistic lines to produce the definite effects aimed at, and were not the result of accidental growth. 'It is likely that this theory is being pushed further than the evidence will support', commented Unwin. 'There is however, no doubt that in the Middle Ages there was such a strong and widely prevalent tradition of the right and wrong in building at any period, that the builders seem at least to have been generally capable of seizing upon accidental irregularities, and making something definitely fitting and beautiful out of them.'[7] We are presented with a mystery, said Sitte. 'The mystery of the innate, instinctive aesthetic sense that worked such obvious wonders for the old masters without resort to narrow aesthetic dogma or stuffy rules. We, on the other hand, come along afterward, scurrying about with our T square and compass, presuming to solve with clumsy geometry those fine points that are matters of pure sensitivity.'[8] Sitte and Unwin are pointing to the role of culture in the planning process, something picked up by Christopher Alexander in *A Pattern Language*. Alexander thinks of towns, streets, buildings and so on as orders of connecting relationships. In the

[4] Mumford, *City*, p. 348.   [5] Ibid., p. 483.   [6] Ibid., p. 450.
[7] R. Unwin, *Town Planning in Practice: An Introduction to the Art of Designing Cities and Suburbs*, 2nd edn (London: Fisher Unwin, 1911), p. 194.
[8] Sitte, *Birth*, p. 159.

older European towns, he argues, all the patterns had certain qualities in common based on shared human emotional and psychological needs: the need for greenery, sunlight, places to be with other people, spaces to be alone, spaces for the young and old to mix, spaces for excitement and tranquillity. To build well again, he argues, we need to recover the culture. To build beautiful places, 'It is essential that the people of a society, together, all the millions of them, not just professional architects, design all the millions of places. There is no other way that human variety, and the reality of specific human lives, can find their way into the structure of places.'[9] What he wants to avoid is the tyranny of the expert. 'As soon as a few people begin to build for "the many", their ideas about what is needed become abstract; no matter how well meaning they are, their ideas gradually get out of touch with reality, because they are not faced with the living examples of what the patterns say.'[10] Similarly, in a town where the common language has vanished and the construction is in the hands of a few, the design is clumsy.[11] When working properly, 'millions of individual acts of building will together generate a town which is alive, and whole, and unpredictable, without control. This is the slow emergence of the quality without a name, as if from nothing.'[12]

The question is, of course, whether the degree of cultural consensus this implies would ever again be possible and whether, in a society where everything has to be done at once, a process of designing over centuries would make sense.

PLANNING AND THE COMMAND ECONOMY

Modern town planning was born out of a reaction to the squalor and anarchy of the nineteenth-century industrial town. We get a glimpse of the moral fervour that produced it in Thomas Sharp's call for planning in 1940. 'For fifteen years and more in places like Rhondda, Jarrow and Bishop Auckland', he wrote, 'hundreds of thousands of Englishmen have been eating their hearts out in squalid, dole-supported unemployment spent among fouled landscapes and filthy slum-built towns with hardly a hand lifted to help them.' The English refusal to plan, he felt, was ignoble

---

[9] Alexander, *Timeless Way*, p. 164. Kunstler echoes this. 'We have lost so much culture in the sense of how to build things well. Bodies of knowledge and sets of skills that took centuries to develop were tossed in the garbage and we will not get them back easily. The culture of architecture was lost to Modernism and its dogmas. The culture of town planning was handed over to lawyers and bureaucrats and with pockets of resistance mopped up by the automobile, highway and real estate interests.' *Geography*, p. 245.
[10] Alexander, *Timeless Way*, p. 236.   [11] Ibid., p. 355.   [12] Ibid., p. xiv.

and inhuman. Such planning as there had been was 'haphazard, unrelated, short-term, small visioned' when what was needed was big-visioned, long-term, comprehensive. He went on,

> It is no overstatement to say that the simple choice between planning and non-planning, between order and disorder, is a test choice for English democracy. In the long run even the worst democratic muddle is preferable to a dictator's dream bought at the price of liberty and decency. But the English muddle is nevertheless a matter for shame. We shall never get rid of its shamefulness unless we plan our activities. And plan we must – not for the sake of our physical environment only, but to save and fulfil democracy itself.[13]

He almost certainly had in mind Daniel Burnham's famous advice to 'make no small plans' on the grounds that they lacked the ability to stir people's imaginations. His connection between planning and democracy was prescient, though it may not have seemed obvious at the time. The war made a command economy essential and set the scene for the 'golden age of planning' which followed. Planners knew what was best for people; they drew up their plans and executed them; and the population was improved. In contrast with organic planning this kind of planning has implicit moral purpose. John Burns introduced the Housing, Town Planning Bill of 1909 with the words 'The object of this Bill is to provide a domestic condition for people in which their physical health, their morals, their character, and their whole social condition can be improved . . . The Bill aims in broad outlines at, and hopes to secure, the home healthy, the house beautiful, the town pleasant, the city dignified, and the suburb salubrious.'[14] Kantorovich in 1967 claimed that town planning 'is dedicated to the promotion of an efficient and life-enhancing relationship between man and his physical environment'.[15] Even today, in a much more sceptical age, planning can still be defined as 'managing change in order to try and achieve a better future'.[16] Better according to whom, and according to which standards, is, of course, the question. Talk of morals, character, something being life-enhancing, things being better or worse, presupposes an accepted vision of what it means to be human, a contested issue since such visions are culturally constructed.

As a way of examining the assumptions which underlay planning in its 'golden age' I shall look at Patrick Abercrombie's plan for Plymouth of 1943. Plymouth was the heart of Royal Navy operations in World War II and

[13] T. Sharp, *Town Planning* (Harmondsworth: Penguin, 1940), p. 143.
[14] Quoted in P. Hall, *Cities of Tomorrow* (Oxford: Blackwell, 1988), p. 53.
[15] Quoted in J. M. Simmie, *Citizens in Conflict* (London: Hutchinson, 1974), p. 183.
[16] T. Kitchen, *Skills for Planning Practice* (Aldershot: Ashgate, 2007), p. 88.

naturally attracted the attentions of the Luftwaffe. Air raids lasted a week, and when they were finished the whole of the nineteenth-century town was destroyed and roughly 70,000 people made homeless. The mayor, Lord Astor, was a friend of Abercrombie's, the most famous British planner of the day and in charge of the rebuilding of London. He persuaded him to take on Plymouth as well, and the plan appeared within a year.

Today consultation is part of every planning process, although it may not amount to very much. Abercrombie, however, scarcely consulted at all. This was not because he disdained the public but because he was intent on preventing land speculation and wanted to keep land prices down. His plan envisaged re-housing 69,000 people.[17] It helped to pioneer many new ideas including landscaping to an overall plan, the inner-ring road strategy for minimising through traffic, the attempted co-ordination of building design and the use of the city's landlord powers to control advertising and land use. Although it does not set out its philosophy we can, I think, discern six main principles behind it.

The plan rests on a coherent anthropology. Abercrombie learned from planners like Clarence Perry and from Lewis Mumford, whose wartime pamphlet *The Social Foundations of Post-war Building* he cites. 'We forget the human spirit and the changes of the human spirit to which everything should be adjusted', wrote Mumford, 'and we tinker too much with mere structure... The City must be planned for a community life... and not as a mere repository of industry.'[18] During the war years, Abercrombie commented,

there has been a decided trend of public opinion back to the spirit of the com-munity, and increasingly insistent demands are being made for better and more efficient use of the land to the benefit of the people as a whole... Experience in the war has exemplified the fact that when the cause of the community is at stake, individualism must be subordinated.[19]

Sprawling cities, it was argued, had encouraged an anonymous way of life deficient in community activities and loyalties. Abercrombie believed that Perry's neighbourhood units were the means to recreate community. Industry and housing should be zoned rather than mixed promiscuously as they had been in the old town. 'Here are to be found in close juxta-position, but properly segregated, Home, Work, and Play, Administration and Business, National and Local life.'[20] The new neighbourhood was to be a 'development of the medieval community around the village green'.[21]

---

[17] J. Paton Watson and P. Abercrombie, *Plymouth* (London: Underhill, 1943).
[18] Ibid., p. 4.   [19] Ibid., p. 28.   [20] Ibid., p. 7.   [21] Ibid., pp. 81–2.

Each neighbourhood should have between 6,000 and 10,000 people. These figures were based on the numbers necessary to sustain a primary school. Traffic would be diverted round the edge but shops and other community facilities would be at the heart. Each precinct should have a neighbourhood centre with a community building, a church or chapel, a small library, a cinema, a restaurant, a café or hotel, shops, a laundry and child welfare and other clinics.[22] The community building should be a comparatively simple affair, the main purpose of which is that it should be the place where the citizens amuse themselves rather than listen to performances by experts. In the hilly environment of Plymouth, Abercrombie used the valley floors for open space, put housing on the slopes and used the hill-top sites for industry, schools and playing fields.

Second, Abercrombie was concerned for human scale. He noted that

It is not generally appreciated that it is the community spirit developed from that inherent characteristic of all races in the form of mutual aid which has been mainly responsible for the development of art and knowledge in the best periods of progress in personal industry, craftsmanship and science...A perversion of this wholesome spirit of community life has driven the human race to congregate together and, despite a natural love of the country, we are still enlarging our towns, until we now have forty-four towns in the world with a population of over a million.[23]

In that case human scale is lost. Grouping the city in neighbourhoods counteracted this. Abercrombie believed with Unwin that nothing was gained by overcrowding. He believed that density should not exceed a hundred persons per acre.

Third, he maximised the amount of recreational space and insisted that this was not just for games. He quoted Mumford: 'There is not a village or a housing estate that is well planned, unless it has made provision for places of withdrawal – solitary walks, devious woodland paths – no less than

---

[22] These principles were abandoned thirty years later as it was found that they had not taken sufficient account of demographics. Primary schools were faced with falling rolls and had to be closed. However, with 'new urbanism', we seem to be reinventing the wheel. The major principles of new urbanism are to create compact, walkable neighbourhoods with clearly defined centres and edges with a public space, a square or green, at its heart surrounded by public buildings. There should be a focus on diverse mixed activities in close proximity: living, shopping, schools, work-places and parks. Streets should be reclaimed, with building entrances fronting the street rather than parking spaces. A wide spectrum of housing options should enable people of a broad range of incomes, ages and family type to live within a single area. Landry, *Art of City-Making*, p. 306. Brian Walker points out that Alexander's *A Pattern Language* takes up these ideas in Pattern no. 12, 'Community of 7000'. Here the community buildings function to decentralize political power. Walker, 'Another Kind of Science', p. 1061.

[23] Paton Watson and Abercrombie, *Plymouth*, p. 78.

places where people can gather together in groups for social communion.'[24] These open spaces were networked across the city, so that it was virtually possible to walk from north to south through parkland and woodland.

Fourth, Abercrombie believed his was the first plan to rank agriculture equal to city extension. Town and farm were visualised as complementary parts of an indivisible whole, each with its own use and each with its distinct and clearly marked boundaries.[25] He believed that agriculture would continue to be one of Britain's main industries and that indiscriminate spread of urban growth, which often took the best and most fertile land, must be stopped.

Fifth, he gave thought to beauty. In the neighbourhood units, he argued, 'there is opportunity for the latest thought in seemly community design. They must be absolutely first rate; each with a pre-determined optimum population, but having sufficient area to give a reasonable choice of site and not conceived as a single housing scheme to be built at once'.[26] His plan for the centre was based on a grid with two main axes, Armada Way, running from north to south between the railway station and the Hoe, and Royal Parade, running from east to west between the main shopping area and a cluster of civic buildings; the former was to be a 'Garden Vista' making use, with terraces, slopes, steps, pools, avenues and other contrasting features, of the varying levels. Abercrombie wanted 'one of the finest railways stations . . . in the Kingdom' at the top of Armada Way. The railway hotel was to be planted with palms so that travellers knew they had arrived in the warm south-west.

Abercrombie wanted his streets to bear comparison with the streets of Nash and Wood the Younger in London and Bath and therefore wanted them designed as a whole. The openness and modernity of the new centre was intended to stand in sharp contrast to the antiquity of the Barbican quarter to the south-east, which had escaped the bombs. The city as a whole was intended to counterpoint the beauty of coast and moor, between which it was sandwiched. It was intended to show what human beings are 'capable of in the way of artificial design for purpose and delight'.[27] In contemporary terms we can say that Abercrombie understood that the city plan had to enhance the ecology of the whole region rather than to damage it.

Sixth, Abercrombie wanted to escape the tyranny of the motor car. He proposed segregation of traffic and pedestrians, the provision of dual carriageways, separate cycle tracks and pedestrian ways and the restriction of side road and riparian access on to main traffic routes. He further

[24] Ibid., p. 4.   [25] Ibid., p. 3.   [26] Ibid., p. 4.   [27] Ibid., p. 9.

proposed pedestrian precincts, accessible only by bus and delivery vehicles, areas for the civic centre, the theatre, shops and banks and insurance firms. In Abercrombie's vision, no child would have to cross a main road on the way to school.

This plan, therefore, gives us six key themes: an anthropology on which it rests, which is what we would today call 'communitarian'; human scale; recreational space; the importance of agriculture, or the town–country theme; beauty; and the need to deal with traffic. We can see that there is a strong commitment to an overarching common good behind the whole plan. Eliot had written in 1925 (in *The Hollow Men*):

> Between the idea
> And the reality
> Between the motion
> And the act
> Falls the Shadow

One of the problems with Abercrombie's plan was the shabbiness and lack of imagination, in turn linked to lack of cash, of the realisation. Neither the station nor the station hotel was ever built. Instead, tawdry tower blocks marked both the station and the civic centre. The buildings of the centre are dull and uninspiring and the city lacks legibility. In the opinion of some, the box-like architecture is partly conditioned by the rigid geometry of the street pattern. The absence of alleyways compels long walks round the main blocks, and the absence of narrow streets means that there is no protection from westerly gales.[28] Traffic flows were seriously underestimated, so road and footpath patterns fail to separate traffic and pedestrians. In terms of aesthetic and landscape the neighbourhood units do recall village greens, but are let down by the shabby buildings around. The community facilities so essential to the neighbourhood idea were not provided on the scale envisaged, and the reconstruction of the village community spirit proved elusive.

PLANNING FOR THE AGE OF THE CAR

The dirigisme of this type of plan gave way, in the 1960s, to 'systems' planning, in which 'cities and regions were viewed as complex systems . . . while planning was seen as a continuous process of control and monitoring of

---

[28] M. Brayshay (ed.), *Post-War Plymouth: Planning and Reconstruction*, South West Papers in Geography, University of Exeter, 1983.

these systems derived from the then new science of cybernetics'.[29] One of the key figures in this change was Melvin Webber, who was called in to lead seminars in the preparation of the plan for Milton Keynes, a third-generation new town. Webber was described by the city's first architect as its 'true father'.[30] Peter Hall has remarked that systems plans had a distinctly blueprint tinge, and this is certainly true of Milton Keynes, despite the sharing-out of architectural design between different architects.[31] For Simmie systems theory rests on 'hidden ideological foundations, requires impossible feats of functional rationality, and is substantially irrational . . . It contains the idea that the natural or normal state of the system is some kind of integrated equilibrium to which the system itself is, or policies should be, directed. Thus it contains an implicit reification of the status quo.'[32] The idea behind the original garden city had been to create 'an environment as conducive as possible to good health, happiness, stimulation and satisfaction during their youth and working lives, and contentment and care in their old age'.[33] The area designated for the city, the act for which was passed in 1967, was forty-nine square miles, which incorporated nineteen old communities including eleven villages.

As with Abercrombie's plan there is a clear anthropology, which is individualism. The idea of the common good was simply abandoned. Webber believed that, in the age of the car, community would be based on voluntary association rather than propinquity. The logic of this was a suburban city. Villages were all very well, Webber taught, but their horizons were narrow. The voluntary community made possible by mass car transport represented social gain. Both in theory and practice this became the heart of the Milton Keynes vision. On the one hand the rationale for the city was re-housing. People were moved to the city and old networks were thus broken. In this situation they relied first and foremost on their partners. At the same time the priority of 'family-based activity' was part of the philosophy. 'If the average English family want a suburban life without excessive imposition of noise, overcrowding and movement problems', wrote Walker, 'a suburban city such as Milton Keynes can be encouraged.'[34] Densities were very low, typically between thirty and thirty-three houses to the hectare (more or less the same as that recommended by the Tudor Walters Report in 1918 and favoured by Unwin).

[29] Hall, *Cities of Tomorrow*, p. 327.
[30] D. Walker, *The Architecture and Planning of Milton Keynes* (London: Architectural Press 1982), p. 8.
[31] Hall, *Cities of Tomorrow*, p. 330.   [32] Simmie, *Citizens in Conflict*, p. 185.
[33] T. Bendixson and J. Platt, *Milton Keynes: Image and Reality* (Cambridge: Granta, 1992), p. 37.
[34] Walker, *Architecture*, p. 138.

The social vision of the new town was egalitarian. When Margaret Thatcher came to power in 1979, and told the Milton Keynes Development Corporation that it should bring in 'a better class of people', its head insisted that Milton Keynes wanted 'no nob's hill'. But the old socialist idea of the priority of community took a back seat, in part against the wishes of the planners. The first goal of the master plan was opportunity and choice, which referred to both jobs and housing. The plan's idea was that community facilities and shops would be placed on neighbourhood borders, so that people could cross from one area to another, a process made easier by the construction of underpasses. Design considerations led to their being situated away from roads, and thus the idea was never really implemented. An attempt to see that there were no class ghettoes failed, again, partly for reasons of design. 'Netherfield and Coffee Hall were not at all what was envisaged in the master plan. These huge, repetitive "worker housing" schemes reduced choice while the siting, for reasons of architectural form, of pubs, shops and schools away from the main roads isolated each square from its neighbours.'[35] Others represented the triumph of design over common sense and, like the development in Fullers Slade, failed to give people privacy. The use of flat aluminium roofs and profiled aluminium panels suggested prefabs. Some of the failures in design stemmed from tight budgets imposed by government. This led to barrack-like terraces and the loss of footpaths and adequate landscaping. Writing in 1982, Walker confessed that it was difficult to build huge numbers of houses successfully.

Meanness of scale has become apparent; the quality of generosity is not there. Dimensions have become tighter; bay windows have disappeared; the paper thinness of current detailing, and the lack of surface modelling have led to an architecture of cosmetics where colour and ultimately blanket landscape form a camouflage . . . Mass housing requires a Messiah not a Minister to thread us through the eye of the blind needle. APPLICATIONS PLEASE.[36]

It is hard not to feel that some of the failures rest in design. The severely modernist Netherfield, built in 1973, quickly became one of the most deprived estates in Britain, attracting large regeneration funding which was spent on putting on pitched roofs.

The emphasis on choice was a reaction to the old bureaucratic socialism, which denied people any autonomy if they were in corporation housing, but it fitted seamlessly into the Thatcherite era, for which 'opportunity'

---

[35] Bendixson and Platt, *Milton Keynes*, p. 99.　　[36] Walker, *Architecture*, p. 41.

and 'choice' were watchwords. During the 1980s the local Conservative MP described people in Milton Keynes as 'apolitical' and 'classless', the 'new Britain'.[37] For the first decade more public than private housing was built. By the end of the 1980s the reverse was true. Shared ownership – part mortgage and part rent, with a view to perhaps taking on a 100 per cent mortgage at some point – played a large part in this move. The overall result was to create what some have described as a middle-class ghetto, where it becomes increasingly difficult to get people to do menial jobs.

Milton Keynes is hardly an eco-town, but ecological considerations were part of its initial brief. By 1990 there were 5,000 energy-efficient houses in Milton Keynes, and all new houses are built to exacting energy conservation standards. However, the arguments for a city based on a light rail network, advocated by the county planner in the early days and long the preferred option, were overruled in favour of the car. The idea had been to provide a free monorail service, paid for out of the rates, which would link small townships of 5,000 to 7,000 like beads on a string. This was finally overruled as too expensive but today seems like a missed opportunity. The roads have been as expensive, and have determined the social ethos of the city. Walker insisted that the city was designed for the resident rather than the motorist, but the plan for the centre was predicated on mass car ownership, with wide boulevards, parking areas and walkways. Against the suggestions of the original plan the corporation allowed itself to keep parking in the centre. Today, English Partnerships is seeking to put parking on the outskirts and to build more housing on the boulevards. Bendixson considers that making public transport central to the city 'would have turned it into a glorified council estate' but this judgement looks very odd from the perspective of the rest of Europe, where public transport is much better provided and used.[38]

The main problem for Milton Keynes was to work out what it stood for. Plymouth, like many old towns, grew up around an industry – the naval dockyard. Such industries gave the towns their character and their raison d'être. The original reason for building Milton Keynes was the need for housing, driven by a prediction, which turned out to be grossly inaccurate, that Britain's population would grow by 20 million before 2000. The job of the corporation was to attract industry to the town in order to keep pace with the development of housing. In this it has been outstandingly successful, for the town now has more than 3,500 firms operating in it,

---

[37] Bendixson and Platt, *Milton Keynes*, p. 253.   [38] Ibid., p. 266.

including the Open University, one of its biggest employers.[39] However, this back-to-front development meant that the planners had to ask what they understood by urbanity. Derek Walker's answer was 'physical largeness; a feeling of intensity of use, of gathering together; a certain range of opportunities made possible by an urban scale; a positive contrast with the countryside; the celebration of urban detail; an enjoyment of the properties as an end in itself'.[40] This does not yet take us to the meaning of the city; some have suggested that this has been defined in terms of consumerism and leisure, with one journalist describing the shopping mall, the first of its kind in Britain, as a 'huge glass cathedral . . . a 21st century shrine to imaginative entrepreneurship'.[41] Milton Keynes, writes Bendixson, is not a place for the quaint, the mystical and the old. 'It is bold, new, shiny, rational, progressive and materialist . . . The rational in us admires its logic. The romantic in us fears its order.'[42] But is Bendixson confusing what is rational and progressive with the centrality of consumerism and leisure? Of course, all cities have markets and places for leisure, but if they become the heart of the city is not the heart hollow? In the past, great cities have usually had places for defence, places for civic debate or religious shrines as their symbolic centre. As it happens, the city's most notable landmark is its ecumenical church, but architecturally this represents a colossal missed opportunity, a lightweight quotation of earlier forms which represents no attempt to think through what a church for a new city ought to look like. Bendixson commends the fact that it was partly financed by the building of two nearby office blocks: it shows.

The lack of vision for the town is reflected in the planning of the centre. The master plan originally envisaged a rambling place around pedestrian squares and malls, with parking at the fringes. In fact the planners opted for broad boulevards flanked by parking and then by footways, 'classic city streets expanded to provide room for the age of the Ford Sierra'.[43] The centre has been called 'a celebration of the right angle'. Walker sought human scale and wanted to provide an environment which, while not requiring the users to learn new or strange urban skills, 'may offer some urban delights: space, greenery, legibility and the opportunity for peace and quiet'. He wanted legibility, but this is notoriously missing, a problem compounded by the preservation in street maps and terminology of the 'verticals' and 'horizontals' of the plan. The centre is let down by the

---

[39] Today the main industries include electronics, computing, food processing, distribution and business services, just as Melvin Webber predicted. Unemployment is nominal at 1.5 per cent.

[40] Walker, *Architecture*, p. 8.   [41] Lee Scriven, *Independent Guide to Milton Keynes*.

[42] Bendixson and Platt, *Milton Keynes*, p. viii.   [43] Ibid., p. 131.

absence of any truly inspiring buildings. There are no skyscrapers here, indeed few buildings higher than the trees, but modernism is the primary inspiration. There were no pitched roofs in central Milton Keynes until 1989.

The master plan was committed to consultation, but this took the form of obtaining feedback every six or seven years, when people asked, unsurprisingly, for privacy, kitchens big enough to eat in and lots of storage space, and expressed concern about noisy neighbours. Today English Partnerships, the quasi-autonomous non-governmental organisation (quango) which eventually took over from the Milton Keynes Development Corporation, is committed to much greater consultation, but the results of this are still awaited. The plan turned its back on zoning, aiming instead to 'restore a natural balance and interrelation' between city living, working, learning and playing. The result, however, is suggestive of either a suburb situated in an industrial estate, or vice versa, and the buildings of the industrial estates are not always very clearly distinguishable from those of the centre.

Where the realisation of the plan has been outstandingly successful is in the incorporation of park land, which constitutes almost a quarter of the total area. Because the city is built on flood plain, it has had to incorporate a network of large lakes, which are now used for leisure activities. Walker described Milton Keynes as 'a soft city set in open countryside where the quality of the grid road offers a neutral counterpoint to the external countryside and to less ordered roads within'. The park land is arranged so that cyclists, horse riders and water-borne transport can move across the city. The valleys of the Ouze and the Ouzel cannot be built on, and existing woodlands were conserved. The city was divided into six zones, each of which is planted with different major species of tree and shrub, emphasising a natural difference between areas.

The city has solved the problem of congestion, but finding one's way around as a motorist remains a problem. Generous tree planting helps deal with air pollution, but also cuts down vistas. The undifferentiated nature of the grid system means that all roads feel much the same. There is an outstanding footpath and cycle system, the 'red route', which runs for 320 kms. and incorporates existing village routes and towpaths, but it is used by only 3 per cent of the population.

In sum, in Milton Keynes we can see a return to individualism, a commitment to egalitarianism, but also a lack of any coherent idea of what it is which makes a town or city. 'Where there is no vision the people perish.' People like living in Milton Keynes, we are told, but what does the city tell its people about who they are and what they should become?

Critique of top-down planning began directly after World War II, even as Plymouth was being rebuilt, on the grounds that such planning stifled individual initiative, imposed rigid lifeless solutions and gave planners too much power.[44] Above all the results seemed dismal. Why should Utopia have been such an all-pervading failure, asked Alice Coleman, when it was envisaged as a form of national salvation? 'It was conceived in compassion but has been born and bred in authoritarianism, profligacy and frustration. It aimed to liberate people from the slums but has come to represent an even worse form of bondage. It aspired to beautify the urban environment, but has been transmogrified into the epitome of ugliness.'[45] She pointed to ideologically driven bureaucracy as the heart of the problem.[46] But in the United States, with a very different political history, the same period had also produced

a crisis of the human habitat: cities ruined by corporate gigantism and abstract renewal schemes, public buildings and public spaces unworthy of human affection, vast sprawling suburbs that lack any sense of community, housing that the un-rich cannot afford to live in, a slavish obeisance to the needs of automobiles and their dependent industries at the expense of human needs, and a gathering ecological calamity that we have only begun to measure.[47]

Kunstler, the author of this critique, points the finger not at bureaucracy but at the values of modernism.

All over the world many planners adapted the basic idea of Le Corbusier, of towers in a park, 'the maddest of all Utopian schemes', 'where streets are replaced by empty spaces from which towers arise, towers bearing

---

[44] Cited in G. Cherry, *Town Planning in Britain since 1900* (Oxford: Blackwell, 1996), p. 119.

[45] A. Coleman, *Utopia on Trial: Vision and Reality in Planned Housing* (London: Shipman, 1985), p. 180.

[46] 'The introduction of planning suppressed spontaneous progress, and the Department of Environmet and its predecessors have presided over one counter-productive policy after another. Housing shortages have been perpetuated by compulsory eviction, leaving large numbers of dwellings unoccupied for years; by massive demolition programmes; by diversion of potential building investment funds into lavish spending on housing bureaucracies; by insistence on pointless density standards; by planning delays; by the squandering of public money on superfluous common parts dictated by the obsession with flats; and by absorbing resources to deal with large-scale building defects that would not have occurred if we had followed our tradition of homes in individual houses.' Ibid., p. 183.

[47] Kunstler, *Geography*, p. 60.

neither the mark of a communal order, nor any visible record of the individual house, and demonstrating in their every aspect the triumph of that collective individualism from which both community and individual are abolished'.[48] Popular outrage at these things, Scruton remarks, is not a matter of taste but much more a re-affirmation of injured moral feeling.

These critiques produced a marked disenchantment with planning. For neo-liberalism planning itself was the problem, and the way forward was to leave things to private enterprise.[49] Planning was an unnecessary interference in the market. As this worked out in a scheme like the redevelopment of London's Dockland, however, investing in industry and public housing was not attractive to the private sector, which favoured luxury housing, tourism and office development. Any community benefits which accrued were not intended but a spin-off of the market. The idea of the common good was not simply abandoned but ridiculed as old-fashioned and counter-productive. The result was a mixture of tragedy and farce. Transport needs were not thought through and had to be put in late at immense cost to the taxpayer, who thus underwrote the financial sector. Moreover, market forces have produced a place 'with no real soul and without the saving grace of classical architecture, good transport or public spaces'.[50] A study of the episode concludes that

Market led planning does not work. It does not work on its own terms because it is not market led but dependent on public activity and investment. It does not work on the private sector's terms because the necessary infrastructure is not planned sufficiently and it does not work from the point of view of local residents whose needs have not been met and who have been faced with the threat of being replaced by another community while all the time being excluded from decision making.[51]

One of the lessons to be drawn from the whole exercise is that the principles of strategic planning are vital and that their abandonment leads to 'the anarchy of the market' and costly and unpopular mistakes.[52]

If we ask what anthropology underlies this form of planning we come up with some form of Social Darwinism. Charles Landry remarks that

The internal logic of the unfettered market reveals a limited story of ambition and no ethics or morality. It has no view of the 'good life', of social mixing, of mutual

[48] Scruton, *Aesthetics*, p. 250.
[49] S. Brownill, *Developing London's Docklands: Another Great Planning Disaster?* (London: Chapman 1990), p. 5.
[50] Ibid., p. 177.   [51] Ibid., p. 13.
[52] Ibid., p. 180. The same has been found to apply in Minneapolis and Sydney. A. MacLaran (ed.), *Making Space: Property Development and Urban Planning* (London: Edwin Arnold, 2003).

caring or nurturing the environment . . . Like a veil the market system shrouds our consciousness while plumping up desire and consumption. The market logic has a tendency to fragment groups into units of consumption and enclaves, and in so doing to break up social solidarities. But the latter are needed if intractable urban problems such as meeting responsibility for the public realm or natural surveillance are to be achieved.[53]

As we saw in Chapter 1, the unfettered market was one of the acids which dissolved earlier commitments to the common good. Landry is effectively arguing that cities cannot function in the absence of such an idea.

PLANNING, IDEOLOGY AND POWER

Early town planners, like Raymond Unwin, a utopian socialist who had sat at the feet of William Morris and Kropotkin, wanted to undermine class prejudice through planning. 'There is nothing whatsoever in the prejudices of people to justify the large covering of areas with houses of exactly the same size and type', he wrote.

The growing up of suburbs occupied solely by any individual class is bad socially, economically and aesthetically. It is due to the wholesale and thoughtless character of town development and is quite foreign to the traditions of our country; it results very often in bad municipal government and unfair distribution of the burdens of local taxation, misunderstanding and want of trust between different classes of people and in the development and exaggeration of differences of thought and habit; it leads, too, to a dreary monotony of effect which is almost as depressing as it is ugly.[54]

Attempts at social engineering which followed this advice proved unpopular. Surveys in the 1960s showed that two-thirds of respondents preferred single-class streets to streets of mixed social classes.[55] Simmie argues that the new towns movement was based on essentially middle-class ideas, namely that the solution to the problems of inner urban areas was to be found in planned suburbanisation and decentralisation; that there was a mechanical link between environment and human behaviour; and that 'happiness could be promoted by mixing all sections of the population together in socially balanced neighbourhood units, thus ameliorating the divisions in society'. 'The main attraction of these ideas is that they are platitudes which do not challenge the existing order.'[56]

Planners during the 'golden age' were by and large committed to 'the public interest', a version of 'the common good', but this has incurred

[53] Landry, *Art of City-Making*, p. 3.   [54] Unwin, *Town Planning*, p. 294.
[55] J. M. Simmie, *Citizens in Conflict* (London: Hutchinson, 1974), p. 31.   [56] Ibid., p. 75.

criticism from two directions. First, it assumes that society is essentially co-operative and that people share common values and aspirations. Second, the assumption of public interest often represented no more than 'the aggregated interests... of the most powerful coalition of participants in any given cause'.[57] The poor, the sick, the old, the inadequate, the immobile and the under-housed do not compete in the struggle for power and resources and they thus were overlooked in town planners' definitions of public interest.[58] Thus, even if this was not their overt aim, planners could be seen as agents of the ruling classes. The planning system, on this analysis, complemented and reflected the class structure, giving most to those who already had a lot and giving least to those who needed the most.[59] Town planning, in fact, put knowledge at the service of power.[60] Already in 1951 a study of Stevenage found that planners translated into 'sociological terms and architectural forms middle and upper class ideologies of a conservative or liberal-reformist nature', and that the balanced community they supported 'served the forces of law and order, middle class morality, and the social status quo'.[61] Plans presupposed social consensus when they should have been acknowledging the reality of class conflict.

A study of market-driven 'rejuvenation' in Minneapolis found that the question of power ran much more deeply than was usually appreciated:

It is vital to appreciate the hegemonic role of prevailing ideology. Influence in public affairs is based on a profound belief, common to government officials and public alike, on an unquestioned taken-for-granted faith that capitalist relations of production are not simply the best, but that they represent the only possible system. This is a pervasive, unspoken and largely unrecognized power grounded upon an uncritical ideological reflex. It is a conception of reality which directs public policies in certain directions because they are regarded as self evidently 'realistic', thereby effectively eliminating the potential of alternative radical actions by relegating them to the garbage can of 'unreality' itself.[62]

This is hardly surprising. Plans are policies and policies imply politics. 'The question is not whether planning will reflect politics but whose politics it will reflect.'[63]

[57] Ibid., p. 130.   [58] Ibid., p. 137.

[59] J. G. Davies, *The Evangelistic Bureaucrat: A Study of a Planning Exercise in Newcastle upon Tyne* (London: Tavistock, 1972), p. 229.

[60] Simmie, *Citizens on Conflict*, p. 151.

[61] H. Orlans, *Stevenage: A Sociological Study of a New Town* (London: Routledge, 1952), p. 94.

[62] A. MacLaran and D. Laverny-Rafter, 'The Rejuvenation of Downtown Minneapolis: Urban Planning as a Creature of Private-Sector Interests', in MacLaran (ed.), *Making Space*, p. 117.

[63] Quoted in B. Cullingworth and V. Nadin, *Town and Country Planning in the UK*, 13th edn (London: Routledge, 2002), p. 355.

PLANNING AND DEMOCRATIC PROCESS

The criticism that planning colludes with power takes us back to Sharp's remark about planning as vital to democracy. When he wrote that, the difficulties implicit in the idea of democracy were certainly not uppermost in his mind. In the United States, where modern democracy first took root, representative democracy was preferred to participative democracy because of the perceived danger of faction. Rule by the whole people was quite clearly made impossible by this strategy. Meanwhile, in France, Michele Buonarotti made a distinction between the order of equality, which in his view constituted true democracy, and the order of egoism or 'the English doctrine of the economists'. According to this critique, laissez-faire economics systematically undermined democracy by replacing it with the pursuit of wealth in which class distinction could not but be strengthened. For sixty years free markets and democracy have been twinned in North American rhetoric but, as John Dunn remarks, 'The market economy is the most powerful mechanism for dismantling equality that humans have ever fashioned.'[64]

The critiques of planning's collusion with power, developed in the 1970s, and the return to market anarchy in the following decade, have issued in a new planning orthodoxy which develops Sharp's dictum in a way that he would probably have found surprising. Participative democracy, sometimes called 'Jeffersonian democracy', is government by discussion and consent. De Tocqueville argued that town meetings are to liberty what primary schools are to science.[65] Taking a cue from this, it has been argued that planning decisions should be shared at local council level – and in Britain they are indeed considered at parish councils, though without any final power of veto.

Democratisation was at the heart of John Forester's study of 'planning in the face of power' in 1989. Following Habermas, he understood planning as an exercise in communicative action. The planner's key activity, quite unlike that of Abercrombie's, or even that of the Milton Keynes Development Corporation, is focussing and shaping attention, talking and listening. It is fundamentally about relationships. Critical planning theory, he argued, reveals true alternatives, corrects false expectations, counters cynicism, fosters enquiry and spreads political responsibility, engagement

---

[64] J. Dunn, *Democracy: A History* (New York: Atlantic, 2005), p. 137. This is rhetorically splendid but one would imagine that feudalism would mount a very credible challenge.
[65] De Toqueville, *Democracy in America*, bk I, ch. 5, p. 61.

and action. This process, he recognised, rests on agreement about goals.[66] If this is the case then planning represents the sharp end of decision making in what today is called a pluralist society.[67]

A notion of the common good is vital to any political society, Leonie Sandercock recognises, but this must be generated not by transcending or ignoring cultural and other differences (the liberal position) but through their interplay in a dialogical, agonistic political life. She gives an example from East St Louis of 'empowerment planning', which is the commitment to participatory action research, direct action organising and education for critical consciousness. There is, she argues, a core story here about the organisation of hope.[68] Planning is geared to community empowerment. Planners bring to the table skills in research and critical thinking, knowledge of legislation and the workings of state agencies, specific skills in fields like housing and local economic development, organising and financial skills and a commitment to social and environmental justice. Planning strives to be open about the values and visions it stands for and defends.[69] This summarises the vision of the United Nations Conference on Environment and Development held in Rio in 1992, which wanted a 'continuous dialogue between the actors involved in urban development and the participation of local communities in the identification of public services needs, the provision of urban infrastructure, the enhancement of public amenities and the protection and/or rehabilitation of older buildings, historic precincts and other cultural artifacts'.[70]

But what level of consultation are we thinking of? Christopher Day argues that consensus design processes can work even at a town level. The process involves getting groups to work out together what they want and to bring all differences to the surface and to continue discussion until they are resolved. If delegated power is to respond to community needs rather than just build its own power structure, he argues, it is essential that the upper layers make as few decisions as possible. Everything that can be passed down for more local decision making must be – this is the principle of subsidiarity. With this sort of structure, he claims, participatory planning is possible even at a town scale, if not on a larger one, with the nut-and-bolt decisions made by street, block and apartment floor

---

[66] J. Forester, *Planning in the Face of Power* (Berkeley: University of California Press, 1989), pp. 162, 199.

[67] MacIntyre reminds us that the problem of medieval society was 'how to educate and civilize human nature in a culture in which human life was in danger of being torn apart by the conflict of too many ideals, too many ways of life'. *After Virtue*, p. 165.

[68] Sandercock, *Cosmopolis II*, pp. 104, 172.   [69] Ibid., p. 210.

[70] N. Robinson (ed.), *Agenda 21 and the UNCED Proceedings* (New York: Ocean, 1993), ch. 7.

sub-groups.[71] Consensus design, he argues, reconnects people with place, and the buildings that result from this process revere both people and place, the life of nature and of human activities.[72] Prioritising such processes would be consistent with the return to localism, and the network of small, self-reliant communities which Giddens concedes may be bound up with the planning of the future.[73]

This level of democracy represents an aspiration in most places, if it is not something which is actively opposed. Market anarchy still dominates in planning situations all around the world, and at a local level money always talks. Kitchen notes that 'throughout the world . . . planners have generally found it very difficult to involve effectively other than a tiny minority of the population in the process of development plan-making'.[74]

Democracy is tiresome and time-consuming. 'In building the new towns', Peter Hall remarks, 'freedom for managerial enterprise and energy had to be given priority over the principle of democratic accountability.'[75] But if such freedom is at the cost of public distrust the gains are pyrrhic. D. M. Hill argues for a balance between representative and participative democracy. Decentralisation has its limits, he points out. It can reinforce the position of self-interested groups with little concern for the wide community. When participation rates are low the result is elitist domination, and this participation is inegalitarian. Without an overall strategy and resources, participative democracy reinforces the status quo. The key question is what structures and procedures exist to facilitate people's involvement in decisions, provide them with adequate information and ensure the quality and equity of those decisions.[76]

The Town Planning Institute in Britain recognises that planning cannot always, or indeed often, be achieved through consensus. Planning, like the law, and sometimes through the law, is charged with mediating difference. Nothing could more starkly emphasise its political character. Kitchen argues that 'top-down' processes of thinking holistically about a place and its people and 'bottom-up' processes of working with local people to draw from them full contributions based upon their knowledge and understanding need to meet in the middle and to inform each other. But he rightly adds that this is most unlikely to satisfy everyone's wishes in a pluralist society.[77]

---

[71] C. Day, *Consensus Design: Socially Inclusive Process* (Oxford: Architectural Press, 2003), p. 207.

[72] Ibid., p. 32.   [73] Giddens, *Politics*, p. 160.   [74] Kitchen, *Skills*, p. 67.

[75] P. Hall, *Urban and Regional Planning* (London: Routledge, 1992), p. 76.

[76] D. M. Hill, *Citizens and Cities: Urban Policy in the 1990s* (New York: Harvester Wheatsheaf, 1994), p. 249.

[77] Kitchen, *Skills*, p. 61.

GRACE AND PLANNING

Looking at this brief review of plans and some of the debates over planning in recent years, I shall argue that there would be five hallmarks of a planning process which bore the marks of grace.

We saw in our consideration of grace that beauty is one of its hallmarks, and this I take to be an important goal of planning. To the architect, wrote Unwin, town planning specially appeals as an opportunity for finding a beautiful form of expression for the life of the community.[78] The bye-law houses built after the Public Health Act of 1875, he said, though their sanitation is adequate, are not really homes for people.

There is needed the vivifying touch of art which would give completeness and increase their value tenfold; there is needed just that imaginative treatment which could transform the whole . . . It is the lack of beauty, of the amenities of life, more than anything else which obliges us to admit that our work of town building in the past century has not been well done. Not even the poor can live by bread alone.[79]

Beauty, he acknowledged, is an elusive quality, not easily defined, not always easily attained by direct effort, 'and yet it is a necessary element in all good work, the crowning and completing quality'.[80]

Camillo Sitte had tried to analyse the nature of the beauty in old town squares as a contribution to a practical aesthetics. If with Aristotle we are to make a people both secure and happy, he wrote, city planning cannot be merely a technical matter but should in the truest and most elevated sense be an artistic enterprise.[81]

To approach everything in a strictly methodical manner and not to waver a hair's breadth from preconceived patterns, until genius has been strangled to death and joie de vivre stifled by the system – that is the sign of our time. We have three major methods of city planning – the gridiron system, the radial system, and triangular system . . . Artistically speaking, not one of them is of any interest, for in their veins pulses not a single drop of artistic blood.[82]

---

[78] Unwin, *Town Planning*, p. xiv.   [79] Ibid., p. 4.   [80] Ibid., p. 9.
[81] Sitte, *Birth*, p. 142. Independently of Sitte, Fourier in France also gave thought to beauty. 'The view at the end of each road shall be of a country landscape or of a public or private architectural monument; a regular network of streets will be forbidden. Some will be curved and winding, to avoid monotony. At least one eighth of the surface area will be occupied by squares. Half the streets will be planted with trees of various kinds. The minimum width of the streets will be nine toises; to accommodate the pavements, if they are only for pedestrians, they may be reduced to three toises, but the other six shall be kept as flower beds.' L. Benevolo, *The Origin of Modern Town Planning* (London: Routledge, 1967), p. 58.
[82] Sitte, *Birth*, p. 229.

Unwin learned from Sitte, but also from the north German towns that he loved, that street junctions could be arranged to give enclosed views and to render possible the erection of irregularly picturesque groups of buildings. If we can give to our streets some individuality, he argued, 'may we not find that our people, going to and from their work, will change their route, taking the almond-planted street in the early spring, the plum, the crab, and the hawthorn streets later; and later still the streets planted with acacia and catalpa, or with the trees whose early foliage is their glory, such as the sycamore.'[83] 'No beauty can arise from the mere aggregation of detached units; there must be something crystalline in the structure, some relationship and grasping of the parts before there can be beauty.'[84]

Modernism turned its back on these insights. Giedion spoke sneeringly of 'Camillo Sitte's "sermons"', and Le Corbusier thought his insights worthy only of a pack donkey. However, as urbanists slowly became aware of the charmlessness of the environment that had been created there was a return to them. We need an environment which is not simply well organised, but poetic and symbolic as well, wrote Kevin Lynch.

It should speak of individuals and their complex society, of their aspirations and their historical tradition, of the natural setting, and of the complicated functions and movements of the city world. But clarity of structure and vividness of identity are first steps to the development of strong symbols. By appearing as a remarkable and well knit place, the city could provide a ground for the clustering and organization of these meanings and associations.[85]

As Nicholas Wolterstorff argues, aesthetic delight is a component within, and a species of, that joy which belongs to the shalom God has ordained as the goal of human existence, and which here already, in this broken and fallen world of ours, is to be sought and experienced.[86] Beauty may not be strictly speaking more important than bread, but equally it cannot be dismissed as politically and theologically unimportant. Practically speaking there was for centuries a view that the upper classes of course took beauty (fine houses and parks, clothes, painting, etc.) for granted, while the poor could whistle for what they might. But beauty is part of 'life in all its fullness' and it is there for all. To ignore it is to ignore a key aspect of the divine command. The question of beauty is the question of imagination

---

[83] Unwin, *Town Planning*, p. 278.   [84] Sitte, quoted in Jackson, *Sir Raymond Unwin*, p. 98.

[85] K. Lynch, *The Image of the City* (Cambridge, Mass.: MIT Press, 1960), p. 119. A key part of the contemporary problem is traffic. 'Try to imagine a building of any dignity surrounded by six acres of parked cars. The problems are obvious. Obvious solution: Build buildings without dignity.' Kunstler, *Geography*, p. 121.

[86] N. Wolterstorff, *Art in Action* (Carlisle: Solway, 1997), p. 170.

and of spirit, words which Abercrombie was not frightened to use of Plymouth, though the realisation seems to deny them. The impact of beautiful buildings is obvious in Frank Gehry's Guggenheim Museum in Bilbao, which both has helped regenerate the city and commands intense local affection. People respond to first-class building and planning as Sitte argued. The need for good design has become a town planning axiom, and was expressed by John Gummer when Minister of the Environment in 1994:

Quality affects us all... Good urban design can reinforce a sense of community, whereas anonymous grey and alienating surroundings isolate the individual... quality attracts quality, good design attracts life and investment and a strong community stands out against crime... if we improve our buildings and the streets and spaces which they define, we surely improve the quality of all our lives.[87]

The idea that good design would mitigate crime proved illusory, but that is not in itself an argument against it.[88]

A second mark of gracious planning is justice. In planning we can see that the order of egoism has prevailed over the order of equality but we cannot accept that as fate. Simmie argues that 'There is no reason to suppose that once the real basis of society has been exposed as conflict over the distribution of resources and power that the forces of history cannot be altered to make these distributions more equal. The problem is to find the will.'[89] Although the socialist argument has been lost over the past thirty years, Naomi Klein notes that the dream of economic equality remains popular, and is difficult to defeat in a fair fight. In her view that is the reason for what she calls 'disaster capitalism's need to rely on terrorist or other shocks to justify its policies'.[90] In place of the grand visions of human equality which inspired socialism she finds local movements 'that do not seek to start from scratch but from scrap, from the rubble that is all around... Radical only in their intense practicality, rooted in the communities where they live, these men and women see themselves as mere repair people, taking what is there and fixing it, reinforcing it, making it better and more equal.'[91] Christopher Day's practice of consensus design, though time-intensive, is surely the way in which planning has to look. It is not intoxication and grandiloquence that we need now, says Joseph

[87] J. Gummer, introduction to *Quality in Town and Country: A Discussion Document* (London: Department of Environment, 1994), p. 2.
[88] Hall, *Cities of Tomorrow*, p. 406.   [89] Simmie, *Citizens in Conflict*, p. 227.
[90] N. Klein, *The Shock Doctrine* (Harmondsworth: Penguin, 2008), p. 451.   [91] Ibid., p. 466.

Rykwert, but sobriety and effective action. 'Therefore, make little plans, say I – and lots of them.'[92] Brian Walker understands Alexander's *A Pattern Language* as an attempt to weigh up the advantages of devolved decision making and the need to make sure that this does not result in worse outcomes, for example in denser traffic flows. The heart of his response is a mixture of incrementalism and the imperative to make sure that every new development contributes to the richness and beauty of the whole. As such it may not be purely utopian.[93]

A third is human scale. Coleman pleaded for 'an arrangement of space that enables human beings to master their immediate environment and not be enslaved by it . . . autonomy for each household, with a garden large enough to be defensible and to accommodate changes that make the resident's mark independently of the designer'.[94] The idea of human scale looks back to Babel and the human attempt to build a city which scales the heavens, and forward to a world built to 'the measure of Christ'. But what counts as human scale in the built environment? Are Manhattan and Chicago human-scale or not? It could be argued that Milton Keynes is human-scale, but at the same time it is somewhat boring and insipid, devoid of any truly daring imagination, and daring imagination is also part of humanness. We need architecture to take our breath away. Abercrombie wanted a city which would match the beauties of the natural environment. He did not get it but his aspiration was right.

A fourth is sustainability. The understanding of human beings as part of creation, given us in Genesis 2, will be a key part of any theological account of town planning. We are part of the whole, and if we try to live as masters and possessors we will destroy ourselves. Early town planning is accused of an anti-urban bias.[95] Certainly more recent town planning has been 'anti-rural' and scoffed at, for example in the 1942 Scott Report's emphasis on the need to preserve rural land. But the assumption that we live in a world where the market can answer all our problems is no longer sustainable. In the light of peak oil and climate change the question of what count as the hinterlands of a city will become more and more pressing. Abercrombie was right: agriculture needs to be given a place equivalent to that of the town. Sustainable development provides a potentially radical philosophy to guide

[92] J. Rykwert, *The Seduction of Place* (Oxford University Press, 2000), p. 246.
[93] Walker, 'Another Kind of Science', p. 1068. Alexander's suggestions are developed in C. Alexander, H. Neis, A. Anninou and I. King, *A New Theory of Urban Design* (New York: Oxford University Press, 1987).
[94] Coleman, *Utopia on Trial*, p. 118.
[95] Thus Simmie argues that the organicism of the garden city movement 'is materially responsible for the anti-urban animus of British town planning'. *Citizens in Conflict*, p. 21.

planning.[96] In Britain the Royal Town Planning Institute thus adopts the precautionary principle and notes that 'Planning decisions cannot be based exclusively upon an open-ended presumption in favour of development.' The problem is in addressing the culture which underwrites such a view.

The perennial wisdom of humanity honours mystery and acknowledges the need for caution and large margins. It knows that human intelligence is always and everywhere woefully inadequate and that we need large margins. Much of this old and ecologically sound knowledge is embedded in scriptures, law, literature, and ancient customs. But how is this to be made vivid for an entire culture suffering from attention deficit disorder?[97]

An ecological account of planning means that transport will be at the heart of it. 'Too often it is the motor car which dominates planning', laments one of Plymouth's planners.

It might be foolishly courageous to suggest . . . that in the future the motor car will become the servant of mankind rather than its master; that it will be taken by the scruff of the neck and forced to behave itself. This has long been the hope of most planners, who have suffered decades of derision from highway engineers and the road lobby for questioning relentless road building.[98]

Milton Keynes would have been better off for its integrated public transport network.

Finally, for all its difficulties, on which I will have more to say in the next chapter, Christianity cannot get away from community. 'There is growing up a new sense of the rights and duties of the community as distinct from those of the individual', wrote Unwin. 'It is coming to be more and more widely realised that a new order and relationship in society are required to take the place of the old, that the mere setting free of the individual is only the commencement of the work of reconstruction, and not the end.'[99] We saw that community was at the heart of Abercrombie's vision, rejected in Milton Keynes in favour of the dispersed community made possible by car ownership. 'The idea of building a "neighbourhood", "village" or "cluster" as a functioning social unit is now properly discredited', wrote Walker in 1982.[100] But what is the alternative to the neighbourhood unit? As he wrote, an area designed under his aegis was contradicting him. Norman Foster's suburb of Beanhill has problems with the tawdriness of its aluminium

[96] D. Warburton, *Reinventing Planning* (London: TCPA, 1999).
[97] D. Orr, *The Nature of Design* (Oxford University Press, 2002), p. 73.
[98] C. Shepley, 'Planning Plymouth's Future', in B. Chalkley, D. Dunkerley and P. Gripalos (eds.), *Plymouth: Maritime City in Transition* (Newton Abbot: David & Charles, 1991), p. 224.
[99] Unwin, *Town Planning*, p. 375.   [100] Walker, *Architecture*, p. 10.

materials, but people have liked the houses and have chosen to stay, and a real community has emerged, now covering four generations. Community has emerged willy-nilly, and design has something to do with this. The gospel puts community at the heart of its vision of human life. There are challenges here both to our understanding of town planning and to our understanding of ministry and of the shape of the church in new estates. For the theologian, I suggest, the possibilities of modern communication cannot be the driving factor in our understanding of community, as they were for Webber. This is individualism writ large. What has happened at Beanhill shows that community is not a dead letter and that design can enable it.

Surveying the scene in 1996, the Professor of Urban and Regional Planning at the University of Birmingham, Gordon Cherry, felt that planning had lost its legitimacy and was likely to be reduced to a form of management. But planning is a central matrix for politics, ethics and aesthetics. It is, or should be, the most immediate form of practical politics, where, as the Royal Town Planning Institute recognises, the movement between local, regional and central is non-stop. As such it is applied wisdom, phronesis, wisdom quite literally where Proverbs puts it, in the market place. It is a practice not defined by the goods internal to it, but reliant, rather, on society's exercise of the virtues, and, as MacIntyre notes, practices cannot flourish in societies where the virtues are not valued.[101] In the next chapter I turn to the exercise of such planning in the creation of public space.

[101] MacIntyre, *After Virtue*, p. 193.

CHAPTER 6

Grace and public space

As we saw in Chapter 2, *koinonia* is one of the key words in the Greek New Testament, and in relation to the notion of public space we may take from it a threefold significance. First, it reflects the fact that for Paul, especially, fellowship or community was one of the markers of the new reality called into being by the life, death and resurrection of Christ. Community is not an optional extra, something which can equally be replaced by the free choice of individuals, but is central to the human good. In that case public space is not simply a place where a crowd of individuals can gather, as opposed to private space where you have to be known, or where money buys you entry. Public space is bound up with the common good. In terms of the discussion of multiculturalism in Chapter 1, public space is somewhere where all the various 'publics' and sectors of the community are free to come and go. As we go through the various aspects of public space in this chapter it can be seen that, while there are places in which some members of a multicultural society might feel uncomfortable – Christians in Mosques, Jews and Muslims in churches, Muslims in pubs and so on, in fact the public spaces of squares, streets, parks and museums do function very effectively to provide space for the entire community. But, second, *koinonia* comes from *koinos*, meaning common, vulgar, unclean. The *koinonia* of the New Testament was the fellowship of the *ochlos*, the crowd, and not of the educated and cultured. Public space has often had this connotation, as in the 'pub', the public house which was needed by the poor but irrelevant to the gentry. Lastly, as we also saw in Chapter 1, the idea of what was common led to an understanding of the earth as a common treasury, of the importance of common land. This understanding derived especially from Leviticus 25.23:

The land (*erets*) shall not be sold in perpetuity, for the land is mine; with me you are but aliens and tenants.

Erets, here, we may take as a metaphor for all created reality, the whole earth. Ton Veerkamp calls this perhaps the most important verse in Scripture.[1] The denial of absolute possession of the land, on the ground that 'the land is mine', means that there are no absolute property rights, and that therefore no class structure is other than provisional. 'In every society there is a God, that is, that which finally undergirds everything, the ground order, and at the same time the limiting instance of the right to property.'[2] Theologically the fact that 'the land is mine' means that all is public, set aside for the common good, and individual property owners are only stewards on behalf of God, their neighbour and the whole earth. 'Land', created reality, for the biblical writers, is not a form of private property with its exclusive character and absolute right of use and abuse. Israel did not have this right, at least according to the authors of Leviticus. Understanding 'land' in this extended way, we can follow Bas Wielenga when he argues that 'The land is the aim of YHWH's ways with Israel. It is and remains his gift, and the fruits of its soil are his blessing. It is meant to be the basis of a new society, of fellowship in freedom and equality.'[3] The Levitical writers proposed institutions to make sure that the land did not become alienated, namely the remission of debt provisions and the limitation of domestic service. The remission codes are based on faith in YHWH, the God who frees from Egypt, a metaphor for all places dominated by Pharonic rule. That YHWH is God means that the gods of possession are not absolute. In terms of my Trinitarian scheme, public space falls under the appropriation of God the Reconciler. Public space is a way of making the goods of place concrete, and of providing the physical structure which will help community to flourish.

PUBLIC SPACE AS THE SPACE OF COMMUNITY

Both history and experience tell us that community is fragile and difficult. Zygmunt Bauman suggests that the longing for community is peculiarly characteristic of postmodern times: living with contingency and uncertainty community is the search for shelter, a port in a storm. We regroup in temporary tribes, and the ethnic group in particular provides a refuge against a hostile uncaring world.[4] A century before him, Ferdinand Tönnies contrasted the anonymous society of the big city with the imagined

[1] T. Veerkamp, *Autonomie & Egalität: Ökonomie, Politik, Ideologie in der Schrift* (Berlin: Alektor, 1993), p. 98.
[2] Ibid., p. 101. [3] B. Wielenga, *It's a Long Road to Freedom* (Madurai: TTS Press, 1981), p. 125.
[4] Z. Bauman, *Modernity and Ambivalence* (Cambridge: Polity, 1991), p. 246.

fellowship of the country village.[5] This was not an elective community, neo-tribalism, but organic and deep-rooted. But this vision of community was always a myth: class divisions meant that that earlier *Gemeinschaft* was always unjust, and often savage. It policed difference and lent itself to persecution. Community, in fact, is fleeting and elusive, only partially and imperfectly realised over and again. In its totality it is an eschatological reality: only in the Kingdom of God will there be perfect shalom with everyone reconciled and dwelling in peace and justice (Ps. 85.10). Here and now we only have signs and sacraments of community, and perhaps it was in some such way that Paul thought of *ekklesia*. Certainly the Bene-dictine communities understood themselves sacramentally, not as perfect realisations of community in a wicked world but as sober attempts to see how community might be fashioned and modelled, imperfect realisations which needed constant work.

If there is a romance of *Gemeinschaft* there is equally a romance of danger. Richard Sennett argues that the demand for 'community', purified of all that might convey a feeling of difference, is built on an adolescent fear of the pain of challenge and participation.[6] The family in particular, he believes, acts as a shield from diversity. To grow to adulthood we need to be able to tolerate painful ambiguity and uncertainty, and we therefore need the anarchy the city can provide. 'The great promise of city life is a new kind of confusion possible within its borders, an anarchy that will not destroy men, but make them richer and more mature.'[7] In the healthy city there will be no escape from situations of confrontation and conflict, and this depends on diverse and ineradicably different kinds of people being thrown together and forced to deal with each other for mutual survival.[8] Dense disorderly cities challenge the capacity of family groups to act as intensive shelters, as shields from diversity, and create the need to move outside the domestic circle into the wider world.[9] There is truth in this, of course, but it does not acknowledge how destructive, even murderous, conflict might be. Dense, disorderly cities are not so wonderful for the victims of knife crime. People who celebrate the edginess of the city usually live in safe places.

David Harvey argues that we should not necessarily regard face-to-face relations as more pure and authentic than relations mediated across time and distance. Not all mediating relations are alienating, and the intimacy

---

[5] F. Tönnies, *Community and Civil Society*, tr. J. Harris and M. Hollis (Cambridge University Press, 2001).
[6] R. Sennett, *The Uses of Disorder* (New York: Norton, 1970), p. 42.   [7] Ibid., p. 108.
[8] Ibid., p. 163.   [9] Ibid., p. 169.

of place is not the only locus of authentic socio-ecological relations.[10] Community, he says, is as much part of the problem as the panacea. 'Communitarianism rests on mythic beliefs that a thing called community can be created as some freestanding and autonomous entity endowed with causative and salving powers. Entities like communities, while not without significance, cannot be understood independent of the social processes that generate, sustain and also dissolve them.'[11] Richard Sennett deplores the search for cosy community, arguing that it rests on an emotional narcissism which debilitates a proper politics. We need the mutual distance of impersonality. 'The belief in direct human relations on an intimate scale has seduced us from converting our understanding of the realities of power into guides for our own political behaviour.'[12] There is some truth in these criticisms, but they underestimate the degree of alienation experienced without genuine community, and they tend to elide community and communalism, the situation in which community solidarity is turned against others. Sennett's proposal that the impersonal city is more liberating than the engaged community is deeply implausible, though the point that internal conflict strengthens the bonds of community can be true. It was not true in Northern Ireland or the Balkans, nor is it in caste villages, but it may be true in intentional communities or work-places.[13] In the absence of such a community we resort to rugged individualism or affinity groups which relate to one another by the internet or which travel to meet one another. We have to ask whether there are realistic options for surviving the global emergency which do not depend on learning co-operation. If that is the case, then genuine community is indispensable.

Because we are embodied creatures, and do not simply meet over the internet, we cannot have community without public space. In a variant on Aristotle's introduction to the *Politics*, Scruton remarks that it is the public life which prompts us to build, which marks us off from the animals.[14] Although people cannot be made better by building, it remains true that

The net effect of beautiful, well designed, high quality physical environments is that they feel restorative, more care is taken of them, feelings of stress and fear of crime is reduced, and social mixing increases, as does hope, motivation and confidence in the future and thus well being. By contrast ugly environments increase crime and fear of crime and lead to stress, vandalism, untidiness, feelings of depression, isolation, loneliness, worthlessness, a lack of aspiration and a drained will. The consequence is a self-reinforcing negative cycle, the likelihood of less

[10] Harvey, *Justice*, p. 311.   [11] Ibid., p. 425.
[12] R. Sennett, *The Fall of Public Man* (New York: Knopf, 1974), p. 339.
[13] Sennett, *The Corrosion of Character*, p. 143.   [14] Scruton, *Classical Vernacular*, p. xv.

employment, reduced social capital and less social bonding . . . A core question to any architect is then, How does your structure help build social capital?[15]

There is, in other words, a vicious circle between poor environments and lack of community, and a virtuous circle between love of place and strong community. Alexander argues that social capital can be promoted by the development of promenades, shopping streets, town halls, pubs, cafés and other meeting places.[16] We should add that public toilets are also an important part of the common good, an essential recognition of our bodiliness. Their replacement by 'pay toilets' is a sign of the loss of the sense of the public and common good in our society. Arguing that the essence of developing as a human being is developing the capacity for ever more complex experience, Richard Sennett comments that the American individual is a passive person and that monotonous space is what a society of passive individuals builds for itself.[17] He believes that public space in the contemporary city is either about consumption or about tourism and that this trivialisation of the city as a stage of life reflects fear of that exposure through which we learn how to weigh what is important and what is not.[18] Michael Sandel argues that public spaces are not primarily for those who cannot afford facilities themselves but are sites 'for the cultivation of a common citizenship, so that people from different walks of life encounter one another and so acquire enough of a shared sense of a shared life that we can meaningfully think of one another as citizens in a common venture'.[19]

Approaching the same point slightly differently, van Pelt argues that without a place where people can face the ultimate questions there could be no freedom, no autonomy, no responsibility and therefore no citizenship.[20] 'The creation of community has as much to do with mundane issues such as the placement of streets as it does with broader questions of the values which people hold in common. A sense of community depends to a very large degree on the existence of certain types of urban experience. That, in turn, entails the creation of a particular type of urban infrastructure.'[21]

---

[15] Landry, *Art of City-Making*, p. 245.
[16] C. Alexander, S. Ishikawa, M. Silverstein, M. Jacobson, I. Fiksdahl-King and S. Angel, *A Pattern Language* (New York: Oxford University Press, 1977), pp. 311–14, 349–52.
[17] Sennett, *Conscience of the Eye*, p. 65.   [18] Ibid., p. xiii.
[19] 'Markets and Morals', BBC Radio 4, 9 June 2009.
[20] Van Pelt, in Westfall and van Pelt, *Architectural Principles*, p. 180. Robert Lifton argues that 'we affirm life in the face of death through the construction of cities: the human problems of mastering death anxiety and achieving a sense of immortality are tasks that individuals cannot accomplish alone. These are issues at the common boundary of the individual life project and the collective historical project.' Quoted in ibid., p. 179.
[21] Walker, 'Another Kind of Science', p. 1062.

PUBLIC AND PRIVATE SPACE

Public space is defined over against private, and this separation, unknown in hunter-gatherer society, certainly emerged in the city, and specifically in Athens in the reforms of Solon in the sixth century which parallel the biblical Jubilee legislation. Hebrew Bible scholars do not agree on the date of the Jubilee proposals, but we know that Solon became archon in 594 BC, facing a fragmented and disheartened society where debt was a key problem. He addressed this through a *seisachtheia*, a 'shaking-off of burdens', and through legislation to make sure the situation would not be repeated.

The differences from the biblical procedure are interesting. First, the biblical authors assumed that the situation would recur. They therefore proposed remission of debt either every seven or every fifty years. The Jubilee is about the 'conservatism of revolution', the return to the original situation, the dismantling of class and the return to equality. This 'permanent revolution' never happened, as we can see from Ezekiel 48, but the call to it is based on a perception of what is worthy and what is unworthy of the human, which is the bottom line of every economic order.[22]

Second, the biblical authors linked the Jubilee to the Day of Atonement, when Israel confessed its sins. 'This confession and acknowledgement of sin is no spiritual and moral inner opportunity of individual men, but is robustly material in the return to relations of freedom in the economy of the land and the return to the family unit, which is being renewed.'[23] We are beginning to get accustomed to confession of sin in relation to slavery, to the genocide of indigenous populations and to Christian treatment of the Jews. Slavery, of course, was part of a particular economy. We are still far from facing up to the relations of oppression implicit in most economies, and in particular our own. Without this facing up, addressing our shadow, which is the purpose of the Day of Atonement, we cannot begin on more just economic relationships. The Jubilee proposals envisage, then, a fundamental heart-searching in regard to economics, asking where the vehicle we are travelling in is going, whether it has got any brakes and what the purpose of the journey is.

Third, and most important for this chapter, the biblical vision thought in terms of a society of smallholders, much as Jefferson seems to have imagined the United States. In Athens, by contrast, Solon's legislation was based on the idea of the polis and on the distinction between private and public

[22] Veerkamp, *Autonomie*, pp. 93, 94. [23] Ibid., p. 94.

property. This is a distinction which was certainly not there in hunter-gatherer society and cannot be mapped easily on to ancient Israel, where families are considered as tenants of the deity who is the owner of the land.

In Athens the sanctity of the home was marked in Solon's reforms: 'The boundary line that enclosed one's property, the nomos, was from now on to be sacred. Without this protection of a citizen's place in the world there could be no guarantee of justice.'[24] To have property meant

no more or less than to have one's location in a particular part of the world and therefore to the body politic, that is, to be the head of one of the families which together constituted the public realm . . . To own property meant here to be master over one's own necessities of life and therefore potentially to be a free person, free to transcend his own life and enter the world all have in common.[25]

The threshold of the house was what separated the private realm and the political realm. 'Without the private realm of the house there can be no citizenry, and there can be no city.'[26]

In the Hebrew Bible there is no such distinction: the framework of the law, the covenant, is with the whole people. Private property forms no part of it. Similarly, for Christians 'the Domus Dei (the Church) offered a home to all citizens of the Civitas Dei (the State) and thus gave the destitute and the homeless a basis for dignity. No one was a slave in the house of God since it offered a place for all.' Paradoxically, van Pelt traces the idea of private property to this strategy: 'The church's spiritual answer to the dilemma Solon had addressed became the foundation of the modern ideology of property. If for the church a person's property had its source in the baptised soul, in the modern age it became one's possession of one's own body, or one's "labour power".'[27]

Because private property made the city possible van Pelt reads it positively, but Howard Kunstler understands its present manifestation in more or less an opposite way. The identification of the extreme individualism of property ownership with all that is sacred in American life, he argues, 'tends to degrade the idea of the public realm, and hence of the landscape tissue that ties together the thousands of pieces of private property that make up a town, a suburb, a state'.[28] American town planning privileged the private, and the result was that 'the public realm counted for nothing. This spawned towns composed of blocks unmodified by devices of civic art, checkerboard towns without visible centres, open spaces, odd little

---

[24] Van Pelt, in Westfall and van Pelt, *Architectural Principles*, p. 178.
[25] H. Arendt, *The Human Condition* (Chicago University Press, 1958), pp. 61, 65.
[26] Van Pelt, in Westfall and van Pelt, *Architectural Principles*, p. 211.   [27] Ibid., p. 179.
[28] Kunstler, *Geography*, p. 27.

corners, or places set aside for the public's enjoyment.'[29] In order to have a worthwhile civilisation, he argues, we have to give up the fetish for extreme individualism and rediscover public life, public manners and some notion of the common good.[30]

Private space was from the beginning gendered. Home might be 'the woman's realm' but 'inside, the paterfamilias ruled with absolute authority'.[31] In Athens the support of one autonomous citizen required the labour of many individuals: relatives, hired workers, agents and slaves. This provided the material basis for the continuation of individual life. Women could not enter public space except for religious ceremonies and funerals.[32] The celebrated contrast between poor homes and public splendour was 'the material manifestation of the ideology of separate spheres for men and women'. The division of life space into two spheres, the public and the private, was in fact a psychological and ideological support for the legitimacy of political and social hierarchies. It dressed up domination as protection.[33]

Despite the presumption against ostentation in ancient Athens (which followed from the need to spend money on public works and festivals), we may assume from the remarks at the beginning of Plato's *Republic* that class difference was from the start very marked in relation to private property. In Israel the prophetic denunciations of ostentatious building likewise indicate severe class division.

On the positive side we have intimations in Horace and Cicero that privacy, the ability to retreat, to get on with humble domestic affairs without being bothered with the dangerous world of politics, quickly became a treasured aspect of private space:

> Happy he who, far from business,
> Like the ancient race of mortals,
> Works his ancestral estate
> With his own oxen freed from all debt interest,
> And is not roused as a soldier by the fierce trumpet
> And does not shudder at the sea's rage,
> And avoids the forum
> And the proud thresholds of greater citizens.[34]

---

[29] Ibid., p. 30.   [30] Ibid., p. 275.

[31] Van Pelt, in Westfall and van Pelt, *Architectural Principles*, p. 177.

[32] Mary Ann Tétreault, 'Formal Politics, Meta Space and the Construction of Civil Life', in A. Light and J Smith (eds.), *The Production of Public Space* (Lanham: Rowman & Littlefield, 1998), p. 83.

[33] Ibid., p. 90.

[34] Horace, Epode 2.1–8. Stephen Harrison's translation. As he points out, this famous sentiment is ironised by the fact that it is spoken by a money lender. See 'Town and Country', in S. Harrison (ed.), *The Cambridge Companion to Horace* (Cambridge University Press, 2007), p. 238.

Over against all this stood the public realm. The temples, markets, playing fields, meeting places, walls, public statuary and paintings of the ancient city represented the culture's values in religion, politics and family life.[35] Van Pelt divides public space into four: the emporium, the stela, the Acropolis and the agora (which included the stoa). There are analogies with all these in contemporary public space but there is no precise analogy here with space for leisure, though the agora also saw the celebration of games. Spaces for leisure were found in the ancient world at Olympia, at the Colosseum and at the theatre even if, in all these cases, the religious dimension was far more significant than in contemporary society.

In contrast to van Pelt I shall divide public space into eight areas, by no means exhaustive, beginning with churches, mosques and temples.

CHURCHES, MOSQUES AND TEMPLES

In many ancient societies temples were the first great common buildings to be erected. On one level they were a marker that the community had a reference point beyond itself, in 'eternity', which is to say in values of justice, mercy and truth. In classical Athens the Acropolis was 'the shrine of the city as it celebrated within the imperfect setting of the actual city the enduring idea of the city, of the city Athens ought to be'.[36] In Israel the Temple was quite clearly the ideological focus point of the newly established Davidic monarchy. After the division of the kingdom Jeroboam had to try to do a similar job with Samaria, though never so successfully. Solomon's prayer at the dedication of the Temple, a later account of course, is a naked piece of Judaean ideology. Perhaps in the same way the Acropolis was the guarantor of the success of the city state of Athens, the statue of Athena a projection of the city's persona. The civic function of many cathedrals and town churches, the connection between city corporation and church, continues this ideological function. In the biblical witness this was always a suspect enterprise. The construction of buildings does play an important role in the Bible, argues van Pelt, but the buildings were seen as impeding the spiritual progress of the people.[37] The Temple might invite paganism (as with Manasseh) or suggest that the covenant could be maintained by ritual observance. Jeremiah warned people to put no trust in the Temple. It was the people's response that mattered, not the Temple in itself. That this perception was internalised is indicated by the fact that Judaism survived

---

[35] Sennett, *Conscience of the Eye*, p. xi.
[36] Van Pelt, in Westfall and van Pelt, *Architectural Principles*, p. 190.   [37] Ibid., p. 94.

the destruction of the Temple without a problem. In the New Testament Jesus is the true Temple and it is the living body, the people of God, which is important. Christianity managed without major buildings for upwards of 200 years.

In medieval Europe church buildings were everywhere the most important symbolic markers, for reasons we shall explore further in Chapter 11. Medieval church towers were like gigantic stelae, says van Pelt, pointing to the earth and the heavens, disclosing the absolutes of death and immortality.[38] Even in the Renaissance sacred architecture was taken to be the most important, at least for Alberti, who argued that the church should be the noblest ornament of a city and its beauty should surpass imagination. The Byzantine builders had adopted the palace model of a basilica for a church to avoid confusion with pagan temples. Alberti had no such scruples.

I would have the temple made so beautiful, that the imagination should not be able to form an idea of any place more so; and I would have every part so contrived and adorned, as to fill the beholders with awe and amazement, at the consideration of so many and so excellent things, and almost force them to cry out with astonishment.[39]

It is this staggering beauty which awakens sublime sensations and arouses piety in people. Something analogous had been believed by the Gothic builders, as we shall see in Chapter 11. Alberti's churches are all modelled on pagan temples. For him, Wittkower remarks, 'humanism and religion were fully compatible and he conjures up a serene, philosophical and almost puritanical architecture'.[40]

In the rebuilding of London after the Great Fire, Wren envisaged that the Stock Exchange would be the focal point rather than St Paul's, but he was overruled and the Cathedral remained the dominant symbol of the City until after World War II, when the symbols of capital at last took the ultimate point which had been intended for them.

The great temple cities of south India perhaps give a flavour of what religious foci might have been like in Europe in earlier ages. In Madurai, in Tamil Nadu, for example, the Temple stands at the centre of the city, ringed by concentric streets, its great eighteenth-century towers (*gopurams*) surrounding the twelfth-century core. Corridors of profound shade mean that parts of the Temple are cool even in the hottest months, though the 'tank' where worshippers should be able to take a ritual bath is almost

---

[38] Ibid., p. 189.   [39] Alberti, *Ten Books*, bk VII, ch. 3, p. 136.
[40] Wittkower, *Architectural Principles*, p. 10.

always dry. The whole Temple is a place of bustle, as worshippers perform *puja*, listen to the exposition of texts or simply talk in family groups. A huge market is part of the complex, along with fortune tellers, musicians and holy men. For most of the day the Temple is thronged and represents the permeability of sacred and secular space, as people move easily from the surrounding streets into the Temple and out again. Its endless iconography, centring on Siva and his consort Meenakshi, provides the symbolic focus for the whole city. In the same way medieval cathedrals were often the centre for trade and discussion. When St Paul's burned down, much of the printed stock in London went with it; the hushed silence of modern-day churches is a relatively new thing. Temples, mosques and churches were public, though what has been meant by 'public' has often been circumscribed. Hindu temples, for example, did not allow Dalits entry, and mosques and synagogues put restrictions on the entry of women.

Churches and mosques, if not temples, have also provided places for reflection. The cloister plays a key role in cities, said Mumford. 'Without formal opportunities for isolation and contemplation, opportunities that require enclosed space, free from prying eyes and extraneous distractions, even the most extroverted life must eventually suffer. The home without such cells is but a barracks; the city that does not possess them is only a camp.'[41] Sir Henry Wotton noted that temples are usually dark, 'Devotion more requiring collected than defused spirits';[42] in Christianity, at least, churches have been places where 'prayer has been valid' – places where people's deepest needs and fears could be addressed. They have also been places, at least since the days of Ambrose and Chrysostom, where, in the sermon, they have provided a public place to reflect on the condition of society, to bring it to the bar of absolute moral value and call for change.

Churches and temples have always been cultural centres. Cathedrals maintained sophisticated musical traditions; the town church of Leipzig was the site of much of Bach's work, and village churches hosted bell ringers, choirs and the bands that Hardy memorialises in *Under the Greenwood Tree*. Throughout the Middle Ages they were also sites for meetings and celebrations which were not in the strict sense religious – or rather, the boundary between religious and secular was much more blurred than it later became. Churches also were, and continue to be, places of refuge. In the Middle Ages criminals could claim sanctuary. Today in North America many churches are active in helping illegal immigrants. In Latin America during the Terror, many churches were active in helping relatives of the

---

[41] Mumford, *City*, p. 311.   [42] Wotton, *The Elements of Architecture*, p. 44.

disappeared, or people who were in opposition. This was another political function, in direct contrast to the legitimising function bound up with their origin.

Today, in Britain at least, the need to charge admission to cathedrals in order to cover the enormous costs of maintenance blurs the gap between religion and heritage. The charge has the same deterrent effect as museum charges, putting off many who might otherwise idle in and browse around. It assimilates the building to a museum so that the tourist who thinks that the mass in a side chapel is merely a 'historical re-enactment' can be forgiven for thinking so. It likewise blurs the distinction between sacred and secular, but in the direction of the commodification of everything. In the villages where the local stately home is owned by a banker or is part of the National Trust, the church, if it is unlocked, may be the only public space which people can visit for nothing and where they can sense the continuity of the generations. Questions relating to the importance of religious buildings are central to both Jewish and Christian scriptures, and the assimilation of church buildings to heritage only underlines these. As congregations shrink even the need for shelter or for large meeting spaces is questioned. And at the same time the human need for symbols nags away. To replace cassock and alb with a business suit is to lose rather than to gain, and perhaps the same may be said of the move to the school hall or the empty cinema on Sunday mornings. When the church meets, as it did in the second century, in private homes, icons, crosses or other symbols very often mark the space off as sacred but then, too, the relation between public and private space is blurred in another direction. In that case, as in Corinth right at the beginning of church history, it may turn out that some members are more equal than others, and that some parts of the church cannot be comfortable and do not have the freedom which they would have in genuinely public space.

THE PUBLIC SQUARE

The agora in the ancient Greek city was the space for free speech and debate. It may have originated in the practice of the warrior class gathering in a circle and each one having his say and then stepping back into the circle. Jean Pierre Vernant comments,

the human group creates this image of itself: along with the private dwellings there is a centre where public affairs are discussed, and this centre represents everything that is 'common', the collectivity as such. In this centre all persons are on a footing of equality, no one is inferior to anyone else . . . We see here the birth of a society in which the relationships between man and man are perceived as identical, symmetrical, interchangeable . . . It could be said that by having access to this circular space known as the agora, citizens become part of the political system, based on balance, symmetry, reciprocity.[43]

In Athens the agora was where the ecclesia, the assembly of free citizens, met to decide on policy and to elect its leaders. Located halfway between the necropolis and the Acropolis, it stood 'between the city of eternal ends and the city of eternal beginnings. The agora brought the two together. It was the location of government and the seat of sovereignty.'[44] South of the agora was the Areopagus or Hill of Ares, where Paul set out his account of the gospel according to Luke, believed to be the original meeting place of a prestigious council of elders who, even after Solon's reforms, judged murder cases and symbolically represented 'a force of moderation, of reconciliation and of the supremacy of the polis over the blood feuds of the past'.[45] The Areopagus was the seat of the law which guaranteed the freedom and order of the city.

There are two ways in which public squares still fulfil their political function. First, in North America and mainland Europe it is common for civic buildings, especially courts and town halls, to front on to great squares. Symbolically, then, they mark the space as political. In Spanish colonial towns, says Jackson, 'the Plaza is not a stage set but a manifestation of local social order, of the relationship between citizens and the authority of the state'.[46] Statues, inscriptions and other symbols remind people of their civic duties and privileges. Sitte hoped that his squares might inspire civic virtue and help to create a better future free of philistinism and utilitarianism.[47]

The sheer problem of size means that the idea of debate among an entire citizenry is normally impossible. Nevertheless, political opinions are often voiced as protest in public squares, sometimes in epochal ways, as at Wenceslas Square, Tiananmen Square and the Brandenburg Gate, but also in scores of rallies held each year in Trafalgar Square in London. This square, along with Hyde Park, is the focus for (mostly peaceful) political protest. This could be read cynically as a safety valve for political emotions, enabling the status quo to be maintained, or it could be read (as I would prefer to see it) as a vital extension of representative democracy.

On exceptional occasions public space can also fulfil important political or symbolic functions. Thus after the bombing of Plymouth in 1942, once

---

[43] Quoted in Jackson, *Discovering*, p. 19.
[44] Van Pelt in Westfall and van Pelt, *Architectural Principles*, p. 205.   [45] Ibid., p. 200.
[46] Jackson, *Discovering*, p. 17.   [47] Sennett, *Conscience of the Eye*, p. 176.

the fires were all put out, the mayor, Lord Astor, magnificently ordered a public dance on the Hoe to show that Plymouth's spirit was unbroken. In Exeter on the millennium eve, thousands of people gathered on the Cathedral green, known locally as the city's beach. They did not quite know why they were there but they wanted to be in some symbolically significant place. At the end of midnight mass the bishop processed down the Cathedral and the great west doors were opened. Silence fell over the huge crowd. The bishop blessed them. No one understood what this was about and the silence continued. Then he said, 'Happy New Year!' and a vast roar, like that of football crowd in full swing, filled the night sky.

By and large the significance of public space has, however, been lost. J. B. Jackson cites a description of public space as 'a gathering place for the people, humanizing them by mutual contact, providing them with a shelter against the haphazard traffic, and freeing them from the tension of rushing through a web of streets'. This, he says, is a characteristically modern definition of the public square: 'a place of passive enjoyment, a kind of playground for adults, an urban form which acts to draw people together and give them a momentary pleasure and sense of well being'.[48] The London Eye, a fairground attraction, becomes a permanent feature of a 'monumental city centre', a confession both of the vapidity of government purpose and of a craven populism.[49] In our time, said Mumford,

the ultimate fate of the commercial city is to become a backdrop for advertising: a fate well symbolized by the recent transformation of New York's two railroad stations from great public monuments to exhibition halls for a commercialism whose tawdriness by contrast gives almost a regal dignity to the financiers who originally conceived these stations with some sense of public obligation.[50]

'City after city discovers that its abandoned industrial waterfront or out-moded city centre contains enormous tourist potential and refurbishes it as a leisure time spectacle and sightseeing promenade. All of these sites become culinary and ornamental landscapes through which the tourists – the new public of the late twentieth century – graze, celebrating the consumption of place and architecture, and the taste of history and food.'[51]

---

[48] Jackson, *Discovering*, p. 16.
[49] Joseph Rykwert quite rightly expresses astonishment at this development and notes the contempt for the Greater London Council expressed in the sale of County Hall and its subsequent use. *Seduction*, p. 265.
[50] Mumford, *City*, p. 507.
[51] Christine Boyer, 'Cities for Sale: Merchandising History at South Street Seaport', in M. Sorkin (ed.) *Variations on a Theme Park: The New American City and the End of Public Space* (New York: Hill & Wang, 1992), p. 189.

Public space, by and large, is reduced either to leisure – perhaps a place to eat one's sandwiches at lunchtime on a nice day, or a place to enjoy buskers, as at Covent Garden, or a place of pageantry, as in Siena's Campo, where the Palio, the twice-yearly horse race, is still celebrated.[52] It becomes part of a theme park, a substitute for the democratic public realm. In this sense we could argue that the attempt to reclaim public space as a place of serious encounter 'is the struggle for democracy itself'.[53] Alternatively it might be felt that the public sphere of political contest 'is more real as fantasy, and ideal type, than as historical achievement'.[54]

THE STREET

These comments lead on to a consideration of the street, which Roger Scruton regards as 'the most important of open public spaces'.[55] A street, he says, should be regarded not simply as a means of access but as an end in itself – a place that can be enjoyed for its own sake.[56]

There are, of course, many types of street. There are 'mean streets', sites of crime, drugs and prostitution, which need to be reclaimed. In Barcelona Las Ramblas, one of the most famous avenues in the world, has become criminalised, 'charmless, tawdry and dangerous'. The newspaper *La vanguardia* describes it as 'A dark boulevard where drunks impose their style, where wallets disappear and there are fights and muggings . . . The sensation is of chaos, of a lost city. Barcelonans are turning their backs on it.'[57] The Barcelona authorities are trying to restore it to its former family-friendly status. 'Reclaim the streets' has been a feminist campaign for more than forty years now. Jane Jacobs argued that overlooked streets, not abandoned to either business or commerce, were by and large safe streets.

There are also a great many unpleasant streets. In high-rise cities people live 'in an aural state of siege', with traffic and other noises amplified by the canyons which pass for streets, full of 'bad breath', the smells from air conditioning, extractor fans and exhausts.[58] Many streets are impossible for pedestrians to negotiate because of the speed and volume of traffic. Contrast these with pedestrianised areas where it is a pleasure to stroll,

---

[52] In August 2010 the Italian government sought to ban the Palio, but this move is being hotly contested by the Sienese.
[53] M. Sorkin, in Sorkin (ed.), *Variations*, p. xv.
[54] J. Hartley, 'The Sexualization of Suburbia', in R. Silverstone (ed.), *Visions of Suburbia* (London: Routledge, 1997), p. 181.
[55] Scruton, *Classical, Vernacular*, p. 32.   [56] Ibid., p. 37.   [57] *The Observer*, 24 July 2009.
[58] Landry, *Art of City-Making*, p. 53.

meet and talk. A boulevard is different from an urban expressway, Kunstler argues. It is properly part of the urban fabric of the city.

It celebrates the idea of the city as a place with value, a place where a human being would want to be, not just a one-dimensional office slum to be fled after the hours of work. It defines a space in a way that allows for multiple functions: motoring, strolling, shopping, business, apartment living, repose. The subtleties of its design make all the difference.[59]

There are streets of charm and surprise: the small stepped alleyways which drop down Italian hill towns or British seaside towns, with glimpses into hidden courtyards or places of work. 'Have a care', warned R. S. Thomas,

> This wealth is for the few
> And chosen. Those who crowd
> A small window dirty it
> With their breathing, though sublime
> And inexhaustible the view.[60]

Prettying such streets for tourists is the surest way to kill them. Trees and water beautify streets: the pollarded trees of southern France, the chestnut avenues of London, the water which flows from the rebuilt synagogue in Freiburg, symbolically taking the water of life of repentance and new life around the city, the leats of south-west British towns, reflecting the sky and changing hour by hour.

The street is different from the grand avenue, which is associated above all with the baroque city. 'With the development of the wide avenue the disassociation of the upper and the lower classes achieves form in the city itself. The rich drive; the poor walk. The rich roll along the axis of the grand avenue; the poor are off centre, in the gutter... The rich stare; the poor gape: insolence battens on servility.'[61] However, Mumford also noted the irony that these great streets served as a diminishing glass so that the baroque despot soon reached 'his political vanishing point'.[62] Later, broad streets were carved out for political reasons. Between 1827 and 1852 barricades were thrown up in Paris on nine occasions. The wide boulevards which Haussmann created were designed to make riots more difficult and access for troops easier.[63]

---

[59] Kunstler, *Geography*, p. 125.
[60] R. S. Thomas, 'The Small Window', in *Selected Poems 1946–1978* (London: Granada, 1973), p. 125.
[61] Mumford, *City*, p. 424.   [62] Ibid., p. 447.
[63] Giedion, *Space, Time and Architecture*, 5th edn (Cambridge, Mass.: Harvard University Press, 1974), p. 746. He seems to think that this was a good thing.

Postmodern thought celebrates 'erotic' space. The city is understood to be about enjoying spectacle and chance meetings. The city, says Iris Marion Young,

offers delights and surprises. Walk around the corner, or over a few blocks, and you encounter a different spatial mood, a new play of sight and sound, and new interactive movement. The erotic meaning of the city arises from its social and spatial inexhaustibility. A place of many places, the city folds over on itself in so many layers and relationships that it is incomprehensible. One cannot 'take it in', one never feels as though there is nothing new and interesting to explore, no new and interesting people to meet.[64]

Equally, however, in this postmodern world, streets may be abandoned for skyways or underpasses often formally policed, which furthers the privatisation of space.[65] Marginal social groups and political activity are excluded from what now passes for the public domain. 'Under the guise of convenience, we are imposing a middle class tyranny on the last significant urban realm of refuge for other modes of life, other values: downtown streets.'[66] Contrast these with the arcaded streets of Bath and Chester, originally a product of gentrification but now elegant, comfortable, sociable and available for all. The street, Scruton argues, should reflect the desire for a common public order, the façade being a recognition of that order.[67] The abandonment of the façades shows that we have lost that sense, and our projects testify to a collective loneliness and isolation. Public order, however, is not given but is achieved, and there is no public order until people can see it. The loss of a proper vocabulary with which to express this is therefore a serious matter.[68] The façade is the public face of a building and allows it to negotiate a street or to stand comfortably in constricted places.[69] The face represents the values of publicity, order and felt representation of human life. A building without a façade is not just a building without a face – it is a building without expression and hence a building without life.[70]

Life-giving streets, however, cannot be created simply by façades. They are an expression of a culture, and as the Barcelona example shows, this cannot be taken for granted but has to be fought for and continually re-appropriated. Our streets tell us what we believe about ourselves – whether

[64] I. M. Young, *Justice and the Politics of Difference* (Princeton University Press, 1990), p. 240.
[65] T. Boddy, 'Underground and Overhead: Building the Analogous City', in Sorkin (ed.), *Variations*, p. 140.
[66] Ibid., p. 150.   [67] Scruton, *Aesthetics*, p. 249.   [68] Ibid., p. 250.
[69] Scruton, *Classical Vernacular*, p. 22.   [70] Scruton, *Aesthetics*, p. 254.

we are manic and driven, careless of the public good, or whether we have pride in ourselves and sufficient confidence and generosity to be inclusive.

PARKS AND SPACES OF LEISURE

The 'paradise' of Genesis 2 and 3 is taken from the Persian royal gardens. The walled garden with flowers and trees, places to sit and take leisure or to make love, is one of the deepest cultural archetypes not simply in Europe but in Asia as well. The medieval European nobility aspired to such gardens, and they began to be opened up to the public in the seventeenth century. They kept in view 'the aristocratic concept of space and verdure, as an essential part of urban life: not to be covered over without biological impairment, as well as aesthetic dreariness and depression'.[71] There were *Volksgärten* in Vienna and Berlin and the Vauxhall Gardens on the South Bank in London. The idea of public parks spread partly to improve the conditions of factory workers; partly as part of the belief that moral benefit derived from the natural environment; and partly to improve the value of real estate: both Regent's Park and Hyde Park in London were real estate ventures.[72] Public parks were 'an expression of a growing sense of the urban public as a body politic'. They symbolised civic culture and aspiration.[73]

In the second half of the nineteenth century and the first half of the twentieth 'pleasure grounds' were laid out in every British town and city, maintained by the rates and with special facilities for children. For many years they were maintained by park keepers, who were local council employees. The abandonment of this form of employment was not principally about budgets, as was claimed, but about priorities, about the devaluation of the public realm. In many places, both in North America and in Britain, parks quickly became unsafe places, abandoned to drug users. There is a paradox here which S. Kaviraj has explored in relation to Calcutta. There the Maidan was laid out as a Victorian formal park, for people to enjoy a shaded stroll. In colonial times it was largely used by the white inhabitants. After Independence its railings were slowly ringed by small shops and shacks, and then these invaded the park because it was 'pablik' space, space for everybody, as opposed to the private space from which they could

---

[71] Mumford, *City*, p. 436.
[72] J. B. Jackson, *A Sense of Place, a Sense of Time* (New Haven: Yale University Press, 1994), p. 114.
[73] L. Greenhalgh, 'Greening the Cities', in A. Barnett and R. Scruton (eds.), *Town and Country* (London: Jonathan Cape, 1998), p. 263.

be chased off. But the park now disappeared.[74] *Koinonia* relates to what is common, the sphere of the *ochlos*, the crowd, the poor, what Marx called the Lumpenproletariat, but the idea of the public presupposes normative values, of what is good for the citizenry as a whole. The debate as to the nature of these is at the heart of democracy.

Scruton argues that parks represent the idea that our primary civil need is to escape from the pressure of others; that they represent a concealed hostility to the city and its works; and that they presuppose a libertarian idea of human ends.[75] He thinks the park does not bear the imprint of any particular sets of values. Charles Landry's Comedia group, on the other hand, which studies culture in cities, takes the very opposite line, regarding parks as places where competing groups have to find ways of co-existing.[76] They afford the many who have no garden, and who either have no place for children to play or cannot afford expensive equipment, with beautiful and gracious places. Most visits to a park are with children and, if it is the case that children's play helps form basic sensibilities, then qualities of trust, fairness, justice and loyalty vital to civil society may be significantly developed in the play spaces that parks make available.[77] Nothing better expresses our commitment to a non-utilitarian public philosophy, an acknowledgement that beauty is important for its own sake, and that trees and flowers are one of our chief sources of delight. Far from manifesting a hostility to the city they provide its counterpoint, spaces without which a city can easily become dreary and inhuman. Far from their being libertarian, their very existence and maintenance express the strongest belief in an ordered and beautiful common life. In some of these parks the beauty and magic of paradise are truly made available for all.

Dickens records how working-class Londoners spent their Sundays going to Greenwich or Richmond, boisterous places with plenty of liquor and oysters on sale. As opposed to the moral orderliness of the park, what we now see, J. B. Jackson argues, is the proliferation of ad hoc public spaces where the interaction and confrontation of the market place prevails: the flea market, the competitive sports event, the commercial street in the blue-collar part of town temporarily transformed into a fairground, the parking lot transformed into spaces for games and spectacles and the places where the presence of others is the main source of pleasure and stimulation. 'The park as a total experience for all classes of citizens is gradually becoming

---

[74] S. Kaviraj, 'Filth and the Public Sphere: Concepts and Practices about Space in Calcutta', *Public Culture*, 10/1 (1997), 83–113.
[75] Scruton, *Classical Vernacular*, p. 36.   [76] Greenhalgh, 'Greening the Cities', p. 264.
[77] So Ken Worpole in Greenhalgh, 'Greening the Cities', p. 265.

merely one space out of many, now serving an invaluable function primarily for children, older people and the dedicated student of nature.'[78] Jackson is right to point to rumbustious 'unofficial' places in which order is not tightly preserved, in which people are inventing themselves and their entertainment as necessary places in the public realm. Without order no life is possible, but where there is perfect order there is death. To some extent wise councils in Britain have acknowledged this in tacitly allowing places for skateboarding or jump-biking. Maintaining the public realm requires a balancing act in which the need for creative disorder is acknowledged and allowed on the margins. It cannot be provided for, because as soon as this happens it is brought within the realm of order and ceases to fulfil its function. Neither can it be allowed to take over, because space ceases to be public and is given over to the strong.

Nothing makes clearer that the public realm requires wisdom, generosity and courage for its maintenance and that what can easily be sneered at as a realm of 'middle-class values' can be a very precious as well as a very fragile possession.

MUSEUMS AND ART GALLERIES

Museums have their origins in the temples and treasure houses of the ancient world. Nebuchadnezzar, we are told, 'carried off all the treasures of the house of the Lord, and the treasures of the king's house' (2 Kings 13.13). Collections of curiosities were places where one could reflect or muse. Such collections were amassed by monarchs, the wealthy, but also by abbeys and churches in the Middle Ages. Modern museums often began with private collections – for example, the British Museum began with the collection of Sir John Soane. It is to the Victorian passion for education that we owe the wonderful museum quarters of cities like London. Late-night opening was introduced in the Victoria and Albert Museum as early as 1857 to allow the working classes entrance. It was hoped that the museum would stimulate productive industry and improve morals. 'In the burgeoning cities of the industrial north, museums and libraries began to be founded as a distraction and refreshment for the working population. They were to raise the moral and educational tone of cities – and counteract drunkenness and fornication.'[79] The Victoria and Albert was the first museum anywhere to provide a café, the magnificent William

---

[78] Jackson, *Sense of Place*, p. 116.
[79] R. Hewison, *The Heritage Industry: Britain in a Climate of Decline* (London: Methuen, 1987), p. 86.

Morris, Gamble and Poynter rooms, still in use. Museums and galleries were vehicles for Arnold's sweetness and light, the infusion of the work ethic by the values of high culture. My impression, as a gallery user, is that museums have become less middle-class spaces than they used to be. To be in the Tate Modern, on any day of the week, is to observe the full gamut of an extremely lively and diverse multicultural society, though I suppose it is not a favourite venue for *Big Issue* sellers. Judging by other societies where museum entrance is not free, it has to be said that museum charges are a key way of introducing or enforcing class distinctions in such places.

After a period when museums were considered dull and fuddy-duddy they have been rejuvenated all over the world and are now prime tourist sites. Frank Gehry's Bilbao museum is one of the world's most iconic buildings and has done much to regenerate the city. The current mass popularity of the museum and art gallery can partly be understood as a function of the change in education from discipline to enjoyment. Museums and galleries are often spoken of as providing entertainment but in fact they appeal to what Aristotle considered the innate human pleasure in learning. In religiously divided cultures, or in secular societies where churches no longer speak, museums and galleries provide a way of thinking about the purpose of life, allowing glimpses of higher values. During World War II Kenneth Clark persuaded the government to allow one work of art at a time to be displayed in London, while all the rest were kept safe deep in slate mines in Wales: the public thronged to see these pictures. More dubiously they provide an ersatz religious experience, as was evident at the Vermeer exhibition at the National Gallery in 1996 when there was a positively devout silence in front of many of Vermeer's pictures, which were treated as icons.

Increasingly museums play a more significant educational role. Daniel Libeskind's Jewish museum in Berlin traces the history of German Jewry over more than 1,000 years, its design incorporating the 'voids' or discontinuities of that experience; it is built over the three axes of continuity, exile and the Holocaust, and ends with the small but thriving German Jewish society of today. It speaks to the whole of German, and indeed European experience. The International Slavery Museum in Liverpool fulfils a similar function. In facing up to the forced mass migration of the slave trade, the museum hopes to shape contemporary consciousness about both race and slave labour.

All public space is educative but the museum and gallery put education at the heart of public life, many of them in extremely creative ways. Museum shops, as well as generating income, act reflexively, raising questions about taste, beauty and significance in the population at large. That the museum has replaced the cathedral as a centrally significant public space may be taken as a working-out of Lessing's preference for the quest for truth over absolute truth.[80] To keep them free of charge is a commitment to public life at the centre of a generous and egalitarian culture.

THE WAR MEMORIAL AND THE CEMETERY

It is odd to us, though it would not have been to the Victorians, to regard cemeteries as public space. Van Pelt gives the funeral monument, or stela, a central place in his account of the public space of ancient Athens. 'It was the place where the citizen returned into the order of nature and where his actions, undertaken for the city, were subsumed into an immutable past.'[81] The annual public funeral of the citizens who had fallen in war for the city's sake was one of the most important civic events in ancient Athens and addressed the question of why people should die for the city. The answer was that to live in a city meant to live within the city's collective body after the death of one's physical body. The dead lived on as an example of excellence that provided a normative foundation for the political life of the city. People went through the cemetery on the way to school, and this provided a lesson in citizenship. Care for the dead was a mark of character, and no one could hold public office if they had not been seen to honour the dead. In this way the necropolis was the moral and pragmatic foundation of the public realm.[82]

In the Middle Ages, Ariès claims, the cemetery took the place of the forum. 'The cemetery served as a forum, public square, and mall, where all members of the parish could stroll, socialise, and assemble. Here they conducted their spiritual and temporal business, played their games, and carried on love affairs.'[83]

The cenotaph, the war memorial and the Holocaust memorial offer us analogies with the cemetery in ancient Athens. 'Forgetfulness leads to exile, while remembrance is the secret of redemption', it says at Yad Vashem. The words of Primo Levi, survivor of Auschwitz, preface the Holocaust memorial in Berlin: 'It happened once and therefore we know it can happen again: this is the core of what we have to say.'[84] Its designer,

---

[80] Lessing wrote: 'If God held all truth in his right hand and in his left hand the everlasting striving after truth, so that I could always and everlastingly be mistaken, and said to me "Choose", with humility I would pick on the left hand and say, "Father, grant me that. Absolute truth is for thee alone."' *Lessing's Theological Writings*, ed. H. Chadwick (London: A. &. C. Black, 1956), p. 43.

[81] Van Pelt, in Westfall and van Pelt, *Architectural Principles*, p. 183.   [82] Ibid., p. 185-7.

[83] P. Ariès, *The Hour of our Death* (New York: Oxford University Press, 1981), p. 62.

[84] P. Levi, *The Drowned and the Saved* (London: Abacus, 1988), p. 167.

Peter Eisenman, wrote that he wanted it to be a part of ordinary, daily life and not a holy place. He envisaged it being used for short cuts. In this respect the idea behind it was close to that of the Athenian necropolis.

The war memorials of Europe came into being as a response to the trauma of World War I and to that extent answered the same question about dying for one's country as they did in ancient Athens. Originally they gave an occasion for collective grieving, as the Vietnam wall in Washington still does. As memory fades they give an occasion to remember past or present national greatness. But the idea that they might be an important educational device is not credible in the undialectical way which van Pelt seems to think obtained in Athens. Today people are much more aware of the fact that wars are fought to gain commercial advantage, to save or extend empires, to advance great fortunes, in the interest of megalomaniac dictators, directed by generals dining on silver while tens of thousands of ordinary troops die in bombardment. The lesson that war memorials teach may be the opposite of what was originally intended. Monuments which speak powerfully to one generation later lose their power. For the first few years after its erection former soldiers required people to doff their caps before Edith Cavell's memorial near St Martin-in-the-Fields in London. It is now lost in the swirl of traffic, and few remember who she was or why she was 'shot at dawn'. In Exeter streets, pubs and a statue commemorate Sir Redvers Buller, a hero of the Zulu wars, now completely forgotten. The main function of the statue seems to be to invite students to place traffic cones on Buller's cockaded head.

Where they exist Victorian cemeteries are still visited. Famous cemeteries like Highgate, where Marx is buried, or Père Lachaise in Paris, where the remains of Abelard and Heloise were interred in the nineteenth century, are places of pilgrimage. They are often places of wild, untended beauty, full of a pleasant nostalgia as one decodes stories of the good and the great of a past era. From the start they were intended as places where one might walk, an extension of the park.[85] Modern cemeteries, on the other hand, are harmless places, tidy, with their clipped lawns and rose beds, and completely without evocative power. The privatisation of death has its inevitable correlate in the public realm, and this reflects a modern pathology. 'The suppressions of death make modern men and women callous, apathetic and infantile. They produce forced pretences of enjoyment, and fanatical performance neuroses. These suppressions kill the love for life as a whole. If we suppress our fears, and don't take time to mourn our dead, the pain of other

---

[85] K. Worpole, 'In the Midst of Life', in Barnett and Scruton (eds.), *Town and Country*, p. 312.

people will leave us unmoved too.'[86] The disappearance of the Victorian cemetery was bound up with the scarcity and therefore the price of land, but forgetfulness of the dead is another way in which the public realm is trivialised, for if we do not know where we come from, we cannot know who we are. 'For the first time in history we are in danger of creating a culture lived in the continuous present, with the past eradicated or denied in modern urban architecture and planning, and the future, similarly, rendered off limits by the reaction against all forms of teleological or utopian idealism.'[87] Ken Worpole argues that local burial makes clear the meaning of the city as a site of historical consciousness. No cemetery, no city! as the Parisian citizens told Haussmann. When friends visit the grave, the cemetery remains part of the symbolic urban realm. The urban cemetery is a reminder of another world, 'a vegetative, entropic, timeless world, that is beyond human or bureaucratic control'. Without this reminder the city remains ungrounded and therefore incomplete.[88]

PUBS AND CAFÉS

Originally the Athenian agora was surrounded by all kinds of different buildings, but one architectural form came to predominate as a special type that connected the centre of deliberation from the periphery of administration: the stoa or portico. Stoas were the natural resort for people wanting shelter from rain or sun, people waiting for a friend or talking to acquaintances. Philosophers also found they could meet in the stoa.[89] Are there analogies to the stoa in contemporary public space? Leonie Sandercock remarks that the city's public spaces are not natural servants of multicultural engagement. Sites for coming to terms with difference are the 'micro publics' such as work-places, schools, colleges, youth centres, sports clubs, community centres, in which people from different cultural backgrounds are thrown together in new settings, which disrupt familiar patterns and create the possibility of initiating new attachments.[90] Among these 'micro publics' I want to think of pubs and cafés as analogous in some way to the stoa, as places which allow for the real formation of community through the invisible filigree of debate and argument.

The 'public house' was so called because in small communities it provided a fire, which the poor often could not afford, a room big enough to

---

[86] J. Moltmann, *The Coming of God* (London: SCM, 1996), p. 57.
[87] Worpole, 'In the Midst of Life', p. 307.   [88] Ibid., pp. 309, 314.
[89] Van Pelt, in Westfall and van Pelt, *Architectural Principles*, p. 209.
[90] Sandercock, *Cosmopolis II*, p. 94.

meet and talk in, and refreshment. Public houses were also the forerunners of the local general store. Worry about these places as centres of agitation or rebellion is well documented throughout early modern Europe: they were not just, or even centrally, about eating and drinking but about conversation, often political. In the same way the coffee houses of the Enlightenment were the places where political parties met and where insurance companies like Lloyds of London began. These places are public space, but space which is hosted. The licensee, as the British publication *The Good Pub Guide* insists over and over again, is the person who makes or breaks a good pub. You are not entering his or her home and yet his or her personality is impressed on the place. The licensee both acts as a focus for the hospitality of the community and facilitates it. He or she does so through the provision of food and drink, two of the most elementary human needs, as Christian sacramental thinking has always recognised. Successful community needs public, shared, welcoming, non-tribal space. Good pubs and cafés provide a space for congeniality, oil the wheels of community by encouraging good humour, laughter and space for friendly discussion and enable social classes to mix. In different ways in most countries (think of the *taverna*, the Parisian café, the *Kneipe*, the pub) these places often express a strong sense of identity. Under postmodern conditions, writes Bauman, where community is always hard work and an uphill struggle,

We console ourselves and summon our wilting determination by invoking the magic formula of 'tradition' – trying hard to forget that tradition lives only by being recapitulated, by being construed as a *heritage*; that it appears, if at all, only at the end, never at the beginning, of agreement; that its retrospective unity is but a function of the density of today's communal cloud.[91]

There are justified attacks on the heritage industry as a sentimental obfuscation of the cruelty and divisions of the past, and therefore as an equally sentimental and mendacious construction of our present. Marx was quite right that all history is the history of class struggles, and this is very obvious in our 'heritage'. But pubs emerge from the underside of history and even today are often working-class. The way in which they focus identity is indicated in their popular name of 'the local'. It is true that *ekklesia* has always been ambivalent about local culture and ethnicity, but on the other hand Pentecost represents a celebration of local difference *as a gift of the Spirit*. What is precluded is chauvinism. Local identity is to be celebrated as a precious gift provided it does not lead

[91] Bauman, *Modernity*, p. 250.

us to suppose that every other identity is inferior or has to be converted into our own. This presupposes what twentieth-century missiologists called 'indigenisation' or 'inculturation'. What, surely, is a sin against the Holy Spirit is the present process of homogenisation which we know as 'McDonaldisation'. If the opposite of sin is grace, and if McDonaldisation is one form of sin, there is grace abounding in the English pub or café.

But is not the pub or the taverna the very antithesis of sacred space? William Blake, for one, thought it was not. In 'The Little Vagabond' he wrote

> Dear Mother, dear Mother, the Church is cold,
> But the Ale-house is healthy and pleasant and warm;
> Beside I can tell where I am used well,
> Such usage in heaven will never do well.
>
> But if at the Church they would give us some Ale,
> And a pleasant fire our souls regale,
> We'd sing and we'd pray all the live long day,
> Nor ever once wish from the Church to stray.
>
> Then the Parson might preach, & drink, & sing,
> And we'd be as happy as birds in the spring;
> And modest dame Lurch, who is always at Church,
> Would not have bandy children, nor fasting, nor birch.
>
> And God, like a father rejoicing to see
> His children as pleasant and happy as he,
> Would have no more quarrel with the Devil or the Barrel,
> But kiss him, & give him both drink and apparel.[92]

The 'micro publics' of pubs, cafés and tavernas provide a space for what Karl Rahner calls 'the liturgy of the world', which is then reflected on by what we know as 'sacraments'. For Rahner, the mass is a sign in miniature of the mass of the world, to which Christ himself belongs. A sacrament is the sign of the *res sacramenti*, the reality designated, which is identical with the whole unfolding history of the world.[93] Pubs and cafés are in no way exceptional in being part of this process but they are not, as some Christians even today might feel, excluded from it. Blake wants to contrast ordinary human warmth and kindliness with the anti-humanist tendency

---

[92] From W. Blake, 'Songs of Experience', in *Complete Writings*, ed. G. Keynes (Oxford University Press, 1969), p. 216.

[93] K. Rahner, 'Considerations on the Active Role of the Person in the Sacramental Event', in *Theological Investigations*, vol. XIV (London: Darton, Longman and Todd, 1976), pp. 161 ff.

of some theology and practice, and he is right to find such warmth in places of public refreshment.

THE MARKET

Van Pelt argues that in ancient Athens the market was the one institution which broke the public–private divide, making that which is produced elsewhere available. Historically markets have been friendly, lively and colourful places. If you have the good fortune to shop regularly at a local market you get to know traders and friends, and markets are usually surrounded by the pubs and cafés just considered. Mumford properly calls them places of human delight. He contrasts them with the 'plastic-coated automation of the American supermarket, with its ghastly fluorescent lighting, its meretricious packaging, its cunningly baited booby traps ("impulse buying"), its poisonous forms of preservative antisepsis, its frozen and flavourless foods, in their artfully arrested decay, [which] present a contrast that betrays both an aesthetic and a physiological as well as a social loss'.[94] Mumford did not live to see the biggest of the malls.

In complete contrast to Mumford, Ira Zepp argues that malls may be understood as sacred space. Drawing on the work of Mircea Eliade, he argues, apparently without irony, that malls are centred places, that their floor plans embody a sacred geometry, that they are places of festival and of pilgrimage, and that they enable community. He even uses Pauline indwelling language of the mall: 'The mall is in you and you are in it.'[95] The mall is a democratic, unifying, universal place which gives spirit and personality to the city and provides, at its best, the most appealing entertainment available. Its playful atmosphere points us beyond commerce, barter and trade and tells us that life is not finally lived at the level of momentary transactions and that such exchanges will take place in an atmosphere of fun and conviviality. Like cathedrals malls define the nature of reality, provide a definition of the good life and status symbols that trigger our desires, and claim to be the centre of meaning and value.[96]

More people go to the Mall of America than go the Vatican and Mecca. For a cultural populist this may be an endorsement but the critics think otherwise. Physically, malls are surrounded by parking lots, dependent on the car and therefore bad for the environment. The old markets maintained

[94] Mumford, *City*, p. 343.
[95] I. Zepp, Jr, *The New Religious Image of Urban America: The Shopping Mall as Ceremonial Centre* (Niwot: University Press of Colorado, 1997), p. 70.
[96] Ibid., p. 125.

continuity with the street, but malls are 'pedestrian islands in an asphalt sea'.[97] Malls are private space, so political speech is strictly controlled; people meet not as citizens in a democratic society but as consumers. Anyone attempting religious or political speech can be quickly removed.[98] 'The enclosure of urban space represents a secession from the larger society that is inspired by (and inspires) fear of crime and social disorder, and it signals a withdrawal from public space and public life.'[99] The policing of malls means that they are predicated on a certain elitism, affluence, luxury and availability of spare time.[100] Many malls now clarify the extent of their public role by posting signs that read: 'Areas in this mall used by the public are not public ways, but are for the use of tenants and the public transacting business with them. Permission to use the said areas may be revoked at any time.'[101] The mall and shopping as the metaphor for a good life cannot sustain the spirit, remarks Landry. Filling emptiness with busyness rarely works, however enticing it may appear at first sight.[102]

A completely private sector approach tends to privatize public space, so you tend to end up with mall-like developments and lose the street in the process . . . However well done, the former has a commercial edge as it is geared to consuming, which allows for some excitement but is essentially barren. The latter done well . . . can exude public values like conviviality, the ability to hang around or the ability to reflect.[103]

Aesthetically malls offer a make-believe world that has no connections with the cultural and ecological realities of the place. 'It is enjoyment without risk; a Brave new world of real life Feelies; the perfect environment supported by unlimited energy resources and technology in the service of the vicarious experience.'[104] The West Edmonton Mall in Alberta, for example, the largest mall in the world, offers flamingos, ibises, sharks, Siberian tigers, Versailles fountains and so on. Air conditioning and artful lighting manipulate space and light to create a fantasy urbanism devoid of the city's negative elements – weather, traffic and poor people.[105] Mumford argued that a constant education of the senses is the elemental groundwork of all higher forms of education. 'When it exists in daily life a community may spare itself the burden of arranging courses in art appreciation. And

---

[97] M. Crawford, 'The World in a Shopping Mall', in Sorkin (ed.), *Variations*, p. 212.

[98] L. Wallin, 'The Stranger on the Green', in Sorkin (ed.), *Variations*, p. 105.

[99] D. Judd and T. Swanstrom, *City Politics: Private Power and Public Policy*, 3rd edn (New York: Addison Wesley, 2002), p. 433.

[100] Zepp, *New Religious Image*, p. 147.   [101] Crawford, 'The World in a Shopping Mall', p. 23.

[102] Landry, *Art of City-Making*, p. 113.   [103] Ibid., p. 303.   [104] Hough, *Out of Place*, p. 96.

[105] Crawford, 'The World in a Shopping Mall', p. 22.

when it does not exist, such efforts are largely banal and self defeating, for they deal chiefly in currently fashionable clichés, not in the underlying realities.'[106]

Malls have no place for small traders. At the mall all rents are necessarily high because of the high cost of construction, maintenance, heating and air conditioning. Only the large chain store operations can afford to be there. These destroy local businesses and in so doing destroy local economies. The chains gave back nothing to the locality except a handful of low-wage service jobs.[107] In Britain an all-party parliamentary group predicted that small shops might vanish from the country's high streets by as early as 2015. 'The erosion of small shops is viewed as the erosion of the social glue that binds communities together.'[108] Paris has a local urbanism plan which seeks to encourage small shops and key workers to stay in the city. Central Paris is far livelier because it has a dense and varied network of shops and people. Half of the 71,000 shops in Paris have restrictions placed on them to prevent inappropriate change of use.[109] The malls claim to offer variety but the chains rigorously repeat the range of products offered at every other shopping mall. Since branches of national chains are the most reliable money makers, individually owned stores are admitted only with shorter leases and higher rents.[110]

The malls are also unsustainable. Alan Durning claims that North America's thousands of shopping malls are the centrepieces of the most environmentally destructive ways of life yet devised. In combination with the suburbs that surround them and the cars that stream into them they cause more harm to the biosphere than anything else except perhaps rapid population growth.[111] The ideological, political and architectural unauthoritativeness of the shop is evident to all, remarks van Pelt, but in the mall we have the apotheosis of postmodern space – consumer-driven, without meaning, ultimately destructive, with the 'public' replaced by the consumer.

This brings us back to the central meaning of public space. It is in public space that a community gives an account of itself. This is one of the reasons why Milton Keynes is so disturbing, having been built inside out, beginning without a purpose and having to find one. A city can be a city only when it knows its meaning. In Siena the magistrates knew it was 'the common good'. In Victorian times courthouses and town halls announced a portentous sense of civic pride. Parks were created for the

[106] Mumford, *City*, p. 343.   [107] Kunstler, *Geography*, p. 120.
[108] Landry, *Art of City-Making*, p. 133.   [109] Ibid., p. 133.
[110] Crawford, 'The World in a Shopping Mall', pp. 4, 9.
[111] During, quoted in Zepp, *New Religious Image*, p. 173.

delight of all citizens. But if all we can think of is a fairground ferris wheel, or if consumerism becomes the meaning of the city, then the city is finished.[112] No grace, beauty, dignity or justice attaches to it. Public places can be gracious, it turns out, only when the citizenry seeks grace. In the next chapter we turn to the way this applies to human settlements.

[112] Van Pelt, in Westfall and van Pelt, *Architectural Principles*, p. 180.

CHAPTER 7

Settlements in grace

In the 1990s the Mayor of Baltimore called for his city to become 'a city in grace'. The phrase is evocative, but what would it mean? In the first place, it implies something about identity. A city, says Daniel Kemmis, is a living organism and therefore capable of something we might call grace.[1] This way of speaking recalls the language about the 'angel' of the various cities in the book of Revelation, a way of talking about their particular spirit, culture or ethos, what it is that makes London, Delhi or Nairobi different, or what accounts for the different moral codes which Thomas Hardy claimed he found in every different village.

Second, when Aristotle talks of a 'polis', which we translate as 'city', he means a settlement very often no bigger than a modern village. When Peter Hall writes about 'cities in civilization', or Saskia Sassen about 'global cities', by and large they mean great cities, often of many millions. Much writing about the built environment is concerned simply with 'the city'; the village is left to anthropologists, the town to planners or historians and the suburb to sociologists. But when Haddon Wilmer asks what sort of humanity is encouraged by different types of city, the question must be applied to all forms of settlement.[2] I shall accordingly take 'city' as a way of talking about human settlements in general and look at villages, towns and suburbs as well as cities proper.

Third, to talk of a city or settlement in grace is to recall its opposite, a sinful or alienated city. It helps to understand a city in grace to understand what it is distinguished from. I therefore want to reflect on what it is that makes cities or settlements fail, the ways in which they destroy life rather than enable it.

[1] Kemmis, *Good City*, p. 25.
[2] H. Wilmer, 'Images of the City and the Shaping of Humanity', in A. Harvey (ed.), *Theology in the City* (London: SPCK, 1989), p. 34.

Lastly, every settlement, from the smallest to the greatest, has an economy, a society, a built form, an ecosystem, a polity and a culture.[3] In virtue of each it can be a settlement 'in grace' or otherwise. Carroll Westfall argues that Ur and Babylon were not cities but settlements. To call something a polis implies a political order. 'A polis is an entity in which three things are brought together into coordination as people live together: a shared purpose, a government they construe in order to exercise power justly while reaching for that purpose, and a physical setting which serves their purposes and facilitates their governing themselves.'[4] But even villages have these things. In each case we have to ask how polity, culture, economy, ecosystem and so forth interact, for the answers for a city and a village will be different. In terms of my fundamental theological scheme all three Trinitarian appropriations are needed in thinking about human settlements: all instantiate particular forms of order, and therefore the values which underlie planning; all are communities which can either foster or hinder reconciliation; many are the product of utopian visions which have set out to make a more gracious world.

By way of introduction to the idea of cities in grace I shall begin with some reflections on the idea of human settlements as educative.

THE POLIS AS EDUCATION

The idea of the divine education is fundamental to both Deuteronomy and the prophets. As Hosea (6.5) puts it,

> I have hewn them by the prophets,
> I have killed them by the words of my mouth.

Deuteronomy reads the whole of history as a way in which God instructs Israel – this is the presupposition of what we call the Deuteronomic history. The city as such plays no part in this education. The Deuteronomists were sceptical of the ideology which had gathered around Jerusalem, but even for those who were not, Jerusalem either signified the centre of the Davidic monarchy or the Temple, which Solomon had made the focus of the YHWH cult. The culture of the Hebrew Bible is emphatically non-urban.

In Greece a century or so after these writers, Thucydides, Aeschylus and Sophocles offer us a very different account of 'the education of the human race'. In Pericles' famous Funeral Oration after the first year of the

---

[3] Landry, *Art of City-Making*, p. 6.   [4] Westfall and van Pelt, *Architectural Principles*, p. 48.

Peloponnesian War in 430, Pericles claims that Athens provides a liberal education for its citizens. As Thucydides records it he said:

Our constitution does not copy the laws of neighbouring states; we are rather a pattern to others than imitators ourselves. Its administration favours the many instead of the few; this is why it is called Democracy. If we look to the laws, they afford equal justice to all in their private differences; if to social standing, advancement in public life falls to reputation for capacity, class considerations not being allowed to interfere with merit; nor again does poverty bar the way, if a man is able to serve the state, he is not hindered by the obscurity of his condition . . . We throw open our city to the world, and never by alien acts exclude foreigners from any opportunity of learning and observing . . . We cultivate refinement without extravagance and knowledge without effeminacy; wealth we employ more for use than for show and place the real disgrace of poverty not in owning to the fact but in declining the struggle against it . . . as a city we are a school to Hellas; while I doubt if the world can produce a man, who, where he has only himself to depend on, is equal to so many emergencies, and graced by so happy a versatility as the Athenian.[5]

The city, says Aristotle, originates in the union of a number of villages which come together for the bare needs of life, 'and continue in existence for the sake of a good life'.[6] The good life is directed towards the goals proper to humans, namely to produce people who embody courage, temperance, liberality, magnificence, greatness of soul, gentleness, urbanity, wittiness and modesty. This can be done only in community because such virtues can be learned only through interaction and fellowship. The urge for community is part of human nature, and therefore to live outside community is to live an unnatural life. Community, for Aristotle, is found in the city, which might be quite small, perhaps three to five thousand people living inside the city wall, though more in the surrounding chora, or rural hinterland.[7] This city exists to promote the flourishing of education and excellence.[8] This accords a significance to the city which was undreamed of in Hebrew thought and which is little enough in evidence in Christian thought either. John Chrysostom, who worked in Constantinople until he was exiled, thought that in cities the devil uses 'lewd sights, base speech, degraded music and songs full of all kinds of wickedness' to lead us on the

---

[5] Thucydides, *History of the Peloponnesian War*, bk II, ch. 6, tr. R. Crawley (London: Dent & Dutton, 1910), p. 93.

[6] Aristotle, *Politics*, 1252b28, *Complete Works*, p. 1987.

[7] M. A. Hansen, *Polis: An Introduction to the Ancient Greek City State* (Oxford University Press, 2006), p. 75. Athens had about 30,000 male citizens and therefore a total population nearer 200,000.

[8] Aristotle, *Politics*, 1283a25, *Complete Works*, p. 2036.

road to damnation.[9] For Augustine, Rome was the archetype of the earthly city and it was fundamentally marked by the *libido dominandi*, the 'lust to control'. In the twentieth century the Calvinist Jacques Ellul regarded the city – clearly distinguished from all other forms of settlement of course – as cursed by its origin, its structure, its selfish withdrawal and its search for other gods.[10] Sin, 'the world' and the powers of hell are all symbolised in the city. 'In the clear vision of the Lord's Spirit the truth about Rome is the truth about Moscow, about Berlin, about Paris and about Washington.'[11] The life of a powerful city is always a constant succession of revolts against God. This is notwithstanding the fact that the city is the product of good will, 'the engineer's bright eye, the urbanist's broad sweep of mind, the hygienist's idealism'.

Affirmation of the city is a less prominent theme. The rebirth of the city in twelfth-century Europe produced positive evaluations in Abelard, for whom cities were 'convents' for married people, where they could live together in charity, and in Aquinas in the next century, for whom the city was the most complete of all human communities (as opposed, say, to monasteries or villages). The study of the city is called politics, 'a branch of practical philosophy which excels all others since it deals with the most perfect means of procuring goodness in human affairs through the use of human reason'.[12] This is as close as we ever get to the Greek theme, made possible by Aquinas' belief that grace perfects nature. In his scheme, however, the educative role of the city cannot play the central part that it does for Aristotle, as the education provided by church and sacraments is more crucial and requires quite different forms of society. The role of church and city is analogous to the role of revealed and natural theology. Ellul's dialectic includes an affirmation of the city. In virtue of the death and resurrection of Christ the city is now a neutral world where human beings have possibilities for constructive action. In particular the person of faith must pray for the good of the city as Jeremiah insisted, and as Abraham did for Sodom.[13]

Many contemporary thinkers take up the Greek idea of the educative impact of the city. 'If we are to have cities', said Mumford in 1961, 'it

---

[9] J. Chrysostom, *De poenitentia*, VI, in J. P. Migne (ed.), *Patrologia graeca*, vol. XLIX (Paris, 1862), p. 313.

[10] J. Ellul, *The Meaning of the City* (Grand Rapids: Eerdmans, 1970), p. 60.   [11] Ibid., p. 50.

[12] P. Abelard, *Theologia christiana*, II.43–56, in *Petri Abaelardi opera theologica*, ed. E. M. Buytaert, vol. II, Corpus Christianorum, vol. XII (Turnhout: Brepols, 1969), pp. 149–55; Aquinas, *Sententia libri politicorum*, Prologue, A 69–70, www.corpusthomisticum.org/iopera.html (last accessed 16 August 2010).

[13] Ellul, *Meaning of the City*, p. 75.

is because they make men.'[14] Cities have been the places where dreams have turned to drama, and 'sexual desire flowered into poetry and dance and music. The city itself thus became a collective expression of love.'[15] Through the spaces of agora and stoa, however these have materialised, the city has promoted significant conversation.[16]

The final mission of the city is to further man's conscious participation in the cosmic and historic process. Through its own complex and enduring structure, the city vastly augments man's ability to interpret these processes and take an active, formative part in them, so that every phase of the drama it stages shall have, to the highest degree possible, the illumination of consciousness, the stamp of purpose, the colour of love. That magnification of all the dimensions of life, through emotional communion, rational communication, technological mastery, and above all, dramatic representation, has been the supreme office of the city in history. And it remains the chief reason for the city's continued existence.[17]

'As we collectively produce our cities', writes David Harvey, 'so we collectively produce ourselves. Projects concerning what we want our cities to be are, therefore, projects concerning human possibilities, who we want, or, perhaps even more pertinently, who we do not want to become.'[18] The 'Educating Cities' network writes that

The city is educative . . . per se: there is no question that urban planning, culture, schools, sport, environmental and health, economic and budget issues, and matters related to transport and traffic, safety and services, and the media include and generate forms of citizen education. The city is educative when it imprints this intention on the way it presents itself to its citizens, aware that its proposals have attitude-related consequences and generate new values, knowledge and skills.[19]

The more traditional way to think of the educational work that cities do is to think of civility, the codes for relationship which emerge from crowded living.[20] Cities are, by definition (though not always in reality), places which 'civilise' us, which teach us the arts of co-operative and creative living. As we shall see, these accounts of the educative role of cities can be extended to other forms of settlement as well.

The tragedies of Aeschylus add an important rider to this account of the city as educative. In the *Oresteia* Orestes is freed from pursuit by the Furies by the due process of law. 'The committal of [Orestes'] case to a legally constituted tribunal of men is the apotheosis of law, of civilization,

[14] Mumford, *City*, p. 127.   [15] Ibid., p. 121.   [16] Ibid., p. 139.   [17] Ibid., pp. 655–6.
[18] D. Harvey, *Spaces of Hope* (Edinburgh University Press, 2000), p. 159.
[19] Landry, *Art of City-Making*, p. 311.   [20] Kemmis, *Good City*, p. 191.

of the polis and of ordered life.'[21] The implication is that it is the city which leads to the structures of law which address the furies of blood vengeance and the never-ending cycle of retribution. Of course in Israel the law is given in 'the wilderness', outside all given structures, marking the fact that it comes directly from God. Even here, however, the probable dependence of the 'Ten Words' on earlier codes such as those of Hammurabi indicates a relationship to the city. The city is essential precisely in its laws, says Aristotle, for without the justice which the laws of the city imposes human beings are 'the most unholy and the most savage of animals, the most full of lust and gluttony'.[22] It is a virtuous circle: it is the city which gives rise to law and it is law which civilises us. Aquinas, followed by the Reformers, endorsed the idea that the law was educative, though they did not tie it in the same way to the city.[23]

In speaking of human settlements as educative we are thinking, therefore, of two things. We are thinking of the kind of community found in a given settlement, its overall culture, its account of human ends, and the way it fashions its citizens. This was Pericles' concern. The city of Athens was educative, for him, in its understanding of the human good. Taking a wider and less chauvinist view, Aristotle argued the same for the polis in general. Second, some thinkers want to tie law to the city, and then to argue that the law is an important part of human education. We can put the point that the city is educative in this way: settlements, like the people who create them, do not live by bread alone.[24] This means that the first thing any settlement needs is faith, something to believe in. 'The crucial step is to be able to define and communicate a bigger role and purpose for the city [or settlement] by defining a common goal based on an integrated emotional, technological, environmental, social, economic, cultural and imaginative story.'[25] There is an analogy with architecture. As we shall see in Chapter 10, postmodernism produces poor architecture because it does not believe in anything. The question of transcendent purpose is crucial and is a key part of the common good. Lack of transcendent purpose in the city is not an absolutely new phenomenon. If Mumford is right,

---

[21] E. T. Owen, quoted in Westfall and van Pelt, *Architectural Principles*, p. 202.

[22] Aristotle, *Politics*, 1253a37, *Complete Works*, p. 1988.

[23] Aquinas writes, 'The purpose of human law is to lead men to virtue, not suddenly but gradually. Some are naturally virtuous but those who are not are trained to virtue by the discipline of laws.' *Summa theologiae*, 1a 2ae 95.1, vol. XXVIII, p. 101. The Reformers discerned a threefold use of the law: it convicts us of unrighteousness, curbs those who, unless forced, have no regard for rectitude and justice and helps believers learn with greater truth and certainty what the will of the Lord is which they aspire to follow.'

[24] Kemmis, *Good City*, p. 65.   [25] Landry, *Art of City-Making*, p. 287.

the Hellenistic city effectively built to celebrate its own achievements, as did Imperial Rome. Perhaps it was because he wrote in the milieu of the Hellenistic city and of Imperial Rome that the author of Hebrews insisted that 'here we have no lasting city, but look for the city that is to come' (Heb. 13.14). With regard to the cities that he knew, he was right, for imperial ambitions, whether colonial or neo-colonial, are no substitute for transcendent purpose. In relation to each form of settlement, therefore, we have to ask what it believes in.

A subset of these arguments relates to the impact of the built form of the settlement, of the hermeneutic circle famously indicated by Churchill when he said that 'we shape our buildings and then they shape us'. Although urbanists are more or less unanimous in agreeing that it is not possible to improve the human race simply by building or planning, equally it is clear that there are dehumanising environments which have to be avoided. The question about cities in grace is also, if not primarily, the question about the most humanising form of environment.

To be a city in grace any settlement also needs to be sustainable, but this is a bigger question than being low-carbon. Cities, says Landry, need to be emotionally and psychologically sustaining, and issues like the quality and design of the built environment, the quality of connections between people and the organisational capacity of urban stakeholders become crucial, as do issues of spatial segregation in cities and poverty. 'Sustainable places need to be sustaining across the range.'[26]

THE VILLAGE

For the past twelve millennia most human beings have lived in villages and it is fair to say, therefore, that the village is mother to the human race. Mumford understood them as above all a feminine creation.

Certainly 'home and mother' are written over every phase of Neolithic agriculture, and not least over the new village centres, at last identifiable in the foundations of houses and in graves. It was woman who wielded the digging stick or hoe: she who tended the garden crops and accomplished those masterpieces of selection and cross-fertilization which turned raw wild species into the prolific and richly nutritious domestic varieties: it was woman who made the first containers, weaving baskets and coiling the first clay pots. In form, the village, too, is her creation: for whatever else the village might be, it was a collective nest for the care and nurture of the young. Here she lengthened the period of child care and playful

[26] Ibid., p. 11.

irresponsibility, on which so much of man's higher development depends. Stable village life had an advantage over looser itinerant forms of association in smaller groups in that it provided the maximum facilities for fecundity, nutrition and protection. By communal sharing of the care of the young, larger numbers could prosper. Without this long period of agricultural and domestic development, the surplus of food and manpower that made urban life possible would not have been forthcoming.[27]

In his study of villages around the world Richard Critchfield assumes that villages are all agriculturally based, but of course there were mining villages, fishing villages, industrial villages, villages based on forestry and so on.[28] It is a mistake to think there was no division of labour in the village beyond the gender division which Mumford, and before him Engels, identified. Even in industrial villages there was a variety of trades, and sometimes formal education. In agricultural villages there were many trades and specialisations, from smithying to carpentry, to wheelwrights, to dairy work, herbalism, cobbling, clothes making and so on.[29] Even today small farmers can turn their hands to most things. The village always was, and often still is, a hive of industry.

In Chapter 4 we noted David Harvey's dismissal of the village as a dehumanising environment, but as an ideal it continues to be extraordinarily powerful. Gillian Darley records more than 400 villages built in Britain in the past three centuries and argues that new settlements should include villages. 'As an ideal aspired to over centuries, the village, traditional or model, cannot suddenly be consigned to limbo, regarded as an irrelevancy and an ineffective solution to the problems of modern life.'[30] Cities have always recruited from the village, said Mumford. 'Once we allow the village to disappear, this ancient factor of safety will vanish. That danger mankind has still to reckon with and forfend.'[31]

The village, Mumford argued, gave us the neighbour, the one who lives near at hand, sharing the crises of life. Precisely because of this, morality

---

[27] Mumford, *City*, p. 21.   [28] R. Critchfield, *The Villagers* (New York: Anchor Doubleday, 1994).

[29] As noted, for example, by Lord Justice Scott, *Report of the Committee on Land Utilisation in Rural Areas* (London: HMSO, 1942) (henceforth 'the Scott Report'), p. 21.

[30] G. Darley, *Villages of Vision*, 2nd edn (Nottingham: Five Leaves, 2007), p. 274. Jeremy Seabrook writes of the migrants coming to the city, 'They do not come willingly . . . They did not leave the mango orchards, the vegetable gardens, the rice fields, the small holdings with their pigs, ducks and chickens, because they were attracted to Bangkok.' And he quotes one immigrant as saying, 'We have come because we have no choice, because the places where we grew up have been ruined.' 'People think they come to the city for money, but actually, the city robs them, traps them into jobs with no skills, no future, for the sake of immediate earnings that must be sent home to the family.' *In the Cities of the South* (London: Verso, 1996), pp. 28, 29.

[31] Mumford, *City*, p. 69.

began in the mores, the life-conserving customs, of the village. He speaks of a 'watchful, identifiable deeply concerned group'.[32] 'Village life is a counterbalance to the blanket of anonymity offered by city life. There is constant potential for neighbourly contact in a village and each person can contribute to his community, according to his wishes.'[33] This would be the village in grace, but the picture is over-romantic. Historically, villages were usually class- and caste-divided, sometimes bitterly so, and over countless generations. In contemporary south India village community is frequently quite literally murderous.[34] In Britain house price inflation has forced out the poor and turned the countryside into a gentrified enclave.[35] Pleading the cause of countryside protection, the affluent have sought to exclude the poor. Here and there, and in the teeth of planning legislation, people have insisted on 'the right of all of us, just through having been born on this earth, to enjoy a right of access to our modest share of it'.[36] They appeal to the Local Agenda 21 objective to 'provide access to land for all households . . . through environmentally sound planning'. In Britain as elsewhere this is a class issue. As in the cities, control of land prices is the key to both social and economic regeneration.

Small communities enforce social conformity. Strict dress codes are imposed on lower castes by higher castes in India. In Britain right up to the 1960s any offenders against sexual mores were at the receiving end of rituals of shaming where other villagers conducted rough theatre outside the offender's house.[37] In twenty-first-century Britain, where the ethos is egalitarian and against deference, it might be thought the village approaches the ideal. The tiny village of Iddesleigh in Devon, for example, has 150 inhabitants but thirteen clubs and societies, all centred on a famously hospitable pub. The most prominent landowner keeps rents low for local people on small incomes and is not interested in making a fortune from wealthy 'quality of lifers'. The extent to which villages are emotionally and psychologically sustaining therefore varies enormously. In parts of the world they are clearly oppressive and places to escape from; in others, richly nurturing. What makes the difference is the local power structure.

---

[32] Ibid., p. 24.   [33] Darley, *Villages*, p. 274.

[34] H. Gorringe, *Untouchable Citizens* (New Delhi: Sage, 2005).

[35] M. Shucksmith, *Exclusive Countryside? Social Inclusion and Regeneration in Rural Britain* (York: Joseph Rowntree Foundation, 2000).

[36] C. Ward, *Cotters and Squatters* (Nottingham: Five Leaves, 2002), p. 174.

[37] However, Laurie Lee claimed in *Cider with Rosie* that Sladd, the village in which he grew up, defended its inhabitants, turning a blind eye to much misdemeanour and shaming only in exceptional circumstances, and never appealing to the police or wider powers of justice, even in cases of murder.

Around the world villages are usually composed of vernacular buildings, of which I shall say more in Chapter 10. Gentrification has accustomed us, at least in Britain, to picture-postcard images of villages. We need to remind ourselves how recently these places were a source of horror. Here is the account of the sanitary inspector of the city of Norwich in 1863, visiting a Norfolk village:

A stranger cannot enter the village without being struck with surprise at its wretched and desolate condition. Look where he may, he sees little else but thatched roofs – old, rotten and shapeless – full of holes and overgrown with weeds; windows sometimes patched with rags, and sometimes plastered over with clay; the walls, which are nearly all of clay, full of cracks and crannies; and sheds and outhouses – where there are any – looking as if they had been overthrown very early in the present century and left in the hopeless confusion in which they fell.[38]

Such villages could be found today in many places around the world, including much of mainland Europe. This is a sober warning against romanticisation. All the same the older villages often manifest the virtues of Mumford's 'organic planning'. 'If the physical framework of the village disintegrates, so too does the social framework and that must be nothing short of disastrous.'[39] Newer villages only too often exemplify the tyranny of the right angle. William Gilpin admitted that regular buildings might be more convenient, but he missed in Nuneham Courtney, the source of Goldsmith's *Deserted Village*, 'the proper appendages of a village, the winding road, a number of spreading trees, a rivulet and a bridge and a spire to bring the whole to an apex'.[40] In Britain villages often have common land which all can share, or a village green. Where they are caste-divided, however, different sections of the community must drink from different wells and are even debarred from some parts of the village.

Mining villages can have their spoil heaps and be as dreary and ugly as any other industrial landscape, but the agricultural village was necessarily built around care for the countryside. Hedging and ditching and all the other activities which keep a place neat and clean were not undertaken for aesthetic effect but because they were essential for efficient farming.

In terms of polity villages were often gerontocracies, and mostly patriarchal. Often the council of elders both made all major decisions and even administered justice. In Britain today the parish council, unpaid and

---

[38] R. Heath, *The English Peasant* (London: Fisher Unwin, 1893), p. 69. Doubtless these very same houses, brightly thatched, now sell for more than half a million pounds, and estate agents extol the virtues of cob.
[39] Darley, *Villages*, p. 274.   [40] Quoted in ibid., p. 28.

voluntary, monitors the affairs of the village and has a wide range of responsibilities. Here some measure of democracy is in place. Landry talks of ways
of enchanting the city, by which he means 'the repetitive acts of kindness
which form the texture and glue from which social capital grows'. 'This is
the only form of capital that grows by frequent use, rather than depleting.
It is the nervous system of the lived city.'[41] By acts of kindness he means
things like the voluntary planting of trees, hanging flower baskets outside
your house or busking.[42] All such acts, as important in the village as in the
city, create a life-enhancing ethos for a place and are about enhancing the
common good.

All over the world Critchfield found religion to be the core of village
life.[43] Following Dominic Crossan he understands Jesus as a principally
rural figure who worked among the farms and villages of lower Galilee.
Prophets, he thinks, mainly emerged from the village. Taking up the idea of
religion as projection, Walter Lippman thought that 'the deep and abiding
traditions of religion belong to the countryside. For it is there that man
earns his daily bread by submitting to superhuman forces whose behaviour
he can only partially control.' The villager understands himself or herself
as part of a greater order, whereas such pieties are dissolved in the city.[44]
Less reductively Redfield suggested that 'peasants find in life purpose and
zest because accumulated experience has read into nature and suffering and
joy and death significance that the peasant finds restated for him in his
everyday work and play'.

> There is a teaching, as much implicit as explicit, as to why it is that children come
> into the world and grow up to marry, labour, suffer and die. There is an assurance
> that labour is not futile; that nature, or god, has some part in it; there is a story or
> a proverb to assure one that some human frailty is just what one ought to expect;
> there are in many cases some serious myths to explain the suffering of the innocent
> or prepare the mind for death. So that although peasants . . . will quarrel and fear,
> gossip and hate, as do the rest of us, their very way of life, the persisting order
> and depth of their simple experiences, continue to make something humanly and
> intellectually acceptable of the world around them.[45]

Today the image of the village as closer to traditional patterns of belief
and ways of life than other forms of settlement has everywhere been challenged by the coming of television and the internet.[46] 'The global village
relentlessly roots out the real villages that still remain and drains away their

---

[41] Landry, *Art of City-Making*, p. 268.   [42] Ibid., p. 379.   [43] Critchfield, *The Villagers*, p. 429.
[44] W. Lippman, *A Preface to Morals* (New York: Macmillan, 1929), pp. 62–3.
[45] R. Redfield, *Peasant Life and Culture* (University of Chicago Press, 1956), p. 74.
[46] Critchfield, *The Villagers*, p. 10.

content, their information.'[47] The sense which was found everywhere in the old village that the future would simply repeat the past has been lost and been replaced by the idea that it can be radically improved. There is no reason, though, why this should spell the death of the village. In some countries, such as Denmark, they remain an important part of future planning.[48] Darley is pessimistic about the future of the village in Britain, though convinced of its importance as a social form. Gentrified commuter villages become 'grotesque over-statements of rural life, laden with sadly ill-used impedimenta of the countryside... At best the village can be preserved or subtly altered, at worst it can be destroyed.'[49] On the other hand the idea of the small community gathered around a central space, with its own amenities, refuses to go away, and is frequently how cities are conceived. New urbanism in many ways seeks to recreate the village, and despite the drift to the cities humanity's ancient home continues to prove inspirational as a vision of a concrete way in which a common good might be crafted.

THE TOWN

'One of the great deficiencies in the whole of west Devon', wrote W. G. Hoskins in 1954, 'is a town large enough to act as a Mecca for the isolated parishes.'

Country people do not want to live permanently in a town, but they like – and need – the complete refreshment that an occasional day-off in town can give: the shops, the lights, the crowded pavements, the theatres and cinemas, the cafes, the exciting variety of things they do not want to buy. To be in Exeter or Plymouth on a winter afternoon just before Christmas is not just a useful or necessary trip to town: it is for country people a spiritual experience, an utterly satisfying re-creation, something to talk about afterwards for weeks, to look forward to for months. And there is no town in that great quadrant of western Devon between Dartmoor and Hartland Point, nothing to satisfy this deep need for a break from country isolation and toil.[50]

Hoskins here puts his finger on the relation between the village and the city as it existed in the days before mass car ownership. The market town was different. It was 'the clearing house of the countryside'. It provided shops, markets, professional services of doctors, solicitors and bankers,

---

[47] Bill McKibben, quoted in Ibid., p. 439.   [48] Darley, *Villages*, p. 270.   [49] Ibid., p. 273.
[50] Hoskins, *Devon*, p. 311.

amusements such as cinemas and dance halls and grammar or secondary schools.[51]

Vance proposed that there has always been an alternative to synoecism (the process by which villages come together to form a city, as proposed by Aristotle), namely what he called diocecism, in which cities dispersed into their rural hinterlands.[52] Perhaps this is what is happening, at least in Britain, and there is no doubt that information technology makes it easier to do so, though there is a legitimate worry that the end result will be 'telesprawl', a further undisciplined spread of suburbia.[53] In Britain market towns are the favourite destination of people leaving the city. Nearly one-third of British people now live in them.[54] What is the attraction, and what would mark out a town in grace?

Small towns are notorious for being sleepy or dull, with 'not much happening', but, perhaps because of the universality of education, or perhaps because of middle-class immigration, small towns, in Britain at least, are vibrant communities with their own newspapers or newsletter, arts centres, arts festivals, mostly centred on local performers, local sports teams and amenities such as swimming pools and libraries. They are lively, involved communities where it is possible to shine without being a star. Ease of information means they are networked to the world. They are large enough to be able to escape if you wish, but small enough to have a good circle of friends. In Europe until the twentieth century, and in other parts of the world even now, towns offer a chance to escape social policing. In Britain they are at the centre of the 'slow city' movement which wants to emphasise the importance of local identity through preserving and maintaining the local natural and built environments, promoting local foods and supporting local cultural traditions.[55]

Kemmis puts political engagement at the heart of his idea of a city in grace, and small towns today, in Britain at least, are vivacious, lively, politically alive, often inclined to independent or 'Green' politics rather than to the politics of the major parties. They are at the forefront of the Transition Town process, which, in England, began in Totnes and which is

---

[51] Scott Report, p. 13.

[52] J. E. Vance, Jr, *The Continuing City* (Baltimore: Johns Hopkins University Press, 1990), p. 74.

[53] P. Hall, *Cities in Civilization* (London: Weidenfeld and Nicolson, 1998), p. 959.

[54] 18 million according to R. Green, 'Not Compact Cities but Sustainable Regions', in M. Jenks, E. Burton and K Williams (eds.), *The Compact City: A Sustainable Urban Form?* (London: Routledge, 1998), p. 146.

[55] Landry, *Art of City-Making*, p. 118. As of 2009 Cittaslow towns included Perth, Ludlow, Diss, Berwick upon Tweed, Mold, Cockermouth and Llinlithgow. Of these only Perth was a city, and it has a population of 43,000.

about political empowerment as much as it is about preparing for a post-carbon future. To be part of this process, to shop at the farmers' markets, drink in the pubs and cafés, attend political meetings and the annual play or pantomime is to be aware of a community pulling together, of a vividly realised common good.

In terms of built form most small towns manifest what Mumford would call an organic plan, whether based on the high street or the square, and there is often next to no modernist architecture. Where they are alive they have not been taken over by the homogenising and destructive advance of the big supermarket chains. The return to the small town may represent a perception about the importance of scale. For centuries, says Kemmis, we have steadfastly denied the fundamental wisdom of the golden mean, insisting that matters of scale could be dealt with in purely abstract or mechanical terms with no reference to the human measure of things.[56] The move back to small towns might signal that people are voting with their feet as regards scale. Kirkpatrick Sale talks of the beanstalk principle, that for every animal, object, institution or system there is an optimal limit beyond which it ought not to grow, and its corollary, that beyond this optimal size all other aspects of a system will be affected adversely.[57] Victor Papanek agrees. 'My primary conviction as a human being, a designer and an ecologist is Nothing Big works – Ever!'[58]

In towns the division of labour was always, more or less by definition, greater than in the village, but what also still marks the distinction is the size of the market. There may be a shop, or perhaps two, in the village but varied shopping is almost definitional for a town, though this will not include the big department stores of the city. The small town, then, a little bigger than Aristotle's polis, has a great deal to offer for a settlement in grace.

THE CITY

Counter-urbanisation may be an important trend in Britain, but world-wide the city is the main focus of migration. Every year another sixty-eight million people move to cities. The push and pull factors which account for this are well known: 'rural life is dull and backbreaking; there are few opportunities and little new arable land that can be developed, especially for women, who are often excluded from land occupancy upon the death

---

[56] Kemmis, *Good City*, p. 139.   [57] Sale, *Human Scale*, pp. 38, 59.
[58] V. Papanek, *The Green Imperative* (London: Thames and Hudson, 1995), p. 24.

of, or their divorce from, their husband. The cities are uniquely able to create jobs, and if the formal sector does not have them, the informal sector will'.[59] In fact, the chance of work is very questionable, as we shall see in Chapter 10, but land has a maximum carrying capacity and when it is exceeded people will eventually be forced off it. The industrialisation of agriculture and enclosure also force people into the cities. But can cities, as the Mayor of Baltimore hopes, be communities in grace? Familiar problems with that suggestion are the sense of alienation, which Tönnies was getting at with his idea of an impersonal *Gesellschaft*; the question of scale; and the question of whether cities are sustainable.

Jane Jacobs believed that cities lay at the heart of all economic creativity and expansion, but in her prioritisation of marginal cities she seems to invoke an economic determinism, a thesis about success breeding decline which cannot be endlessly replicated. There is an analogy with the success of the capitalist economy. Western capitalism was built on the exploitation of cheaper labour elsewhere, but because the world is finite there is a necessary end to the possibilities of this. In the same way, there are not infinite possibilities for marginal cities. Jacobs did not build into her thinking the need to recognise limits, whether of population or resource use. Moreover, the possibility of either cities or cultures over-exploiting their resource base and thus collapsing, as Diamond has documented, shows that Jacobs' thesis does not sufficiently take account of the city's indebtedness, over against its creativity. Much city boosterism is decidedly idealist: it suggests humans can live by creativity alone.

For some, excitement is what lies at the heart of city community. Nothing is so fundamental to a city, says Kemmis, as the concentration of humans and human activity within a small compass. As opposed to towns, cities have a 'demotic cosmopolitanism', a 'street level reinvention of identity'.[60] A city, says Richard Sennett, is 'a human settlement in which strangers are likely to meet. For this definition to hold true, the settlement has to have a large, heterogeneous population.'[61] As the focus of immigration cities continually renew their bloodstream. Peter Hall regards this process as one of the key factors in city creativity.[62] In contrast to the home-grown entertainment of towns and villages, they have first-class music and theatre, famous sports teams and entertainment which the town cannot provide. The coming-together of an enormous variety of individuals and of trades

---

[59] UN Habitat, *The Challenge of Slums: Global Report on Human Settlements 2003* (London: Earthscan, 2003), p. 26.
[60] Paul Gilroy, Quoted in D. Massey, *World City* (Cambridge: Polity, 2007), p. 171.
[61] Sennett, *Fall of Public Man*, p. 39.   [62] Hall, *Cities in Civilization*, p. 285.

and professions develops a synergy which the town cannot aspire to. At the same time cities are often unsafe or downright dangerous places, something which Hall suggests may be the price which has to be paid for creativity.[63] Whether there is any real connection between knife crime, say, or the risk of rape, and a creative milieu must be doubted. Not everyone finds this side of city life exhilarating. The Jain activist Satish Kumar, for example, currently head of Schumacher College, feels 'in exile' in cities but at home in the countryside.[64] Others are more inclined to side with Sidney Smith's description of the countryside as 'a kind of healthy grave'. It is much harder to say of cities, comprehensively, that they are 'sustaining across the range' as Landry urges they should be. They may be emotionally and psychologically draining. Notoriously they are often fractured by poverty and racial, ethnic or religious divisions.

Although the anonymity of the city is often celebrated, as the condition which allows difference of gender or sexuality in particular to flourish, at the same time cities are repeatedly described as 'collections of villages'. Papanek suggests that if we are seeking a benign, neighbourly way of life, rich in interconnections and cultural stimuli, then we should think of networks of neighbourhoods of about 5,000 to 10,000 residents – essentially the vision of the city as a network of villages. For him the 'ideal city' would be a network of such neighbourhoods, each of about 50,000. 'Special functional reasons may decrease city size to 20,000 or increase it to 120,000 – beyond that lies social chaos.'[65] But Abercrombie's neighbourhood districts in Plymouth, which were each of about 10,000 people, complete with village green and facilities, seem never to have become the urban villages he imagined. In most cases where villages within a city are spoken of, what is meant seems to be not the neighbourhood or the borough but that collection of streets where one shops, takes children to school and gets to know people on a day-to-day basis.

People frequently opt for city life for the freedom from social policing of the village, but on the other hand gangs and criminals can enforce their own moral codes, as they did in Belfast for decades, and as they still do in Rio de Janeiro, punishing relationships across confessional and other divides. The free 'erotic' city can be romanticised quite as much as the village.

As we have seen, Aristotle's cities were very small. The London of Dr Johnson, of which he could say that if you were tired of London you were tired of life, was half a million, which Schumacher thought was the limit of

---

[63] Ibid., p. 71.   [64] *Coracle* (Iona Community), July 2009.   [65] Papanek, *Green Imperative*, p. 112.

what was desirable.[66] There are now nineteen mega-cities with populations over 10 million, housing 8 per cent of the world's urban population. Does it make sense to think of such numbers as one city? What do cities of 30 million, like Tokyo, or 20 million, like Mexico City, São Paulo or Shanghai mean?[67] Is a coherent identity possible with those numbers, and without such an identity how could any settlement be a city in grace? Reasons for doubt are given in Chapter 10, as the growth of vast slums leads to divisions between fortified enclaves for the affluent on the one hand and hundreds of thousands of people living without the most basic amenities on the other.

Unlike villages and towns, cities have often been at the centre of the urban planners' vision. The broad avenue, the great boulevard, the embankment, the great gathering spaces, the triumphal arches, all mark off the city. This vision can beautify the city but equally it can lead to what Jane Jacobs called 'the sacking of cities', instantiated all over the world as urban expressways carved up city spaces and made them hostile and inhuman places. To repair the damage it is not urban acupuncture but painstaking urban surgery which is needed to put the city back together again. On the other hand cities, as compared with towns, ought to have architecture to take the breath away. A major problem with twentieth-century urban building, however, has been ignoring the context. Christopher Alexander argues that all new building should help heal and make whole. Every act of construction must create a continuous structure of wholes around itself.[68] The skyline of London would be very different if this advice had been heeded.

The question of sustainability must be the heart of the question of whether cities can be in grace. Cities like La Paz and Kathmandu are threatened by the melting of the glaciers which provide their water. The Colombian Andes will have no glaciers left in ten years, compromising the water supplies of hundreds of towns and cities. Mexico City has already run out of water: taps ran dry during every month of 2009. 'A decaying infrastructure cannot reliably supply its ever-growing populace, and, though water is already harvested from hundreds of miles away, continuing drought in the region is exhausting the supply.'[69]

Some allege that cities are at the heart of the ecological crisis in that they use between two-thirds and three-quarters of fossil fuels world-wide. Mayur describes cities as 'overgrown monstrosities with gluttonous appetites for

---

[66] Schumacher, *Small is Beautiful*, p. 55.
[67] Quoted in H. Girardet, *The Gaia Atlas of Cities*, rev. edn (London: Gaia, 1996), p. 71.
[68] Alexander *et al.*, *New Theory*, pp. 66–7.   [69] Oxfam, *Suffering the Science*, pp. 42, 45.

material goods and fast declining carrying capacities ... Only catastrophe awaits such a system of disharmony.'[70] Herbert Girardet argues that in order for the waste gases they produce to be absorbed through photosynthesis cities need to nurture forests as 'symbiotic partners' to ensure climatic stability. Achieving this, as he says, means making commitments on a global scale.[71] Murray Bookchin, on the other hand, believes that huge cities cannot be adapted to alternative energy. 'To use solar, wind and tidal power effectively, the giant city must be dispersed. A new type of community, carefully tailored to the nature and resources of a region, must replace the sprawling urban belts of today.'[72]

The question of sustainability applies especially to the mega-city. Mumford said that those who believe that there are no alternatives to the present proliferation of metropolitan tissue perhaps overlook too easily the historic outcome of such a concentration of urban power: they forget that this has repeatedly marked the last stage in the classic style of civilisation, before its complete disruption and downfall.[73]

The other side of the coin, however, is the argument that cities provide the most environmentally sustainable way of housing people and providing factories, offices, shops, leisure facilities and many of the other things that society wants.[74] Some argue that it is not cities per se that are the problem but high-income lifestyles. Within United States cities people can have a relatively small carbon footprint, and New Yorkers emit just 30 per cent as much greenhouse gas as the national average.[75] Some even believe that the ecological crisis can be solved only by most people living in cities.[76] Travel in cities is less energy-consuming than in small towns and rural areas, because journey lengths are shorter, so people can walk and cycle more. Inner-city combined heat and power stations are becoming more common, producing hot water and generating electricity. Picking up on the theme of the city as a set of related villages, many cities link their neighbourhoods with light transit systems, aiming for mixed land use, with commercial and residential properties in together; high density, with everything within walking or cycling distance; extensive landscaping, including

[70] G. Haughton and C. Hunter, *Sustainable Cities* (London: Regional Studies Association, 1994), p. 15.
[71] Girardet, *Gaia Atlas*, p. 166.
[72] M. Bookchin, *Post-Scarcity Anarchism* (Montreal and Buffalo: Black Rose Books, 1986), p. 97.
[73] Mumford, *City*, p. 598.
[74] Here T. Burton and L. Matson, 'Urban Footprints: Making Best Use of Urban Land and Resources – A Rural Prespective', in Jenks, Burton and Williams (eds.), *Compact City*, pp. 298–301.
[75] D. Satterthwaite and D. Dodman, 'The Role of Cities in Climate Change', in Starke (ed.), *State of the World 2009*, p. 76.
[76] H. Sherlock, 'Repairing our Much Abused Cities', in Jenks, Burton and Williams (eds.), *Compact City*, p. 295.

rooftop gardens; good provision for children and for the community in the form of libraries, child care, centres for the elderly and perhaps small urban farms; and as high a degree of self-sufficiency for the community as possible.[77] Kemmis suggests that cities need healing, and the ten-step programme adopted by Copenhagen, which prioritises pedestrians, populates the core, promotes cycling and encourages student living, is a way of understanding that in practice. It seeks to convert key main streets into pedestrian thoroughfares; reduce traffic and turn parking lots into public squares; keep densities high but honour the human scale; populate the core; encourage student living; adapt the cityscape to changing seasons; promote cycling as a major mode of transportation; and make free bicycles available.[78] Jaime Lerner, former Mayor of Curitiba in Brazil, speaks of 'urban acupuncture', by which he means the revitalisation of a city without major redevelopment schemes. He seeks to reduce car use by establishing bus rapid transport schemes, encouraging multi-use buildings, and getting back to mixed use where residents live closer to their work-places. All these may be considered ways of creating a city in grace. Such ideas are close to the idea of the compact city, which is advocated as the most plausible way of organising human populations creatively while saving rural land. Sceptics suggest, however, that the compact city meets neither energy efficiency nor economic demands, and that it lacks the popular or political support to make it workable.[79] The need to avoid town cramming and to leave space for urban farms works against them, and 'the miracle of crowded living' is not always so obvious. Among humans, as among animals, crowded conditions often lead to violence. The compact city, then, may not be the new Jerusalem, and the case for it 'remains largely unresolved'.[80]

Landry points out that the fate of cities is bound up with property values. As happened in London's Docklands, and as has happened countless times around the globe, the interest of the global marketplace both prices out less affluent locals and, at the same time, increases the local tax bill. To avoid this the market has to be tamed.[81] No city in grace is possible unless this happens. Amsterdam has survived as a human-scale city because the chain stores cannot impose their templates on to it. 'In Amsterdam the

[77] P. Newman, 'Urban Design, Transportation and Greenhouse', in R. Samuels and D. Prasad (eds.), *Global Warming and the Built Environment* (London: Spon, 1996), p. 82. Munich, Freiburg, Stockholm, Vancouver and Washington DC have such transit systems.

[78] Landry, *Art of City-Making*, p. 384.

[79] L. Thomas and W. Cousins, 'The Compact City: A Successful, Desirable and Achievable Urban Form?', in Jenks, Burton and Williams (eds.), *Compact City*, pp. 53ff.

[80] Editorial comment in Jenks, Burton and Williams, *Compact City*, p. 215.

[81] Landry, *Art of City-Making*, p. 123.

intricate physical patterning and structure dominated by canals cannot be broken up. In addition it is extremely difficult for corporations to buy up large areas. The resulting fragmented ownership means that landlords are not always pumping up rents to their highest levels.' As a consequence Amsterdam is still not a 'clone town'. Its charm includes the presence of a large number of unique shops as well as the fact that it is not dominated by motor traffic.[82]

Cities of course have polities which are sometimes capable of challenging both state and federal power. The 'machine politics' in American cities was 'a system of organized bribery' in which, despite the trappings of representative democracy, power flowed from the top down.[83] Despite the fact that 'patronage is not what it used to be', many cities have powerful mayors who control vast budgets and can decisively shape their city's fortunes for good or ill. The larger the city, however, the more distant representative democracy is. In the United States community organising addressed this democratic deficit, focussing on pragmatic issues – schools, roads, health clinics – and aiming at empowerment.[84] To some extent the Transition Town movement has taken up the baton, though in a less confrontational way. The agenda of the community movement is a recognition of the limitations and dangers of representative democracy at the local level. In the United States cities have ceded power to suburbs, as the percentage of the population in inner-city areas has shrunk to 14 per cent, a fact recognised in presidential elections, which now target 'hometown America'.[85]

THE SUBURB

Could there be a suburb in grace? From the moment the gracious elite suburbs of the nineteenth century were replaced by the mass suburbs of the twentieth this has been doubted both on grounds of community and of form. For Sharp in 1940 suburbs were 'socially sterile, aesthetically empty and economically wasteful', and this judgement has been endlessly repeated.[86]

Suburbs were dormitories in their inception, and thus had no economy of their own, but internet technology now raises the possibility that suburbs themselves can be creative economic centres, and arguably this is true of

---

[82] Ibid., p. 122.   [83] Judd and Swanstrom, *City Politics*, p. 55.
[84] The Transition Town movement could be said to represent a 'nonideological pragmatism' of the type favoured by Saul Alinsky. Judd and Swanstrom, *City Politics*, p. 412.
[85] Ibid., p. 247.   [86] Sharp, *Town Planning*, p. 54.

Silicone Valley. If Milton Keynes is an industrial park within a suburb, or vice versa, then perhaps it is true of that as well. Some believe the city is obsolete. People now frequently commute from suburb to suburb rather than from suburb to centre, and we have a 'polynucleated metropolis'.[87] The balance of power, it is argued, has shifted from centre to suburb. 'Today most urban residents rarely visit the historic city . . . except to play tourist . . . the edge cities with their office towers, hotels and restaurants, the mega malls located at freeway interchanges . . . these supply the backdrop for most people's lives'. The periphery is no longer subordinate, and so strictly speaking there is no 'sub' urb.[88]

Socially the suburb is said to fall between two stalls. The suburb 'has neither the crowded interest of the town, nor the quiet charm of the country, it gives us the advantages neither of solitude nor of society'.[89] Americans, says Kunstler, dream of owning a house on a sacred plot.

But the place where the dream house stood – a subdivision of many other identical dream houses – was neither the country nor the city. It was no place . . . Air, light, and a modicum of greenery came with the package. The main problem with it was that it dispensed with all the traditional connections and continuities of community life, and replaced them with little more than cars and television.[90]

Low density can make community more difficult while the favourite sub-urban device of the cul de sac represents overly optimistic assumptions about people's readiness to get along. There are many examples of informal suburban policing of taste quite as strong as anything to be found in a village.[91] Necessarily dependent on transport to the centre, suburbs are often socially fragmented.[92] Mumford felt that suburbia was based on a flight from reality.

In the suburbs one might live and die without marring the image of an innocent world . . . Here domesticity could flourish, forgetful of the exploitation on which so much of it is based. Here individuality could prosper, oblivious of the pervasive regimentation beyond. This was not merely a child-centred environment: it was based on a childish view of the world, in which reality was sacrificed to the pleasure principle.[93]

[87] Judd and Swanstrom, *City Politics*, p. 167.   [88] Ibid., p. 316.
[89] A. Edwards, *The Design of Suburbia* (London: Pembridge, 1981), p. 223.
[90] Kunstler, *Geography*, p. 105.
[91] P. Langdon, *A Better Place to Live* (Amherst: University of Massachusetts Press, 1994), p. 43.
[92] M. Smith, J. Whiteleg and N. Williams, *Greening the Built Environment* (London: Earthscan, 1998), p. 166.
[93] Mumford, *City*, p. 563.

The suburbs lost the dialectical tensions and struggles which made city life significant.[94] The view of the suburb which emerges in contemporary pop music is little different from that of the older generation of critics:

There's no sense of excess here; no spill-over of cousins, aunts and uncles; no massing on street corners. These are single class communities: people don't know each other but they know what they're like. Neighbours nod across the street, compare cars, keep their salaries to themselves. Suburbia is a place where people live but don't work; rest but don't play (the real jobs, the real shops, the real pleasures, are elsewhere). Geographically, suburbia is, in effect, an empty sign, a series of dots on the map from which people travel – to the office, to the fleshpots, to the city. Suburban living is characterized by what it lacks – culture, variety, surprise – not by what it offers – safety, privacy, convenience.[95]

This is the view, Frith comments, of those who grow up in the suburb and rebel against what they find stifling in it. But the detractors of the suburb often forget that people in their millions opted for them to get away from the city. They wanted a better quality of life for their families. Suburbs are usually regarded as collections of nuclear families but Herbert Gans found a dense network of community groups and organisations, embracing a very high percentage of their occupants. He also found community ethics in good shape:

By any yardstick one chooses, Levittowners treat their fellow residents more ethically and more democratically than did their parents and grandparents. They also live a 'fuller' and 'richer' life. Their culture may be less subtle and sophisticated than that of the intellectual, their family life less healthy than that advocated by psychiatrists, and their politics less thoughtful and democratic than the political philosophers' – yet all of these are superior to what prevailed among the working and lower middle classes of past generations.[96]

All the same suburban culture is said to be centred on home entertainment. It has depended on radio, television and the telephone 'to compensate for loneliness and distance, as well as to make mobilization possible'.[97] Suburbs, of course, have been ecologically a liability as they require commuting, and over the past sixty years this has been increasingly car-based. This is even more the case if, as Silverstone alleges, suburban culture is a consuming culture, 'the crucible of a shopping economy'.[98]

[94] Ibid., p. 563.
[95] S. Frith, 'The Suburban Sensibility in British Rock and Pop', in Silverstone (ed.), *Visions of Suburbia*, p. 275.
[96] H. J. Gans, *The Levittowners* (London: Allen Lane, 1967), p. 419.
[97] Silverstone, 'Introduction', in Silverstone (ed.), *Visions of Suburbia*, p. 10.   [98] Ibid., p. 8.

Many authors agree that suburbs bred a flight from civic or political engagement. 'The suburban dream equalled selfishness, a rejection of obligation and commitment to the city where the suburbanite earned his living. A suburban house bred detachment from civic responsibility. It imperilled community spirit by highlighting class distinctions residentially.'[99] On the other hand, voter turnout rates are higher in the suburbs than elsewhere.[100] Unlike towns and villages, suburbs have no polity as such, though the associations they support will very often have political ends. John Hartley argues that the suburb represents the 'feminisation' of politics, with the media visualising and teaching public issues in the midst of private consumption. For him, the virtues inculcated by 'telebrities' are 'the future of democracy, for good or ill'.[101] Overall the extent to which suburbs instantiate the common good is therefore unclear: there is evidence for Gans' enthusiasm, but the sense of a largely atomised population still persists in critique, not simply from social scientists, but from people who live there themselves.

When it comes to form suburbs are often condemned as dull, lacking imagination or visual delight.[102] Mumford described them as 'a multitude of uniform, unidentifiable houses, lined up inflexibly, at uniform distances, on uniform roads, in a treeless communal waste, inhabited by people of the same class, the same income, the same age group ... Thus the ultimate effect of the suburban escape in our time is, ironically, a low grade uniform environment from which escape is impossible.'[103] However, suburbia has diversified as people have customised their houses and gardens. For Roger Silverstone suburbia is creative. 'The standardization so bemoaned by modernist critics is itself, plausibly, quite superficial. Levittown has now become a passable model of postmodern individuality ... Spaces, both inside and out, are redesigned, reformed into expressions of personal taste and identity.'[104] What they lack, as opposed to all other forms of settlement, are pubs, cafés and neighbourhood stores, the very 'micro publics' which allow community to form.

SETTLEMENTS IN GRACE

In Chapter 1 I spoke of the relation of Cathedral and Campo in Siena as representing an ellipse rather than a circle. An alternative to that 'grace

---

[99] P. J. Waller, *Town, City and Nation: England 1850–1914* (Oxford University Press, 1983).
[100] Judd and Swanstrom, *City Politics*, p. 249.
[101] J. Hartley, 'The Sexualization of Suburbia', in Silverstone (ed.), *Visions of Suburbia*, p. 181.
[102] Hall, *Cities of Tomorrow*, p. 296.   [103] Mumford, *City*, p. 553.
[104] Silverstone, 'Introduction', in Silverstone (ed.), *Visions of Suburbia*, p. 6.

perfecting nature' view is Karl Barth's account of concentric circles of community. 'The civil community shares both a common origin and a common centre with the Christian community . . . It is outside the Church but not outside the range of Christ's dominion.'[105] The church witnesses to this dominion and works to create correspondences with it, including in the built environment. The state, Barth argued, belonged to the order of redemption and should be understood as an institution of the wisdom and patience of God. 'In the sphere of nature there is intended to be an order of the grace of God.'[106] For Barth this was the state, but I am arguing that it includes the built environment as a whole. We have seen that 'grace' refers first and foremost to the quality of divine action, and as such the measure of human action. Grace denotes beauty, justice and also proportion, or scale. Because it characterises the divine action it has the sense of redemptive purpose. All this gives us a yardstick to understand settlements in grace.

Think of Birmingham, England. In the 1960s Joseph Chamberlain's bustling city of a thousand trades, with its grand civic buildings, was truly sacked by road builders with the determination and the imagination of Robert Moses. The Victorian railway station was put under ground and instantly became the most hostile and least-loved railway terminus in Britain. Twenty years later the city planners sought to redeem this hostile chaos, to restore the city to the people and take it back from the car. They refashioned the city, creating hugely important cultural icons like the new hall for the City of Birmingham Symphony Orchestra, reinventing Birmingham's crumbling dank canals and turning them into restaurant quarters and luxury flats. This brought about a certain regeneration and a better feel to the city. All the same, a three-day workshop held in 2001 sought to face up to the fact that the economic development of the 1980s had only benefited the middle class and had not provided a culturally inclusive representation of the city. It now raised the issue of justice and worked hard on anti-racist and anti-gang programmes and on racial inclusion.[107] In Leonie Sandercock's view these initiatives have been a qualified success, and they certainly show willing. Birmingham, then, has tried to meet the demands of beauty and justice. But what about a transcendent narrative, a story to live by? Without this no settlement can be educative. How could any place 'make human beings' in Mumford's words, without knowing what it was about? Birmingham's story had been that of the early industrial revolution, a world of endless trades and crafts. What is to replace that?

[105] Barth, 'The Christian Community and the Civil Community', in *Against the Stream*, p. 21.
[106] K. Barth, 'The Christian Community in the Midst of Political Change', in *Against the Stream*, p. 94.
[107] Sandercock, *Cosmopolis II*, pp. 18, 175, 176.

Sandercock suggests that Birmingham should celebrate its postcolonial history, the fact that it is home to huge settlements of West Indians, Asians and Chinese and a vibrant centre for their economies. Perhaps a successful multiculturalism might provide a story to live by, a lively and engaged working-out of the common good, and this is indeed what the city council seems to aim for. Time is required to see how the creativity of this culture will manifest itself and once again provide identity, pride and purpose,

Grace also implies proportion, the question of scale. To be a city in grace, Kemmis notes, is to have purposes for the common good. But are such purposes possible either for the suburb or the mega city? Schumacher, we saw, thought half a million was the limit of what was possible but Birmingham, with just over a million, shows that larger cities can also have a coherent purpose. In Birmingham much turned on creative engagement in Handsworth, a racially highly mixed area. This raises the question of urban villages. Emerging from the importance of scale is the argument that villages are the foundation stone of the urban order and not destined to be swept away by mega city development. They are this because it is impossible, as some postmodern theorists suppose, to sideline the question of community. Settlements are educative because they bring people together, to learn from their differences and to fashion a future together. Much postmodern thinking is simply individualism writ large. In this respect Frederic Jameson's celebrated description of postmodernism as 'the cultural logic of late capitalism' is well deserved. The priority of purpose and the inescapability of community for any account of the human good consonant with a Christian understanding means that leaving things to the market is not an option. The 'invisible hand' is the negation of such purposes and always prioritises the strong over the weak.

The question of justice is also the question of sustainability because justice is intergenerational. As we have seen there is no simple answer to this question in terms of settlements. Villages in the West are dependent on the car. Compact cities may not be as benign as they claim. Small towns, especially where they have rail links, are an attractive option but they cannot do what the city does. Finding truly sustainable ways of living together, while sustaining human creativity, is a core part of what it means to be a city in grace. New Urbanism represents an attempt to respond to these questions. In Poundbury, in Dorset, Leon Krier has attempted to recapture some of the charm of the older English settlement, with varied roof lines, varied house sizes, narrow lanes and central squares. The attempt is commendable, and perhaps it is better than what the volume builders have produced, but the stark juxtaposition of Scottish baronial,

French chateau and Georgian and Victorian styles, not to mention a market hall which echoes Knossos, recalls Disneyland rather than any grounded settlement.

A proposed settlement which seeks to bring together the demands of justice, beauty and sustainability is Sherford, just north of Plymouth, England. Four thousand new homes were required in an area of outstanding natural beauty. An area of 415 hectares was allotted, and the planners have set aside half of this to be a community park where there will be a wind farm providing between 53 and 90 per cent of the energy for the community, but also organic horticulture to provide vegetables for it. In addition there will be 4 hectares of allotments as well as facilities for sport and other forms of leisure. In the settled part there will be a town centre and three neighbourhood centres designed to ensure that 80 per cent of all the inhabitants are within a five-minute walk of shops and services. There will be a secondary school for 825 pupils, primary schools for 420 pupils each, a library, a youth centre, a health and social care centre, a town hall and a community theatre and/or cinema. There will be one 'worship centre' (sounds ominous) and a cemetery. The development will be compact and is designed to minimise car use as far as possible. A light transit system going to the heart of Plymouth every few minutes will make it uneconomic to drive. Pedestrian and cycle use will be prioritised. The area will be mixed-use: 900,000 square feet of retail, commercial and employment uses are planned, providing jobs for as many as one in three of the households living there. The mistake of Milton Keynes, which is a doughnut, with a retail and civic centre surrounded by suburbs, is thus avoided. A mixture of small and large houses, apartments, shops and offices is envisaged, increasing in density nearer the centre, with varied roofscapes, some buildings of five storeys, and broad streets to make sense of this. Overall densities of thirty-five to forty dwellings to the hectare are planned, increasing to between fifty and sixty to the hectare in the centre. Civic and community buildings will be placed on squares and at key junctions, which will both make them accessible and enable them to function as landmarks. The plan speaks of 'a basic structure of interconnected public streets, squares, greens, open spaces and parks that provide a continuous and varied public realm, overlooked by buildings that provide natural surveillance and contact from those living and working inside, and which are linked by green ways to the community park'. A couple of the more attractive existing agricultural buildings will become pubs. A roadstone quarry will become a large adventure playground (the children will have to share the quarry with rare bats!). Of course planners' drawings are as unreliable as estate agents' photos, but it looks as if the tweeness of Poundbury, and the besetting sin of so much new urbanism, will be avoided while charm will not be sacrificed either.

From the start there has been a high degree of consultation, though whether one can really talk of local ownership of the plan is another matter. Extensive audits of biodiversity have been undertaken and this will be enhanced as far as possible. Buildings will meet exacting standards for ecological design, aiming far higher than existing building regulations require. Given the huge gap between house prices and average earnings in the region, 15 per cent of homes will be social-rented and 35 per cent available on various forms of equity. In terms of design and building specifications these will be indistinguishable from homes bought on the open market. They will be grouped in small clusters throughout the community.[108] This looks like a recipe for maintaining a settled community rather than one where people have to move out as families grow and shrink.

The thought and imagination which have gone into this plan are impressive. Of course, realisation may be quite another matter. Too many plans look wonderful on paper and produce bleak and crime-ridden places in reality. The basic principles that Christopher Alexander laid down for organic growth and urban design have not been followed: the planners are still in charge and architects, rather than master builders, are still going to be given a free hand. Moreover, housing need is often a bad reason for a settlement. What will be its purpose? By what story will it live? And what finally will be its spiritual centre? In addition to all the questions about beauty and justice it is these questions which will determine whether or not this, or any other settlement, could be said to be characterised by grace.

In the next chapter I turn to a key question for any settlement, and a key question for a world of eight billion or more: how is it going to be fed?

---

[108]   The majority of social-rented houses will be for families: as a rough guide the planners are reckoning on 10 per cent having one bedroom, 35 per cent having two bedrooms, 30 per cent having three bedrooms and 15 per cent having four bedrooms, and 10 per cent being sheltered accommodation.

CHAPTER 8

Feeding the city

TOWN AND COUNTRY

'The all pervading disease of the modern world is the total imbalance between the city and countryside', wrote the long-time Chief Economist of the United Kingdom Coal Board, Fritz Schumacher. This was, he said,

an imbalance in terms of wealth, power, culture, attraction, and hope. The former has become over-extended and the latter has atrophied. The city has become the universal magnet, while rural life has lost its savour. Yet it remains an unalterable truth that, just as a sound mind depends on a sound body, so the health of the cities depends on the health of the rural areas. The cities, with all their wealth, are merely secondary producers, while primary production, the precondition of all economic life, takes place in the countryside. The prevailing lack of balance, based on the age-old exploitation of the countryman and raw material producer, today threatens all countries throughout the world ... To restore a proper balance between city and rural life is perhaps the greatest task in front of modern man.[1]

If anything the gap is wider now than when Schumacher wrote, but no city exists without its hinterland; cities have to be fed. David Harvey accuses bioregionalists of being 'hopelessly infected with nostalgia' but the truth is that, as Wendell Berry puts it, 'No matter how urban our life is, our bodies live by farming.'[2] Socrates' idea in the *Phaedrus* that human beings can learn nothing from the stars, stones and trees was, said Mumford, 'a cockney illusion'.

A forgetfulness of the city's visible dependence upon the country, not only for food, for a thousand other manifestations of organic life, equally nourishing to the mind; and not less, we know now, of man's further dependence upon a wide network of ecological relations that connect his life with creatures as obscure and seemingly remote as bacteria, the viruses and moulds; and ultimately with sources of energy as remote as the radiations from distant stars. Babylonian superstition

[1] Schumacher, *Small is Beautiful*, p. 170.
[2] W. Berry, 'The Body and the Earth', in *The Unsettling of America*, p. 97.

183

was closer to the truth in its erroneous associations of the planets' movements and human events than was Greek rationalism in its progressive dissociation of man and nature, polis and cosmos.[3]

All over the Third World cities are growing by the day, harvesting the world agrarian crisis.[4] This crisis follows from the economic policies of neo-liberalism, and in particular the imposition of Structural Adjustment Programmes (SAPs). Sustainable urbanism, Davis recognises, presupposes the preservation of surrounding wetlands and agriculture. As it happens, all over the Third World cities are polluting, urbanising and destroying their environmental support system, thus imperilling food security and their very survival.[5] For this reason alone it is impossible to talk about the built environment without talking about agriculture.

All over the world the growth of urbanisation is mirrored by the decline of farming. Since the Neolithic revolution most humans have been engaged in growing food, and this was true beyond the middle of the twentieth century. Only in the past sixty years has the balance tipped towards urbanisation and industrialisation. In that period the number of farms in England dropped from 500,000 to 158,000. The rate of decline has not noticeably eased: over 17,000 farmers and farm workers – 5 per cent of the workforce – left the land in the twelve months to June 2003, and more than 80,000 jobs have been lost in the past decade.[6] All sectors of farming and cultivation have been affected. There has also been a huge decline in the numbers of those who grow their own food. During the early twentieth century in Britain there were just under 4 million acres of allotments producing about half the food, fruit and vegetables consumed domestically. There are now under 40,000 acres, though rising food prices have led to a modest increase in interest.[7]

The same story applies to Europe as a whole, where, in 1999, 200,000 farmers gave up agriculture. France lost half its farmers between 1982 and 1999. In Germany a quarter have gone in the past ten years. The United

[3] Mumford, *City*, p. 199.
[4] Davis, *Planet*, p. 16. Cf. the manifesto of The Land is Ours: 'Agriculture begets human culture; and cultural diversity, like biological diversity, flowers in obedience to the conditions that the earth imposes. The first and inevitable effect of the global market is to uproot and destroy land-based human cultures. The final and inevitable achievement of a rootless global market will be to destroy itself.' *The Land*, 8 (Winter 2009–10), 2.
[5] Davis, *Planet*, p. 134. In India more than 50,000 hectares and in Egypt 30,000 hectares of croplands are lost every year to urbanisation. In Vietnam disgruntled peasants use industrial effluents to cultivate food in revenge for constant uprooting. Similarly in Colombo unsuitable waste is used to grow vegetables as fast as possible. Ibid., pp. 135–6.
[6] F. Lawrence, *Not on the Label* (Harmondsworth: Penguin, 2004), p. 137.
[7] J. Pretty, *Agri-Culture: Reconnecting People, Land and Nature* (London: Earthscan, 2002), p. 185.

States has lost 4 million farmers since the 1930s.[8] In Africa and Asia the urbanisation trend is predicted to continue so that, according to the Food and Agriculture Organisation, by 2030 the split will be 31 per cent rural and 69 per cent urban. Jerry Buckland puts three questions to this prediction. First, can the 1.3 billion people predicted to pour into the cities all find low-wage jobs as they have done in south-east Asia? If they did, what would be the consequences for resources and pollution? Second, what happens to the countries currently providing the industries which will be displaced by China, south Asia and sub-Saharan Africa? What will happen to their workers? Third, what will be the consequences for food security?[9] Could the world be fed without peasant agriculture? Currently 2.5 billion people still work in agriculture, so it is still the world's largest single source of work, and traditional and 'unimproved' agriculture still supports about a third of the world's population. What urban boosterism seems not to notice is that farming has the possibility to provide work for people, which the city cannot endlessly do.

In the context of this book we need to ask how the relation of city and countryside is to be understood within the framework of grace and the common good. We have seen that grace involves beauty, justice (of which sustainability is a part) and scale. In particular Wendell Berry speaks of sustainable farming as involving 'kindly use': 'kindness' is one of the most familiar translations of *hesed*. We shall have to ask what practices oppose this, and what their consequences might be. In terms of the fundamental theological scheme it might seem that God the Creator was the most obvious appropriation, one that is favoured by our harvest hymns. But the question of justice is urgently raised by farming, as we shall see, and the need for reconciliation by profound antagonisms between town and country. Equally, the question of how we should best farm raises the question of empowerment, which I have called the core concept of the appropriation of God the Redeemer, since the Spirit, in both the Hebrew Bible and the New Testament, is the one who empowers people and calls all to be 'prophets' or leaders. I begin in an unlikely place, with the relation of farming to the beauty of our world.

It might seem that farming was a purely utilitarian affair – simply a question of producing enough food to feed the world's population – but in fact beauty is not irrelevant to the relation of the city and the countryside.

[8] Lawrence, *Not on the Label*, p. 140.
[9] J. Buckland, *Ploughing up the Farm: Neoliberalism, Modern Technology and the State of the World's Farmers* (London: Zed, 2004), pp. 21–2.

Long before set-aside and the idea that farmers were primarily park keepers, rather than food producers, the Scott Report noted that the beauties of Britain (and this will apply to any agricultural landscape) are largely man-made. 'Left to themselves the fields would quickly revert to thickets of scrub and brambles would be interrupted by swamps and bogs choked with reeds and rushes. The British countryside today owes its characteristic features to the fact that it has been used – in other words it has been farmed.' With a sidelong glance at Patrick Abercrombie, the founder of the Council for the Preservation of Rural England, the report notes that

the countryside cannot be 'preserved' . . . it must be farmed if it is to retain those features which give it distinctive charm and character. For this reason neither the farmer nor the forester can be regarded as simply members of an industry or on the same footing with those in other great industries. In addition to their function of producing food and timber from the land, farmers and foresters are unconsciously the nation's landscape gardeners, a privilege which they share with the landowners.[10]

It could be argued that the small scale of the British countryside makes it more beautiful than other rural landscapes, such as those of China, Poland or Russia. It could also be argued that love of 'nature' is a product of Romanticism and should not be generalised as a permanent human trait. On the other hand a readiness for aesthetic experience is certainly part of what it means to be human, and the natural world is so full of stimuli, and the evidences of delight in flora and fauna and in birdsong so widespread, that the attempt to restrict it to modern consciousness seems artificial. The historian G. M. Trevelyan agreed that 'Without vision the people perish . . .'

and without natural beauty the English people will perish in the spiritual sense. In old days the English lived in the midst of Nature, subject to its influence at every hour. Thus inspired, our ancestors produced their great creations in religion, in song, and in the arts and crafts – common products of a whole people spiritually alive. Today most of us are banished to the cities, not without deleterious effects on imagination, inspiration and creative power.[11]

Similar expressions of love for nature are attested in the rest of Europe, in Russia and in Asia.[12] A world without natural beauty would indeed be

---

[10] Scott Report, p. 47.   [11] Quoted in ibid., p. v.

[12] P. J. Asquith and A. Kalland, *Japanese Images of Nature: Cultural Perspectives* (London: Routledge, 1996); S. V. Venkateswaran, *Indian Culture through the Ages* (London: Longmans, 1943), p. 109; G. Hamburg, 'Russian Political Thought 1700–1917', in D. Lieven (ed.), *The Cambridge History of Russia 1689–1917* (Cambridge University Press, 2006), p. 135.

an ungracious world. However, the beauty of the countryside is bound up with human intervention. It is 'agri-culturally' inscribed and is one of the profoundest things the farmer gives to the city, a vital part of the common good.

While the question of beauty is crucial to the human spirit the relation between grace and the town–country question is primarily bound up with questions of justice, scale and sustainability, but I begin with some reflections on grace and food.

GRACE AND FOOD

Probably the most familiar meaning of the word 'grace' is a short prayer of thanksgiving before meals. More honoured in the breach than in the observance, this is a vestige of the thankfulness for food which characterises most peasant cultures, a recognition that the means of life can never be taken for granted. Because the Hebrew Bible emerges from such a culture it is deeply imbued with the understanding that food is gift, that therefore it cannot be monopolised, and that it is given to be shared. In God's blessing of man and woman God says: 'See, I have *given* you every plant yielding seed that is upon the face of all the earth, and every tree with seed in its fruit; you shall have them for food.' The animals likewise are given 'every green plant for food' (Gen. 1.29–30). After the flood this is modified:

The fear and dread of you shall rest on every animal of the earth, and on every bird of the air, on everything that creeps on the ground, and on all the fish of the sea; into your hand they are delivered. Every moving thing that lives shall be food for you; and just as I gave you the green plants, I give you everything. Only, you shall not eat flesh with its life, that is, its blood. (Gen. 9.2–4)

The story makes clear that killing is never normal, never to be taken for granted. Flesh eating is regarded as a permission, not a right, and kosher killing is a sign or sacrament of this. Isaiah famously dreamed of an end to all violence, and a return to the original paradisal state, where no creature preys on another (Is. 11.6–9).

The sense of food as gift was strongly linked with a knowledge of the fragility of the food supply. The key story of the Hebrew Bible, the exodus, turns on famine and a threat to survival. The stories of the wilderness wanderings in the book of Numbers constantly return to hunger and thirst, contrasting it with the well-fed slavery of Egypt. Israel lyrically celebrated its well-watered Jordan valley as God's primary gift:

The Lord your God is bringing you into a good land, a land with flowing streams, with springs and underground waters welling up in valleys and hills, a land of wheat and barley, of vines and fig trees and pomegranates, a land of olive trees and honey, a land where you may eat bread without scarcity, where you will lack nothing . . . You shall eat your fill and bless the Lord your God for the good land that he has given you. (Dt. 8.6–10)

In the New Testament Paul appeals to the fertility of creation as one of the evidences for God's existence. He tells the crowd in Lystra: 'God has not left himself without a witness in doing good – giving you rains from heaven and fruitful seasons, and filling you with food and your heart with joy' (Acts 14.17).

The gift of plenty is, however, contingent on practices of justice: '*If* you follow my statutes and keep my commandments' all this will follow (Lev. 26.3). Jesus' depiction of God as the giver, 'pressed down, overflowing', draws on the description of Leviticus, where the harvesters can barely keep pace with the abundance. It is a key part of the realisation of shalom, that situation of peace and justice which is God's will for Israel (Lev. 26.6). For Jesus, as for the authors of Leviticus, the demands of justice follow the gift, something the first community recognised according to Luke (Acts 4). To understand justice in relation to food and farming we need to draw on the idea of the ecological footprint. Given a population of 7 billion this is now 1.89 gha per person. As we saw in Chapter 2, a United States footprint is currently 9.5 gha, and a British one is 5.5 gha. 'Each year, as the population rises and as our demands increase, our individual share of the earth reduces in size and so we move further back in time. Eventually we will have a world that can support us all only with the simplest possible lifestyle.'[13] Interestingly, a World Wildlife Fund survey showed that the only country which combines a good Human Development Index (HDI, measuring well-being in terms of a nation's ability to provide conditions for its people to live long, healthy and creative lives) with a sustainable footprint is Cuba. 'This sends a clear message that capitalism and democracy are not necessarily a viable route towards achieving sustainability.'[14] 'Justice' will involve both relying less on food flown in or trucked from great distances and learning to eat differently. Meat and fish have a bigger footprint than vegetables; local food has a smaller footprint than imported food. If justice is an issue then this requires that we change our eating practices.

---

[13] R. and B. Vale, *Time to Eat the Dog? The Real Guide to Sustainable Living* (London: Thames and Hudson, 2009), p. 37.

[14] Ibid., p. 39. In 2001 the United States had an HDI of 0.94 and a footprint of 9.5 gha; the Netherlands an HDI of 0.94 and a footprint of 4.7 gha; Cuba an HDI of 0.81 and a footprint of 1.4 gha.

To know food as gift is not only to be aware of the immense amount of labour, of justice and injustice, which lies behind everything we eat. It is also about our self-understanding. The 'fast food nation' anatomised by Eric Schlosser, which applies to the United Kingdom as well as to the United States, represents a culture which knows nothing of food as gift.[15] Amazingly diverse cuisines represent millennia of experimentation which, through the alchemy of art, turn virtually anything which can provide nourishment and which is not positively toxic into delicious food. Food is not a mere commodity, writes Gilles Luneau:

Eating is an intimate, daily activity, a source of pleasure, a means of survival, and a critical aspect of the way in which we relate to the earth. Food has its rituals in every culture, creed, religion and philosophy. Wheat, maize and rice are more than just crops. They are the outcome of the fusion of sun, water and soil. In eating, humans inscribe themselves in the cycles of the universe, and this is far more profound and basic than just making money. Wheat was growing long before coins were cast.[16]

Fast food, on the other hand, subjects food to the routinised processes learned first in car factories, cuts costs so that food is produced dangerously and unhealthily, pays as low wages as possible and is not made to be eaten with reverence.

Contemporary Western attitudes to food are challenged by a Christian understanding focussed in the eucharist, which derives its name from the Greek verb 'to give thanks' (*eucharisteo*). The eucharist emerges not simply from the 'last supper', as Western theology has tended to argue, but from the whole table fellowship of Jesus, his meals with all and sundry, including social outcasts. Jesus used meals to include people like Zacchaeus once more within the wider society, to effect reconciliation. We learn from the Emmaus story that thanking God before meals, which is what is meant when it is said that Jesus 'blessed' bread and wine, was characteristic of him. The disciples after the resurrection do not recognise him until he does this absolutely characteristic action – this is the giveaway. Because it is so important to him he teaches his disciples to pray for *ton arton ton epiousion* (daily bread). This much debated phrase seems to refer back to the story of the manna, where God gives Israel its food for the coming day in a way that cannot be hoarded. When people attempt to hoard the food it is corrupted, loses its nourishment and becomes a source of death. Thus

[15] E. Schlosser, *Fast Food Nation* (Harmondsworth: Penguin, 2002).
[16] Introduction to Bové and Dufour, *The World is Not for Sale*, p. xii.

Jesus is teaching his disciples to remember the manna, to live from the gift, to share and not to hoard.

The eucharist also looks back to the great feedings, which should be read not as a miraculous multiplication of particles but as an acted parable of the miracle of sharing. In Mark's version the disciples note that it is late and it is time to call it a day. They suggest that the people be sent back to their villages so they can buy food. As Ched Myers puts it,

> Jesus' solution has nothing to do with participation in the dominant economic order. Instead he determines the available resources, organizes the consumers into groups, pronounces the blessing, and distributes what is at hand...the only 'miracle' here is the triumph of the economics of sharing within a community of consumption over against the economics of autonomous consumption in the anonymous marketplace.[17]

Most familiarly, the eucharist also looks back to the meal Jesus kept with his disciples before his death. This was either a Passover meal or a meal kept in a Passover context. In other words, it was a feast of freedom, which Jesus linked to his own life and death and to the continuance of his practice by his disciples. At every eucharist we remind ourselves of the fundamental part food plays in the economy of grace, celebrating the whole process of production, and as a feast of freedom we commit ourselves to challenge unjust ways of dealing with this basic resource.

'Grace' before meals, then, epitomises an understanding of the economy as a whole. It points us to a non-exploitative economy organised in the interests of the common good, an economy in which town and country live together symbiotically.

AGRICULTURE AND THE GLOBAL EMERGENCY

What I called in Chapter 1 'the global emergency' is intimately related to farming. Currently world population grows by between 75 and 80 million per year. To feed 80 million people you need to expand the grain harvest by 21 million tons per year. The architects Robert and Brenda Vale calculate that in order to feed a city of 10 million a circle of productive land about 400 km in diameter is needed, a city of 1 million needs 125 km, and a city of 100,000 a circle of land 40 km across.[18] There are two problems with this, namely that the amount of fertile land is finite (arable land constitutes

---

[17] C. Myers, *Binding the Strong Man* (Maryknoll: Orbis, 1988), p. 206.
[18] Vale and Vale, *Time to Eat*, p. 55.

about one-tenth of the total land area of the planet), and also that it is shrinking, in the face of desertification, overgrazing and urbanisation.[19]

Climate change is already affecting food production, and impacts, both negative and positive, are set to increase. Some areas will be able to grow different crops but the staples of rice and maize are likely to be badly affected. Rice yields drop by 10 per cent for every 1 per cent rise in night-time temperature.[20] Maize is extremely vulnerable to drought, and yields may fall all over the world: Mexico may lose 300,000 hectares of maize production by 2020.[21] With shrinking glaciers the Ganges may become seasonal, affecting 40 per cent of India's irrigated cropland and affecting the water supply of 400 million people.[22] Conversely much fertile land all over the world may be flooded by the sea: in England nearly half of the most productive land is in the Fens, the most threatened area. A United Nations report of August 2009 notes the urgent need for better irrigation to feed an expected 1.5 billion people. The Director General of the International Water Management Institute notes that 'If nothing is done, you are going to get an increase in social unrest, migration and a fertile ground for terrorism.'[23]

Pests and diseases may increase. Fish, which currently provides food for nearly half of the world's people, is threatened by the increasing acidification of the oceans. 'Little-understood changes in ocean currents, oxygen levels, and salinity, and the consequent changes in behaviour of marine animals throughout the food chain are also causing alarm.'[24] Increasing acidity means that marine species cannot build shells and skeletons from calcium carbonate. This threatens the plankton at the base of the marine food chain.[25] The Oxfam report *Suffering the Science* concludes that

Hunger will be one of the major impacts of climate change. It may be the defining human tragedy of this century. Millions of people in countries that already have food security problems will have to give up traditional crops and agricultural methods as they experience changes in the seasons that they and their ancestors have depended upon. The social upheavals that result – such as migration and

---

[19] L. Brown, 'Eradicating Hunger', in L. Brown, C. Flavin and H. French (eds.), *State of the World 2001* (London: Earthscan, 2001), pp. 43 ff.

[20] D. Dodman, J. Ayers and S. Huq, 'Building Resilience', in Starke (ed.), *State of the World 2009*, p. 157.

[21] S. Scherr and S. Sthapit, 'Farming and Land Use to Cool the Planet', in Starke (ed.), *State of the World 2009*, p. 31.

[22] Ibid., p. 32.   [23] Quoted in *The Guardian Weekly*, 21–6 August 2009.

[24] Oxfam, *Suffering the Science*, p. 21.

[25] T. Lovejoy, 'Climate Change's Pressures on Biodiversity', in Starke (ed.), *State of the World 2009*, p. 69.

conflict – may mean that this change in the functioning of our planet affects more people than any other.[26]

Thus, though it is true that food production has soared in the past sixty years, constant gains in production cannot be taken for granted. Particularly serious is the fact that the world's two most populous nations have lost the ability to feed themselves. In south Asia 94 per cent of land suitable for farming is already in production. The use of electric pumps by millions of farmers is causing groundwater levels to drop. Around one-third of the world's population already live in water-scarce areas, and this figure is set to rise with expanding populations.[27] Nature's indifferent justice, comments Wendell Berry, is that like other creatures we will ultimately starve down to the carrying capacity of our habitat.[28] Half of the world's population now live in cities, but the fate of all the world's people is bound up with farming. The ancient theme of town and country, and the disciples' question 'how shall all these people be fed?', come back with a new urgency.

FARMING AND THE GLOBAL ECONOMY

The global emergency is driven by the conjunction of spiralling numbers and a particular model of the economy, which includes agriculture as it includes everything else. People are pouring into the cities not because the village is such a dehumanising environment, as Harvey thinks, but because agricultural livelihoods have been destroyed by neo-liberal economic policies. The United Nations report *The Challenge of Slums* remarks that there is probably more confusion about trade and its effects on growth and inequality than about any other aspect of globalisation.[29] Following Structural Adjustment Programmes fledgling urban industries in developing countries have often been crushed and agriculture converted to export crops. 'SAPs devastated rural smallholders by eliminating subsidies and pushing them sink or swim into global commodity markets dominated by heavily subsidized First World agribusiness.'[30] In Andhra Pradesh, in 2004, 500 farmers committed suicide by drinking pesticide that was purchased with loans they could not repay.[31] All over the world small farmers are swamped by cheap imports. Indian farmers are driven under by soya

---

[26] Oxfam, *Suffering the Science*, p. 10.
[27] J. Vidal, 'Asia Lacks the Means to Feed Extra 1.5bn People', *The Guardian Weekly*, 21–6 August 2009.
[28] W. Berry, 'Getting Along with Nature', in *Home Economics*, p. 8.
[29] UN Habitat, *Challenge of Slums*, p. 40. [30] Davis, *Planet*, p. 15. [31] Ibid., p. 171.

imported from the United States; Mexican beef producers likewise go under to United States producers, whose inroads into Mexico's markets have tripled since the North American Free Trade Association was formed. A Kenyan study says that liberalised trade, including World Trade Organization agreements, benefits only the rich while the majority of the poor do not benefit but are instead made more vulnerable to food insecurity.[32] Farmers in both rich and poor countries are caught between rock-bottom prices for their products and rising costs for inputs.[33] Globally, the price index of commodities declined by 47 per cent between 1982 and 2001. In sugar alone exporters to the global market lost nearly two billion dollars owing to falling prices in the four years up to 2002. Less than 10 per cent of the retail value of coffee stays with the countries that grow it whereas ten years ago they kept 30 per cent of its value. Auction prices for tea in India have fallen by a third in the past six years, and the tea workers' union has had to negotiate a 12 per cent wage cut. Low rice prices have affected rural economies in Thailand, Vietnam and China. A World Bank study estimates that the divergence between the farm and retail prices costs commodity-exporting countries more than $100 billion a year and that anti-competitive behaviour by the dominant transnational corporations is the key cause. Developing countries are being forced to open their markets to imports in basic commodities in which they are self-sufficient, a situation leading to massive disruption to their small farmers and thus to their ability to feed themselves. Food dumping continues apace and food security is being sacrificed on the altar of free trade.[34] The situation is exactly as it is represented in the book of Proverbs: 'A poor man's field may produce abundant food, but injustice sweeps it away' (Prov. 13.23).

The logic of free trade rests on four major mystifications, remark Herman and Kuper. Agricultural markets are supposed to be self-regulating, but they are not. They have a spontaneous and chaotic character due to climate variations, and therefore public intervention is necessary to assure their regulation. Second, subsistence farmers are pitted against highly subsidised and mechanised farmers in the West. Third, prices for commodities are both unstable and substantially dumped, and they are sold below their production costs. And finally, free trade is not the engine of economic development it is supposed to be, since exporting countries keep only a

---

[32] J. Madeley, *Food for All* (London: Zed, 2002), p. 120.

[33] P. Herman and R. Kuper, *Food for Thought: Towards a Future for Farming* (London: Pluto, 2003), p. 91.

[34] Ibid., p. xvii.

small part of the revenues generated by exports. Profits go mainly to the corporations which 'add value'.[35]

As Berry puts it, when you have a free market in food, 'Every farmer in every nation is thrown into competition with every other farmer.' Competitive pressures will mean that conservation practices will be dropped and the exploitation of labour and the use of toxic chemicals will increase.[36] The free market, he concludes, cannot assign a value to the things that matter to agriculture – topsoil, ecosystem, the farm, the farm community. An exclusive focus on production leads to over-production. The free market is economic Darwinism, but to say that both predator and prey are beneficiaries of the free market idea 'is the result of a lazy (when not villainous) wish to found the human economy on natural law'. In Berry's view there are two human laws of economics. The first is that money must not lie about value. 'It must not, by inflation or usury, misrepresent the value of necessary work or necessary goods. These values must not, by any devices of the market or banks, be made subject to monetary manipulation.' The second is that 'There must be a decent balance between what people earn and what they pay, and this can be made possible only by control of production. When farmers have to sell on a depressed market and buy on an inflated one, that is death to farmers, death to farming, death to rural communities, death to the soil, and death to food.'[37]

What we call globalisation is a system where giant corporations acquire assets transnationally with a view to making profit. These assets include food and water. The issue of the economy is a fundamental question about who controls the means of production, and primarily food, and for what reason. Six corporations handle 85 per cent of world trade in grain. Brewster Kneen, a Canadian beef farmer and food campaigner, writes:

If five or six corporations have control over every seed of all major commercial crops planted anywhere on earth, this is totalitarian. Add to seeds control over the genetics of all major lines of commercial animals and it will be somewhat more totalitarian. Then engineer all the genetics – plant or animal – to be hybrids, sterile or both, and the achievement will be without question totalitarian. It will amount to the occupation of the land – the earth itself – by foreign troops and their local mercenaries.

At the other end of the chain there is a growing occupation of the land by a handful of global supermarket chains, and an occupation of the supermarkets themselves by transgenic foods and food products, unlabelled, so that the public cannot identify the invaders and thus avoid and reject them.[38]

---

[35] Ibid., pp. 13–19.   [36] Berry, 'A Big Bad Idea', in *Sex, Economy*, p. 47.
[37] Berry, 'Six Agricultural Fallacies', in *Home Economics*, p. 127.
[38] B. Kneen, *Farmageddon* (Gabriola: New Society, 1999), pp. 179–80.

The irony is that most trade is unnecessary. Herman Daly points out that more than half of all international trade involves the simultaneous import and export of essentially the same goods.[39] The inefficiency of this and the impact on climate change ought not to need pointing out.

Colin Tudge comments that 'If all the world's countries opted for systems of agriculture that were aimed at national self-reliance, with trade restricted mostly to non-essential delectables, and achieved this primarily via the mixed farm, world food production as a whole could be biologically robust and the general standard of nutrition and gastronomy could and should be very high indeed.'[40] It is hardly surprising that Berry argues that a sound agricultural economy cannot be based on any market that it does not control. The best thing for any country is to grow its own food. As much as possible of the food that is consumed locally ought to be locally produced on small farms, and then processed in small, non-polluting plants that are locally owned.[41]

It is rightly pointed out that Third World food production is adversely affected by subsidies paid to European and North American farmers. This is true but needs qualification, as many farmers in the developed world have also suffered through low commodity prices. The truth is that subsidies have gone to the biggest farmers. Under the previous terms of the Common Agricultural Policy 80 per cent of UK farm subsidies went to 20 per cent of farmers with the largest farms. The smallest 30,000 farmers received a third of all support, and poultry and pig farmers did not qualify at all. Even under the new single farm payment size is still disproportionately rewarded. In the United States only 120,000 farms, out of a total of 2 million, receive 60 per cent of all income. Subsidies have been very selective, therefore, and in any case, the cost of inputs has meant that by and large they have ended up in the pocket of agribusiness. Appealing to his understanding of the common good, Albino Barrera argues that there is a moral imperative to subsidise smaller farmers to cope with 'negative externalities'.[42]

Trade impacts on the built environment in another way in the power of the large supermarket chains in relation to local suppliers. In Britain the building of thousands of out-of-town supermarkets has led to the demise of 238,000 small shops. A thousand independent food shops close each year. Family greengrocery shops are now only 12 per cent of the United Kingdom market in fruit and vegetables. A Friends of the Earth report

[39] H. Daly, 'Free Trade: The Perils of Deregulation', in J. Mander and E. Goldsmith (eds.), *The Case against the Global Economy* (San Francisco: Sierra Club, 1996), p. 231.
[40] C. Tudge, *So shall we Reap* (Harmondsworth: Penguin, 2003), p. 89.
[41] Berry, 'Conservation and Local Economy', in *Sex, Economy*, p. 17.
[42] Barrera, *Economic Compulsion*, p. 204.

of June 2005 concludes that supermarkets' need to push prices down is forcing suppliers to use labour which is poorer, more desperate and likely to be more compliant. The report concludes that there is a direct connection between concentration of retail power and deterioration of working conditions. These developments, which increase car dependency, also destroy the viability and social fabric of towns. The dominant economic model, therefore, wreaks havoc in different ways in both rich and poor worlds, actively destroying any understanding of the common good.

FEEDING THE CITY

The agricultural improvements of the eighteenth century were the essential precondition for the industrial revolution and for rising populations, first in Europe and then elsewhere. Farming shared in that process in the increasing number of machines able to do agricultural jobs, although worldwide the process is extremely patchy.[43] The most important of all was the tractor: the Fordson went into mass production in 1919. An unforeseen consequence was larger farms. As machines got bigger, so did the farms they could manage, and equally the number of workers to run the farms shrank.

On the face of it, big farms are very efficient. In the United Kingdom 10 per cent of farms produce 80 per cent of the food. In Europe just 12 per cent of all farms produce 60 per cent of all agricultural output, and a mere 1 per cent rear 40 per cent of all animals.[44] Output has soared in the past seventy years. In the United Kingdom farms produce three times the amount of wheat and barley per hectare and more than twice as much potato and sugar beet as they did in the 1940s, and cows produce twice the milk per lactation. However, this efficiency is only part of the story. I shall argue that there are other respects in which large farms have to be regarded as inefficient, unsafe, inhumane and unsustainable. To feed the world's population using conventional methods would use 40 per cent of the world's total energy consumption.[45]

A first problem is that this kind of farming is on the whole monocultural. Farmers specialise in one thing, whether it be cereals, livestock or poultry. Sometimes the specialisation is even more narrow, so that one farmer will rear pullets and then sell them on to someone who keeps laying hens; or livestock is sold on to be fattened and killed and so forth.[46] Monocropping

[43] In Sudan, for example, populations are only just learning to use the ox plough. Starke (ed.), *State of the World 2009*, p. 95.
[44] J. Pretty, *The Living Land* (London: Earthscan, 1998), p. 4.
[45] Vale and Vale, *Time to Eat*, p. 33.   [46] Bové and Dufour, *The World is not for Sale*, p. 64.

is supposed to be more efficient because it allows for economies of scale, but monocultures fail to respect the checks and balances which characterise the natural world, as Rachel Carson noted in *Silent Spring*. The traditional mixed farm has more effective resistance to pests and diseases. It is also more efficient in that it is able to grow food for its animals and use their manure on the fields. Cattle feedlots, by contrast, have to find ways of getting rid of the manure they produce and import food for their animals. Huge feedlots hold as many as 100,000 animals, generating 100,000 tonnes of waste per year and using 4 million litres of water a day in summer.[47]

Monocultures rely on high inputs both in terms of fertilisers, pesticides and cattle feed. In 1994 every acre of wheat in Britain received an average of eight sprays. Of course these inputs help explain the rise in productivity, but against that the cost of removing agrochemicals from water is nearly £120 million per year. United States agriculture, hugely reliant on pesticides, is also highly efficient at producing food, but agricultural run-off into the Gulf of Mexico means that parts of it are a dead zone which can no longer support marine life. In Spain the downside of a highly 'successful' horticulture development is that nitrate levels are ten times higher than the World Health Organisation permits. Some 30 per cent of acid rain in the Netherlands is a product of the country's industrial livestock operations.[48] Soils with nitrogen fertilisers release nitrous oxide, which has 300 times the warming capacity of carbon dioxide. Fertilised soils release more than 2 billion tons of greenhouse gases each year.[49] The catastrophic decline in bees around the world is linked to monocropping and to the globalisation of agriculture. In California's Central Valley 700,000 acres are planted to almond orchards. They cannot bear fruit unless they are pollinated, and bees are trucked in from all over the United States to do this. But bee colonies are simply collapsing. 'Bees need a varied diet to thrive. No single pollen source contains the vitamins, proteins, minerals and fats necessary for good nutrition. That's exactly what they're not getting with today's massive mono-crops and rampant suburbanization.'[50]

Keeping animals in huge numbers means that they cannot be reared on their normal diets: cattle cannot feed on grass, pigs root around and poultry peck around for grubs and grains. At present it takes 7 kg of cereals to produce 1 kg of feedlot beef, 4 kg to produce one of pork and 2 kg to produce one of poultry.[51] At the same time, as Colin Tudge points out,

[47] Pretty, *Agri-Culture*, p. 105.
[48] Lawrence, *Not on the Label*, pp. 54–62; Pretty, *Agri-Culture*, p. 62.
[49] Scherr and Sthapit, 'Farming and Land Use', p. 35.
[50] W. Ellwood, 'Why are they Dying?', *New Internationalist*, 425 (September 2009), 6.
[51] Pretty, *Agri-Culture*, p. 5.

livestock consume as much grain as 2 billion people, meaning that we are already actually looking at the task of finding food sufficient for nearly 9 billion people, and this is set to increase exponentially. Thus, if meat consumption stays at its present levels (and it is has doubled in China in the past twenty years, and is set to double again) it will not be 9 billion people we have to feed by 2050 but the equivalent of 12 billion.[52]

Industrial agriculture is also inefficient because it does not respect the natural limits of animals. As José Bové puts it, 'If you drive your car at breakneck speed with savage acceleration it won't last long. Farmers are encouraged to drive their herds at their maximum capabilities. Intensive milk production means that a cow has three calves in five years. With sustainable farming a cow lives over 10 years.'[53] In general, it applies a completely false paradigm to agriculture – false because animals and plants are not machines, and because a properly managed farm does not have the life expectancy of a piece of machinery. It resorts to what Aldo Leopold called a 'Pax Germanica of the agricultural world'.[54] 'The damages of our present agriculture', writes Berry, 'all come from the determination to use the life of the soil as if it were an extractable resource like coal, to use living things as if they were machines, to impose scientific, that is, laboratory, exactitude upon living complexities that are ultimately mysterious.'[55] Industrial agriculture relies on an energy supply that lies outside biological cycles and integrities and is predicated on the continuance of cheap oil, which, as we saw in Chapter 2, cannot be taken for granted. It also requires a level of work from the farmer which is inappropriate because 'The faster we work the less attention we can pay to its details and the less skill we can apply to it.'[56] One of the effects of climate change is that rising temperatures are likely to make agricultural work more onerous and even dangerous.

What all this amounts to is that industrial agriculture is 'efficient' only if loss of soils, damage to biodiversity, pollution of water and harm to human health are ignored. In the West at present it gives us 'cheap' food, but food is not cheap. 'We actually pay three times for our food: once at the till, a second time through taxes that are used to subsidize farmers and a third time to clean up the environmental and health side effects.'[57] Though industrial agriculture looks impressive it entails 'the loss of active rural communities (and ways of life and cultural diversity), the despoliation

[52] Tudge, *So shall we Reap*, p. 78.　　[53] Bové and Dufour, *The World is not for Sale*, p. 68.
[54] Aldo Leopold, *A Sand County Almanac* (New York: Ballantine, 1970), p. 199.
[55] W. Berry, 'The Use of Energy', in *The Unsettling of America*, p. 90.　　[56] Ibid., p. 93.
[57] Pretty, *Agri-Culture*, pp. xvi, 52.

of traditional landscape, the loss of wild species – and the greatest flaw of all – the fact that it is not sustainable'.[58]

Second, industrial agriculture is inhumane. Adam Smith famously eulogised the division of labour in a pin factory, and this principle was one of the key factors in the industrial revolution. Many people, however, feel that this is deeply distasteful in farming as it implies an instrumentalisation of living creatures. Battery farming is the most notorious example, where poultry are reared in sheds holding up to 50,000 birds. Each bird has an area the size of an A4 sheet of paper, and may never see daylight. Keeping livestock in overcrowded conditions also leads to stress and aggressive behaviour.[59] Agriculture is trivialised to become 'a manufacturer and supplier of component parts for the transnational food assembly corporations'.[60]

Third, it is unsafe. It is unsafe partly because industrial farming has led to the loss of biodiversity. This is serious because it reduces possible resistance to disease. When India's rice crop was devastated by a virus in the 1970s, scientists examined 17,000 varieties of rice before finding one wild rice strain which was resistant. The Irish potato famine could have been avoided if there had been more varieties of potato.[61] In India ten varieties of rice are cultivated, out of 30,000. In Zimbabwe two maize varieties form 90 per cent of the crop. During the twentieth century in the United States 91 per cent of field maize varieties, 94 per cent of pea varieties and 81 per cent of tomato varieties have been lost. In the last fifty years in Britain 60 per cent of ancient woodlands, 90 per cent of meadows and 50 per cent of birds that depend on agricultural fields have gone. One-third of 6,500 breeds of domesticated animals are under threat of extinction. Two-thirds of England's hedgerows were lost between the 1950s and the 1990s. In Europe some 750 breeds of domestic animal became extinct in the twentieth century. In Britain twenty-six breeds of farm animal were lost.[62] These losses are not an aesthetic issue: they could be life-threatening if we cannot find varieties resistant to disease.

Some think that loss of biodiversity can be ignored because technique will make up for it. The biotechnology firms believe that drought- or disease-resistance can be engineered by genetic manipulation, but no one knows the upshot of this technology. It is not necessarily a guarantee of better yields: conventional soya is still outperforming genetically modified (GM) varieties. The main problem, however, is that it puts too much power

---

[58] Tudge, *So shall we Reap*, p. 277.   [59] Lawrence, *Not on the Label*, p. 22.
[60] B. Kneen, *From Land to Mouth* (Toronto: NC Press, 1993), p. 86.
[61] Madeley, *Food for All*, p. 140.   [62] Pretty, *Living Land*, p. 68.

over food into too few hands. Control is the central issue. Because of corporate control over the food chain GM technology could worsen rather than improve prospects for hungry people. The Director of Novartis, one of the world's biggest biotech companies, said: 'If anyone tells you that GM is going to feed the world tell them that it is not . . . to feed the world takes financial and political will – it's not about production but about distribution.'[63] Genetic engineering, writes Brewster Kneen,

is an expression of ingratitude and disrespect, if not contempt. It is a vehicle, in practice, of an attitude of domination and ownership, as expressed in the assumption that it is possible, reasonable, and morally acceptable to claim ownership over life. The claim that it is possible to own life, at least to the extent of being able to claim a patent on a life process or life form, is so outrageous socially and ethically as to be hardly worth debating.[64]

In reality, Colin Tudge comments, genetic engineering has so far contributed nothing that can truly be said to be of any significant use at all in feeding the world. 'Agriculture is primarily craft. Science is the gilt on the gingerbread.'[65]

Industrial agriculture is unsafe also because the toxins used in industrial agriculture affect people's health. The Royal Commission on Environmental Pollution, reporting in September 2005, called for further research on the impact of pesticides on human health and dismissed the idea that there are 'no scientific concerns' about spraying. Many illnesses and allergic conditions, and possibly cancer, may be linked to it. Keeping animals in large numbers, getting them to grow faster than they would normally do, to have more offspring than they would normally do and to produce more milk, requires huge quantities of antibiotics. 'If you wanted to create the maximum possible disease among animals then, in principle,' comments Colin Tudge, 'you would do as factory farmers do.' United States farmers give six times more antibiotic to their livestock purely as growth promoters than are used in human medicine.[66]

The use of toxins inevitably leads to accidents. In the United States the Sacramento river was poisoned by a carload of agricultural poison which was supposed to be safe in small doses. As Berry notes, this

ignores the fact that it has to be stored in large quantities somewhere and accidents are inevitable. Such chemicals are used to replace the work and intelligence of people and such a deformed agriculture is made necessary by the public demand

---

[63] Quoted in Madeley, *Food for All*, p. 64. The remark was made at a public meeting in Norfolk in 2000.
[64] Kneen, *Farmageddon*, p. 29.   [65] Tudge, *So shall we Reap*, pp. 264–5.   [66] Ibid., p. 161.

for a diet that is cheap and luxurious – too cheap to support adequate agricultural communities or good agricultural methods and yet so goofily self-indulgent as to demand in every season out-of-season foods produced by earth-destroying machines and chemicals.[67]

The well-publicised disasters of the past two decades are linked to what Colin Tudge calls 'cut-price husbandry' and to making farming subservient to the market.[68] Bovine spongiform encephalopathy (BSE), for example, is caused ultimately by using feed supplements which include produce from dead animals. No instances of BSE have been found in organic herds.

The foot-and-mouth disease epidemic in Britain in 2001, which was the worst in recorded history and was even more expensive than BSE, was not caused by poor husbandry, but was bound up with a technocratic and bureaucratic approach to agriculture, with the closing of small abattoirs and therefore with long-distance trucking of animals. The cost of the cull was a staggering £8 billion, but this overlooks the toll taken in ruined lives, farmer suicides, wrecked communities and the loss of many small businesses dependent on rural tourism.

The ability of farming to feed huge numbers of people, says Berry, has been made possible 'by the substitution of energy for knowledge, of methodology for care, of technology for morality'.[69] By contrast we have to learn the need for limits. The Amish, he comments, 'have mastered one of the fundamental paradoxes of our condition: we can make ourselves whole only by accepting our partiality, by living within our limits, by being human – not trying to be gods. By restraint they make themselves whole.'[70]

SERVING AND KEEPING

Notoriously, Lynn White suggested that our ecological problems sprang from the use of the 'dominion' verse in Genesis 1.28.[71] This suggestion, endlessly debated, overlooks the basic exegetical rule that 'Redactor is rabbenu', that we have to interpret texts as the redactor teaches us to. In relation to Genesis 1.28 it is certain that the redactor wanted us to read it in the light of the second creation story, according to which, 'God put Adam in the garden to till and keep it'. (Gen. 2.15). I suggest that this account points us in the direction of a sustainable agriculture.

[67] W. Berry, 'Conservation is Good Work', in *Sex, Economy*, p. 31.
[68] Tudge, *So shall we Reap*, p. 174.
[69] W. Berry, 'The Ecological Crisis as a Crisis in Character', in *The Unsettling of America*, p. 33.
[70] W. Berry, 'Word and Flesh', in *What are People For?*, p. 201.
[71] L. White, 'The Historical Roots of our Ecological Crisis', *Science*, 155/3767 (March 1967), 1203–7.

The word 'garden' (*gan*) is, of course, a metaphor for the whole earth. The verb translated 'till' is the verb *abad*, which means to work, serve or worship. It is not only human beings who do this, but God as well. 'I have not made you serve,' says God in Isaiah, 'but you have made me serve with your sins' (Is. 43.23). The noun from it is *ebed*, servant, a word fundamental for the theology of second Isaiah and taken up by Jesus in Mark: the Son of Man came not to be served but to serve (Mk 10.43). Serving, in Scripture, is key to being fully human, and farming, serving the earth, serving the whole human community, is part of this.

The verb 'to keep', *shamar*, is another crucial word. It is the word invariably used for keeping God's commandments. It is the root of the word Cain uses in reply to the divine question 'Am I my brother's keeper?' To keep in this sense likewise goes to the very heart of human identity. To be truly human is to keep my neighbour; it is to keep the commandments and thus to keep the gift, God's earth. Keeping the earth, in fact, is the practical application of keeping the commandments. From a secular standpoint Colin Tudge recognises this in his argument that 'unless we keep morality and aesthetics firmly in view, then they will go by the board. The idea that human values simply install themselves by default is another illusion. In agriculture as in all things, human values must be written specifically into the act.'[72]

If there are practices of domination then serving and keeping begin with a completely different approach. 'The agrarian mind begins with the love of the fields and ramifies in good farming, good cooking, good eating and gratitude to God . . . the industrial-economic mind begins with ingratitude, and ramifies in the destruction of farms and forests.'[73] This is an account of sin and grace in relation to farming.

At the heart of good husbandry is care for the soil. Sir Albert Howard insisted that the heart of both agricultural and human health lay in healthy soil. He summed up a lifetime's research in the following propositions:

1. The birthright of all living things is health.
2. This law is true for soil, plant, animal, and man: the health of these four is one connected chain.
3. Any weakness or defect in health of any earlier link in the chain is carried on to the next and succeeding links, until it reaches the last, namely man.

---

[72] Tudge, *So shall we Reap*, p. 101.
[73] W. Berry, 'The Whole Horse', in *The Art of the Commonplace* (Washington: Shoemaker and Hoard, 2002), p. 241.

4. The widespread vegetable and animal pests and diseases, which are such a bane to modern agriculture, are evidence of a great failure of health in the second (plant) and third (animal) links of the chain.

5. The impaired health of human populations (the fourth link) in modern civilized countries is a consequence of this failure in the second and third links.

6. This general failure in the last three links is to be attributed to failure in the first link, the soil: the undernourishment of the soil is at the root of all.[74]

Wendell Berry credits topsoil with a Christ-like nature

in its passivity and beneficence, and in the penetrating energy that issues out of its peaceableness. It increases by experience, by the passage of seasons over it, growth rising out of it and returning to it, not by ambition or aggressiveness. It is enriched by all things that die and enter into it. It keeps the past, not as history or as memory, but as richness, new possibility. Its fertility is always building up out of death into promise. Death is the bridge or the tunnel by which its past enters its future.[75]

Ultimately the world will be fed by good husbandry, and good husbandry is kindly use: 'To treat every field or every part of every field, with the same consideration is not farming but industry. Kindly use depends upon intimate knowledge, the most sensitive responsiveness and responsibility.'[76] It will not be saved by technological miracles. Soil loss, says Berry, 'cannot be saved by heroic acts of gigantic technology but only by millions of small acts and restraints, conditioned by small fidelities, skills and desires. Soil loss is ultimately a cultural problem; it will be corrected only by cultural solutions.'[77] Such small acts might be instanced by education in kitchen gardening and organic farming in Nepal, which has increased vegetable production threefold, or rainwater harvesting in Zimbabwe, which has allowed maize to be grown and has led to self-sufficiency.[78]

Kindly use would lead to a farming which generated fewer greenhouse gases than industrial farming currently does. Scherr and Sthapit outline five strategies to this end. The first is to minimise inorganic fertilisers by increasing soil carbon through composting, green manures, livestock manures and nitrogen-fixing crops. Practices which reduce tillage also reduce carbon emissions. In Brazil 'No-till plots yielded a third more wheat and soybean than conventionally ploughed plots and reduced soil erosion by up to

---

[74] Sir A. Howard, *The Soil and Health* (Lexington: University Press of Kentucky, 2006), p. 12.

[75] W. Berry, 'A Native Hill', in *The Art of the Commonplace*, p. 25.

[76] Berry, 'The Ecological Crisis as a Crisis of Character', in *The Unsetting of America*, p. 31.

[77] Berry, 'Conservation and Local Economy', in *Sex, Economy*, p. 15.

[78] Dodman, Ayers and Huq, 'Building Resilience', pp. 154, 158.

90 per cent.'[79] Second, ways of producing food which store carbon in the biomass of roots, trunks and branches have to be explored. This can be done by cultivating perennial grains, through agroforestry intercrops and tree crop alternatives for food, feed and fuel. Third, livestock production can be managed so that greenhouse gas emissions are reduced. Some feed supplements reduce methane emissions.[80] Fourth, existing carbon stores in natural forests and grasslands can be protected, and lastly vegetation can be restored in degraded areas. In Niger, the authors report,

a 'regreening' movement, using farmer-managed natural regeneration and simple soil and water conservation practices, reversed desertification, increased tree and shrub cover 10 to 20 fold, and reclaimed at least 250,000 hectares of degraded land for crops. Over 25 years, at least a quarter of the country's farmers were involved in restoring about 5 million hectares of land, benefiting at least 4.5 million people through increased crop production, income, and food security.[81]

GRACE AND SCALE

Throughout the book so far we have seen that grace involves scale. In a post-carbon world the question of whether small mixed-use farms are more efficient than big monocultural units is moot. To suggest this is not to forget the terrible drudgery involved in much traditional farming. It is a realistic question about how the world is going to be fed. It is not identical to the argument over the virtues of organic farming either. It is going back to Leviticus and suggesting that good husbandry is the key to human flourishing.

Taking the problems involved in industrial agriculture one by one we can see how they match up when set alongside the small mixed farm. In the first place, as we have already seen, mixed farming keeps checks and balances in place. There is less chance that disease will affect every aspect of a farm's production. Rotation of crops means that the life cycle of pests is disrupted. Integrated pest management finds ways of dealing with pests

---

[79] Scherr and Sthapit, 'Farming and Land Use', p. 36.

[80] Simon Fairlie has shown how unsubstantiated is the claim that livestock produce 18 per cent of man-made greenhouse gases. Methane stays in the atmosphere for only twelve years; carbon dioxide for 200. In terms of quick fixes this makes methane a good target. The alternatives proposed, which include soya, would actually produce more carbon dioxide. 'Carbon Colonialism and the Mathematics of Methane', *The Land*, 8 (Winter 2009–10), 13–17. The new Food and Agriculture Organisation report *Livestock in the Balance* recognises the role livestock play in enhancing smaller livelihoods and 'protecting the poorest households for whom livestock serve as a crucial safety net'. *The Land*, 8 (Winter 2009–10), 12.

[81] Scherr and Sthapit, 'Farming and Land Use', p. 44.

that are not solely reliant on chemical sprays. Beekeepers, for example, have found that introducing mesh floors to their hives is a more effective way of dealing with varroa than the annual use of one or other of the patent chemical insecticides. Planting a wider range of crops is also a hedge against the more erratic weather that global warming is bringing us.

Second, mixed farms recycle their wastes and make more effective use of their resources. They pay more attention to nitrogen fixation and soil regeneration. In other words, they rely more on good husbandry than on the agrochemical companies, an independence which may prove crucial as more and more of the food chain falls under corporate control. They also rely on far fewer inputs than industrialised agriculture. Where monocultures need 300 units per 100 units of food, polycultures need only five.

The small farm has no need to Taylorise production. As they have always done, farmers know their animals and their individuality. Respecting animals is not sentimentality. If there is a moral ecology in which 'everything is connected to everything else' then we are sure to pay for disrespectful practices. To treat animals as items on a production line does damage to the whole of society, for ultimately we cannot live schizoid lives. The call for a more integrated agriculture, therefore, is also a call to live with greater integrity across the board.

Not only do mixed farms produce few external impacts, but it has been calculated that organic agriculture produces between 75 and 125 pounds of positive externalities per hectare, in terms, for example, of the preservation of hedgerows, biodiversity and topsoil. 'Give me spots on apples but leave me the birds and the bees', sang Joni Mitchell, in response to Rachel Carson's polemic against the blanket use of DDT. It is also argued that small ecological farms have a productivity far higher than that of large industrial farms. Intercropping results in more efficient utilisation of resources (light, water, nutrients) by plants of different height, provides insurance against crop failure, provides effective cover to soil, reduces the loss of soil moisture and helps keep pest and weeds under control.[82] The question of real efficiency is crucial. We cannot afford to be romantic about agriculture. The question for the future must be as to what counts as true efficiency, and present rules of accountancy cannot give the answer to that. New measures of efficiency are required. Tudge argues that what we need to do to feed the world is to give the best land to pulses, cereals and tubers (that is, to arable farming); to fit in horticulture in every spare pocket – and be

---

[82] Madeley, *Food for All*, p. 26.

prepared to spend a lot of time and effort on it, and to invest capital for example in greenhouses; and to allow livestock to slot in as best it can.[83]

Again, small mixed farms generate more robust rural communities and on the whole employ more people. Given that eight billion people cannot all live in cities and find things to do there the question of human community, and what people are meaningfully going to do, is quite as urgent as the question of how people are to be fed. Jules Pretty has documented the growth of community food systems and rural partnerships around the world, which both develop more vibrant local communities and are involved in massive increases in agricultural productivity using locally adapted and sustainable technologies.

Following W. P. Hedden, Jules Pretty speaks of the emergence of food-sheds: self-reliant, locally or regionally based food systems composed of diversified farms using sustainable practices to supply fresher, more nutritious foodstuffs to small-scale processors and consumers to whom producers are linked by the bonds of community as well as economy.[84] The growth of farmers' markets around Europe and in North America may be an instance of these arriving on our doorstep.

Finally, small-scale agriculture is nowhere near as energy-dependent as industrial agriculture, a key factor in a world faced by global warming. Agriculture plays a significant part in global warming through deforestation, fertiliser use and the methane from cattle and rice paddies. Sustainable farming can do much to reduce these emissions. For all these reasons small mixed farming may be more truly economic than anything achieved by economies of scale. After a century of industrial agriculture, Jules Pretty argues, the time has come for the next agricultural revolution, a return to tilling and keeping and an end to practices of domination.[85] This will represent a return to a common-sense agriculture: rooted in good husbandry; traditional in structure, yet making all the use it chooses to of the very best science and (where appropriate) the highest technology; guided by biological reality (ecology, physiology) and by the human values of kindness, autonomy and justice.[86]

In her *History of Alternative Agriculture* Joan Thirsk shows that agriculture has gone through many cycles over the last 700 years, now going for big units, now for small. She thinks we are ripe for another round of small-scale, more labour-intensive agriculture. She argues that the strong assumption of our age that omniscient governments will lead the way out

---

[83] Tudge, *So shall we Reap*, p. 357.   [84] Pretty, *Agri-Culture*, p. 117.   [85] Ibid., p. xvi.
[86] Tudge, *So shall we Reap*, p. 380.

of economic problems will not serve. This would apply a fortiori to technology, and at present to the 'promise' of genetic engineering. She believes that solutions are more likely to come from below, and she quotes William James: 'I am against bigness and greatness in all their forms, and with the invisible, molecular, moral forces that work from individual to individual, stealing in through the crannies of the world like so many soft rootlets, or like the capillary oozings of water, and yet rending the hardest monuments of man's pride, if you give them time.'[87] Given the likely impact of feedback loops, time is not necessarily something we have much of, but in relation to industrial agriculture peak oil may spell out the need to follow the small-scale option. If Jules Pretty, Colin Tudge and the other authors quoted here are right it may be possible to feed the city in a sustainable way, and to have an agriculture based on kindly use which would be an agriculture 'in grace' and which would, in both town and country, genuinely serve the common good.

In the next chapter I turn to a key question for both rural and urban areas, that of transport.

[87] J. Thirsk, *A History of Alternative Agriculture* (Oxford University Press, 1997), p. 226.

CHAPTER 9

Connecting the city

Humans have always been on the move, but since the mid-nineteenth century at increasing speeds and in unparalleled numbers. For getting on for a century those in the West have become accustomed to taking ease of travel for granted: roads are for the most part well surfaced, well maintained, created by huge machines, paid for by taxation; likewise other forms of transport like trains and aeroplanes, with all the infrastructure that they need. This is a very recent development. As noted in Chapter 4, a novel set in the 1880s can still turn on the difficulty of an eight-mile journey. Jane Austen's *Sense and Sensibility*, published in 1811, cannot be understood outside the background of the difficulty of the 170-mile journey from London to Exeter, or the 70-mile journey from Bristol. In the world where rapid travel can be taken for granted there is, it is true, still a romance of the road, celebrated in 'road movies', but there is little romance in the airport waiting lounge, especially as security checks have made air travel more and more tiresome. Compared with a harbour an airport is a sterile place, dominated equally by security and check-in procedures and by shopping, with poor-quality, standardised and over-priced food and no real humanity.[1] 'Modern airports are for the most parts places of panic and dismay. This is largely because they are architecturally taciturn. They rely on labels to shepherd people from place to place: arrows, direction signs, arresting explanations, everything in short but architecture.'[2]

In harbours one finds the dense jostle of hotels, pubs, cafés, shops, seamen's missions, doss houses and brothels, with the cry of gulls, the smell of the sea and the sparkle of sun on water, often giving out directly on to the town. All this is impossible for the airport, which is a pallid

---

[1] Perhaps the nearest to an airport of any interest is Amsterdam's Schiphol, with its exhibits from the Rijkmuseum and instant train connections to Amsterdam ten minutes away, but even then it is hardly a place one might choose to wander around and in which one might want to linger, as in most harbours.

[2] Scruton, *Classical Vernacular*, p. 51.

and anodyne replacement with all the allure of a Wimpy bar, the smell of aviation fuel and acres of tarmac.

The actual structures of modern travel seem to be purely utilitarian. How can they be an object of theological reflection? The answer is that connections are a fundamental part of the common good: humankind hardly exists without them. These connections can be imperial or humble, routes of power or routes of pilgrimage, songlines or sites of constant deep noise, sustainable or unsustainable. Issues of justice are raised by the exclusion which follows from bad connections. According to my fundamental theological scheme I will understand 'ways', which include all forms of travel, under the appropriation of God the Creator, as the creation of order, but the two other Trinitarian appropriations, reconciliation and redemption, or community and hope, also come into play. I begin where humanity begins, with the pedestrian.

THE PEDESTRIAN

Any walk in the countryside will disclose numerous paths and tracks made by animals in search of food and water: such tracks are the origin of our roads.[3] Long-distance tracks mark the course of annual migrations. Homo sapiens and her ancestors lived for some two million years as hunter-gatherers and presumably had analogous tracks. The !Kung bushmen follow migrating animals for food, and this may have been a common practice. It was not until the agricultural revolution, some time around 12000 BC, that settled patterns of life emerged and place may have taken priority over journeying. For the vast bulk of our history we have been pedestrians, though this does not rule out the covering of large distances. The pedestrian way of life, says J. B. Jackson, 'formed our ideas of community, of time and space and our relationship with the environment'.[4] 'For untold thousands of years we travelled on foot over rough paths and dangerously unpredictable roads, not simply as peddlers or commuters or tourists, but as men and women for whom the path and road stood for some intense experience: freedom, new human relationships, a new awareness of landscape. The road offered a journey into the unknown that could end up allowing us to discover who we were and where we belonged.'[5] Gerry Hughes suggests that walking on foot to holy places answers a deep religious need.

[3] C. Taylor, *Roads and Tracks of Britain* (Letchworth: Aldine, 1979), p. 6.
[4] J. Jackson, *Sense of Place*, p. 198.   [5] Ibid., p. 192.

It is a symbolic gesture, a search for our real destination, a kind of sacramental journey, a sign that we are in search of an answer to our deepest longings . . . On the road the pilgrim learns that searching for God is already to have found him and that direction is much more important than destination, because God is not just an end, not a beginning, but for us he is always a beginning without end.[6]

The road Edward Thomas celebrates belongs to the pedestrian:

> Often footsore, never
> Yet of the road I weary,
> Though long and steep and dreary,
> As it winds on for ever.[7]

This is despite the fact that, as he wrote, 'all roads lead to France' and he, with millions of others, walked to his death.

The increase in wheeled traffic for members of the upper class which began in the mid-seventeenth century changed attitudes to pedestrians: 'those travelling on foot were increasingly viewed as members of the lower class – they were footmen, footboys, footpads, foot soldiers; persons belonging at the foot of the social order; in critical writing, pedestrian came to mean laboured, commonplace, and without style'.[8] Jackson thinks that the advent of rapid transport makes our pedestrian history a fact of merely archaeological interest but this is not the case. In the first place, in the first decade of the twenty-first century about one-third of the world's population are still primarily pedestrian and have little access even to bus transport. Their sensibilities are largely untouched by modernity. Second, John Bowlby argued that babies are still programmed to go to sleep while being walked, a profound memory of our nomadic or at least pedestrian past.[9] The century in which we have got used to rapid transport is a mere blink in evolutionary time, and it is questionable how far earlier ideas of community, time and space have been changed. Third, still today the only way really to get to know an area is to walk it. Walking discloses a level of detail, of flora and fauna, of the lie of the land, unavailable in any other way. The fact that a third of the population of Great Britain 'go for a walk'

---

[6] G. Hughes, *In Search of a Way* (London: Darton, Longman and Todd, 1986), p. 50.

[7] E. Thomas, 'Roads', in *Collected Poems* (London: Faber, 1974), p. 163.

[8] Jackson, *Sense of Place*, p. 204.

[9] 'The fact that, if it is to terminate crying, rocking must be at sixty cycles a minute or above may perhaps be related to the rate at which an adult walks. Sixty steps a minute is in fact a very slow walk and is almost always exceeded. This means that, when carried on his mother's back or hip, a young baby is rocked at not less than sixty cycles a minute and so does not cry – unless he is hungry or in pain. This happy consequence might be due to chance: more likely, it seems, it is a result of selective pressures that have been operating during the course of man's evolution.' J. Bowlby, *Attachment* (Harmondsworth: Penguin, 1969), p. 353.

at weekends, usually in the countryside, may represent a response to such facts. Of course, this astonishes many Third World people, who may have to walk miles for water. In general the modern economy could not work by walking: it depends on rapid transport, which also makes the shorter working day possible. However, it is still true that the fastest way to move people in cities is on foot or on bicycles. As Mumford noted, the slowest is to put them all in cars: 'The entire day-time population of historic Boston could assemble by foot on Boston Common, probably in less than half an hour if the streets were clear of motor traffic. If they were transported by motor car, they would take many hours, and unless they abandoned their unparkable vehicles would never reach their destination.'[10] The pedestrian, then, is still very much with us, still shaping our ways of life. The latest idea of urban form, pedestrian pockets, tries to see that people are all within ten minutes' walking distance of basic facilities such as shops, schools, clinics and public transport.

WAYS AND THE STRUCTURE OF LIFE

Around 5000 BC came the invention of the wheel, and perhaps a thousand years after that the domestication of the horse. These two developments were essential for the emergence of empire and for the development of what we would properly call roads as opposed to tracks. 'The horse-drawn chariot made the conquest of foreign countries an easier undertaking. Rural paths serving small and often primitive communities ceased to play a historic role. Their obsolescence marked the beginning of modern Western history based on urbanization, imperialist expansion and continent-wide trade and the spread of agriculture.'[11] With the rise of empire, Jackson argues, two patterns of roads emerged. On the one hand there were centripetal systems based on the village, vernacular roads which followed the topography and bent to skirt a tree or cross by a ford, 'playing [an] insignificant role in the history of material progress'.[12] On the other hand were centrifugal road systems which ignored topography, built bridges and viaducts and were often only for use by imperial armies and officials. 'These roads lead from the imperial city and are built to extend and consolidate power.'[13] Such great roads characterised the Incan and Persian empires, but it was Rome which made them its trademark, setting a golden marker in the Forum at Rome and tracing milestones from there to the furthest reaches

---

[10] Mumford, *City*, p. 578.   [11] Jackson, *Sense of Place*, p. 198.   [12] Jackson, *Discovering*, p. 22.
[13] Ibid., p. 23.

of the empire. Both kinds of roads, Jackson thinks, served much the same purpose – 'the strengthening and maintenance of social order, the tying together at one central place all the spaces which constitute the territory of a community or a state'.[14] If we go far back enough, to the very emergence of roads, we have to talk about the creation of social order, indeed of a human world in which communities trade with one another, share skills, and cross-fertilise cultures. In this sense roads are the instruments of the 'economy of redemption'. Paul would probably have recognised this in relation to sea roads, and John may have had such a sense in mind in calling Jesus 'the way'. This is clearer in centripetal than in centrifugal roads. The maze of tiny roads in the area in which I write, for example, Dartmoor in England, links farms to villages, villages to market towns, and market towns to the cathedral town, from which, anciently, roads run to London and, somewhat circuitously, to the port of Bristol. The roads are a mass of tiny tributaries carrying life backwards and forwards, food in one direction, manufactured goods, books and music, preachers, ideas in the other. The roads breathe life. Without them no farm, village or market town survives: there is no human community. They are a physical instantiation of the common good. John Knox, travelling in the Scottish Highlands in 1786, noted that 'Through a considerable part of the year the inhabitants of each respective glen or valley may be considered as prisoners strongly guarded by impassable mountains on one side, by swamps and furious torrents on the other.'[15] Roads brought strangers with them. These could be a threat to established order but, when travel was difficult and relatively scarce, and when one might see no one but one's kin for months if not years on end, guests were welcome, as they were for Abraham (Gen. 18). The road was not a threat but a blessing, bringing news and stories from unfamiliar places. The centripetal roads are small, and the smaller they are the slower they are. They are subordinate to the purposes of agriculture. Some of their banks and hedges are among the oldest things in Britain, reaching back to the Iron Age.[16] Even in the age of mass motoring they are places of great beauty. The centrifugal roads, on the other hand, are not so simply positive: Roman roads were made for conquest and tribute. Order here is imposed. The Pax Romana (or that of any other empire) implies subjugation. Here we are concerned not with a common good which emerges through trade and conversation, but with the need to conquer,

---

[14] Ibid., p. 22.
[15] Quoted in A. R. B. Haldane, *New Ways through the Glens* (London: Nelson, 1962), p. 12.
[16] Hoskins, *Making*, p. 29.

exploit and, if necessary, repress. Yet even these roads brought ideas with them, and cultural change. So Constantine travelled from York to the battle of the Milvian Bridge when the sun worship with which he was familiar in Britain was transposed into worship of Christ the unconquered Sun.

Of course, not all roads are clearly centrifugal or centripetal. On the whole Jackson is right that 'without a specific destination, a road has no reason for existing', but this needs to be qualified with the awareness that tracks leading out of medieval villages often stopped at fields, forests or springs, the places of labour.[17] Even today there are many 'no through roads', though these characteristically lead to houses or settlements.

Some roads seem to have had largely religious or ritual functions, like the roads leading to Stonehenge or Avebury in England. On Dartmoor and in Cornwall, again in England, there were 'churchways' which linked parish churches to outlying farms. Remote areas had corpse roads or lichways over which the dead had to be carried for burial. Some of these involved carrying coffins for up to twelve miles over mountainous country.[18] A bishop who took his job conscientiously could not travel if the roads were too bad, and the Bishop of Carlisle, in 1354, offered forty days of remitted penance to anyone who would help repair the boggy road between Carlisle and Penrith.[19] Some pilgrim routes, like the road to Compostella or to Walsingham, might be considered as primarily religious roads, though the route followed by the Canterbury Pilgrims was a Roman road. Occasionally there are monastic roads which link monasteries with their outlying properties, as in Mastiles Lane in Yorkshire, which runs from Fountains Abbey right through to the monastic estates in the Lake District. Jackson argues that the warpath of the North American Indians was a place of ceremony and ritual when war was declared, and was thus a form of religious road. When not used for war it was a place of dread and was avoided.

There were some roads, like the drove roads, which went very considerable distances but were not imperial roads. On the contrary, they skirted the big roads in order to avoid tolls and they begot their own network of way stations to care for the drovers. In eighteenth-century England 40,000 Highland cattle were driven each year to Norfolk to be fattened up before going to London; 30,000 black cattle came from Wales through Herefordshire to south-east England. Geese were driven in flocks of thousands from Norfolk to London after the corn harvest when they could graze on the stubble. From the same direction 150,000 turkeys were likewise

---

[17] P. Hindle, *Medieval Roads and Tracks* (Princes Risborough: Shire, 1998), p. 46.
[18] Ibid., p. 12.   [19] Ibid., p. 20.

driven.[20] Since long distances could not be covered, stops were at seven- to twelve-mile intervals, and in England are often recorded by pubs such as the Drovers Arms, or others which recall the type of cattle: the Scotch Inn, the Craven Heifer or the Welsh Arms.[21] Roads thus created communities on the way where other trades could flourish and villages spring up.[22]

More than empire, trade was the great creator of roads. This applied, obviously, to the drove roads, but also to the salt roads. Salt was an important commodity in medieval England, and the inland salt producers, or wiches, such as Droitwich, Nantwich, Middlewich and Northwich, had roads to deliver salt to other places characterised by this trade, such as Saltersford and Saltergate.[23] The Fosse Way, which runs from the south coast of Devon towards Lincoln and the Humber, catered for trade with northern Europe. Towns poorly placed in relation to the road system failed. Before the advent of the railway perishable goods had to be carried by courier. In 1710 320 horses galloped through Tonbridge in Kent every day, bringing fish up to London for the hotels and clubs.[24]

In terms of engineering Roman roads were unequalled for almost 2,000 years. Until the nineteenth century most roads in most places in the world were unmetalled, presenting huge problems for wheeled traffic in wet weather. In Britain, although there were notable medieval bridges, and even a religious order devoted to bridge building, bridges had to wait until the early nineteenth century. Before that rivers had to be forded.[25] Giedion rightly comments on the beauty of many modern bridges.[26] In medieval Britain roads were not physical objects but 'a perpetual right of passage in the sovereign, for himself and his subjects, over another's land'. A road was a right of way, and if the road became 'foundrous' travellers had the right to go off it into standing corn. 'That the ways, in winter, must be impassable for wheel traffic was habitually taken for granted.'[27] As late as 1740 in the county of Aberdeen 'there was no road . . . on which wheels of any kind could be dragged'.[28] In 1792 in Cumberland the Road Surveyor, a local farmer forced to occupy this office for a year on behalf of the parish,

---

[20] S. and B. Webb, *The King's Highway* (London: Longman, 1913), p. 68.
[21] Hindle, *Medieval Roads*, p. 15.
[22] In 1686 Salisbury, a small town in Wiltshire, could accommodate 548 travellers and 865 horses in its inns. F. Braudel, *The Wheels of Commerce* (London: Collins, 1985), p. 353.
[23] Hindle, *Medieval Roads*, p. 8.   [24] Webb, *King's Highway*, p. 66.   [25] Ibid., p. 85.
[26] Speaking of the Swiss engineer Maillart, Giedion says, 'His shapely bridges spring out of the shapeless crags with the serene inevitability of Greek temples. The lithe, elastic resilience with which they leap their chasms, the attenuation of their dimensions, merges into the coordinated rhythms of arch, platform and the upended slabs between them.' *Space, Time and Architecture* (Cambridge, Mass.: Harvard University Press, 1967), p. 461.
[27] Webb, *King's Highway*, p. 6.   [28] Haldane, *New Ways*, p. 3.

had to call on local people to open the tracks over the common so that carts could once again use them.[29] This meant that until the invention of the railway engine, travel was invariably slow. 'Napoleon moved no faster than Julius Caesar', as Paul Valéry remarked. Using the utmost exertion, with relays of horses, it was the general rule to cover at most sixty miles in a day.[30] Until the seventeenth century people mostly travelled either on foot or on horseback. When Luther was sent by his order to Rome he walked. Ten years later he walked to his trial in Worms. Hackney carriages were first used in London in 1634; post chaises in 1664.[31] But coaches had no springs until 1754 and were slow, uncomfortable and dangerous. Arthur Young, travelling in Lancashire in 1770, recorded:

I know not in the whole range of language, terms sufficiently expressive to describe this infernal road. Let me most seriously caution all travellers who may accidentally propose to travel this terrible country to avoid it as they would the devil; for a thousand to one they break their necks or their limbs by overthrows or breakings down. They will here meet with ruts, which I actually measured, four feet deep, and floating with mud only from a wet summer. What, therefore, must it be after a winter? The only mending it receives is tumbling in some loose stones which serve no other purpose than jolting the carriage in the most intolerable manner. These are not only opinions, but facts; for I actually passed three carts broken down in these eighteen miles of execrable memory.[32]

The increase in traffic and in the number of public coaches, and the development of the postal service, meant that better roads were urgently needed, and Telford and Macadam were the ones who provided them. It was the latter who insisted that roads must be made to accommodate traffic and not traffic regulated to preserve roads.[33] The improvements they introduced in the 1820s heralded the great age of the stagecoach, when the fastest coaches, such as the Exeter Telegraph and the Devonport Mail, reached the astonishing speed of ten miles per hour. We have a vivid picture of this period from De Quincy:

From eight fifteen or twenty minutes later, imagine the mails assembled on parade in Lombard St . . . On any night the spectacle was beautiful. The absolute perfection of all the appointments about the carriages and the harness; their strength, their brilliant cleanliness, their beautiful simplicity – but more than all, the royal magnificence of the horses – were what might first have fixed the attention . . . Every

---

[29] Webb, *King's Highway*, p. 6.
[30] F. Braudel, *The Structures of Everyday Life* (London: Collins, 1981), p. 424.
[31] Webb, *King's Highway*, p. 70.
[32] Quoted in Jane Oliver, *The Ancient Roads of England* (London: Cassell, 1936), p. 135.
[33] Webb, *King's Highway*, p. 172.

moment are shouted aloud by the post-office servants, and summoned to draw up, the great ancestral names of cities known to history through a thousand years... Lincoln, Winchester, Portsmouth, Gloucester, Oxford, Bristol, Manchester, York, Newcastle, Edinburgh, Glasgow, Perth, Stirling, Aberdeen... every moment you hear the thunder of lids locked down upon the mail bags.[34]

Richer passengers travelled inside, the poorer on the roof, often without a proper seat and without protection from the weather. The noise of the riff-raff outside and the drumming of their feet on the carriage roof occasioned this advertisement:

<blockquote>
For Portsmouth
A New Carriage on Springs
Called
The LAND FRIGATE
</blockquote>

Sets out from the Bell Savage, Ludgate Hill, to the Red Lyon At Portsmouth, every Tuesday and Saturday, at 6am. Fare 15s each Passenger. Ladies and Gentlemen Are requested to observe that the Frigate is elegantly sashed all Round, and that in order to Preserve the respectability of the Vehicle no outside passengers are Carried.[35]

The Devonport mail covered 227 miles in twenty-four hours; the Edinburgh coach 400 miles in forty hours.[36] The artist J. M. W. Turner, who had a strong constitution, travelled all over Europe in these contraptions.

Medieval Europe tried to finance the making of roads through local levies. In eighteenth-century Britain turnpike roads, paid for by local entrepreneurs but making money by charging tolls, spread all over Britain. By 1830 there were 22,000 miles of such roads. In Wales this provoked the Rebecca riots, appealing to Genesis 24.60 – 'you shall possess the gate of your enemies'. Men in women's clothes assailed the turnpikes at night, cut them down and burned the gatekeepers' cottages. One woman gatekeeper was murdered, but the jury refused to convict the assailant. With the advent of the railways the turnpikes lost their revenues and parishes were once again required to pay for their maintenance. The turnpike trusts had to be abandoned and were replaced by County Road Boards, the eventual solution to road maintenance throughout Britain.[37]

The heyday of the stagecoach lasted only a dozen years, and was then eclipsed by the railway boom, which revolutionised the speed of travel.

---

[34] Quoted in Oliver, *Ancient Roads*, p. 186.   [35] Quoted in Ibid., p. 177.
[36] Webb, *King's Highway*, p. 72.   [37] Ibid., p. 218.

'Every coach had to be taken off the road the moment the railway was open to the towns along its route.' The last mail coach between London and Birmingham ran in 1839; the last between London and Bristol in 1843; the last to Plymouth in 1847; and the last mail coach of all, between Thurso and Wick, in 1874.[38] By the time of George Stephenson's death in 1848 railways had already covered most of England. The motive was trade. The preamble to the bill authorising the Stockton and Darlington Railway in 1821 noted that 'the making and maintaining of a railway or tramroad for the passage of wagon and other carriages will be of great public utility by facilitating the conveyance of coal, iron, lime, corn, and other commodities'.[39] By the end of the nineteenth century the time for a journey between London and Edinburgh was six hours and eighteen minutes, at an average speed of sixty-three miles an hour. Not everyone approved. 'We have too much hurrying about in these islands', complained William Wordsworth; 'much for idle pleasure, and more from over activity in the pursuit of wealth, without regard to the good or happiness of others.' When the railway was extended from Kendal to Windermere he asked indignantly:

> Is then no nook of English ground secure
> From rash assault?

And he went on:

> Proud were ye, Mountains, when, in times of old,
> Your patriot sons, to stem invasive war,
> Intrenched your brows; ye gloried in each scar:
> Now, for your shame, a Power, the Thirst of Gold,
> That rules o'er Britain like a baneful star,
> Wills that your peace, your beauty, shall be sold,
> And clear way made for her triumphal car
> Through the beloved retreats your arms enfold!

> Heard YE that Whistle? As her long linked Train
> Swept onwards, did the vision cross your view?
> Yes, ye were startled; – and, in balance true,
> Weighing the mischief with the promised gain,
> Mountains, the Vales, and Floods, I call on you
> To share the passion of a just disdain.[40]

Forty years later Ruskin agreed with him. 'The whole system of railroad travelling', he wrote, 'is addressed to people who, being in a hurry, are therefore, for the time being, miserable.'

---

[38] Ibid., p. 216. [39] J. Pendleton, *Our Railways* (London: Cassell, 1894), vol. I, p. 31.
[40] Hoskins, *Making*, pp. 262–3.

No one would travel in that manner who could help it – who had time to go leisurely over hills and between hedges, instead of through tunnels and between banks: at least those who would, have no sense of beauty so acute as that we need consult it at a station. The railroad is in all relations a matter of earnest business, to be got through as soon as possible. It transmutes a man from a traveller into a living parcel. For the time he has parted with the nobler characteristics of his humanity for the sake of a planetary power of locomotion. Do not ask him to admire anything. You might as well ask the wind. Carry him safely, dismiss him soon: he will thank you for nothing else . . . there never was more flagrant nor impertinent folly than the smallest portion of ornament in anything concerned with railroads or near them.[41]

Such disdain did nothing to stop the triumphant progress of the railways, however, and they carried all before them until World War I. They represented the first real democratisation of travel. Tourism began with them, and the mass expansion of suburbia. The railway, said John Pendleton in 1894, 'has become the chief agent of the nation. It runs for everyone'.[42] The historian G. M. Trevelyan considered the railways 'England's gift to the world'.[43] After World War II a combination of the power of the road lobby and cost benefit analysis led to their decline both in North America and in Britain (though not in mainland Europe). In Britain a physicist, Dr Beeching, was brought in to chair British Rail, and closed one-third of the network. His report, published in 1963, appeared just six years before E. J. Mishan popularised environmental economics. The nostalgia generated by the old branch lines, memorialised in Flanders and Swann's song 'Slow Train', would have astonished Ruskin.

Just as the railways put an end to the stage coach, so mass car ownership has had a severe impact on the railways. Henry Ford's Model T went into general production in 1908 and was soon leaving the production line at a rate of one every three minutes, priced so that ordinary people could afford it.[44] More than any other vehicle it was what made mass motoring possible. By the 1960s the private car had begun to supplant public transport everywhere in Europe, and it has now begun to do so in Asia. For the free marketeers, car travel promised liberation from the vulgar masses. The great thing about cars, according to the transport minister in the Major government, was that 'you don't have to put up with the dreadful human beings sitting alongside you'.[45] Margaret Thatcher was of the same

[41] Ruskin, *Seven Lamps*, p. 121.   [42] Pendleton, *Our Railways*, vol. I, p. 8.
[43] C. Barman, *Early British Railways* (Harmondsworth: Penguin, 1950), p. 5.
[44] The price represented four months' wages for a worker on the assembly line.
[45] Quoted in J. Moran, *On Roads: A Hidden History* (London: Profile, 2009), p. 229.

mind. Left-wing commentators spoke of 'the organization of individual isolation'.[46] Mass car ownership, and even more the transfer of freight from rail to road, required a new type of road: freeways, *Autobahnen* or motorways. Everywhere they were at first seen as symbols of triumphant modernity, 'a terrestrial take on the space race'.[47] In Britain a socialist transport minister could refer to motorways as 'the cathedrals of the modern age', just as the great railway stations had been regarded as the cathedrals of the nineteenth century.[48] Not everyone was enthralled. Mumford noted sourly in 1961,

The multiplication of motor vehicles capable of high speeds has in fact resulted in the progressive retarding of transportation and the piling up of costs. Horsedrawn vehicles in New York, according to a traffic study made in 1907, moved at an average of 11.5 miles an hour: today automobiles crawl at the average daytime rate of some six miles per hour; and as the density of building per acre increases in both business and residential areas, even this speed will slow down further.[49]

Road protests already began in the 1960s. The cultural theorist Fred Inglis described urban motorways as a symbol of 'intellectual tunnel vision', comparing their procedures to United States policy in Vietnam.[50] Echoing Mumford, another protestor described them as 'a consummate evil, the product of the "Divine Right of the Technological Imperative"'.[51] Road protests, the cultural historian Joe Moran argues, never managed to stop any particular development, but they did change the cultural mood. In the 1960s prime ministers turned out with champagne and a press corps to open a new stretch of motorway. Thirty years later it happened at night, without any fanfare, for fear of demonstrations. The triumphal slogan of twenty years ago, 'If you've got it, a lorry delivered it', has been quietly dropped.

Mass car ownership furthered the development of suburbia, which had already begun with the railways. The car, however, changed it. 'Instead of buildings set in a park, we now have buildings set in a parking lot... Unwin's salutary demonstration, Nothing Gained by Overcrowding, must now be countered with a qualifying admonition: "Something Lost by Overspacing".'[52] In changing settlement patterns, mass car ownership also contributed to the rise of a new form of social exclusion.[53] As

---

[46] The Situationist International, quoted in Moran, *On Roads*, p. 201.
[47] Moran, *On Roads*, p. 23.   [48] Barbara Castle, quoted in ibid., p. 45.   [49] Mumford, *City*, p. 626.
[50] Quoted in Moran, *On Roads*, p. 204.   [51] Quoted in ibid., p. 206.   [52] Mumford, *City*, p. 576.
[53] J. Hine, 'Transport and Social Justice', in R. Knowles, J. Shaw and I. Docherty (eds.), *Transport Geographies: Mobilities, Flows and Spaces* (Oxford: Wiley Blackwell, 2007), p. 49.

noted earlier, about one-third of the world's population are still pedestrian. For them the question of justice is not so much about access as about education or sanitation. But in developed countries the poor can be excluded from health facilities, local job markets and leisure activities by lack of car ownership.[54]

The bioregional proposals explored in Chapter 4 address this problem through re-localisation, envisaging a future where carbon-driven transport may well be restricted to the emergency services or at least to public transport. Assuming that oil remains relatively cheap and plentiful, or that a substitute for oil is found, one possible response to social exclusion is demand-responsive transport, used in rural areas for hospital visits and for group meetings, lunches, etc. Another is the service route, targeted at health centres, hospitals and shops. Such schemes have been implemented in Denmark, Finland, Norway, the Netherlands, Canada and the United States.[55] Trade-offs then have to be debated between economic, environmental and social sustainability. Policy makers have to decide whether to try and decrease social exclusion and enhance social justice or to promote a shift from car to bus, train, walking and cycling.[56]

ROADS AS METAPHOR

Roads are so central to human experience that in some cultures, including both the Greek and the Judaeo-Christian, they provide a key metaphor for understanding human existence. The Greek word *hodos*, like the English 'road', applies to sea routes as well as land, and Homer's Everyman, Odysseus, is fated to be a wanderer. The *Odyssey* is counterpoised between journey and place. Throughout his journeys Odysseus longs to come back home, but when he finally does so he has to tell Penelope that his fate involves more wandering. Although Odysseus' journeys are mainly at sea, land roads were also important for the Greeks. For them 'the way of the road builder was seen as dedicated to the gods and was sponsored and directed by priests. According to Greek belief the gods themselves first traced the alignment of roads and Delphi, the centre of the cult of Apollo,

---

[54] Hine (ibid.) points out that there is a high correlation between transport deprivation and factors such as low incomes, low levels of car ownership and public sector housing. People from households on low incomes in the United Kingdom make fewer journeys overall but about twice as many journeys on foot and three times as many journeys by bus as households in the top two income groups. There is lower car ownership among women and people of black and mixed ethnic origins. The disabled also have problems. In rural areas public transport schedules can make it difficult to keep a job.

[55] Ibid., p. 59.   [56] Ibid., p. 61.

was never thought of as his home but as the terminus and goal of all the ways he followed.'[57] Hermes was the god of roads and travellers and at the same time the god of the pastoral landscape, carrying a lamb on his shoulders.

He was the mediator between two worlds: the world of the living and the dead, the rural and the urban, public space and the secret space of home. Perhaps we could say he was the god of country roads – roads which shifted location but always led eventually to the temple and the agora; the centripetal roads which farmers and herders use to go to market. Hermes the god of mediation, the god of contracts and agreements, seems to symbolize the road as a mean, the way to a chosen end.[58]

Modern roads, very different from these, can be places of alienated solitariness, comments Joe Moran, 'But they are also about the inextinguishable desire for connecting with other human beings and sharing our experiences of the world.'[59]

In the biblical tradition it is Cain who becomes a wayfarer and a vagabond after the murder of his brother. Abraham is sent out from his homeland to a place he does not know and journeys down to the Negev. The second book of the Torah is called in the Septuagint *Ex-odos*, 'the way out', or 'the way from', and records forty years of wanderings in the desert. Already in this culture journeying is so fundamental that of the more than 560 uses of the word *derekh*, way, in the Hebrew Bible, about three-quarters are metaphorical. Humans must walk in God's ways; Israel persists in its stubborn ways; it must wait on the Lord and keep his ways. Second Isaiah promises that God will prepare a way for Israel to return, an imperial highway where cuttings are made through the hills and the rough places are macadamised. In the New Testament Jesus is depicted as constantly on the way, walking around Galilee with his disciples, and finally up to Jerusalem. According to Luke Christianity is first known as 'the Way', and John applies this description to Jesus. The narrative of Paul's experiences is given in terms of journeys, with a goal in Rome, or in Spain, which he probably never reached. Journeying, therefore, is used to characterise the very meaning of faith and the self-revelation of God. God journeys, accompanies God's people, calls them to dangerous but ultimately liberating journeys. Discipleship is itself journeying. If God is 'the Way', and not the end of the road then, as Gerry Hughes puts it, 'faith does not give final answers to questions but the courage to face them'.[60]

[57] Jackson *Discovering*, p. 21. [58] Ibid., p. 22. [59] Moran, *On Roads*, p. 259.
[60] Hughes, *In Search of a Way*, p. 152.

Given this background in the foundational texts it is hardly surprising that in medieval times pilgrimage becomes a metaphor for life. In the seventeenth century an itinerant pedlar, John Bunyan, makes the vicissitudes of seventeenth-century travel an illustration of the Christian life. Not Odysseus, the cunning macho hero, but the pilgrim becomes Everyman, journeying towards a goal which he or she reaches only in the next life. Note that this is not travel for travel's sake: this does not emerge until the nineteenth century. But life is understood teleologically. Whatever we do, even if it be only mending pots and pans, we move towards a goal. Today this teleology has been abandoned. What takes its place is the rationality of the market, where the ultimate source of value is choice between different providers.

We have produced a new kind of road and a new metaphor, a vast network of smooth, efficient highways leading to every conceivable destination. At the same time we have largely ceased to believe in one universally accepted religious goal, usually identified with Christianity and the notion of spiritual redemption and of an afterlife. Heaven is no longer our destination. A third interpretation is taking shape: a multitude of roads, each with its own destination, obliges us to choose, to make decisions of our own.[61]

This gives an existential dignity to choice as an end in itself. For Edwin Muir the great road becomes a metaphor for society's mistaken turning. Unable to go back we travel on, but as we do so

> These words rang in their ears as if they said
> 'There was another road you did not see'.[62]

PLACE AND FREEDOM

Jackson puts the question of whether the house, or the road leading to the house, came first. A theologian might argue, he suggests, that

if God had meant us to stay home, to be sedentary, to put down roots as farmers or husbands (a word which once signified house-dwellers), he would have first commanded us to build a house. But if he had intended us to be forever on the move – hunters or herders or pilgrims in search of an elusive goal – he would have ordered us to beat a path, to make a road and follow it.[63]

---

[61] Jackson, *Sense of Place*, p. 204.
[62] E. Muir, 'The Road', in *Collected Poems* (London: Faber, 1960), p. 163.
[63] Jackson, *Sense of Place*, p. 189.

The choice, he thinks, is between a sense of place and a sense of freedom. Certainly human history can be charted between the ellipse of rootedness and movement, and this continues today in the tension between global travel on the one hand and the struggle to recover an authentic sense of place on the other, between the celebration of local vernaculars and a world awash with refugees.

Jackson's question as to the priority of road or house is surely answered in evolutionary terms in terms of the road, because hunting and gathering support only around ten people per acre, and even with very small populations there is a constant need to move on. Only with the agricultural revolution and the growth of cities did place become more central. When Cain is banished after the murder of Abel he loses 'the place ... which ... provided the means for life to be lived, for nourishment, prosperity, security, protection'.[64] His lament shows that he already takes settlement, or place, for granted. The promise of the land, and of 'rest' in the Hebrew Bible, is a recognition of the goods of place, the flourishing of particular cultures, vernaculars, cuisines, languages. After entry into the promised land it seems as if rest is attained, but it proves elusive. Israel's actual experience is of being 'harried among the nations, from one end of the earth to the other' (Dt. 28.64). Human beings as political animals, comments Jackson, are 'always inclined to be footloose, inclined to leave family and home for a more stimulating spot', but though this is true for Abraham the Deuteronomic perspective is that loss of place, the need to wander, is a curse, not a blessing.[65]

The priority of freedom has been anciently celebrated by some nomadic cultures, such as that of the Roma, but at the cost of constant hostility from settled populations. The romance of travel celebrated since the Enlightenment, 'the joy of the open road', is possible only for those with a secure background, a passport, an embassy which will come to their aid if they are in difficulties. Robert Louis Stevenson represents the new kind of traveller. *Travels with a Donkey* is the record only of a twelve-day holiday, and it is in the course of that modest journey that he remarks, 'For my part, I travel not to go anywhere, but to go. I travel for travel's sake. The great affair is to move; to feel the needs and hitches of our life more nearly; to come down off this feather-bed of civilisation, and find the globe granite underfoot and strewn with cutting flints.'[66]

---

[64] C. Westermann, *Genesis 1–11* (London: SPCK, 1984), p. 310.　　[65] Jackson, *Discovering*, p. 27.
[66] R. L. Stevenson, *Travels with a Donkey in the Cevennes* (London: Nelson, 1950), p. 57 (the section on Cheylard and Luc).

It is he, too, who tells us that it is better to travel hopefully than to arrive. Stevenson writes as a Bohemian, like his contemporary Gauguin, who also ends up in the South Seas. Travel ceases to be a metaphor for life but is subsumed under the search for new pleasures, new sensations to titivate jaded palates. Thomas Cook's invention of the holiday excursion had at first been to aid the ancient goal of pilgrimage, but it soon became recreation – a real liberation against the background of a six-day week and long hours, increasingly meaningless against the background of rising affluence. Freedom becomes market freedom, so-called freedom of choice, the choice of Spain, Italy or perhaps north Africa for my holidays. If necessary I can now pay extra to feel the 'needs and hitches of our life' by opting for an 'adventure holiday', but I will certainly be insured to the hilt. Of course, such travel is a justice issue, for it can be enjoyed only by a minority and is indeed parasitic on the labour, and perhaps even the poverty, of the majority.

The vivid characters of medieval wayfaring life have their modern representatives: truckers, salesmen, seamen, air crew, railwaymen, migrants of all kinds, refugees. The tourist replaces the pilgrim. For the Western traveller the great change is speed: the travel lodge replaces the inn; the motorway service station the wayside hostel. Speed means that the endless storytelling of the old journeys is lost, except, perhaps, for the migrants and refugees for whom travel remains dangerous and slow. They now have a new destination, unknown in the Middle Ages: the detention camp.

TRANSPORT AND THE ENVIRONMENT

The building of roads and the channelling of water have, at least since Roman times, produced monuments of great beauty. With the exception of a few medieval bridges this was little added to between the Roman period and the eighteenth century. Then the forty-year boom in canal building brought stretches of water where there were none, with consequent changes in bird and plant life and also aqueducts, cuttings, embankments and tunnels, locks, lifts and bridges.[67] Thomas Pennant observed in 1782 that the Grand Junction Canal between the Trent and the Mersey had improved both housing and pasture: 'the cottage, instead of being half covered with miserable thatch, is now covered with a substantial covering of tiles or slates, brought from the distant hills of Wales or Cumberland. The fields, which before were barren, are now drained, and by the assistance of manure,

[67] Hoskins, *Making*, p. 247.

conveyed on the canal toll-free, are clothed with a beautiful verdure.'[68] In 1932 J. Pearman devoted three large volumes to the subject of 'Railways and Scenery', minutely detailed journeys of what he could see from the window of trains throughout the world, when he was not looking at his stopwatch to see how many minutes a particular stretch of line had taken, and how far behind schedule the train was.[69]

Ruskin complained of 'your railroad mounds, vaster than the walls of Babylon', but as Christian Barman points out, 'the people who made these broad and dignified new roads were conscious both of their architectural opportunity and their architectural obligations'. Euston arch, in his view, 'gave to London a new dignity and a new sense of magnitude it had never known until then'.[70] Contemptuous of such dignity, the modernisers of the 1960s took it down and dumped it in a canal, whence it has only recently been retrieved. Hoskins was almost moved to poetry:

The great gashes they inflicted on the landscape in their cuttings and embankments healed over and wild flowers grew abundantly once more ... one can enjoy the pleasure of trundling through Rutland in a stopping train on a fine summer morning: the barley fields shaking in the wind, the slow sedgy streams with their willows shading meditative cattle, the elegant limestone spires across the meadows, the early Victorian stations built of the sheep grey Ketton stone and still unaltered, the warm brown roofs of the villages half buried in the trees, and the summer light flashing everywhere. True that the railways did not invent much of this beauty, but they gave us new vistas of it.[71]

Ironically this was written just eight years before Beeching, the elimination of the 'stopping train' and the dereliction of much fine railway architecture.[72]

Hoskins did not extend his support to the new roads: 'Great by-pass roads ... now plunge straight across the country, regardless of contours, using cuttings and embankments to keep as even a gradient as possible. They are entirely without beauty. Is there anything uglier in the whole landscape than an arterial by-pass road, except an airfield? Old Roads have been straightened, and have lost all their character, historic and otherwise.'[73] Perhaps a later historian will celebrate these roads; but a major difference

---

[68] Quoted in ibid., p. 254.   [69] J. Pearman, *Railways and Scenery*, 3 vols. (London: Cassell, 1932).
[70] Barman, *Early British Railways*, p. 32.   [71] Hoskins, *Making*, p. 265.
[72] On the negative side Hoskins lamented the way in which the railways eliminated vernacular styles. 'All regional styles and all local materials were exterminated except where the well-to-do could afford to build deliberately in the old manner, with the aid of an architect. What had been the living style of a whole region, modified to suit all classes of people, became a piece of pleasant antiquarianism for a rich man.' Ibid., p. 269.
[73] Ibid., p. 247.

from earlier roads is, of course, the fact that to pay attention to the view is to invite an accident.

When Henry Ford began production of the Model T he envisaged it as a boon to ordinary people so that 'no man making a good salary will be unable to own one – and enjoy with his family the blessing of hours of pleasure in God's great open spaces'.[74] It was a dream which has struck a chord with countless millions, offering freedom to go anywhere when one wants, without consulting timetables, queuing, waiting for delayed trains or buses and sharing sometimes very crowded or uncomfortable coaches. Unfortunately it has costs of which Ford was unaware. The World Health Organisation estimates that about 250,000 people die every year on the world's roads, more than half of these fatalities being pedestrians and cyclists. About 50,000 Americans die every year in road accidents, a total equal to the number of Americans killed in the Vietnam War.[75] It estimates that road accidents will be the third most common cause of death by 2020.[76] Buses, coaches and trains in Britain are seven times safer than cars in terms of passenger fatalities per kilometre.

Transport analysts speak of first- and second-order effects of travel. First-order effects include accidents, pollution, global warming, noise from vehicles and land take by roads, airports and railways as well as the extraction of materials to manufacture vehicles and the waste products when they are scrapped. Second-order impacts relate to how societies and economies create and adapt to increasingly transport-intensive lifestyles. These include effects such as suburbanisation, out-of-town shopping and even obesity. The negative effects of travel are often unrecognised. Thus air pollution from traffic causes more deaths than road accidents. Air pollution in cities may be responsible for as many as a quarter of all deaths of children under five world-wide.[77] Traffic noise has been shown to seriously affect moods, learning and work-place performance and contributes to raised blood pressure, minor psychiatric illnesses and other stress-related illness.[78]

Another form of damage to the environment from the priority we give to transport is that it involves very high land take. Cars need parking space, in Britain 24 square metres per car. A block of 10,000 parking spaces, as provided at the Merry Hill shopping centre in Dudley, England, uses 36 hectares of land, which could provide 648 housing units.[79] As more and

[74] H. Ford, *My Life and Work* (London: Heinemann, 1924), p. 73.   [75] Smith *et al.*, *Greening*, p. 127.
[76] Davis, *Planet*, p. 133.   [77] Haughton and Hunter, *Sustainable Cities*, p. 135.
[78] S. Potter and I. Bailey, 'Transport and Environment', in Knowles, Shaw and Docherty (eds.), *Transport Geographies*, p. 33.
[79] Smith *et al.*, *Greening*, p. 106.

more heavy goods traffic is put on the roads, so the implications for land take expand. An area the size of Leicestershire is now taken up by roads in the United Kingdom, with an additional fifth given over to parking, but 'Asphalt is the land's last crop'.[80]

Roads designed to take 38 tonne, 15 metre long lorries need more space for their junctions and curves than do roads designed for cars or smaller lorries . . . Increases in lorry weight require more substantial structures and road pavements which in their turn demand more of the raw materials of construction . . . a lorry requires 0.007 square metres of space per tonne kilometre in comparison to rail which needs 0.0025 square metres. The lorry, therefore, requires almost three times as much space to do the same work as the train.[81]

Ford's dream of escape to the great open spaces has resulted in a vicious circle where traffic makes more and more places unliveable, resulting in the use of still more traffic to escape from them.[82] The pleasures of travel, and of exploring new places and different situations; the ease with which one can visit friends and family compared with the situation only a generation ago; and the privilege of a fresh and varied diet all year round, which all previous generations could only have dreamed of: all have to be set against the cost to future generations. Transport as we now have it poses major questions of inter- and intra-generational equity.

Currently transport accounts for over 30 per cent of all energy use and is predicted to be the largest contributor to the growth of carbon dioxide emissions in the twenty-first century.[83] Roads 'kill the earth twice – eating up vast amounts of energy to produce and lay the asphalt, and then choking the atmosphere with the carbon from car exhausts'.[84] Because they are impermeable, water run-off is also a problem when it rains, taking pollutants from vehicles.[85] Three-quarters of Britain's carbon dioxide emissions come from road transport. A single tank of petrol produces between 120 and 180 kg of carbon dioxide, and motor vehicle traffic is responsible for about 15 per cent of the world's carbon dioxide output. John Adams talks of 'Carmageddon', by which he means that the human scale of settlements is everywhere threatened by the growth of car dependence, and public transport is on the retreat.[86] In Britain both out-of-town shopping centres and large hospitals developed in the last twenty years have seen a shift away from

[80] Landry, *Art of City-Making*, p. 87.   [81] Smith *et al.*, *Greening*, p. 102.
[82] S. Crowe, *The Landscape of Roads* (London: Architectural Press, 1960), p. 27.
[83] Potter and Bailey, 'Transport and Environment', p. 29.   [84] Moran, *On Roads*, p. 238.
[85] Vale and Vale, *Time to Eat*, p. 113.
[86] J. Adams, 'Carmageddon', in A. Barnett and R. Scruton (eds.), *Town and Country* (London: Jonathan Cape, 1998), pp. 217–32.

locations accessible by bus or on foot towards car-based locations.[87] Sub-urban, urban fringe and rural developments are car- and lorry-dependent, and are therefore antithetical to energy efficiency. Fifty years ago in Britain passenger mileage by bus was twice that of the car; now mileage by car is fourteen times that of the bus.[88] A double-decker bus carries the same number of people as twenty fully laden cars and takes up to a seventh of the road space of the equivalent number of cars, but over the past twenty years the overall cost of motoring has in real terms remained at or below the 1980 level while bus fares have risen by 31 per cent and rail fares by 37 per cent.[89] The shift of freight from rail to road transport is part of the trend to unsustainability. Lorry and air freight are hugely inefficient ways of transporting goods. The land take of a double railway line is metres, compared with 47 metres for a three-lane motorway. A typical freight train can move over 1,000 tonnes of product, equivalent to the capacity of fifty heavy goods vehicles, and moving a tonne of freight by rail produces 80 per cent less carbon dioxide than moving it by road.[90] The Vales recommend increasing use of the passenger cargo ship, a relatively efficient means of transport.[91]

In the West we have constructed a society dependent on the long-distance transport of food. Supermarkets are full of fruit, flowers and vegetables flown in from Latin America, Asia and Africa, all of which contribute to the ecological footprint of the communities who buy them. In a famous piece of research Stephanie Böge, in 1993, established that one pot of strawberry yoghurt involved 8,000 km of transportation, and the distances covered by more exotic foods would be far greater, often involving air travel, which poses a serious threat to the ozone layer.[92] It is aviation, in particular, which 'symbolizes the global rush towards non-sustainability cloaked in a rhetoric of green concerns'.[93]

'Future generations', wrote Mumford, 'will perhaps wonder at our will-ingness, indeed our eagerness, to sacrifice the education of our children, the care of the ill and aged, the development of the arts, to say nothing of ready access to nature, for the lop-sided system of mono-transportation,

---

[87] Smith, Whiteleg and Williams, *Greening*, p. 95.

[88] M. Hillman, 'In Favour of the Compact City', in Jenks, Burton and Williams (eds.), *Compact City*, p. 36.

[89] Landry, *Art of City-Making*, p. 86   [90] Ibid., p. 25.

[91] Container ships use 0.12 megajoules per tonne-km, lorries 2.80 and aeroplanes 9.70. Vale and Vale, *Time to Eat*, p. 43.

[92] E. von Weizsacker, A. Lovins and L. Lovins, *Factor Four* (London: Earthscan, 1996), p. 117.

[93] Smith, Whiteleg and Williams, *Greening*, p. 28. The carbon dioxide released by aircraft at altitude has a global warming effect 2.7 times higher than that of ground-level emissions.

going through low density areas at sixty miles an hour, but reduced in high density areas to a bare six':

But our descendants will perhaps understand our curious willingness to expend billions of dollars to shoot a sacrificial victim into planetary orbit, if they realize that our cities are being destroyed for the same superstitious religious ritual: the worship of speed and empty space. Lacking sufficient municipal budgets to deal adequately with all of life's requirements that can be concentrated in the city, we have settled for a single function, transportation, or rather for a single part of an adequate transportation system, locomotion by private motor car.[94]

Roads, which are vital to the structure of life, which play a key part in the economy of redemption, themselves need redeeming. Structures of grace become structures of sin. Instantiations of the common good become part of the 'common bad', contributing significantly to the global emergency. The centrifugal roads, in particular, become cancerous: as they grow they produce more traffic, take more land, need widening, choke the feeder roads and so on. In making car-dominated societies possible they also contribute to the growth of obesity, and to that situation where, as currently in the United States, under 3 per cent of all trips are made by walking. In continental Europe figures still range from 35 to 45 per cent.[95] More roads get us nowhere. The ellipse of journey and place has shaped human history, but unless we can learn to journey more lightly humankind will destroy its habitat. Technology alone is not the answer. What is needed is a swing of the pendulum towards place rather than journeying, and the growth of an ethic of responsibility and of limits as regards travel. 'If development means a car for every Chinese, then sustainability is no longer possible', Daly and Cobb noted thirty years ago.[96] The same could be said of the growth of air travel. But that day has come, and so far there is no sign that the consequences are heeded. As with the city and as with farming, recovering a sense of our proper limits is an aspect of grace without which we will simply not survive. We need to learn to dwell rather than to be footloose. With that in mind I turn to the question of housing.

[94] Mumford, *City*, p. 580.   [95] Landry, *Art of City-Making*, p. 319.
[96] Daly and Cobb, *Common Good*, p. 76.

CHAPTER 10

Housing by people

Liberation theology has both a critical and a constructive dimension. The passion of liberation theology is the indignation at injustice, the inhuman ways of living visited on some by others in the name of class, race or gender. In Scripture we find this indignation clearly related to housing (Amos 5.11–12; Jer. 22.13–16), and the contemporary world gives cause for such indignation as never before. At the same time I shall argue that we also find clear imperatives for the constructive side, the creation of a world not only of justice and peace, but of beauty.

GRACE AND THE COMMON GOOD IN HOUSING

Over the centuries the church has had little to say about housing. It provided palaces for its bishops, which would have incurred the wrath of Church Fathers like John Chrysostom, not to mention prophets like Amos, but ordinary housing never seemed to be an ethical issue.[1] Perhaps the ideology of hierarchy – the rich man in his castle, the poor man at his gate – made the difference between the hovels of the poor and the mansions of the rich seem inevitable, though the historical record makes that doubtful.[2] Today those theological assumptions are no longer tenable. In terms of my theological scheme I understand the issue of housing to fall

---

[1] John Chrysostom wrote, 'Let us . . . adorn not our houses, but our souls in preference to the house. For is it not disgraceful to clothe our walls with marble, vainly and to no end, and to neglect Christ going about naked? . . . Do you wish to build large and splendid houses? I forbid it not; but let it be not upon the earth. Build yourself tabernacles in heaven, and such that you may be able to receive others; tabernacles which never fall to pieces.' 'Second Homily on the Statues', in P. Schaff (ed.), *Nicene and Post-Nicene Fathers*, vol. IX (Grand Rapids: Eerdmans, 1983), p. 349. Chrysostom could appeal to 1 Sam. 7, which insists that YHWH has 'no house', to Amos 5.11, a critique of luxury housing built on oppression, and to the evangelical teaching that the Son of Man has nowhere to lay his head (Mt. 8.20) and to the warning not to lay up treasures on earth (Mt. 6.19).

[2] There were peasant revolts protesting the injustice of class division from the twelfth century onwards. Some leaders, like the priest John Ball in 1381, appealed to an understanding of human equality based on the creation narrative.

under the appropriation of God the Reconciler, because issues of community and justice are primary, but as we shall see, issues of empowerment, of vision and hope, which I understand under the appropriation of God the Redeemer, are equally important.

In thinking theologically about housing I want to begin at an unlikely place, the famous text of Matthew 16.18, 'You are Peter, and on this rock I will build my church.' Through the twentieth century this was regarded as probably a late interpolation, designed to bolster the Petrine primacy, but Ulrich Duchrow points out that such a reading ignores the likely Aramaic that Jesus would have used.[3] The word 'church' translates Greek 'ecclesia', which in turn translates *quahal*. The *quahal YHWH* was the meeting of the tribes of Israel to discuss policy, to work out what they ought to do. The word 'ecclesia' was presumably chosen to translate it because it was the word for the free assembly of Athens, which met for precisely the same purpose. What did Jesus understand his task to be? How did he envisage his mission? The symbolism of 'twelve' gives us a clue. In calling twelve disciples he reconstitutes the 'people of God', Israel. Along with the prophets he is asking what the point of Israel is, what its purpose might be. In the prayer he teaches his disciples it is clear that it is the realisation of the divine will, the situation where the reign of God, as envisaged by Deuteronomy, Leviticus and all the rest, is realised on earth 'as in heaven'. That will, we have seen already, is life in all its fullness. What would that mean for housing? John Ruskin was perhaps not far out when he spoke of the Christian God as a household God as well as a heavenly one. 'He has an altar in every man's dwelling; let men look to it when they rend it lightly and pour out its ashes.'[4]

For Paul bodies are 'temples of the Spirit' (1 Cor. 6.19). This includes the bodies of the one billion people who live in slums, as well as everybody else. We have to ask, how do we care for bodies? This is not simply a medical question or a question of sexual ethics but the question, how do we house them? What kind of house accords with human dignity? How do we house seven or nine billion people? The United Nations Habitat agenda has five goals: that there should be adequate shelter for all; that settlements should be sustainable; that dwellers should participate in decisions relating to housing; that there should be adequate finance for this; and that gender perspectives should be taken into account.[5] Even in the rich world we are very far from fulfilling any of these requirements, and they are also a rather

---

[3] In private conversation.   [4] Ruskin, *Seven Lamps*, p. 181.
[5] UN Habitat, *Challenge of Slums*, p. 138.

thin realisation of the beauty and justice which we saw to be key aspects of grace. Is there a common good in housing, or is it each person for himself or herself? What would the common good look like?

In attempting to develop a theological ethic of housing I shall begin by considering what the United Nations calls 'the challenge of slums'. I shall then turn to the idea of the vernacular, to empowerment and to co-operation, before turning to the question of gracious building.

SLUMS AND THE NEW WORLD ORDER

'Slum, semi-slum and super slum, to this has come the Evolution of Cities', wrote Patrick Geddes in 1915.[6] Geddes was one of many who looked forward to an escape from Kipling's 'City of Dreadful Night' through the building of garden cities. Others looked to the Radiant City envisaged by Le Corbusier, but nearly a century later one of our foremost urban commentators notes that 'The cities of the future, rather than being made out of glass and steel . . . are instead largely constructed out of crude brick, straw, recycled plastic, cement blocks and scrap wood. Instead of cities of light soaring toward heaven, much of the twenty-first-century urban world squats in squalor, surrounded by pollution, excrement and decay.'[7] One-sixth of the world's population, 1 billion people, currently live in slums, and the number grows by 20 million per year. One of the fastest areas of growth is in the former Soviet Union, where those living in poverty shot up from 14 million to 168 million in the early 1990s, 'an almost instantaneous mass pauperization without precedent in history'. Sofia, the capital of Bulgaria, has Europe's largest slum, mostly populated by Roma.[8]

The 2003 United Nations report *The Challenge of Slums* draws on the distinction between 'slums of hope' and 'slums of despair'.[9] The authors point out that in the developing world slums are the dwelling place of much of the labour force, are interesting communities in their own right and are melting pots for different racial groups and cultures. 'Many of the most important movements in music, dance and politics have their origin in the slums. Many people who are not so poor also live in slums.'[10] Landry instances the Katha organisation in Delhi, which 'works to turn the slums into the gold mines they are' and seeks to empower slum dwellers

[6] P. Geddes, *Cities in Evolution: An Introduction to the Town Planning Movement and to the Study of Civics* (London: Williams & Norgate, 1915), p. 74.
[7] Davis, *Planet*, p. 19.   [8] Ibid., pp. 66–7.
[9] Drawing on P. C. Lloyd, *Slums of Hope* (Harmondsworth: Penguin, 1979).
[10] UN Habitat, *Challenge of Slums*, p. xxxi.

with a commitment to nine 'Cs': Curiosity, Creativity, Critical Thinking, Competence, Confidence, Concentration, Concern, Cooperation, and Citizenship.[11] However, Gita Verma is much more sceptical of attempts at empowerment, and the United Nations report notes the ease with which slums of hope turn into slums of despair. *The Challenge of Slums* notes that the sixth of humanity living in slums face the greatest dangers from transport, pollution, earth movement, garbage dumps, fires and floods.[12] It is the pedestrian poor – more than one million a year – who are disproportionately the victims of traffic accidents. Dangerous industries, like the Union Carbide plant in Bhopal in India, are situated near slums. 'Almost every large Third World City . . . has a Dantesque district of slums shrouded in pollution and located next to pipelines, chemical plants, and refineries.'[13] The slums are built on marginal land, often unstable and at risk of earthquake, so that geographers talk of 'classquakes' because it is the urban poor who generally suffer from these events.[14] Similarly floods largely impact the poor. Those in power speak of them as 'acts of God' but in fact they are a direct result of land ownership patterns and wealth differentials.[15] Slums are extremely vulnerable to fire because of their density and the inflammable nature of the materials used in them, but many fires are started deliberately as a form of slum clearance.

These dangers are only the tip of the iceberg, however. This sixth of humanity have to live with minimum water and for the most part without sanitation. The global sanitation crisis, says Davis, defies hyperbole. 'Today's megacities are stinking mountains of shit that would appal even the most hardened Victorians . . . Constant intimacy with other people's waste . . . is one of the most profound of social divides.'[16] One of the great achievements of neo-liberalism, he says, with savage irony, has been to turn public toilets into cash points for paying off foreign debts: pay toilets are a growth industry throughout Third World slums.[17] The privatisation of

---

[11] Landry, *Art of City-Making*, p. 109.   [12] UN Habitat, *Challenge of Slums*, p. 69.

[13] Davis, *Planet*, p. 129.

[14] Thus in the 1978 earthquake in Guatemala City 'nearly all of some 59,000 destroyed homes were in urban slums built on ravines, above and below steep, unstable bluffs, or on poorly consolidated young fluvio-volcanic sediments. Losses to the rest of the city, and among more expensive homes, were negligible, since they occupied much more stable sites.' Kenneth Hewitt, 'Regions of Risk', pp. 217–18, quoted in Davis, *Planet*, p. 126.

[15] When floods caused 900 deaths in slums in Algiers the president put it down to 'an act of God'. 'Locals knew that this was nonsense. As civil engineers immediately pointed out, the hillside dwellings were a disaster waiting to happen: "These were weak structures vulnerable to heavy rain. Across the country, these kinds of housing constructions have suffered much damage from rain because of degradation, inadequate repair, aging and neglect".' Davis, *Planet*, p. 125.

[16] Ibid., p. 138. In 1990, 480,000 people in Delhi had only 160 toilet seats and 110 mobile toilet vans.

[17] Ibid., p. 141.

water has had a particularly crushing effect. One slum in Nairobi pays for a litre of water up to five times the price paid by the average United States citizen. In Dhaka and Chittagong around one-third of the population are thought to be ill at any one time.[18]

Slum dwellers live under the constant threat of eviction and resettlement. In Shanghai alone more than 1.5 million people were moved between 1991 and 1997 in order to make way for skyscrapers, luxury apartments, malls and new infrastructure.[19]

Healthcare in the slums has everywhere deteriorated in the wake of neo-liberal 'restructuring'. 'Everywhere obedience to international creditors has dictated cutbacks in medical care, the emigration of doctors and nurses, the end of food subsidies, and the switch of agricultural production from subsistence to export crops.'[20] In Kinshasa the population refer to basic public services as 'memories'. Structural Adjustment Programmes, Davis remarks, 'cynically exploit the belief that women's labour power is almost infinitely elastic in the face of household survival needs. This is the guilty secret variable in most neoclassical equations of economic adjustment: poor women and their children are expected to lift the weight of Third World debt upon their shoulders.'[21] Peri-urban poverty, he goes on, a grim human world largely cut off from the subsistence solidarities of life of the traditional city, is the radical new face of inequality.[22] With no possibility of employment and no social security these people are simply redundant, as Malthus declared them to be at the beginning of the nineteenth century. In his chilling phrase, there is no place for them at the world's table. In some slums people turn to selling their kidneys to raise money to survive. In others they turn to gambling and, when this fails, to charismatic religion. In Kinshasa belief in child witches has taken hold. The children, who internalise the accusation and believe they are guilty of causing harm, are cast out or murdered. The charismatic churches, says Davis, have been deeply complicit in promoting and legitimising fears about such children. 'The child witches of Kinshasa, like the organ-exporting slums of India and Egypt, seem to take us to an existential ground zero beyond which there are only death camps, famine and Kurtzian horror.'[23]

Violence permeates the lives of the very poor. In Colombia, street urchins who vandalise the property of the wealthy are killed by death squads. At the same time, children run around killing each other with homemade shotguns and grenades. A World Bank study, *Voices of the Poor*, found that

---

[18] Ibid., p. 147.   [19] Ibid., p. 107.   [20] Ibid., p. 148.   [21] Ibid., p. 158.
[22] Ibid., p. 201.   [23] Ibid., p. 198.

crime, violence and insecurity are the primary concerns of low-income populations. Throughout Latin America a Hobbesian social order has emerged, 'where the principal concern of those inhabiting them is material survival, and only the strongest and fittest can attempt to establish means of enrichment that go beyond mere subsistence, for example through violent economic practices such as drug trafficking'.[24]

It is no longer the culture of poverty which prevails; it is the culture of violence, of hostility, of disintegration, of despoliation, the life expectancy of being a second-class citizen. It is the living and the pursuit of livelihood in enclaves of insecurity and violence. It is the emergence of a new kind of proletarian class, belonging to their own segregated territories, not immediately revolutionary because they are intent on survival, on making a decent or maybe indecent living, on coping with precariousness and despair, with violence and fear . . . The long-term absence of legitimate authority is a multiplier that transforms governance into a variety of other voids: a segmented or fragmented labour market, a standard career of income instability, a disintegration of social protective networks associated with decency and human security.[25]

For Gita Verma, writing from New Delhi, slums are the result primarily of unjust land distribution. She is scathing about the 'slum upgrading' which is the orthodoxy championed by *The Challenge of Slums*. The right to stay in slums, she says, is tantamount to confinement. Urban slumming is not about poverty to be fought with virtuous charity and kindness but about injustice to be fought with vicious intolerance.[26] We need, she says, a different view of the common good, and she pleads for restoring rights, responsibilities and sanity in development systems 'that seem to be hurtling at breakneck speed towards complete anarchy'.[27] Whatever their creed it is impossible not to hear Davis and Verma as speaking in the accents, and with the convictions, of the Hebrew prophets. What motivates them is a concern for human dignity, arguably exactly the same concern which underlies Amos' condemnation of cruelty and injustice and certainly analogous with it. Liberation theology has taken both from the prophets and from Torah the notion of God's solidarity with the poor. As noted in Chapter 2, the idea of the common good in situations of injustice involves struggle for a different, and egalitarian, social order so that, in the words of Deuteronomy, 'there shall be no poor among you' (Dt. 15.4).

[24] D. Rogers, 'Managua', in K. Koonings and D. Kruijt (eds.), *Fractured Cities: Social Exclusion, Urban Violence and Contested Spaces in Latin America* (London: Zed, 2007), p. 83.

[25] Epilogue by the editors in Koonings and Kruijt (eds.), *Fractured Cities*, pp. 138–9.

[26] G. Verma, *Slumming India: A Chronicle of Slums and their Saviours* (New Delhi: Penguin India, 2002), p. xxiii.

[27] Ibid., pp. 149–50.

The poverty and violence of the slums have, of course, a mirror image. Gated communities are the 'most significant development in recent urban planning and design' in China.[28] What Tunde Agbola calls the 'architecture of fear' in relation to the fortified lifestyles of the rich in Lagos reaches a global extreme in large urban societies with the greatest socioeconomic inequalities: South Africa, Brazil, Venezuela and the United States.[29] Conspicuous consumption by the rich 'reached hallucinatory levels in Latin America and Africa during the 1980s as the *nouveaux riches* went on spending sprees in Miami and Paris whilst their shantytown compatriots starved'.[30] Naturally this provokes unrest, and global turmoil can be mapped to cities and regions that experienced the sharpest increases in inequality.[31] Observing this, and planning for the 'New American Century', the Pentagon thinks in terms of a low-intensity world war of unlimited duration against criminalised segments of the urban poor. This, says Davis, is the true 'clash of civilizations'.[32]

ADDRESSING THE CHALLENGE OF SLUMS

Before the neo-liberal turn the English architect John Turner, an enthusiast for the work of Patrick Geddes, had worked in the Peruvian slums between 1957 and 1965. At that time slums were built on marginal land which had not been claimed. He argued that the way to deal with them was not to go for expensive schemes of state housing but to support people in building for themselves. 'Housing', he said, was a verb. 'Questions about the consequences of housing in people's lives can only be asked in words that describe processes and relationships.'[33] He wanted to get away from the obsession with the number of housing units and insisted that the key question was what housing does in people's lives. 'When dwellers control the major decisions and are free to make their own contributions to the design, construction and management of their own housing', he and his fellow contributors wrote, 'both the process and the environment produced stimulate individual and social well being. When people have no control nor responsibility for key decisions in the housing process dwelling environments may instead become a barrier to personal fulfilment and a burden on the economy.'[34] He argued that only local people and

---

[28] Davis, *Planet*, p. 115. [29] Ibid., p. 116. [30] Ibid., p. 157. [31] Ibid., p. 165. [32] Ibid., p. 205.
[33] J. F. C. Turner, *Housing by People: Towards Autonomy in Building Environments* (London: Marion Boyars, 1976), p. 62.
[34] J. F. C. Turner and R. Fichter (eds.), *Freedom to Build: Dweller Control of the Housing Process* (London: Macmillan, 1972), p. 241.

organisations could provide the necessary variety in housing and the great range of production techniques needed to build it.[35]

Turner was a friend of Ivan Illich, who argued that the professionalisation of knowledge makes people dependent on having their knowledge produced for them and leads to a paralysis of the moral and political imagination.[36] Creativity is supposed to be for the gifted few, and the rest of us are compelled to live in environments constructed by them. Building upon this lie, says Simon Nicholson,

> the dominant cultural elite tell us that the planning, design and building of any part of the environment is so difficult and so special that only . . . those with degrees and certificates in planning, engineering, architecture, art, education, behavioural psychology and so on – can properly solve environmental problems. The result is that the vast majority of people are not allowed (and – worse – feel that they are incompetent) to experiment with the components of building.

The majority of the community have been deprived of a crucial part of their lives and lifestyle.[37] Alice Coleman alleged that the utopia of mass housing was 'essentially a device for treating people like children, first by denying them the right to choose their own kind of housing, and then by choosing for them disastrous designs that create a needless sense of social failure'.[38]

Turner's thesis was founded on secure philosophical and political premises but it was co-opted by the World Bank. 'By demonstrating the ability, the courage and the capacity for self help of slum people the way was prepared for a withdrawal of state and local government and support.'[39] Mike Davis accuses Turner of romanticising the poor and of playing into the hands of the neo-liberal agenda. 'Throughout the Third World . . . the (John) Turnerian frontier of free land for poor squatters has ended: the "slums of hope" have been replaced by urban latifundia and crony capitalism.'[40] He shows that the upper and middle classes have seen an opportunity for profit in the slums and now own most of the land, making huge profits out of rents. Ninety-one people, for example, control the majority of all vacant land in Mumbai. More than half of the

---

[35] Turner, *Housing*, p. 83.
[36] Cited in C. Ward, *Talking Houses* (London: Freedom Press 1990), p. 20.
[37] Cited in Ibid., p. 23.   [38] Coleman, *Utopia on Trial*, p. 184.   [39] Ibid., p. 72.
[40] Ibid., p. 92. Davis draws on Seabrook, who writes, 'To emphasize the ability of people to do things for themselves, to become proactive in achieving levels of health care, reconstruction, organization, may create an impression that everything is really best left to the people themselves, without resources from outside. In this way the stress on the positive elements of popular mobilization can in reality serve the purpose of aggravating the position of the poor.' *In the Cities of the South*, p. 196.

dwellings in one Nairobi slum are owned by politicians and civil servants, and the shacks are the most profitable housing in the city.[41] In the slums 'Petty landlordship and subletting are major wealth strategies of the poor', and landlordism is a fundamental and divisive social relation in slum life world-wide.[42]

The Challenge of Slums recognises that no improvement in slums can be made if there is no employment and that therefore the fundamental questions are economic and political. When a million Irish starved in Ireland during the potato famine the British government called a general fast of repentance afterwards. This did not bring back the dead, but it recognised that blind adherence to the Corn Laws was wicked. The child witches of Kinshasa, the selling of organs in Chennai, the millions of people living without hope, are the result of a truly diabolical economic doctrine which has enriched a few and brought death and despair to a sixth of humanity. While nations are still required to spend the whole of, or huge amounts of, their GDP financing the interest on International Monetary Fund debts there can be no hope for the slums. There is now an even more ghoulish development, 'vulture capitalism', where investment corporations buy up Third World debt and then enforce it through the courts. Currently at least twelve of the world's most indebted countries have been ordered by courts to pay money to a handful of obscenely rich people. Quite clearly, hope for the slums can begin only with a new economic order. In turn that might lay the ground for a politics of hope.

A favoured strategy for slum improvement in the past decade has been the proposal of Herman de Soto that slum dwellers should be given entitlements, so that they immediately become property owners and have some capital. De Soto's bootstrap model of development is especially popular, Davis comments, because of the simplicity of his recipe: get the state out of the way, add microcredit and land titling for squatters, then let markets take their course to turn poverty into capital.[43] It rests, however, he argues, on a whole series of fallacies. In the first place de Soto's microentrepreneurs are usually displaced public sector professionals or laid-off skilled workers. But these are only 10 per cent of the economically urban population and not the truly poor. In addition, most participants of the informal economy work

---

[41] Davis, *Planet*, p. 87.

[42] Ibid., p. 42. Davis seems to imply that Turner was complicit with the World Bank. In fact, even in 1973 he answered the questions about romanticising slum living, and of course recognised that justice was central. He continued to insist, however, that control and decision making were the key issues. *Housing*, p. 128.

[43] Davis, *Planet*, p. 179.

for someone else, and not for themselves. Petty exploitation turns out to be the essence of informal employment. Informality, in turn, ensures extreme abuse of women and children. We are talking not about shared poverty but about a situation in which women and children bear the brunt. Moreover, the informal economy generates work not by elaborating new divisions of labour but by fragmenting existing work and thus subdividing incomes. Informal labour ceaselessly wars for economic space. Next, the poor turn, as we have seen, to lotteries and other 'quasi-magical' schemes of wealth appropriation. Under such conditions initiatives such as microcredit have little impact on the reduction of poverty even in Dhaka, the home of the Grameen bank. Increasing competition within the informal sector depletes social capital and dissolves self-help networks and solidarities essential to the survival of the very poor. It destroys the tradition of mutual giving. Davis suggests, therefore, that de Soto's slogans lead to ethno-religious or racial violence. Politically, he says, in the absence of enforced labour rights, the informal sector is a semi-feudal realm of kickbacks, bribes, tribal loyalties and ethnic exclusion.[44] Without decisive public intervention in real estate markets, titling by itself cannot raise the fortunes of the great mass of urban poor dwellers.[45]

The World Bank has looked for empowerment to work through NGOs, but as these have become more professionalised so they have impeded the mobilisation of ordinary people. 'Syrupy official assurances about "enablement" and "good governance" sidestep core issues of global inequality and debt, and ultimately they are just language games that cloak the absence of any macro strategy for alleviating urban poverty.'[46] Once again we have to acknowledge that the misery of so many is not the result of fate, nor of idleness or inability, but of structures of injustice, and sometimes of wickedness, which have to be politically addressed. A theology of housing has to begin here, where the prophets begin.

Having said this, I want to go on to argue that Turner's insistence on empowerment is absolutely right and that it represents the only way to house eight billion or ten billion people with beauty and dignity. In *A Theology of the Built Environment* I argued that the extraordinary story in Numbers 11, where Moses wishes that 'all the Lord's people were prophets', had to be understood in terms of such empowerment, and that the story of Pentecost takes this up. We see the outworking of Pentecost in a passage like 1 Corinthians 12, where a motley group, containing few who were educated or socially powerful (1 Cor. 1.26), are considered to be mutually

[44] Ibid., pp. 179–84. [45] Ibid., p. 81. [46] Ibid., p. 79.

empowered for the creation of the common good, for the realisation of the ends of the church. When it comes to housing, the presupposition of empowerment is, I want to argue, the idea of the vernacular.

THE IDEA OF THE VERNACULAR

Curating a celebrated exhibition of photographs of vernacular architecture, Bernard Rudofsky drew a distinction between pedigreed and non-pedigreed architecture, usually simply called 'vernacular'.[47] In appealing to this tradition I do not romanticise it or forget that some of it was very poor.[48] However, all over the world vernacular architecture has much to recommend it. In the first place vernacular space is, says J. B. Jackson, space to be shared, not exploited or monopolised. 'It is never a source of wealth or power, it is in the literal sense a common ground, a common place, a common denominator which makes each vernacular neighbourhood a miniature common wealth.'[49] Vernacular architecture, in other words, partakes of the common good. It manifests no *libido dominandi*, none of the desire to dominate which Augustine believed characterised the earthly city.[50] It is close to what Alexander called 'the timeless way of building', which, as we saw in Chapter 2, represents patterns of building which have been successful in a particular culture over the centuries.

Second, we have seen in relation to cities and to farming that limits are crucial to the common good. Vernacular architecture embodies limits in a way that pedigreed architecture does not. Rapoport speaks of the 'amazing skill' shown by primitive and peasant builders in dealing with

---

[47] B. Rudofsky, *Architecture without Architects: A Short Introduction to Non-Pedigreed Architecture* (Albuquerque: University of New Mexico Press, 1964), p. 1.

[48] Cf. the account of a report on cottages in Shropshire in the 1860s: 'In the majority of parishes that I visited, they may be described as tumbledown and ruinous, not watertight, very deficient in bedroom accommodation, and indecent sanitary arrangements. On many estates cottages are to be found belonging to the owners of the soil which are a disgrace to any civilised community.' In Herefordshire the cottages 'are generally constructed of wattle and dub [sic], and thatched, and contain only bedroom and sitting room. In one village many of the cottages were found in the last stage of decay, windows broken, doors far from windtight, roofs not water tight, bedrooms unceiled.' Heath, *English Peasant*, pp. 71–2. Later evidence confirms this. J. W. Robertson Scott, *England's Green and Pleasant Land* (Harmondsworth: Penguin, 1947).

[49] Jackson, *Sense of Place*, p. 67.

[50] Here it contrasts with conventional building, where, according to Alexander, even where there is a concern for beauty there is something remote from feeling, an almost disgusting concern with opulence, with the taste of the market place, with fashion so that the simple values of the human heart do not exist. C. Alexander with H. Davis, J. Martinez and D. Corner, *The Production of Houses* (New York: Oxford University Press, 1985), p. 14.

climatic problems and their ability to use minimum resources for maximum comfort. 'The Eskimo has only snow and ice, fur and bone, and some driftwood; the Sudanese have mud, reeds and some palm logs . . . the marsh dwellers of Iraq have only reeds. While this scarcity does not determine form, it does make some solutions impossible and reduces the choice to an extent, depending on the severity of the limitations.'[51] Ecologically there are many advantages in making a virtue out of necessity.

Traditionally we built according to our limits. Today, however, there are no apparent limits. Building form is defined by our technology, by global markets and by consumer taste. Traditionally, resources had to be used wisely, because their scarcity and the effort needed to manufacture them were automatically understood. We now use more and more of them, and bring them from further and further away.[52]

Third, the vernacular tradition responded to local climate conditions and embodied a deep knowledge of, and respect for, its materials but also represented a response to social form and tradition. 'The folk tradition', says Rapoport, 'is the direct and unselfconscious translation into physical form of a culture, its needs and values – as well as the desires, dreams and passions of a people.'[53] Calling for a change in the culture of building, Howard Davis argues that a healthy culture can arise only when buildings of meaning and value are being made by people who are themselves improving their lives through making those buildings. 'The various parts of the culture reinforce each other and make it stronger, its customs and rules are understandable and make sense, and the culture's stability and its ability to change according to new conditions are in balance.'[54]

Fourth, there are two advantages which accrue from the vernacular tradition's dependence on craftsmanship. In the first place it tends to rely on local industry and materials rather than relying on imported materials and complex machinery. This in turn prevents the build-up of distant structures of power.[55] Further, dependence on craftsmanship leads to what Simon Fairlie calls 'irrectitude': vernacular building is not dominated by smooth surfaces and the straight line. The lines of vernacular buildings are 'soft, blurred, gently inclined or wavering; they are distinct from the landscape,

---

[51] A. Rapoport, *House, Form and Culture* (Englewood Cliffs: Prentice Hall, 1969), p. 105.
[52] Smith, Whitelegg and Williams, *Greening*, p. 63.
[53] Rapoport, *House*, p. 2. Cf. Vance: 'Self-conscious architecture withers without public adulation, so only the vernacular form can live in the crowded area of organic growth.' *Continuing City*, p. 50.
[54] H. Davis, *The Culture of Building* (New York: Oxford University Press, 2006), p. 13.
[55] H. Glassie, *Vernacular Architecture* (Bloomington: Indiana University Press, 2000), p. 31.

yet remain at home within their setting of rolling hills or burgeoning foliage'.[56]

The modern brick-built villa, whatever stylistic concessions it may make to the local vernacular, imposes an artificial geometry upon the landscape. Its rigid outline, its mechanical tiling, its machined window frames, its telephone wires and TV aerial . . . all speak of another world. Distinctiveness has turned into intrusion, aspiration has become arrogance, and Nature has been relegated to the status of backdrop – a 'view'.[57]

Loos famously suggested that peasant houses were produced by 'the hand of God' but in fact, said the Irish playwright J. M. Synge, the Kerry peasantry 'would discuss for hours the proportions of a new building – how high a house should be if it was a certain length, with so many rafters in order that it might look well'.[58] Vernacular building, in other words, shared the concern for beauty of pedigreed architecture, but appealed to different canons of beauty. These canons were not imposed by those who knew what was good for 'the masses'.

Fifth, we can say that all architecture manifests a spirituality, but that this can be good or bad, deep or shallow. Christopher Day argues that the methods and materials of modern building militate against repose. 'In smooth plastered, gloss painted rooms you need a radio, hi-fi or television for company, to fill the empty space.'[59] Buildings can promote social and individual healing 'where the environment can offer interest, activity and intriguing ambiguity, timeless durability and a sense of roots (in place, past and future) in the wider natural world with its renewing rhythms, sociable places and relaxing atmospheres for the socially shy, and harmony, tranquillity and quiet soothing spaciousness'.[60] Much contemporary building is the equivalent of a diet of E numbers, which make people manic. Day argues that we need a recovery of the sacred in the broadest sense, which involves the ability of our senses to tell what is good and bad for us. Unless we are just providing containers for people, he remarks, we should have rooms

---

[56] S. Fairlie, *Low Impact Development* (Charlbury: Jon Carpenter, 1996), p. 4. Harries likewise speaks of the 'war against straight lines' waged by the Viennese painter Hundertwasser. *Function*, p. 241. Cf. Alexander: A building in which angles are all perfectly right angles, in which all windows are exactly the same size, and in which all columns are vertical, and all floors perfectly horizontal can reach its false perfection only by ignoring its surroundings utterly. The apparent imperfections of a place which is alive are not imperfections at all. They follow from the process which allows each part to be fitted carefully to its position. *Timeless Way*, p. 152.

[57] Fairlie, *Low Impact Development*, p. 4.

[58] D. Hardy and C. Ward, *Arcadia for All: The Legacy of a Makeshift Landscape* (London: Mansell, 1984), p. 28.

[59] Day, *Places*, p. 142.   [60] Ibid., p. 26.

which are congenial places for silence and meditation. To sum up, 'Unself-consciousness, lack of pretension or desire to impress, direct response to a way of life, climate and technology, use of the "model and variations" method of building, the attitude towards nature and landscape, all play a part in the beauty, simplicity and effectiveness of vernacular architecture.'[61]

The understanding of the vernacular I have just outlined differs from the vernacular celebrated by J. B. Jackson and Robert Venturi. For them the cheap roadside building of contemporary North America is a valid expression of the vernacular. One can see the point, but such building evinces none of the skill and respect for climate and culture of the buildings Rudofsky had in mind. It is also different from the idea of the vernacular which John Summerson dismissed as a chimaera in 1947, and in some respects from Roger Scruton's 'classical vernacular'.[62] Scruton argues that architecture is primarily a vernacular art, to be understood as a process in which ordinary people participate as they build, decorate or arrange their rooms.[63] Buildings ought not to be designed for cognoscenti, but for the mass of mankind; and the practice of architecture does not lie in the hands of geniuses, but in those of ordinary and half-talented people whose task is to make us feel at home.[64] His argument that the vernacular is 'a tradition of patterns, adapted to the uses of the ordinary builder and capable of creating accord and harmony in all the many circumstances of potential conflict' accords with Rapoport's and Day's account of the vernacular, and echoes Alexander's ideas in *The Timeless Way of Building*, but is unnecessarily glossed by the idea of 'the ruling principle' of civility. Civility is certainly welcome but it is too limited a description of what is accomplished by vernacular architecture.

Paul Oliver describes vernacular architecture as that which responds to the values, mores, building skills, experience and wisdom of the cultures whose housing needs are to be met.[65] The problem is that in the West it is

---

[61] Rapoport, *House*, p. 77.

[62] 'A "vernacular" is an intuitive discipline in language or the arts, widely shared in any given historic period. It is conceived to have been a good thing in the past and therefore, by analogy, a worthy objective in the present. "A vernacular architecture of today" is sought. The word is really in the nature of an apology for inadequate knowledge of the workings of the past periods concerned. We speak of a "Georgian vernacular" when we find that certain rules of expression were adopted throughout England in the eighteenth century whereas we are ignorant of the precise means by which these rules came to be accepted. In so far as we do succeed in plotting architectural history we cease to have occasion to use the word "vernacular". Its use in relation to contemporary architecture is absurd. As an objective it is a chimera.' J. Summerson, *Heavenly Mansions* (New York: Norton, 1963), p. 212.

[63] Scruton, *Aesthetics*, p. 17.   [64] Scruton, *Classical Vernacular*, p. 25.

[65] P. Oliver, 'Ethics and Vernacular Architecture', in W. Fox (ed.), *Ethics and Built Environment* (London: Routledge, 2000), p. 115.

precisely these values which are in question, as we saw in Chapter 1. 'The vernacular is dead in the developed countries', wrote Colin Ward, 'though tribute is paid to it in neo vernacular . . . or volks vernacular buildings.'[66] He goes on to say at once, however, that the crisis of energy and resources may lead to a new vernacular. Hassan Fathy argued that such a vernacular would be inspired by a responsive and sensitive balance between the know-how and wisdom of the past and what was sustainable and modern:

Being faithful to a style . . . does not mean the reverent reproduction of other people's creation. It is not enough to copy even the best buildings of another generation or another locality. The method of building may be used, but you must strip from this method all the substance of particular character and detail, and drive out from your mind the picture of the houses that so beautifully fulfilled your desires. You must start right from the beginning, letting your new buildings grow from the daily lives of the people who will live in them, shaping the houses to the measure of the people's songs, weaving the pattern of a village as if on the village looms, mindful of the trees and crops that will grow there, respectful to the skyline and humble before the seasons.[67]

At the heart of this process is not only respect for the context but also faith in human creativity.

FAITH IN CREATIVITY

John Turner, from whom I have taken the title of this chapter, argued in 1973 that the key political issue was that of autonomy versus heteronomy, by which he meant the freedom of people to shape their lives as opposed to having every decision made for them by others, and in particular by an omnicompetent state. Nearly forty years later we have to say that having decisions made for us by omnicompetent corporations, including the big building firms, is no improvement. To treat housing as a commodity is silly enough, Turner argued, but to assume that it must or should be supplied by 'ever-larger pyramidal structures and centralizing technologies is suicidal'.[68] 'Aesthetically hideous, socially alienating and technically incompetent architecture is bound to displace that with traditional values when fossil-fuelled heteronomy takes over.'[69]

Turner's ideas were shared, quite independently, by a number of architects in Egypt, the Netherlands, Britain and the United States. What they were proposing was not just an architectural but a social revolution.

[66] Ward, *Talking*, p. 12.
[67] H. Fathy, *Architecture for the Poor* (Chicago: University of Chicago Press, 1973), p. 45.
[68] Turner, *Housing*, p. 37.   [69] Ibid., p. 49.

In the Netherlands John Habraken published his ground-breaking book on supports in 1961. He looked back to the end of World War I, when standardisation was proposed as the way forward to meet the housing crisis. From the start this was opposed by workers, who 'saw in the dreadful monotony of endless rows of identical houses and bungalows an assault upon their personality, upon their freedom, upon their humanity; this kind of housing turns one into a herd animal, a serf, a dependent'.[70] Habraken agreed with this critique, arguing that mass housing reduces the dwelling to a consumer article and the dweller to a consumer. He wanted personal involvement in housing both as a way of recognising human creativity and as a way of creating vibrant towns and cities. His suggestions rested on a philosophy of everyday life for which housing was a key expression. 'To build dwellings', he said, 'is par excellence a civilised activity . . . civilisation is first and foremost rooted in everyday actions of ordinary people going about their business.'[71] Analagously to Turner's idea of 'housing' as a verb, he insisted that it was a process, one in which there ought to be a public–private partnership. The public element took the form of 'supports', platforms which provided foundations and basic services, on which people could then build as they chose.[72]

Habraken's ideas were taken up in the Netherlands, and elsewhere they were adopted in the form of sites and services. This was a major programme in the effort to regenerate slums in the 1990s but, according to *The Challenge of Slums*, was never popular; we are not told why, apart from the fact that costs could not be recovered. Davis argues that slum upgrading and sites-and-services projects have largely failed to have a visible impact on the housing crisis in the Third World.[73]

In Britain Colin Ward has consistently opposed volume building and has urged, instead, 'a mass of small, local, small-scale solutions that draw upon the involvement, the ability and the ingenuity of people themselves'.[74] Rod Hackney and Nick Wates led a successful wave of community architecture in the 1970s and 1980s, in a deeply unpropitious environment. Wates

---

[70] J. Habraken, *Supports: An Alternative to Mass Housing* (London: Architectural Press, 1972), p. 1. Cf. Howard Kunstler speaking of the way in which the balloon frame transformed the craft of house building into an industry: 'In so doing it turned houses into commodities, things made above all to be sold at a profit, so that those who ended up living in them were not the same ones who built them, meaning that they were houses built without affection.' If the ordinary house of our time seems like a joke, he writes, 'remember that it expresses the spirit of our age. The question, then, is: what kind of joke represents the spirit of our age? And the answer is: a joke on ourselves.' *Geography*, pp. 163, 166.
[71] Habraken, *Supports*, p. 11.   [72] Ibid., p. 60.   [73] Davis, *Planet*, p. 74.
[74] Ward, *Talking*, p. 142.

cites Jefferson, not only a politician but an architect: 'I know of no safe depository of the ultimate power of society, but the people themselves; and if we think them not enlightened enough to exercise their control with a wholesome discretion, the remedy is not to take it from them, but to inform their discretion.'[75] In the wake of bitter inner-city riots the judge commissioned to investigate them noted a link between social unrest and the degree of control people have over their environment. 'Local communities', he suggested, 'should be more fully involved in the decisions which affect them. A "top down" approach to regeneration does not seem to have worked. Local communities must be fully and effectively involved in planning.'[76] Community architecture involved both regeneration of older housing stock and self-build. On the one hand, when the architect Rod Hackney regenerated his early nineteenth-century street, together with a tenants' association, 'crime and vandalism were virtually eliminated, common areas remained spotless, people's health improved dramatically'.[77] On the other hand, when the local residents are excluded in favour of the 'experts' the results have often been economically wasteful, socially inept and sometimes disastrous.[78] An architect, Wates and Knevitt argued, is a professional enabler, a person with technical expertise who uses that to help people to plan their environment themselves. He or she is like a gardener tending plants. The gardener knows he cannot make plants but can only help them grow and become healthy.[79] An outstanding example of such a process is the architect Ralph Erskine's design of the Byker Wall flats in Newcastle upon Tyne, now a grade one listed building. Erskine sat for months in a hut on site listening to tenants and asking them to draw what they wanted to get his result. Wates and Knevitt give many shocking examples of government at all levels refusing to adopt a truly consultative approach, either because ordinary people were despised as stupid or because big business interests would be compromised. 'The stumbling block has been local authorities' persistent failure to devolve sufficient power to their tenants or to allow council officers and other professionals to work properly with them.'[80]

The worry about allowing self-build is explored in Douglas Hardy and Colin Ward's book *Arcadia for All*, an account of the building of the 'plotlands' between the wars, when old railway carriages, disused buses and ramshackle huts became the basis of whole new settlements. One writer in 1936 found on the English coastline 'congeries of discordant

---

[75] N. Wates and C. Knevitt, *Community Architecture* (Harmondsworth: Penguin, 1987), p. 15.
[76] Ibid., p. 16.   [77] Ibid., p. 74.   [78] Ibid., p. 115.   [79] Ibid., p. 78.   [80] Ibid., p. 77.

huts and caravans laid out without any consideration for the amenities, without any thought given to the question of access, design, water supply, sanitation, litter disposal and so on. Their cumulative effect is to produce a shoddy, unplanned and unsightly blight, entirely opposed to the natural character and beauty of the seaside.'[81] Hardy and Ward allow that in an area of the country with a high density of population and growing demands on a fragile environment, preservationists undoubtedly had a case. 'What is debatable is whether restrictions and standards needed to be applied uniformly and indiscriminately in the way they were.'[82] Like Habraken and Turner they insist both that standards are not immutable and that it is wrong to think that people need everything from day one. The Director of the Milton Keynes Development Corporation had at one stage thought that half of the town might be made up of self-build owner starter homes, shared equity schemes, co-operative owner-designed schemes and homes incorporating workshops and other employment.[83] Hardy and Ward comment that 'One of the essentials of a do-it-yourself New Town would be a relaxation of building regulations to make it possible for people to experiment in alternative ways of building and servicing houses and in permitting a building to be occupied in a most rudimentary condition for gradual completion.'[84] Milton Keynes would certainly have been a much more interesting place if this had happened.

Both Ward and Wates cite Sherry Arnstein's 'ladder of participation', which begins with manipulation and ascends to citizen control via therapy, informing, consultation, placation, partnership and delegated power.[85] Today, at the beginning of the second decade of the twenty-first century, 'consultation' is de rigueur, but it is in most cases a purely cosmetic exercise with no real involvement and leaves most people virtually certain that results have been decided in advance. We have in general moved no further forward than placation, if, indeed, we have gone beyond manipulation.

More or less at the same time as Wates was writing, Christopher Alexander was working out his ideas. Like Habraken he begins from the alienating impact of mass housing. In today's production of houses, he writes, the actual construction is essentially factory-like, and labour is related to the building process entirely through the medium of money. The process of house construction as a fundamental part of human life has gone, replaced by large-scale contractors, building inspectors, safety inspectors and all the things which are necessary for large-scale access by heavy equipment and

---

[81] Hardy and Ward, *Arcadia for All*, p. 36.   [82] Ibid., p. 282.   [83] Ibid., p. 297.
[84] Ibid., p. 32.   [85] Ward, *Talking*, p. 126.

machinery.[86] Building a house, he argues, ought to be more like having a child, and celebrated in the same kind of way.[87] He calls for a more human operation in which the joy of building becomes paramount, in which the builders have a direct human relation to the work itself, to the houses, to the place of the houses and to the people that the houses are for.[88] Improving design is not the issue. The alienated character of the buildings stems from the system of production, and it is this which needs changing. Christopher Day instances the rehabilitation of condemned housing in Hackney, east London. Prior to rehabilitation 90 per cent of residents wanted to move out. Following intensive architect–resident collaboration the area became a positive place. As Rod Hackney found, vandalism, theft and muggings virtually disappeared, tenants' health improved, communal areas were looked after, and dignity and respect were re-established.[89]

Alexander asks what kind of processes might be able to produce millions of houses all over the world which are better than current mass housing, whether of the state or of the volume builders, and which take account of the psychological and social nature of the environment and the individuality of the people for whom the houses are built. In *The Timeless Way of Building* he argues that 'It is essential only that the people of a society, together, all the millions of them, not just professional architects, design all the millions of places. There is no other way that human variety, and the reality of specific human lives, can find their way into the structure of the places.'[90] We cannot house people with any semblance of human dignity unless we destandardise, argued Hassan Fathy.

It is a pity government authorities think of people as 'millions'. If you regard people as 'millions' to be shovelled into various boxes like loads of gravel, if you regard them as inanimate, unprotesting, uniform objects, always passive, always needing things done to them, you will miss the biggest opportunity to save money ever presented to you. For of course, a man has a mind of his own, and a pair of hands that do what his mind tells them. A man is an active creature, a source of action and initiative, and you no more have to build him a house than you have

---

[86] Alexander *et al.*, *Production*, p. 297.

[87] Hassan Fathy agrees. 'Once, when a man wanted to build a house', he wrote, 'he would launch into some of the most complex and prolonged decision making of his life. From the first family discussion of the idea to the day when the last workman left the completed house, the owner would be working with the builders – not with his hands, perhaps, but suggesting, insisting, refusing – maintaining a running consultation with them and making himself responsible for the final shape of the house. Indeed, this continuous interest of the owner in his house would continue indefinitely, for there was a superstition to the effect that once a house was quite finished, its owner would die; so the prudent householder would go on for ever altering and adding to the structure and putting off the laying of the last fatal brick.' *Architecture*, p. 28.

[88] Alexander *et al.*, *Production*, p. 298.   [89] Day, *Consensus*, p. 12.

[90] Alexander, *Timeless Way*, p. 164.

to build nests for the birds of the air. Give him half a chance and a man will solve his part of the housing problem – without the help of architects, contractors, or planners – far better than any government authority can.[91]

There is an extraordinary agreement between Fathy and Alexander in the idea of the revival of the master builder, in the deployment of local building yards and in the insistence that designer ('architect'), craftsman and client have to work together. Fathy wrote that he wanted to encourage 'an attitude of busy, interfering concern' among the peasants with whom he was working.[92] Alexander records how, when he explained to his Mexican clients that each house would be different, and that they would each be responsible for the design of their house, 'an incredible light came into their faces when they realized that each house would be adapted to their specific needs, and desires and imagination'.[93]

Fathy built using ancient Nubian techniques, whereas Alexander seeks to use the pattern language, which, he claims, has the capacity to unify the generic needs which are felt by every family and which make a house functional and sensible, with the unique idiosyncrasies that make every family different, and thus to produce a house which is unique and personal but also which satisfies the basic needs of a good house. The building process is governed by a system of steps or operations so defined that they can be applied freely to each plan and will, when properly executed, make a complete and structurally sound building from each plan without the need for working drawings of each building.[94] A house, he argues, is an organic system, like a living creature. Its fabric cannot be properly adapted to its needs and functions unless the process of adapting goes all the way down to small details. It is the operations that are standardised, not the components.[95] The process has a human rhythm. It is not merely a mechanical process in which a building which has already been designed now gets assembled. 'It is instead a human process which allows spirit, humour and emotion to be a part of it and to enter the fabric of the buildings themselves, so that the buildings are felt, in the end, as the products of the rhythm which produced them.'[96] This process could be extended to the world-wide production of houses.[97]

---

[91] Fathy, *Architecture*, p. 32.   [92] Ibid., p. 40.   [93] Alexander *et al.*, *Production*, p. 166.
[94] Ibid., p. 209.   [95] Ibid., pp. 221, 222.   [96] Ibid., p. 291.
[97] Alexander argues that one person could not at any one time work with more than about twenty families and still manage to keep on top of the site planning, design and construction. This means that in a city like Mexicali with half a million people there would be 100 builders' yards and 1,000 new clusters of four or six or ten working together, designing their common land, taking responsibility for their own houses, 'conscious of their own creative power, having a genuine deep-seated relation to the soil on which their houses stand'. Alexander *et al.*, *Production*, p. 349.

Both Fathy and Alexander encountered opposition from the local bureaucracy. Fathy had to leave Egypt and work with Constantin Dox-iadis in Iraq. Alexander commented about the opposition he encountered in Mexico,

When we compare the bookish dissatisfaction which the government officials have with the palpable reality of the families and their delight, and we realize that the officials continue in their distaste and opposition even though they know that the families love their houses and are completely satisfied, must we not then wonder at the frightful arrogance which allows these officials to continue their opinion? Does it not become utterly clear, then, that the game of housing, the production of housing, is indeed a game, recklessly played by banks and realtors and building inspection departments in total disregard of the feelings of the people . . . I myself, when I look at these five houses and the cluster of these houses, am filled with something which is as close to a religious feeling as any social act in our society today can bring me to.[98]

Both architects see the need for a social revolution.

It is as if the rebirth of society itself might start again . . . as if the people, hungry for a conscious, sensible relation to their daily lives, would find it, and be capable of sharing it, so much that finally the entire city comes to life with the pulse of groups of people in every neighbourhood making and shaping their own existence.[99]

One of the key aspects of this is re-learning the need for co-operation.

CO-OPERATION

In an essay published in 1901 Raymond Unwin urged co-operation in building, which, he said, would add character and dignity to both towns and houses. 'What more satisfactory town buildings could one desire than some of the old colleges? Yet these consist primarily of rows of small tenements grouped round quadrangles or gardens with certain common rooms attached.' Instead of having a useless front parlour why not have a common room in which a fire might always be burning in an evening, where comfort for social intercourse, for reading or for writing could always be found? The growth of co-operation would soon bring the common bakehouse and kitchen. Common meals would then evolve.[100] He proposed this for Hampstead Garden Suburb but the idea came to nothing.

---

[98] Ibid., p. 320.   [99] Ibid., p. 349.
[100] R. Unwin, 'Co-operation in Building', in B. Parker and R. Unwin, *The Art of Building a Home* (London: Longmans, 1901), p. 104. In *Town Planning in Practice* Unwin argued that co-operation was possible in heating, provision of play areas and cooking. 'Why should 40 housewives heat up 40 ovens and cook 40 scrappy dinners . . . by co-operation it is quite possible to combine all

Unwin wrote at a time when co-operation was both in the air and much more of a necessity than it is when technology eases so many burdens. In the days before machinery, remarks Henry Glassie, human co-operation was essential to get anything done. The need for it led to compact settlement, which rationalised itself through an economically useful ideology of oneness derived from Scripture.[101]

Seventy years after Unwin wrote, and in an entirely different social atmosphere, these ideas began to be tried out, first in Scandinavia, in the Netherlands, and then in the United States in the cohousing movement. Cohousing is the product of a group of people who build their houses together, shape their common space, just as Alexander imagines, and include a common house as part of the project. Many ideas feed into it. Partly it is a response to changing family patterns and partly to the sense of isolation many experience in the city, partly it represents a search for a community, and partly it is about taking control of life and therefore about direct democracy.[102] Cohousing uses an architect rather as Alexander envisages the role of the master builder. In *Utopia* Thomas More describes a city of co-operatives each consisting of thirty families who share common facilities and meals and who organise child care and other practical functions. Jan Gudmand-Hoyer, the architect for one of the developments in Denmark, commented, 'This will be the first city in the world where Thomas More's idea of Utopia is realized some five hundred years after it was conceived.'[103] A review of cohousing projects found that nearly every community wanted a larger common house to provide extra guest rooms, or rooms for renting out to teenage children or to a couple having relationship difficulties, or to people needing more work space. In Copenhagen there are forty-eight resident-managed cohousing communities. The first phase, completed in 1990, included eleven cohousing communities of twenty to forty dwellings (300 units). Of these eleven, six are non-profit owned rentals, three are co-operatively financed, and three are privately financed. Three of the communities are designed around covered streets. People car-share and jointly own leisure items like boats. The idea is to have the family as a base but open it up to community. It turns out that such

---

the valuable elements of private family life with advantages of a more varied diet, less engrossing domestic labour and care, and a greater degree of social intercourse.' *Town Planning*, p. 383. Unwin himself, of course, lived in the large and beautiful old farm house on the edge of what became Hampstead Garden Suburb.

[101] Glassie, *Vernacular Architecture*, p. 92.

[102] K. McCamant and C. Durrett, *Cohousing: A Contemporary Approach to Housing Ourselves* (Berkeley: TenSpeed Press, 1994), p. 121.

[103] Ibid., p. 145.

cohousing plays a strong role in local community, with members active in the local theatre, politics, schools and sports teams. The idea has since taken root in the United States.

In Britain housing co-operatives allow people unable to afford to buy their own homes to have direct control over the provision of their own housing while at the same time receiving public subsidies.[104] As with Alexander's process, physical involvement is usually part of the process and is good for raising morale and for getting people working together. It, too, has social consequences: 'Decentralization rather than centralization; self help rather than dependency; participatory democracy rather than representative democracy; networking rather than hierarchy; setting long-term objectives rather than short-term.'[105]

BUILDING GRACIOUSLY

In the face of the global emergency, gracious building is also sustainable building. Daniel Williams makes a distinction between sustainable design and green design. 'Green design incorporates ecologically sensitive materials and creates healthy buildings and processes . . . but still functions primarily through the use of fossil fuels . . . Sustainable design goes further to become a passive and active structure that is designed to maximize the use of sites' natural renewable resources.'[106] As we have seen, vernacular building was for the most part sustainable building.

Architecture up until 100 years ago had to be ingenious in providing comfort by integrating passive elements of the natural place into design solutions. Passive elements include warm air rising, prevailing breezes, ventilation chimneys, floor plans proportioned and oriented to provide daylight and fresh air to all users, unique methods of construction, virtual elimination of waste, a symbiotic relationship between the structure and materials needed to build it, and the reuse or return to the earth of the materials after their use.[107]

The most ingenious form of housing ever devised is probably the igloo, but there are many other examples. Mikonos in Greece is subject to gales of up to 75 mph but one can light a match twenty feet inside the town. 'Form itself is acting as a labyrinth, creating a back force – dampening the wind velocity and mitigating its force.'[108] Fathy found in his Nubian houses a form of ventilation which anticipated the most sophisticated knowledge of

[104] Wates and Knevitt, *Community Architecture*, p. 122.   [105] Ibid., p. 155.
[106] D. Williams, *Sustainable Design: Ecology, Architecture and Planning* (Hoboken: Wiley, 2007), p. 16.
[107] Ibid., p. 103.   [108] Ibid., p. 109.

aerodynamics and which had worked out seemingly counterintuitive ways of keeping houses cool, presumably by trial and error.

On Williams' definition a sustainable house is autonomous, which is to say it provides its own energy and recycles its own wastes. Such houses have been around for more than forty years. Today 'eco-houses', which make use of solar panels, windmills, passive solar gain and natural cooling, are fairly common (at least in Britain) but are still not mainstream. Even in the Netherlands, where there have been rigorous sustainability standards for many years, sustainable building measures are still not 'truly embedded in daily construction practice'.[109] In Britain the government's plan for four and a half million new houses required higher standards of thermal efficiency than in the past, but stopped well short of anything that might be called an eco-house. One can only guess at the reason for this. Perhaps it is that those in power really do not believe either in global warming or in the coming energy crisis. Perhaps it is the long shadow of that faith in modernity which marked the whole of the twentieth century and thus a conviction that nothing worthwhile is to be learned from vernacular models. Whatever the reason, it is clear that gracious building cannot be non-sustainable because it breaches the commitment of justice to future generations. Robert and Brenda Vale, designers of the United Kingdom's first autonomous house, argue that the single most important requirement is to downscale. 'What is needed is for small, beautifully designed, flexible houses to become objects of desire.'[110] Where possible they advocate 'timesharing' in buildings – using buildings for more than one function. Thus, schools can host other community events in the evening, and churches can host a wide range of community events.

Gracious building is also, as we saw in Chapter 3, beautiful building. 'It would be grossly discourteous of an architect whose imagination had been enriched amid the loveliness of Siena or Verona, or the Cathedral close of Wells', writes Fathy, 'to scamp his work and fob his clients off with something less than the most beautiful architecture he can create.'[111] The question is, of course, what constitutes beauty. It cannot be without addition the *integritas* and *claritas* which Aquinas proposed nor even Alberti's *concinnitas* (harmony). William Morris insisted that pleasure in work was the secret of beauty. 'Nothing else can make the common surroundings of life beautiful, and whenever they are beautiful it is a sign that men's work has pleasure in it, however they may suffer otherwise. It is this lack of

---

[109] *Frameworks for the Future* (Rotterdam: National Dubo Centrum, 2000), p. 9.
[110] Vale and Vale, *Time to Eat*, p. 149.   [111] Fathy, *Architecture*, p. 72.

pleasure in daily work which has made our towns and habitations sordid and hideous.'[112]

Fathy found the secret of beauty in his Egyptian houses partly in the individuality of the craftsman-made details. Handmade products appeal to us because they express the mood of the craftsman. 'Each irregularity, oddity, difference is the result of a decision made at the moment of manufacture; the change of design when the craftsman gets bored with repeating the same motif, or a change of colour when he runs short of one colour or thread, witness to the constant living interaction of the man with the material.'[113] He dismissed the idea that the old skills had been lost as 'claptrap', designed to fend off awkward enquiries and hide the fact that most architects are acquainted only with industrial materials.[114]

The vernacular he drew on used domes, whose curving lines were a source of delight, but it was above all in the courtyards that he found the 'quality without a name'. 'In enclosed space, in a room, or in a courtyard', he writes, 'there is a certain quality that can be distinctly felt, and that carries a local signature as clearly as does a particular curve. This felt space is in fact a fundamental component of architecture, and if space has not the true feeling, no subsequent decoration will be able to naturalize it into the desired tradition.'[115] European pagans, he argues, had gods in rivers and trees or mountain tops but Arabs, in desert climates, looked to the sky. In Europe (and North America, we may add) people try to make their house one with the landscape and its vegetation through gardens or glass, 'so in desert countries men try to bring down the serenity and holiness of the sky into the house, and at the same time to shut out the desert with its blinding, suffocating sand and inhospitable demons'.

The means of doing this is the courtyard. The house is a hollow square, turning blind, windowless walls to the outside, with all its rooms looking inwards into a courtyard from which only the sky can be seen. The courtyard becomes the owner's private piece of sky. The space enclosed by the rooms of his house can, at its best, alone induce a feeling of calm and security that no other architectural feature can, while in every case the sky is, as it were, pulled down into intimate contact with the house, so that the spirituality of the home is constantly replenished from heaven.[116]

The patterns outlined by Alexander seek to outline a grammar of building which is based on 'rightness of fit', characterising those places where people

---

[112] Quoted in Davis, *Culture of Building*, p. 18.   [113] Fathy, *Architecture*, p. 27.
[114] Ibid., p. 36. Scott argued that the variety of crafts was 'irrecoverably lost'. Fathy, *Architecture*, p. 43.
[115] Fathy, *Architecture*, p. 55.   [116] Ibid., p. 56.

come to life and feel comfortable. In many ways they represent an appeal to common sense but they also turn out to be essentially aesthetic criteria. For example, natural light is what makes houses beautiful, and this means that, wherever possible, there should be light from two sides and rooms should not be more than twelve to fifteen feet deep. Light on two sides, Alexander argues, helps people to understand each other. Even in the days of central heating the fire (the *focus* in Latin) remains important as something which gives life to a room and around which people gather. Buildings need to have variable ceiling heights in order to make people feel comfortable. He agrees with Fathy that the individuality of craftsmanship matters.

There is a character in natural things which is created by the fact that they are reconciled, exactly in their inner forces. For from the play of repetition and variety at every level it follows that the overall geometry is always loose and fluid. There is an indefinable roughness, a looseness, a relaxedness which nature always has: and this relaxed geometry comes directly from the balance of the repetition and variety.[117]

There need to be places where people may be alone without making others feel left out. 'To this end there must be two small places, perhaps rooms, perhaps large alcoves, perhaps a corner, screened off by a half wall – places which are clearly understood as private territories, where each person can keep to himself, pursue his or her own activities.'[118] It is almost, dare one say, 'form follows function', but the function is understood as a joyous common life.

Rules for building like this were already anticipated by Raymond Unwin, who noted the need of the architect to 'design a house to fit the habits of life of those who are to occupy it'.

Knowing that the family will practically live in the kitchen, he would think out the space needed to give room for doing work, taking meals and resting. He would consider what of the work must be done most tends to make the living room uncomfortable and dirty; and he would banish that to a scullery or washhouse. In the living room he would plan so that there might be warm seats round the fire in winter, free from draughts, and seats for summer near the window; a good dresser for work, well lighted and supplied with cupboards, plate rack and perhaps a small washing up sink for crockery. Then he would allow space for a table for meals, and a few shelves for books; perhaps he might even find a corner for a piano or a desk, in case either should be wanted. Instead of the sitting room, he would either build a little den for quiet reading or writing, if any member of the family desired to study, or more probably so plan one of the bedrooms that a portion of it could be

---

[117] Alexander, *Timeless Way*, p. 148. [118] Alexander, *Pattern Language*, p. 386.

made cosy for such a purpose, about the only one for which a sitting room would be at all likely to be wanted.[119]

Perhaps learning from Alexander, or perhaps just drawing on common sense, the cohousing projects mentioned above incorporate design factors that encourage neighbours to meet or that provide children with safe and challenging play areas. Providing small gardens and comfortable sitting places overlooking shared outdoor areas makes it easier for people to meet their neighbours.[120] Sensitive transitions from the most intimate to the most public gathering spaces encourage an active community life. None of this is or ought to be remarkable except that, in volume building, it is mostly overlooked and then people wonder why they cannot settle, need to be constantly on the move or need to surround themselves with television or loud music.

THE NEW VERNACULAR AND THE COMMON GOOD

The eighty million extra human beings each year need somewhere to live. Is it possible that they could have ecologically sensitive and beautiful houses, and not end up in slums? Are the millions pouring into the cities condemned to live in the appalling conditions that Mike Davis documents? Would the provision of decent housing be economically unfeasible? In the rich countries housing development pushes on apace, but much of it is dreary and dispiriting. Is it possible that this could be done better, more sustainably and more beautifully? As we have seen, many architects from around the world argue that 'another world is possible' if we will only trust people's creativity, learn to work and live co-operatively rather than as isolated individuals, reconnect with regional traditions which represent responses to local climate and conditions, and disavow both mass solutions and the technological imperative. Effectively the Rio summit agreed. All countries should, it said,

strengthen the indigenous building materials industry, based, as much as pos-sible, on inputs of locally available natural resources... promote the increased use of energy efficient designs and technologies and sustainable use of natu-ral resources... promote the use of labour-intensive construction methods... develop policies and practices to reach the informal sector and self-help

[119] R. Unwin, 'Art and Simplicity', in *Art of Building*, p. 64.
[120] McCamant and Durrett, *Cohousing*, p. 173.

builders... discourage the use of construction materials and products that create pollution during their life style.[121]

All the architects whose work I have considered argue that housing which would be a delight, which would foster community, enrich lives and be sustainable, is perfectly possible if only the common good is prioritised over profit. All over the world both the skills and the will are there. Just as with agriculture, top-down solutions are not the answer. A new vernacular could be possible, not identical with the old, but standing in traditions which evolved, often over millennia, and capable of recreating a more just and more beautiful world. This possibility is something that a liberation theology, seeking the common good and committed to human survival, would have to listen to. Liberation theology seeks to realise its vision in particular projects, to avoid what it regards the daydreaming of utopianism. The detailed work on low-impact development carried out by Simon Fairlie, and many of the co-operative housing schemes and schemes for social housing, all involve such projects in ways which have the most substantive (I am avoiding the word 'concrete') impacts on the lives of the poor. Their impact on our understanding of society is, I believe, radical, though they can be achieved without those revolutions which 'devour their own children'. If we give them priority, however, as I believe we should, what is the place of 'great' architecture? Is there any place for it in a just and egalitarian society? I turn to this question in the final chapter.

---

[121] Robinson (ed.), *Agenda 21*, ch. 7. Unfortunately, Simon Fairlie notes, in Britain 'it is becoming increasingly clear that the planning and housing system... is not going to budge to accommodate truly affordable self-build unless... the demand for it is manifested in an unmanageable number of unlawful settlements'. *The Land*, 7 (Summer 2009), 59.

CHAPTER II

The virtues of architecture

THE PEDIGREED TRADITION

Given the Christian gospel's 'bias to the poor' it could be argued that Christianity has an elective affinity with vernacular architecture as I have understood it in the previous chapter.[1] In all aspects of culture there is a little tradition, often called the folk tradition, and a great tradition, the tradition of great art, music, literature and also building. In Scripture it is above all the example of Solomon which has been used to justify the great tradition in architecture – Eusebius of Caesarea was the first of many to hail his emperor as a 'new Solomon' – but no support for this could be derived from the gospels. Jesus was born in a stable and died on the cross. Not only did early Christianity have no shrines and altars, it had no grand buildings either. Throughout the history of Christianity there have been those who have felt that the prophetic critique of such building was primary. As we have seen, John Onians considers that Christianity has been consistently opposed to the great tradition in building. If this were true it would invite the Nietzschean criticism that Christianity emasculates a virile humanist culture. As it happens, of course, from Constantine right up to the present Christianity has proved the spur to much high art and architecture. As we shall see, the medieval builders had a closely reasoned theological rationale for their cathedral building, and Alberti, himself an abbot, gave pride of place to the building of churches. At the end of the sixteenth century the Jesuit exegete Juan Bautista Villalpanda believed that God had revealed the proper way of building to Moses in exactly the same way in which he had given the tables of the law. This turned out to be a recommendation of classical architecture, and, although we cannot set it down to the influence of his work, classical styles remained normative for Catholic church building for two and a half

---

[1] I do in fact argue this in *A Theology of the Built Environment*, but have since come to the view that I failed to do justice to the pedigreed tradition.

centuries.[2] In the eighteenth century John Wood the Elder, responsible for the most important developments in Georgian Bath, also believed that God had revealed 'such precepts as were necessary to enable [Man] to arrive at perfection in architecture'. These turned out to be identical with Palladian architecture.[3] He defended classical architecture by chapter and verse, mostly appealing to the Pentateuch and even offered a synopsis aligning Vitruvius with Holy Scripture. Christianity has not always been an enemy of the great tradition, therefore.

The prejudice in favour of the vernacular might, however, find other grounds. Thus John Summerson could argue that the chief function of contemporary architecture is not monumentality but bringing 'a sense of dignity, refinement, subtlety, gaiety, to all places where we live and work'.[4] The view that 'we shall build no new cathedrals' cropped up again and again in the twentieth century, even as candidates for new cathedrals, from shopping malls to skyscrapers, from motorways to airports, were being suggested. Again, there is Roger Scruton's view that architecture is primarily a vernacular art, concerned with the mundane and the repeatable.[5] Modesty therefore becomes it.

Despite these objections there seems to me to be good reason to defend the need for architect-designed building. Imagine a world where there was nothing but vernacular building. Not only would it be poorer, but something crucial to what it means to be human would be missing. Christopher Day distinguishes the vernacular from an architecture which concerns itself with cosmic rules – proportion, geometry, relation to the earth, to the vault of the heavens, to the vertical boundaries of free-stretching space – that of temples, cathedrals, sometimes palaces and civic buildings. Both traditions are artistic, 'but neither is complete or balanced without the other: they need to be brought into conversation'.[6] Pedigreed architecture, Harries argues, sets the everyday in contrast and sends us back to it with eyes more open, with greater awareness of what everyday routines inevitably obscure.[7] Thus, 'The churches of Wren are used as landmarks to punctuate the unbroken line of the vernacular buildings they were intended to grace.'[8] Unlike Alexander, the Christian tradition has also traced imagination and creativity to the divine Spirit, and we find precisely this in

[2] J. Rykwert, *On Adam's House in Paradise: The Idea of the Primitive Hut in Architectural History*, 2nd edn (Cambridge Mass.: MIT Press, 1981), p. 122.

[3] J. Wood, *The Origin of Building or the Plagiarism of the Heathen Detected* (Bath, 1741), p. 233.

[4] Summerson, *Heavenly Mansions*, p. 209.

[5] To maintain that such and such an architect is a creative genius, Scruton thinks, should be a chargeable offence. *Classical Vernacular*, p. 80.

[6] Day, *Places*, p. 28.   [7] Harries, *Function*, p. 281.   [8] Scruton, *Aesthetics*, p. 214.

the greatest building. For these reasons, though Christianity may not be entirely comfortable with the high tradition, it cannot ignore it. We have to ask what theological sense we can make of it. In terms of my theological scheme I understand pedigreed building under the appropriation of God the Redeemer, with its key concern in the gift of creativity. The ethical question, of course, is the end to which this creativity is used. This is not something we can dismiss as an academic issue. In Britain for the past thirty years the heir to the throne has infuriated leading architects and cultural critics, and delighted many members of the public, by attacking both modernist and post-modernist designs and championing neo-classicism. People care passionately about the built environment, and react with either enthusiasm or anger to new monumental building.

In thinking of the pedigreed tradition we need to make a distinction between iconic building, which gives us the Taj Mahal, Hagia Sophia and St Paul's in London, but also the Bilbao Guggenheim, on the one hand, and Scruton's 'classical vernacular' on the other, which might include the work of both Woods in Bath and Nash's Regent Street, but also the work of lesser architects who gave us both Georgian and Victorian suburbs. Both of these are to be contrasted with the vernacular as I have defined it.

VIRTUES IN ARCHITECTURE

In Chapter 1 I spoke of an ellipse between the church and the public square. Harries finds the ellipse, rather, between the house and the church or temple. The ethical function of architecture for him is the provision of a context for the individual's dwelling. 'Sacred and public architecture provides the community with a centre or centres. Individuals gain their sense of place in a history, in a community, by relating their dwelling to that centre.'[9] In the Western world the church occupied this function until the Enlightenment, but it now caters only for a subcommunity. Today no building very obviously addresses the entire community. This means that pedigreed architecture loses its function, which is to recall the values presiding over our lives as members of a society, calling us towards a better life.[10] Summerson agrees, arguing that 'architecture is no longer required to give symbolic cohesion to society'.[11] That was written in 1947, and one could argue that the aspiration to find iconic buildings proves him wrong. Does not Gehry's museum fulfil this function in Bilbao, and perhaps the

---

[9] Harries, *Ethical Function*, p. 287.   [10] Harries, *Ethical Function*, p. 291.
[11] Summerson, *Heavenly Mansions*, p. 209.

Opera House in Sydney? As we saw in Chapter 7, the less dogmatic space of museum or theatre, a space dedicated to education or art, takes the place of an overtly sacred building.

A very different take on the ethical nature of architecture was suggested in the nineteenth century, especially by Pugin and Ruskin. Classical architecture was denounced as pagan, or read as an architecture of the rich and powerful. A particular architectural style, in other words, was associated with a particular polity and ethical stance. Since society was a whole, architecture could not be good if it was achieved at the expense of some part of that society. Reacting to this, Geoffrey Scott satirised what he considered the 'ethical fallacy' in architecture. The prophets Samuel and Jeremiah usurp the authority of Vitruvius. 'Dangers no less desperate than unexpected are seen to attend the carving of a capital or the building of a door; and the destruction of Gomorrah is frequently recalled to indicate the just, if not the probable, consequences of an error in these undertakings.'[12] He did not, however, argue for an exclusively aesthetic importance for architecture. 'Morality deepens the content of architectural experience. But architecture in its turn can extend the scope of morality.'[13] We need to make this concession because for good or ill buildings embody values. Think of the fibreglass and steel structures which have replaced the Victorian railway stations in Oban, Dundee or King's Cross in Britain. The earlier buildings were dignified, drew on the classical vernacular and expressed both civic and corporate pride; the later expressed a 'contemptuous concept of life's value', as if no one were betting on the future.[14] Buildings, says Lewis Mumford, 'speak and act, no less than the people who inhabit them; and through the physical structure of the city past events, decisions made long ago, values formulated and achieved, remain alive and exert an influence'.[15] Keynes' famous remark that practical men, who believe themselves to be quite exempt from any intellectual influences, are usually slaves to some defunct economist can be varied by replacing the last word with 'architect'. Buildings communicate, and they shape relations between people.[16] Ruskin spoke of 'the virtues of architecture', by which he meant that buildings should do their job well and should do it

---

[12] Scott, *Architecture*, p. 104.

[13] Ibid., p. 125. Cf. Westfall: 'What we should want to know about architecture is – how does it serve the most important purpose, that of fulfilling the task that is unique to people, namely perfecting their nature and pursuing the pleasures that are uniquely available to people as people.' Westfall and van Pelt, *Architectural Principles*, p. 152.

[14] Scruton, *Aesthetics*, p. 127, speaking of municipal housing in Kensal Green. Richard Sennett argues that 'no long term' is the watchword of contemporary capitalism. *Corrosion of Character*, p. 22.

[15] Mumford, *City*, p. 135.   [16] Glassie, *Vernacular Architecture*, p. 22.

gracefully. There were, he said, three great branches of architectural virtue in any building, roughly corresponding to Vitruvius' 'commodity, firmness and delight': that it act well, speak well, and look well.[17] What he meant by 'act well' is that the building fulfils its function. A building which is simply 'not fit for purpose' is indeed a bad building. There are concert halls which have poor acoustics, theatres where lines of sight are obscured and communication between actors and audience difficult, tens of thousands of classrooms where communication is impeded rather than facilitated by the architecture. Blake said that Reynolds was 'hired by Satan to depress art', and it often seems that architects have the same job in relation to education. But the ethical question is bound up rather with the idea of the language of architecture, the notion that it 'speaks'. When we say that buildings 'speak' we are referring obliquely to the intentions embodied in them and the way these intentions are realised in a body of conventions and rules.[18]

For Aristotle and Aquinas ethics begins with the recognition that humans have aims, purposes, goals or ends and that these express themselves, among other things, in building. The aims of architecture are rarely purely functional: they embody more complex human ends – for example, for beauty or worship. Such ends are achieved by the exercise of the virtues which, Alasdair MacIntyre argues, need to be understood in relation to practices, those forms of co-operative human activity including, for example, architecture, through which the world is shaped. In this shaping co-operation is crucial since the virtues can be realised only in interaction.[19] There is a circle here, since, in Churchill's phrase, 'we shape our buildings and then they shape us'. The key question concerns the nature of the ends to be realised. When Geoffrey Scott spoke about the 'architecture of humanism' he had in mind the centrality of human scale. Michelangelo wrote of architecture, 'He that hath not mastered, or doth not master the human figure, and in especial its anatomy, may never comprehend it.'[20] Scott comments,

---

[17] J. Ruskin, *The Stones of Venice*, ed. J. G. Links (Cambridge, Mass.: Da Capo, 1960), p. 29.
[18] Scruton, *Aesthetics*, p. 159.
[19] MacIntyre, *After Virtue*, p. 195. Scruton gives an account of the rooting of ethics in community in more Hegelian terms. 'According to the Hegelian theory self knowledge is a form of publicly accessible activity, the activity of creating and engaging in a public world, and of coming to experience oneself as part of such a world, as one rational being amongst many. There can be no self knowledge in a private world. The theory has immediate consequences for the philosophy of practical reason for it is clear that happiness is possible only if it coexists with sufficient self consciousness... Happiness requires self realization and this only comes through human action.' *Aesthetics*, p. 244.
[20] Quoted in Scott, *Architecture*, p. 165.

The humanist instinct looks in the world for physical conditions that are related to our own, for movements which are like those we enjoy, for resistances that resemble those that can support us, for a setting where we should be neither lost nor thwarted. It looks therefore, for certain masses, lines and spaces, tends to create them and recognise their fitness when created. And by our instinctive imitation of what we see, their seeming fitness becomes our real delight.[21]

Such a rule does not advocate any particular style, though Scott thought that the baroque exemplified it admirably.

Scruton begins his account of morality in architecture by insisting that human beings cannot get away from the question of visual validity. Critical judgement is a form of practical reasoning and consists in judgements about what is or is not appropriate.[22] This builds on the sophisticated taxonomy of my ordinary sense experience, which gives us, by and large, an ordered world rather than a jumble of sense data. At the same time our judgements tend to change; they can certainly be educated, and they may also be coarsened. This process is the acquisition of taste. This is not meant 'in the exclusive, snobbish sense of the recognition of certain fixed values by certain people', a luxury import from abroad, received and cherished by a small group of noblemen and artists.[23] It is rather the question of serious aesthetic discrimination, acquired over years, which involves giving reasons that in turn require further reasons 'until finally the process peters out in the reference to religion, history, morality or myth'.[24] The reference to religion and morality is the reference to Aristotle's ends and purposes. For this reason 'aesthetic judgement fills the world with intimations of value'.[25] All building expresses value, which may be good or bad, redemptive or destructive. The reasons the Christian adduces to defend aesthetic judgements derive in particular from the *lectio divina*, the regular reading of Scripture which has defined the Christian community from the beginning. It is assumed (and this is what Barth shares with virtue ethics) that my reading of the Scriptures will shape my intellectual and emotional life and ground my discernment. The rag-bag nature of these Scriptures goes a long way to explaining why Christian discernment is itself a contest, endlessly argued over, and not in any simple way set over against the non-Christian world.

Ethics gives rise to politics, according to Aristotle, because that tries to discern what form of constitution, or what set of institutions, is necessary

[21] Ibid., p. 174.   [22] Scruton, *Aesthetics*, p. 237.
[23] J. Summerson, *Georgian Architecture* (Harmondsworth: Penguin, 1978), p. 27.
[24] Scruton, *Aesthetics*, p. 202.   [25] Ibid., p. 241.

to make the good life possible and to safeguard it. Carroll Westfall notes that the words people speak provide the basis for the knowledge about how people should live and hence what they should build. To build, he argues, therefore requires the polity. 'Architecture serves politics when politics is the art of living well together.'[26] Commenting on his Jewish museum in Berlin, Daniel Libeskind notes that architecture 'is a political act; it is not a private one. It is not just sitting in a studio and inventing whatever one wants to invent. It is a deeply political act, as it can only be built through agreement, through discussion, through discourse and through a democratic view of what is best for the citizens of a city.'[27] Clearly not presupposing any such democratic participation, Ruskin still felt that 'every form of noble architecture is in some sort the embodiment of the Polity, Life, History and Religious faith of nations'.[28] This does not mean that particular polities, say, democratic, monarchical, republican or fascist, have particular architectural styles which belong to them. What it means is that there has to be a 'public language of form, through which people can criticise and justify their buildings, come to an agreement over the right and wrong appearance and so construct a public realm in the image of their social nature'.[29] This realisation of the moral nature of architecture cannot be translated into a formula: this was the mistake of the Victorian thinkers against whom Scott reacted.

Where there is intention there is interpretation. We can argue over the correct way in which to understand a Wren church, or a Palladian villa. Moreover, buildings often change use over time. Oxford gaol, for example, built in the Gothic castle style, is now luxury flats; chapels become houses, churches mosques, warehouses pubs or nightclubs. Cathedrals have been instantiations of a theology of divine light, repositories for trade, symbols of imperial power, and are now 'heritage'. In his history of the Greek orders John Onians shows how meanings changed so that the Corinthian order, for example, went from having a connection with healing to being the consummate expression of the Christian faith, and the Doric from being the emblem of the loftiness and greatness of a noble mind to representing primitive ignorance.[30] This challenges any claim to make hard and fast connections between particular styles and political or ethical principles.

---

[26] Westfall and van Pelt, *Architectural Principles*, p. 155.
[27] D. Libeskind, *The Jewish Museum in Berlin* (Berlin: Studio Libeskind, H. Bibet and G. & B. Arts International, 1999), pp. 14–15.
[28] Ruskin, *Seven Lamps*, p. 199. Cf. Scruton's argument that 'The god of the temple is not the mystery-god of some cabalistic ritual but the universal god of citizenship, the god of justice and law.' *Classical Vernacular*, p. 107.
[29] Scruton, *Classical Vernacular*, p. 79.   [30] Onians, *Bearers of Meaning*, p. 311.

Looking at the many different styles which have signified political power, Charles Jencks correctly insists that the relation of form to meaning is mostly conventional.[31] When trying to evaluate pedigreed architecture it is nevertheless worthwhile to try and see how some of the most important traditions have been understood. Ruskin thought there were three great architectural traditions: classical, romanesque and Gothic. The notion of such traditions is essential provided that we understand them in the light of something like 'the Christian tradition'. Traditions have a unity, something which makes continuity clear, but there is also very often a stunning amount of divergence so that, both metaphorically and literally, different parts of the same tradition hardly recognise each other or speak to each other. This needs to be borne in mind in the following consideration of classical and Gothic traditions, alongside modernism and post modernism.

THE CLASSICAL TRADITION

The Greek orders, beginning with the emergence of Doric in the sixth century BC, are among the most profound and enduring of architectural forms. What is it that constitutes their appeal?

In the first place the classical tradition seems to be supremely rational. Spiro Kostoff speaks of the Doric temple as 'a luminous presence of right angles and sharp geometries', a 'monument of a vital abstraction' marking freedom from the dark ancient forces of the land and the propitiation of these divinely controlled forces through the act of building.[32] There is a self-evident clarity about classical forms. Appealing to Aristotelian canons, Westfall sees classical architecture as seeking beauty through establishing a mean between excess and deficiency.[33] This rationality, the subtle appeal to geometry, is probably what made the classical style appeal to the American founding fathers as they debated the architecture of their central political building in Washington.

Greek thinking, remarks Kostoff, is both typal and specific. 'It takes on an idea (or a form, which is nothing other than a congealed idea), nourishes and perfects it through a series of conscious changes, and in this way informs it with a kind of universal validity that seems irrefutable... The perfection of the Orders is far nearer nature than anything produced on impulse or accident wise.'[34] This is probably what Lutyens meant when

[31] C. Jencks, *The Language of Post-Modern Architecture*, 6th edn (London: Academy, 1991), p. 60.
[32] Kostoff, *History*, p. 124.   [33] Westfall and van Pelt, *Architectural Principles*, p. 271.
[34] Kostoff, *History*, p. 123.

he said it was not possible to play originality with the orders. 'They have to be so well digested that there is nothing but essence left. When right they are curiously lovely – unalterable as plant forms... The process is in fact ideal, that is, based on "the perfection of kind".'[35] Against this we have to note the way in which the orders have gone on evolving, so that the decoration on 'Corinthian' columns, for example, long ago abandoned simple acanthus leaves.

A particular construal of this rationality reads it, with John Summerson and Roger Scruton, as embodying the virtues of civility, decency, serenity and restraint, 'the creation of a public world of mutual respect'.[36] 'In its humble way, the classical vernacular aims to transform the city into a temple, to spread over the human world the mantle of grace.'[37] As we saw in Chapter 3, the commitment to proportion enshrined a sense of human scale which, we may suspect, is one of the secrets of classical architecture's enduring appeal. The orders, for Roger Scruton, are the visible licence to dwell, the affirmation of our right of occupation and the reminder that we belong to a community not of the living only, but of the dead and unborn. 'That is the secret of their civility, which is no different, in the last analysis, from good manners and decency: for these virtues enshrine the gift of membership. Without manners there is anarchy; where there is anarchy no one belongs.'[38] This is well said, though we have to ask whether other styles might not equally embody good manners and whether good manners are the sum of what we are looking for.

At the same time the paradigmatic significance of the Acropolis means that classical architecture has been identified with the emergence of an ideal of freedom, not for slaves and women to be sure, but marked off from the serfdom of barbarian states such as Persia. It emerged in a political context which allowed private property and individual freedom. 'The message of the temple to the alien world was that of a free people, subject to neither king nor priest: "The whole folk year by year in parity of service is our king", as Euripedes put it.'[39] These democratic pretensions were seized on by the fledgling American and French republics. Lacking in the great Greek designs is the whole hierarchical order implicit, for example, in both Byzantine and Gothic progressions from nave to apse or altar, where hierarchy may be enshrined in stone. At the same time the Palladian villa celebrated a colossally unequal social order. Democratic pretensions were

---

[35] Cited in Summerson, *Classical Language*, p. 27.
[36] So Scruton *Aesthetics*, 256, *Classical Vernacular*, 57, and J. Summerson, *Georgian London* (Harmondsworth: Penguin, 1978), p. 23.
[37] Scruton, *Classical Vernacular*, p. 27.   [38] Ibid., p. 109.   [39] Kostoff, *History*, p. 120.

also subverted when the classical vernacular became the favoured language for commerce, as in Wall Street or the Mansion House, or for court houses, or for state buildings like the Capitol, so that it became in another way a language of power.

To emphasise the rationality of classicism does not mean that it is not at the same time an architecture of great vitality, expressed in a whole gamut of visual subtleties. In Greek temples the groundline of the terrace gently curved upward towards the middle of each side. The columns tapered and had slightly convex profiles. The four corner columns inclined inwards and back and were also made thicker than the rest. 'These were not just corrective measures to counter the appearance that straight lines sag. They are intentional and evident distortions that render the otherwise thoroughly rational design of the temple live and spry.'[40] The carvings on the metopes often showed unfinished conflict, thus expressing a 'violent involvement' at a far remove from eighteenth-century urbanity.[41] This is a rather different thing from the civility which Scruton celebrates and which is embodied in Wren's and Gibbs' churches, expressions of the bourgeois settlement of late seventeenth-century England.

The achievement represented by the classical tradition, Scruton comments, is 'the translation of the aesthetic demand into an agreed and flexible language of signs, a language which facilitates at every juncture the outward projection and realization of the self'. This, he says, is not just a passing object of respect, a temporary speciality in the arcanum of taste, 'but on the contrary, the perfect representative of all that is good in building, all that building contains by way of decency, serenity and restraint'.[42] Contrast this, however, with Summerson's defence of Butterfield, who grew up in Georgian London:

How he hated taste! And how right he was! Just imagine yourself living in late Georgian London . . . Imagine a city in which every street is a Gower Street, in which the 'great' buildings are by smooth Mr Wilkins, dull Mr Smirke or facetious Mr Nash. Imagine the unbearable oppressiveness of a landscape in which such architecture represents the emotional ceiling.[43]

One of the things we learn from this is what ought to be the obvious point that the same thing said in another context is not the same thing. Scruton is right to insist that there is nothing wrong with repeating designs from the past. At the same time using the 'classical vernacular' actually produces quite different styles in, say, sixteenth-century Italy, early eighteenth-century

[40] Ibid., p. 127.   [41] Ibid., p. 155.   [42] Scruton, *Aesthetics*, p. 263.
[43] Summerson, *Heavenly Mansions*, p. 173.

London, mid-eighteenth-century Bath and so on, not to mention the quotation of classical motifs by postmodern architecture. The energy and rationality we find in fourth-century Greek architecture are not replicated in Georgian London or Dublin.

The question of interpretation can be illustrated by the design of churches. In his demonstration that God had revealed classical architecture to Moses, Villalpanda reduced the three orders to one, a mixture of Doric and Corinthian, the 'Temple order'. In this way he sought to bring reason and revelation together. 'Villalpanda's work turned the classical orders into the inevitable archetype for an architecture of grace.'[44] Not so inevitable, we have to add, that the original designs for St Peter's in Rome did not have to be amended. Alberti, who was Abbot of San Sorvino in Pisa, spoke of churches as temples and recommended the Greek cross style, combining circles and squares, which in his view were perfect forms. Bramante and Michelangelo planned St Peter's on this model but Pope Paul V developed cold feet about it in the light of criticisms that classical architecture was essentially pagan. The nave was therefore lengthened to produce the more familiar cruciform pattern. John Summerson remarks that St Paul's is a building into whose form the spiritual history of seventeenth-century England is as firmly built as it is into the writings of Locke and Dryden. 'There is the science of the Royal Society, the Latinity of Restoration Oxford, and the religious equivocation of the House of Stuart.' Equally, James Gibbs' St Martin-in-the-Fields is conceived of as a temple which expresses the 'clear correspondence between English Protestantism, Lockeian philosophy and this kind of building', and Hawksmoor's St George's Bloomsbury provoked ridicule from contemporaries by including a statue of George I clad in a toga on the top of its steeple.[45] I cannot myself make a connection between the virtues of the gospel, or the God revealed in Christ, and the social and emotional order of a Wren or Hawksmoor church, though I understand that they are designed for preaching. To me they speak much more of the high and dry deism of the beginning of the eighteenth century, 'Christianity not mysterious', as Toland put it. Similarly there is enormous dissonance produced when one listens to the letter to the Romans read in a Bavarian baroque church. This does not imply any criticism of classical or baroque styles in secular contexts, but it sharpens the question about the ends which such building embodies.

---

[44] Rykwert, *On Adam's House in Paradise*, p. 122.
[45] Summerson, *Georgian London*, pp. 61, 91. Hawksmoor's tower was modelled on the Mausoleum at Halicarnassus. Horace Walpole called the spire 'a masterpiece of absurdity'.

THE GOTHIC TRADITION

Gothic emerged, it is generally agreed, in the middle of the twelfth century, probably under the influence of knowledge brought back from the Middle East after the crusades.[46] The introduction of Euclid's *Elements of Geometry* to the West about 1120–5, translated by Adelard of Bath, was also a key factor.

In his great book on the Gothic cathedral, Otto von Simson understands the two main impetuses of Gothic architecture to be the use of light and the unique relationship between structure and appearance. In relation to the first he argues that the whole of medieval thought operated according to the principle of analogy. Corporeal light was an analogy of the divine light. Pseudo Dionysus, to whom Suger's cathedral in Paris was dedicated, believed that creation is an act of illumination and that the created universe cannot exist without light. If light ceased to shine, all being would vanish into nothingness. Because the created order is full of light the creation is the self-revelation of God.[47] The great windows of the medieval cathedrals were not simply parables of the divine light, but mediated it, helped realise the divine presence.

At the same time these cathedrals were built according to a rigidly mathematical and musical understanding of proportion.

In Chartres, proportion is experienced as the harmonious articulation of a comprehensive whole; it determines the ground plan as well as the elevation; and it 'chains', by the single ratio of the golden section, the individual parts not only to one another but also to the whole that encompasses them all. The same desire for unification that induced the architect to treat piers and superimposed shafts not as independent units but rather as articulations of a continuous vertical rhythm suggested to him the choice of the proportion that might indeed be called the mathematical equivalent of that unifying design.[48]

This correspondence to proper proportion meant that the cosmic harmony revealed there 'inspires the beholder with the desire to establish a similar harmony within himself'.[49] The purpose of the building, therefore, was not just mystical but moral. In the Cathedral of Chartres, von Simson argues, the architect has realised the cosmological order of luminosity and proportion to the exclusion of all other architectural motifs and with a

[46] John Harvey argues that external impact is the only way to understand its sudden emergence. It may be supposed that returning Frankish engineers from 1099 onwards would have come back equipped with fresh knowledge of structural expedients and that a proportion of Eastern prisoners of outstanding capacity were brought back to the West. *The Master Builders: Architecture in the Middle Ages* (London: Thames and Hudson, 1971), p. 28.
[47] O. von Simson, *The Gothic Cathedral*, p. 53.   [48] Ibid., p. 214.   [49] Ibid., p. 140.

perfection never achieved before. Light transfigures and orders the compositions in the stained glass windows, and perfect proportion harmonises all elements of the building.[50]

Roger Scruton feels that while classical architecture is essentially oriented to the world, the 'sacred meaning' of Gothic means that it is 'not of this world' and that its forms 'lend themselves only precariously to domestic and civil uses and the Gothic vernacular has never been more than a passing dream'.[51] This is to overlook, however, both the wide range of medieval secular Gothic buildings, from the Ducal Palace in Venice to Westminster Hall and to schools and hospitals, but also the work of the Gothic Revival, which embraced Strawberry Hill, St Pancras Station, Keble College, the Houses of Parliament, the 1914 Woolworths building in Manhattan and extraordinary suburban developments like the north Oxford estate. Although there were many nineteenth-century Gothic churches the vast majority of Revival work was secular.[52] The importance of secular Gothic means that von Simson's account of the two great principles embodied in the cathedrals cannot be generalised beyond them. They are not, in any obvious way, what Gothic is 'about'.

Summerson understood Gothic as the product of fantasy, the result of 'a profound desire to escape from the remorseless discipline of gravity, a desire to dissolve the heavy prose of building into religious poetry; a desire to transform the heavy man-made temple into a multiple, imponderable pile of heavenly mansions'.[53] On his account Gothic developed by using the aedicule, the 'little shrine', and this marks a profound continuity with the classical tradition, a metamorphosis rather than a contradiction. As it lost its daring it slowly made its way back to the classical norm. To describe the great Gothic cathedrals as 'religious poetry' is just, but it does not help us to understand the Gothic Revival. If we stick with the metaphor we can say that Strawberry Hill or St Pancras Station perhaps represents the rather florid and not very profound poetry we associate with nineteenth-century medieval romances, but the Revival suburban estates are more prose than poetry and often very dull prose at that.

Ruskin put the emphasis on the daring and liveliness of Gothic. It had 'savageness', 'the look of mountain brotherhood between the cathedral

---

[50] Ibid., p. 235.   [51] Scruton, *Classical Vernacular*, p. 27.

[52] In the countryside in Britain old ways of building continued untouched and 'Walpole little suspected that the average barn was more truly Gothic than his bepinnacled Strawberry'. K. Clark, *The Gothic Revival* (Harmondsworth: Penguin, 1964), p. 11.

[53] Summerson, *Heavenly Mansions*, p. 9. This is written of the Romanesque but it sums up what he says a little later about the fantasy of the aedicular system.

and the Alp; this magnificence of sturdy power'.[54] In Gothic one found a peculiar energy 'which makes the fiercest lightning forked rather than curved, and the stoutest oak branch angular rather than bending'. In contrast to Egyptian and Greek building, we find 'an elastic tension and communication of force from part to part, and also a studious expression of this throughout every visible line of the building'. Gothic ornament 'stands out in prickly independence and frosty fortitude, jutting into crockets, and freezing into pinnacles; here starting up into a monster, there germinating into a blossom . . . even when most graceful, never for an instant languid, always quickset: erring, if at all, ever on the side of brusquerie'.[55] Gothic was not constrained by rigid patterns and was 'capable of perpetual novelty'. Ruskin contrasted this with the alienated machine work of the nineteenth century, which, of course, also characterises the Gothic Revival. In one point of view, he argued, Gothic was the only rational architecture,

as being that which can fit itself most easily to all services, vulgar or noble. Undefined in its slope of roof, height of shaft, breadth of arch, or disposition of ground plan, it can shrink into a turret, expand into a hall, coil into a staircase, or spring into a spire, with undegraded grace and unexhausted energy; and whenever it finds occasion for change in its form or purpose, it submits to it without the slightest sense of loss either to its unity or majesty.[56]

Ruskin also felt that Gothic was marked by naturalism, the love of natural objects for their own sake. Gothic, he argued, turned away from the symbolism of Byzantium but also from the quest for perfection of classicism, its carving resembling the 'warts and all' approach of the biblical narrators. Alongside naturalism, however, was a delight in the fantastic and ludicrous, the grotesque. Finally there was 'a magnificent enthusiasm, which feels as if it never could do enough to reach the fullness of its ideal'.[57] Much of this derived from the dominance of carved form. Such form, says Scruton, 'has a peculiar life, and bears on its surface the mark of human labour. It is this mark which transforms the stone of Gothic cathedral from inert masses into centres of vitality. The Gothic cathedral is, therefore, able to risk the greatest possible height and scale, while never approaching the downcasting inhumanity of the modern skyscraper.'[58]

Very little of this was true of the Gothic which Ruskin himself knew, which often amounted to little except the installation of pointed windows and the occasional turret. Much of it, like Strawberry Hill and even the Houses of Parliament, is a product of romanticism. Clark called the Houses

[54] Ruskin, *Stones*, p. 164.   [55] Ibid., pp. 173–4.   [56] Ibid., p. 168.   [57] Ibid., pp. 176–7.
[58] Scruton, *Aesthetics*, p. 220.

of Parliament 'a great necropolis of style' but at the same time 'a triumph of the picturesque'.[59] By contrast, the Gothic of the Commissioners' churches was 'the most completely unattractive architectural style ever employed'.[60] The truth was that even if the old skills were available, which they were, 'the impulse which once made gargoyles so fierce and saints so unearthly was beyond recapture'.[61] As with classicism, simply following rules does not reproduce a style. 'They tried to revive a style which depended on sentiment as if it depended on rules.'[62] Butterfield, as Clark remarks, was a nineteenth-century architect. His entire sensibility was informed by his own century – how could it not be! For all his piety, a Butterfield church is as difficult to worship in as a church by Wren on account of what Clark calls his ruthlessness, even to the point of a certain sadism.[63] The use of the same grammar or language does not produce similar buildings across the centuries because the spirit which informs them is completely different. Awareness of this difference, and the desire for cultural integrity, constituted one of the spurs in the development of the modern movement.

THE VALUES OF MODERNISM

From the mid-nineteenth century onwards we hear voices lamenting the fact that the nineteenth century lacks its own style. The Gothic Revival was not made without a keen awareness of the 'foul wide gap' between the nineteenth and the thirteenth or fourteenth centuries. We must learn the grammar of the past, said Ruskin, and then a new style might arise. We might, as it were, come to speak Italian instead of Latin.[64] Otto Wagner's *Modern Architecture*, whose first edition was in 1895, assured its readers that 'The task of art and therefore also of modern art, has remained what it has been in all times. Modern art must offer us modern forms that are created by us and that represent our abilities and actions.'[65]

This new style, the modern, in order to represent us and our time, must clearly express a distinct change from previous feeling, an almost complete decline of the romantic, and an almost all-encompassing appearance of reason in all our works... The cleft between the modern movement and the renaissance is already larger than that between the renaissance and antiquity.[66]

The revolution in painting, the 'shock of the new', came slightly later but it expressed precisely this sense. What was needed was a complete break with

---

[59] Clark, *Revival*, pp. 103, 105.   [60] Ibid., p. 89.   [61] Ibid., p. 117.   [62] Ibid., p. 200.
[63] Ibid., p. 174.   [64] Ruskin, *Seven Lamps*, p. 208.
[65] O. Wagner, *Modern Architecture* (Santa Monica: Getty Centre, 1988), p. 75.   [66] Ibid., p. 80.

the perspectivism of the past. In the same way, 'Just as Malevich's painting was in effect a clean slate offered to the world to provide an entirely new set of images, so Mies' glassy façades were giant mirrors held up to the world to reflect an entirely new set of forms.'[67]

Allied to this, we encounter a weariness with prevailing forms and the eclecticism of the *belle époque*. In the Netherlands H. P. Berlage denounced such architecture, drawing on Ruskin, as 'sham architecture, i.e. imitation, i.e. lying'.[68] In this period, said van de Velde, people saw that the reigning architecture was a 'lie', all posturing and no truth, and that greater purity of expression was needed. Giedion is therefore correct to say that the modern movement began as a moral demand.[69] In descriptions of modernist architecture written in the first half of the twentieth century we constantly come across the term 'honesty'. Modernists wanted honesty of structure, honesty in the way form reflected function, honesty in reflecting the true spirit of the times rather than the past. Honesty was expressed in showing materials in their natural state and in not disguising the structure of a building.[70] 'The striving towards truth must be the guiding star of the architect', wrote Otto Wagner. 'Then the character and symbolism of the work will emerge virtually of their own accord: sanctity will be observed in the church, gravity and dignity in the governmental building, gaiety in the amusement establishment, and so on!'[71] The factory which Gropius built 'realized honesty of thought and feeling'. It healed (though it is difficult to see how) 'the break between thinking and feeling which had been the bone sickness of European architecture'.[72] Mies van der Rohe quoted Augustine to the effect that 'Beauty is the splendour of truth'. In 1963 Peter Blake could write of Mies that 'his is the moral code of Augustine and Aquinas'.[73] His Bacardi building in Cuba, we are told, is 'an intensely moral building: Serene, clear, unaffected, pure, and utterly self assured.'[74] While one may doubt the connection with Augustine and Aquinas it is not the case that Modernism could not pose general questions of architectural meaning.[75] It certainly did so: at the heart of the creed was 'progress', variously defined, sometimes in terms of the advance of capitalism, sometimes in terms of greater equality and the welfare state. It represented an aggressive account of the 'religion of reason' in built form. The international style was

---

[67] P. Blake, *Mies van der Rohe* (Harmondsworth: Penguin, 1963), p. 28.
[68] Giedion, *Space, Time and Architecture*, p. 292, quoting Berlage.
[69] Giedion, *Space, Time and Architecture*, p. 293.
[70] B. C. Brolin, *The Failure of Modern Architecture* (New York: Van Nostrand, 1976), pp. 15, 16.
[71] Wagner, *Modern Architecture*, p. 83. [72] Giedion, *Space, Time and Architecture*, p. 482.
[73] Blake, *Mies*, p. 15. [74] Ibid., p. 114. [75] As Charles Jencks argues. *Language*, p. 92.

supposed to help to 'create a new species of human being' and was part and parcel of the advance in human welfare.[76]

A third factor in the development of architectural modernism was the impact of new materials, especially iron, steel and plate glass, which had already shown their potential in the mid-nineteenth century, and were taken up by architects like Sullivan in Chicago to create a new kind of shop, or a new kind of factory. Already by 1889 Anatole de Baudot could write that the engineer, *l'homme moderne par excellence*, was beginning to replace the architect. Ten years later Henri van de Velde could claim that 'The extraordinary beauty innate in the work of engineers has its basis in their unconsciousness of its artistic possibilities – much as the creators of the beauty of cathedrals were unaware of the magnificence of their achievements.'[77] The architect has over-valued his usefulness, said the Bauhaus manifesto. 'The engineer, on the contrary, untrammelled by aesthetic and historical prejudice, has arrived at clear organic forms.'[78] Pugin had defended Gothic architecture on the grounds that none of its details lacked functional purpose. The doctrine was now enunciated that 'form follows function'. The reigning utilitarianism was translated into architecture. The new technology begot an aesthetic which played with 'freely hovering parts and surfaces' and dispensed with the traditional relation between load and support.[79]

In all this there is that heady sense of a new world which characterised the early twentieth century: we have the petrol combustion engine! Radio! The telephone! Cubism! The first air flights! Novelists like H. G. Wells fervidly explored the possibilities of a new world. From the start modernism was excited by the new technology. 'The aesthetic qualities of the machine – simplicity and geometry – became desirable in themselves.'[80]

The new glass and steel boxes, the furniture on which no one could be comfortable, followed suit. The catastrophe of World War I left this cultural mood unchastened. 'A great epoch has begun!' Le Corbusier could write in 1921, 'There exists a new spirit! Architecture is the masterly, correct and magnificent play of masses brought together in light.'[81] 'Together let us conceive and create the new building which will embrace architecture and sculpture and painting in one unity', said the Bauhaus manifesto, 'and which will rise one day toward heaven from the hands of a million workers

---

[76] D. Harvey, *The Condition of Postmodernity* (Oxford: Blackwell, 1989), p. 70.
[77] Giedion, *Space, Time and Architecture*, p. 217.   [78] Rykwert, *On Adam's House in Paradise*, p. 24.
[79] Giedion, *Space, Time and Architecture*, p. 485.   [80] Brolin, *Failure*, p. 33.
[81] P. Blake, *Le Corbusier* (Harmondsworth: Penguin, 1963), p. 37.

like the crystal standard of the new faith.'[82] The whole trend of our time is toward the secular, wrote Mies in 1924. 'We shall build no cathedrals . . . Ours is not an age of pathos; we do not respect flights of the spirit as much as we value reason and realism.'[83]

From capitalism – that system wherein all energies are aimed at increasing efficiency, at getting the most return for the least investment – modernists acquired the intellectual and emotional bias for a practical, functional approach to design. This approach worked toward the exclusion of all elements, such as ornament, that served no demonstrably practical purpose, and the rejection of visual complexity in favour of simple forms that, as it was felt, would serve the simple, basic needs of life.[84]

The irony was that some of the trademarks, such as flat roofs and wrap-around windows, were not functional at all. The flat roofs leaked and accumulated snow, prevented air circulating above the upper rooms and left no storage space. Huge amounts of glass increased the need for both cooling and heating.

The International Style was given its name at the Museum of Modern Art in New York in 1932. 'A universal civilization is in the making', the apostle of modernism, Siegfried Giedion, could say, 'but it is by no means developing in every country at the same pace.'[85] Unaware of the dialectic of enlightenment he could still, in the last edition of his book, tell us that 'Science and art, in so far as they explore the unknown or anticipate the future, reflect the real level, the true being, of our age. They are the real moral forces; they will speak for us to later generations when the horrors of the external world of our period have faded away.'[86] Peter Blake, a one-time enthusiast, commented sourly,

The Modern Movement, with its shining dogmas, its exciting slogans, and, above all, with its absolute self righteousness, was and is, quite clearly, a religion as irrational as all others, from snake handling to psychoanalysis. Like all religious cultists, the members of the sect treat their critics with patient condescension: those who don't want to be ground into the dust don't know what's good for them; but the cultist, to whom the Truth has been revealed, does know, and he or she will ram the new language of Vision down the nonbelievers throats, even if they gag on it.[87]

In contrast to the florid excesses of the *belle époque*, modernism inclined to minimalism. Adolf Loos' *bon mot* that 'ornament was a crime' translated

---

[82] Rykwert, *On Adam's House in Paradise*, p. 24.   [83] Blake, *Mies*, p. 117.   [84] Brolin, *Failure*, p. 15.
[85] Giedion, *Space, Time and Architecture*, p. xxxvii.   [86] Ibid., p. 879.
[87] P. Blake, *Form Follows Fiasco* (Boston: Little, Brown & Co., 1974), p. 149.

into an officious puritanism.[88] The steel I-beam was the basic unit of construction (Mies kept a section in his office) and thus Truth and Beauty had to take the rectangular form of the great skyscrapers.[89] Divisions between storeys were eliminated, and thus at the same time the shadow caused by mouldings.[90] Blake argues that the glass 'skin' of these buildings reflected trees and sun and therefore made them vibrant with life and colour.[91] But do they in any way reflect the 'lamp of life' as Ruskin described it? Are they 'vibrant with life' in the way, say, that a Doric temple is, or the west front of almost any medieval cathedral? Charles Jencks speaks of 'univalence', an architecture created around one (or a few) simplified values.[92]

The modern movement espoused humanism, but almost everywhere its results were anti-humanist. From the mid-1960s modernism faced a barrage of criticism, which makes it particularly lamentable that the Manhattanisation of almost every city continues apace. Geoffrey Scott called the belief that engineering could replace architecture 'the mechanical fallacy'. It confused structure in itself with the effect of structure on the human spirit and disregarded the ways in which the architect will either conceal or emphasise the facts of construction. Construction, he said, is a useful slave but a blind master. It cannot substitute for an aesthetic conception or for overall purpose.[93] According to James Stirling (himself a leading modernist) in 1974, 99 per cent of modern architecture is boring, banal and barren and usually disruptive and unharmonious when placed in older cities.[94] The language of modernism, writes Scruton, is uncouth, unredeemed by detail and utterly indifferent to its surroundings or to the person who is obliged to pass the building by.[95] The obsession with speed encouraged the tendency to omit detail, because that could not be seen when passing in a fast car or an aeroplane.[96] Modernism did its immense damage, says Kunstler,

by divorcing the practice of building from the history and traditional meanings of building; by promoting a species of urbanism that destroyed age-old social arrangements and, with them, urban life as a general proposition; and by creating a physical setting for man that failed to respect the limits of scale, growth, and the consumption of natural resources, or to respect the lives of other living things.[97]

High-rise buildings destroy the balance with nature, causing pollution and wind tunnels, they isolate people, they prevent social units like the family

---

[88] Kunstler, *Geography*, p. 71.   [89] Blake, *Mies*, p. 110.   [90] Scruton, *Classical Vernacular*, p. 10.
[91] Blake, *Mies*, p. 62.   [92] Jencks, *Language*, p. 27.   [93] Scott, *Architecture*, p. 96.
[94] quoted in Blake, *Form*, p. 10.   [95] Scruton, *Classical*, p. 16.   [96] Brolin, *Failure*, p. 27.
[97] Kunstler, *Geography*, p. 67.

or neighbourhood from functioning, they work against networks of transportation because they overload roads, and they destroy the urban landscape by eliminating values which existed in the past. 'Human symbols – such as churches, mosques, temples of all kinds, city halls, which once rose above the city – are now below the skyscrapers. We may not agree that God or government should rise above man, but are we ready to agree that symbols of capital gain should rise above everything else?'[98] This was the key point. The values of modernism originated in the factory and moved on to corporate capital. They were the values of the triumphant dollar, thrusting, aggressive, devoid of charm. The humane intentions of the movement touched nobody's heart, said John Summerson. 'To all except an informed few, architecture communicated nothing but boredom.'[99]

As an ideology modernism has been rejected, but the spiritual foundations on which it rests – capitalism, industrial growth and faith in technology – are still in place, and these are what have prevented the growth of a genuine alternative to it.

ARCHITECTURE IN AN AGE OF NIHILISM

Disenchantment with modernism was already voiced in the 1940s, just after the war, which is when the term 'postmodernism' first began to be used, but its manifesto had to wait for twenty years. Robert Venturi's *Complexity and Contradiction in Architecture* is packed full of illuminating analysis of baroque architecture. He wanted to get away from the puritan orthodoxy of modernism. 'I like elements that are hybrid rather than pure, compromising rather than clean', he announced, 'distorted rather than straightforward, ambiguous rather than articulated, perverse as well as impersonal, boring as well as interesting, conventional rather than designed, accommodating rather than excluding ... I am for messy vitality over obvious unity. I include the non sequitur and proclaim the duality.'[100]

---

[98] Quoted in Blake, *Form*, p. 82. Howard Davis argues that there should be a moratorium on high-rise building. 'These outrageous assaults upon our town and city scapes are launched for one reason only: to generate maximum profit for a handful of hit and run speculators who consider the surface of the earth their private preserve.' Densities of up to 200 persons per acre, he argues, can be achieved in two-storey patio houses with individual gardens. *Culture of Building*, pp. 150, 153.

[99] Summerson, *Classical Language*, p. 114. In Britain after World War II a good many modernist churches were built for the new council housing estates. They are charmless functional buildings, 'multi-purpose worship centres' where space can be used for playgroups or meetings during the week, and where a concession is made to the sacred with some cheap stained glass. Not until the 1960s did architects begin to reflect the new ecclesiology which was coming out of Vatican II and to start building something more interesting, to ask what a church might be about.

[100] R. Venturi, *Complexity and Contradiction in Architecture* (New York: Museum of Modern Art, 1966), p. 16.

This sounded promising. Architecture, he said, should be based on the richness and ambiguity of modern experience, and should reflect a view of life as complex and ironic. Unfortunately what came from this was not complexity at all but the banality of pop art. Venturi reflects the power of cultural populism in American intellectual life. His central proposition was that Main Street was almost all right. 'Indeed, is not the commercial strip of a Route 66 almost all right? The seemingly chaotic juxtapositions of honky tonk elements express an intriguing kind of vitality and validity and they produce an unexpected approach to unity as well.'[101] Later he notoriously drew inspiration from the signage of Las Vegas. Buildings were essentially 'decorated sheds'. What has come to instantiate postmodern building is wildly eclectic architecture, random quotation which makes the *belle époque* look Cistercian, all in the name of 'irony'. 'Eclecticism is the degree zero of contemporary general culture: one listens to reggae, watches a western, eats McDonald's food for lunch and local cuisine for dinner, wears Paris perfume in Tokyo and 'retro' clothes in Hong Kong.'[102]

The 'post' in postmodern can suggest that any building which seeks to differentiate itself from modernism is postmodern; thus buildings such as Erskine's Byker Wall or Gehry's museum in Bilbao are sometimes designated 'postmodern', but this seems to me unhelpful.[103] I shall take Venturi's manifesto as postmodern architecture's classic statement and buildings like Charles Moore's Piazza d'Italia in New Orleans, the Pompidou Centre in Paris or the Lloyd's Building in London as classic instances. Modernism had exemplified triumphant Reason, but after Auschwitz it was no longer possible to believe in this. Deprived of this credo what was left was play, irony and behind these, the market. All over the world an 'architecture of spectacle, with its sense of surface glitter and transitory participatory pleasure, of display and ephemerality, of jouissance' has taken the place of the planned centres of modernism.[104] David Harvey reads them in terms of bread and circuses, part of an attempt to distract populations from serious questions of justice and redistribution. Venturi came to think that

---

[101] Ibid., p. 103.   [102] J.-F. Lyotard, quoted in Harvey, *Condition*, p. 87.

[103] In an otherwise excellent book Mary Acton attempts to read both Libeskind and Gehry through deconstruction, but she can do this only by arguing that any interest in metaphor and meaning is part of the intellectual excitement of this stage of postmodern philosophy. But this is obviously nonsense. The builders of the great Gothic cathedrals or of the Parthenon were also interested in metaphor and meaning. For easily understandable reasons thinkers like Derrida call the permanence of truth into question. Perhaps Venturi's architecture expresses a disbelief in truth. But both Libeskind and Gehry are humanists who make positive statements about the human condition and the human future in their buildings (though sustainability is not top of the agenda for either of them). M. Acton, *Learning to Look at Modern Art* (London: Routledge, 2004), pp. 209–10.

[104] Harvey, *Condition*, p. 91.

American space was not about forms but about symbols, communication, advertising. All this, says Kunstler, was wonderfully fascinating:

Parking lots were fascinating, the vast spaces between the buildings were fascinating, the luridly painted statues ringing Caesar's Palace, the highway, the curbing, even the zone of rusting beer cans at the ragged edge of town had something to reward the patient observer... they were like stoned graduate students on a field trip, their critical faculties gone up in smoke...

Irony was the thing. A little gentle mockery, some good humoured ribbing, mild subversion. As if to say, 'here, you nation of morons, is another inevitably banal, cheap concrete box, of the only type your sordid civilization allows, topped by some cheap and foolish ornament worthy of your TV-addled brains'. It must be obvious there was nothing particularly redeeming about this mind game really. It was simply parody, which is to say the sophomoric urge to ridicule by means of feeble imitation, in an absence of an urge to create something of real quality.[105]

The serious point behind postmodern architecture is the respect for difference of postmodern and multicultural theory. Jencks suggests that postmodernism is developing a radical eclecticism which can appeal to different taste cultures, and that it is multivalent, appealing to opposite faculties of the mind and body 'so that they interrelate and modify each other'.[106] As exemplified by Moore, however, Kunstler is much more to the point. In his Piazza d'Italia we find

ironic reference to the five orders of classical column... by placing them in a subtly coloured continuum, indebted somewhat to Pop Art... their elevation is faced in marble, and their cross section is like a slice of cake. The columns are separated from their Corinthian capitals by rings of neon tubing, which gives them colourful luminous necklaces at night... this is not realism, but a façade, a stage set, a fragment inserted into a new and modern context.[107]

To my mind, however, it is not really multivalent at all, but the architecture of a populist avant garde whose most important cultural reference, as instanced by Disneyland, is Mickey Mouse. This is not respect for difference but the triumph of a particular kind of populism, just as modernism represented the triumph of a highbrow account of progress. Put another way, the 'collapse of metanarratives' is reflected in architecture. Classicism, Gothic and modernism all believed passionately in something even if we do not approve of their creed, but postmodernism has no creed but irony. Postmodern play, says Glassie, takes place in the air above nothing, as

---

[105] Kunstler, *Geography*, pp. 82–3.   [106] Jencks, *Language*, p. 107.
[107] Klotz, *Post-Modern Visions*, quoted in Harvey, *Condition*, p. 93.

opposed to its Victorian predecessor or to the eclecticism of earlier periods, which was all juxtaposed to a profound moral order.[108]

The postmodern claim that metanarratives have collapsed is, of course, false. What remains – and here we have the continuity with modernism – is the metanarrative of the market. Postmodernism is, in Jameson's phrase, 'the cultural logic of late capitalism', and postmodern architecture reflects this.[109] What this means in practice is that the drive for profit rules, and in such a situation, Howard Davis notes, the built environment does not improve.[110] The priority of the decorated shed is a confession of our own emptiness.

THE VIRTUES OF ARCHITECTURE

No more for architecture than for politics can there be a 'Christian' tradition. Pugin's claims that Gothic peculiarly represented such a tradition amount to little more than the argument that soaring arches and the pinnacles of the Perpendicular phase of Gothic testify to the resurrection. For the rest, his arguments are resolutely utilitarian. Scruton correctly insists that it is moralistic to try and translate the moral nature of aesthetic taste into a formula, a simple rule of right and wrong.[111] But if we cannot identify any architectural style as Christian there are still aspects of building which the gospel affirms and aspects which it rejects.

The art of architecture, said Geoffrey Scott, 'studies not structure in itself but the effect of structure on the human spirit'.[112] Much pedigreed architecture is downcasting, a testament to the will to power, to an individual or a corporate ego. By contrast, the gospel affirms architecture which is

---

[108] Glassie, *Vernacular Architecture*, p. 79.

[109] F. Jameson, *Postmodernism: The Cultural Logic of Late Capitalism* (London: Verso, 1991).

[110] Davis, *Culture of Building*, p. 94. In an interview with Christopher Alexander the latter comments that because a particular restaurant was built at arm's length to make money, 'it is not done in a way that actually permits a direct relationship between someone's own inner life and the situation there . . . the kinds of relationship that can generate spirit simply do not survive'. Howard Davis and C. Alexander, 'Beyond Humanism', *Journal of Architectural Education*, 35/1 (1981), 18–24.

[111] 'There is no rule or recipe for good building. We have nothing more than an intimation of what good architecture consists in. We have arrived at a sense of deep, a priori, connection between moral and aesthetic understanding; but we have no rule whereby to translate than sense into a critical canon . . . the reason for the value of taste will not be criteria for its exercise: they will issue in no rules of critical discrimination. It is a mark of moralism in aesthetics that it seeks to translate the moral nature of aesthetic taste into a formula; into a simple rule of right and wrong. (It is moralism, for example, that persuaded Pugin that he was obliged to build in the "pointed" style, and which persuaded the advocates of the modern movement of the moral impeccability, indeed the moral necessity, of their enterprise.') Scruton, *Aesthetics*, p. 252.

[112] Scott, *Architecture*, p. 96.

'uplifting', which affirms our humanity and gives us joy. Such architecture emerges from an affirmative vision, as it did in both classical and Gothic traditions. The architects who gave us the masterpieces of these forms believed in something. This is what Ruskin meant by 'the lamp of obedience' according to which, as we saw earlier, good architecture embodies in some way political and cultural values and what he calls 'the religious faith of nations'.[113] This needs to be qualified because polities and religions, even supposedly 'Christian' ones, can be idolatrous. Everyone agrees that Stalinist architecture is downcasting in this way, and many people feel the same about Le Corbusier. Both represent totalitarian ideologies, though of course in Ronchamps Le Corbusier revealed a repressed romanticism. In London the bleak landscape of the Barbican and the South Bank arts complex all bear witness to a harsh utilitarianism which later generations have, bit by bit, to try and humanise. Life-affirming architecture is, as Scott argues, humanist in that it affirms human beings, even if it induces a feeling of humility. There are, of course, modern buildings like this. Frank Lloyd Wright's houses are loved because of their romanticism, their appeal to a love of nature, a vision of patriarchal hospitality gathered around a hearth and an open and liberal individualism. Their problem is that they are not generalisable: like Renaissance palaces they are for a handful of extremely wealthy people. The best work of Alvar Aalto, like the community centre at Saynätsalo in Finland, is likewise humanised through its appeal to nature. As Jencks correctly insists, the spiritual function of architecture will not go away. I suspect that, as the global emergency intensifies, a new spirituality shaped by respect for the natural world (rather than for 'Nature'), a spirituality which already has deep roots in many cultures, will grow and that this will lead to the emergence of a new, modest, but more serious architecture, shorn of postmodern irony.[114]

Second, we have to ask whether the most successful buildings do not in general emerge from a commitment to the common good. In earlier times there were temples and cathedrals; today there are museums, theatres and opera houses. These places are not private space: they belong to the people. So the people of Bilbao are intensely proud of the Guggenheim, the people of Liverpool of 'Paddy's Wigwam', the new Roman Catholic Cathedral.

[113] Ruskin, *Seven Lamps*, p. 199.
[114] Mary Acton draws attention to Richard MacCormack's garden quadrangle in St John's College, Oxford. It stands, as she rightly says, in the English picturesque tradition. It echoes not only the classical tradition, however, but older English traditions. MacCormack was thinking of old London Bridge in putting the student accommodation on top of the piers below. The building thus cleverly alludes to the many stages of the college's past. Acton, *Learning to Look*, p. 268.

Of course there are iconic buildings which are private. The Pyramids were funerary monuments, and the Taj Mahal was a mausoleum, though both are now tourist space. Norman Foster's Swiss Re building, the 'Gherkin', is built for corporate finance and makes deliberate claims for an alternative narrative to nearby St Paul's. What commands affection, however, is what people feel they in some sense own. As I argued in Chapter 7, this is one of the virtues of church building, that it is genuinely common, public space – or it would be if you did not have to pay to go in. It testifies to the fact that 'the earth is the Lord's' and that it cannot therefore be appropriated for the benefits of a few.

A third criterion I have argued for throughout the book is grace – beauty and proportion. This is not identical to the faithfulness to natural forms which Ruskin called for, but it is perhaps no accident that two of the most popular buildings in the Western world of the past fifty years, Jørn Utzon's Sydney Opera House and Gehry's Bilbao museum, embody curves which recall the natural world. The insistence on the right angle, the tyranny of the I-beam, is part of the charmlessness of modernism. Both these buildings dispense with the canons of modernism, and both disavow irony. Ruskin also looked for 'a severe and in many cases mysterious majesty' in architecture asking that buildings 'express a measure of human sympathy by a measure of darkness as great as there is in human life'.[115] He considered this could be achieved by the proper use of shadow, but perhaps we could say that buildings, to answer the deepest human needs, should not be trite. For this reason the inclusion of the Eiffel Tower, or even Versailles, among iconic buildings seems to me to be questionable.[116] There is a proper dignity about great architecture which is bound up with purpose, broadly speaking with grace as justice.

In pedigreed building we also look, not invariably, but often, for the 'wow!' factor, the design which takes our breath away. Many of the medieval cathedrals have this in spades. Great building expresses that daring by which human beings transcend themselves. Two of Ruskin's architectural 'lamps' are connected with this. His appeal to the 'lamp of sacrifice' means that buildings of any quality cannot be bought from the bargain basement shelf. If we try to do this we end up with shoddy, short-lived 'decorated sheds' in

---

[115] Ruskin, *Seven Lamps*, p. 84.

[116] Scruton argues that 'buildings are not composed of brick and stone and stucco but of light and shade . . . That is why mouldings are essential to the art of building. In the case of architecture there is a far greater distinction between those who use mouldings whether cut in stone, pressed in steel or plaster – and those who eschew them, under the conviction that "ornament is crime". Mouldings are the means whereby we become "sculptors of shadow".' Scruton, *Classical Vernacular*, p. 24.

which no one can believe, and which degrade the whole environment. At the same time it is not possible to build well simply by throwing money at a project. Under the 'lamp of life' Ruskin looked for the energy of mind visible in the building. Considering the façade of Pisa Cathedral he noted the variety, the refusal to be bound by mathematical proportion. 'Now I call that living architecture. There is sensation in every inch of it and an accommodation to every architectural necessity.'[117] The right question to ask of ornament, he said, was whether it was done with enjoyment, whether the carver was happy while he was about it. 'You cannot get feeling by paying for it – money will not buy life.'[118] Life and joy are key aspects of successful architecture. Once again one has to ask whether these are possible without some transcendent purpose. These seem to spring from imagination fired by a particular vision, an account of human ends, which are simply not there in the dreary towers of commercial buildings, celebrating nothing but the power of money.

As we have seen, there is no option but to build for our particular age. We can repeat the classical vernacular, or even the Gothic vernacular, but the result will not be the same as the originals which are copied. Seeking a style which emerges from the culture of the day, as modernism wanted, does not have to imply bondage to some false 'historicism'.[119] The problem is the nature of our fundamental source of inspiration. Modernism failed partly because it looked to engineers to provide its poetry, and partly because its guiding credo, the idea of progress, proved to be illusory.

This list of things we might look for in an architecture which would be commended by the gospel is, of course, not exhaustive, nor does it constitute a check-list which any architect should seek to conform to. In the last event it notes that great building is an expression of faith, and therefore of hope, vision and courage. Architecture, like the other arts, succeeds or fails by its answer to the question: in what, or in whom, do you believe? The virtues may be inculcated only by practice, and faith may be put in a certain set of virtues, as seems to have been the case for Pericles, but virtues ultimately rest on faith, that on which we stake our life, which gives us our reason for living. The promise, says Paul, 'depends on faith, in order that it may depend on grace' (Rom. 4.16). Grace, it turns out, is in every sense the root of edification.

[117] Ruskin, *Seven Lamps*, p. 160. [118] Ibid., p. 173.
[119] As David Watkin argues in *Morality and Architecture Revisited* (University of Chicago Press, 2001).

Conclusion: grace and the common good

As we saw in Chapter 1, the doctrine of the Trinity emerged from a pattern of events taken by Christians to be revelatory. Forced upon the early community, gaining ground little by little in the face of a monotheism it seemed to many to compromise, it is an ex post facto doctrine. However, once arrived at, it was found to yield profound insights into what might be meant by the word 'God'. Among other things it provides the grammar for God's engagement with all that is not God. The doctrine of the incarnation speaks of God's taking materiality upon Godself, and therefore grounds our concern for all materiality, while the doctrine of the Spirit is a way of speaking of God active in the world. As we have seen at a number of places in the book, one of the key ways this has been understood, following the ancient story in Numbers 11, is in terms of empowerment. That has been understood in many different ways – in terms of a theology of mission, or of creativity, or of calling – but I want in these concluding reflections to understand it in terms of prophecy and response.

The Seer of Patmos, in the book of Revelation, has a vision according to which four angels blow trumpets to announce destruction about to fall on earth. 'This text', writes Bas Wielenga, 'may encourage us to listen to the warning voices of ecological researchers and to the news about rising sea-levels, pollution of earth and sea and rivers and to respond to them by repenting and calling to repentance, by changing our lifestyles.'[1]

There is no lack of warning: the trumpets have been sounding for quite some time. We know that ice core records indicate that carbon dioxide levels have been the same for thousands of years, but are now 30 per cent above pre-industrial levels. They have risen almost a degree in the past one hundred years. The ice sheet covering the Arctic Ocean has lost 40 per cent of its volume over the last thirty years and could be completely gone

---

[1] B. Wielenga, *Revelation to John: Tuning into Songs of Moses and the Lamb* (New Delhi: ISPCK 2009), p. 63.

in decades. Nobody has modelled what the effect of this ice loss would be. Andrew Simms, Director of the Climate Change programme at the New Economics Foundation, argued that in a hundred months from 1 August 2008, atmospheric concentrations of greenhouse gases would begin to exceed a point whereby it would no longer be *likely* that we would be able to avert potentially irreversible and catastrophic climate change. He and his fellow researchers believed this calculation to be conservative.[2]

These changes stem from the combination of spiralling populations and carbon-intensive technology which began in the eighteenth century. The optimism these changes both presupposed and caused is perfectly understandable. For millennia people had gone hungry, for millennia they had suffered and died without understanding either cause or cure. The chance to change that had to be grasped, but two factors distorted the development. First, scientific and technological progress gave people the illusion of total control. People thought the so-called natural world could be reduced to questions of input–output, know-how, cost benefits and functionality. Commenting on the imperative for farms to get bigger and on the boast that a tiny percentage of the population could now feed the rest, Wendell Berry condemns the technology of infinity, which makes us all its slaves. A limitless technology, he comments, is dependent on a limitless morality, which is to say upon no morality at all. By contrast, the knowledge of our limits is 'the most comely and graceful knowledge that we have, the most healing and the most whole'.[3] In fact, as more and more scientists have been insisting over the past forty years, many natural processes, and in particular the way in which they interrelate, are very poorly understood. The way feedbacks are hastening climate change comes as a surprise because people thought they had the natural world taped. Rather late they find that they do not at all. Our understanding is much more limited than we supposed. Second, and even more significant, all forms of technological progress since 1760 or so have been harnessed to a profit-oriented economic rationality, or irrationality, which has had the reproduction and accumulation of capital as its primary goal, and this remains true to this day. What this means is that the ecological crisis is a crisis of a whole world-view and a whole world system, which we refer to these days as 'globalisation'. The triumphs of Western technology and of market economics have been exported to the whole inhabited earth but may cost the whole inhabited earth.

---

[2] *The Guardian*, 1 August 2008.   [3] W. Berry, *The Unsettling of America*, pp. 78, 94.

So totally are we enmeshed in this pseudo-rationality that we have diffi-culty in accepting the facts and we take refuge in denial. Alastair McIntosh reminds us that 88 per cent of British people think climate change is hap-pening but only 41 per cent think human beings cause it. Seven out of ten think the government should take a lead but only 21 per cent support increasing the cost of flying and only 14 per cent support increasing the cost of petrol. Energy consumption is actually rising. Distances travelled by pri-vate car increased by 17 per cent between 1996 and 2004; and the number of passenger kilometres by plane rose from 125 billion to 260 billion world-wide between 1990 and 2000.[4] The political will to change things isn't there because the electorate aren't worried enough. The New Labour gov-ernment which ended in 2010 planned to double airport capacity and add 2,500 miles more roads. Our economic system, says McIntosh, is infantile. We have what he calls 'consensus trance reality', drifting around in a quasi-hypnotic state while danger accumulates silently ahead of us.[5] In Walter Wink's terms it is an example of the Domination system in operation. Examining the language of the 'principalities and powers' in Ephesians 6.12, Wink argues that these are the interiority of structures, nations and communities. The outworking of the powers is the Domination system, the whole set of assumptions about money as the most important thing in life, the market as the only way to run things, hierarchy as essential to society, the need for a ruling class, the need for patriarchy and so forth. 'This spirit-killing atmosphere penetrates everything, teaching us not only what to believe, but what we can value and even what we can see.'[6] Like the Deuteronomic preacher, Wink argues that we stand before two ways: any religious message that promises that we can win in the terms laid down by the Domination system is apostate. Any theology that promises success, national supremacy or victory through redemptive violence is apostate. Any piety that equates the gospel with getting ahead, being number one or salvation through patriotism is apostate. We have to add, any theology that believes that either technique or 'the market' will get us out of trouble is apostate.

The Domination system is by definition opposed to the common good because it is opposed to anything which might be held in common, as opposed to being made the preserve of the few. At the same time we have seen that respect for cultural difference grounded a principled opposition to the idea of the common good. Surely, it is argued, the idea of the common

---

[4] A. McIntosh, *Hell and High Water* (Edinburgh: Birlin, 2008), p. 87.   [5] Ibid., p. 99.
[6] W. Wink, *Engaging the Powers* (Minneapolis: Fortress, 1992), p. 53.

good only makes sense in small culturally homogenous societies, like that of thirteenth-century Italy? Even there, it has to be acknowledged, what was truly common was quite limited. Today, however, the facts of the global emergency impact every culture and every individual. Finding patterns of living which would be truly sustainable is the lowest common denominator of the common good. This has to begin with the economy, with agriculture and with lifestyle, but every other aspect of culture is affected, including building and planning, the shaping of our built environment.

In this context I have appealed to a renewed theology of grace. The theology of grace first emerges as Israel's response to the gift of freedom and the gift of good land. Its prophets and wise men realise that justice and kindly use are intrinsic parts of such a response. Paul re-crafts this theology in terms of what he has learned in Jesus Christ: 'grace' denotes the surprising, inventive gifting of God in the crucified and risen one, enabling new patterns of living together which break down community boundaries and go beyond moralism. The insight that moralism is destructive, that it warps and blinds the human will, lies behind Augustine's insistence on grace in response to Pelagius, but combining it with a theology of predestination serves to put a minus sign outside the bracket in which the equation of grace is stated. The same thing happens in the thirteenth century when the idea of grace acting ex opere operato cancels out the free engagement of God which grace must signify. By the end of the century interest was focussed on the divine omnipotence, and theology became ever more absurd and trifling. Wycliffe and Huss were among those who protested at such a theology and sought to find a way back to a more wholesome account of the divine engagement. At the Reformation Luther did this through his theology of the Word, which, in a world newly literate, understood the divine encounter through Scripture and through preaching. In hindsight we can see that this move was part and parcel of an increasing rationalism which prepared the way for the Enlightenment, the fundamental conviction of which was that the good was to be realised through rational thought and action. 'The grace of God was acknowledged, celebrated, and even called upon, but the effectual reality of it was displaced from the centre of the human story, and gradually replaced by another confidence, and another possibility for fulfilment, and another centre of hope.'[7] Pietism was one form of reaction to the over-confidence of the Enlightenment, but here grace was understood primarily in terms of the freeing of the individual from the burden of guilt and sin. This was too narrow a basis to sustain

[7] Sittler, *Evocations of Grace*, p. 147,

a theology of grace, and it was shunted on to an enthusiast siding. Today there are many signs that a new theology of grace is being fashioned.

As in the thirteenth century we can understand grace as a way of speaking of God in Godself. All that is not God depends on the fact that God gifts Godself and gifts a reality which is not God. Creation, that is to say, is gift, calling forth gratitude in return. Grace begets gratitude and graciousness. The connection between grace and beauty represents the result of acknowledging, or responding to, the giftedness of all reality. Gracious building and dwelling have a modesty, a humility, a freedom of line, a joyousness, which building and dwelling that emerge from the *libido dominandi* can never aspire to. Sin, the lust to control, writes itself everywhere into the built environment. In the twentieth century it littered the world with many of the ugliest buildings ever created. Part of their ugliness was their sovereign contempt for what was or was not sustainable, which emerged ultimately from the triumphalism of the Enlightenment.

This theology of grace, and an account of the common good, are essential in responding to the global emergency. What the outcome of this emergency will be is far from clear. Feedback loops are already in operation, melting the Arctic ice far sooner than was expected. Mark Lynas thinks there is only a fifty-fifty chance of avoiding the runaway global warming which would lead to mass extinction.[8] This would be the ultimate account of the tragedy of the Commons, as it would follow from every nation and individual prioritising its need to use carbon. All forms of the common good would collapse before our pursuit of our own interests.

It is possible that the processes which would bring about this end are too far advanced to ameliorate, but it is irresponsible to act as if that were the case, or to resign ourselves to fate. The responsible living which seeks to avert such a threat is not joyless but joyful, grace-filled living. To put it in the language of Christian theology, response to grace, finding gracious and grateful ways of living, farming, trading and building, is the only way to salvation. It cannot be met either by bland optimism or by faith in technology because, as Jürgen Moltmann said, already a quarter of a century ago, the global emergency is not simply a technological crisis but a religious crisis of the paradigm in which people in the Western world, and increasingly Asia as well, put their trust and live. It is a moral and spiritual crisis. For this reason it has to be met with a stronger and deeper faith appealing to quite different grounds of hope. Here the author of Revelation speaks to us. He teaches us to 'lift up our heads' and to be open

---

[8] Lynas, *Six Degrees*, p. 264.

for God's new beginning in the breakdown of the world system constructed in the past 200 years.

The author offers us a vision of the throne of God in heaven. As Wielenga argues, what the author wants to convey is the message that there is not only the power of Rome or Washington, not only the power of the giant transnational companies, but a different reality beyond the grasp of those destructive powers. The throne in heaven is a symbol of an alternative power at work in history, the power of love which aims at redeeming life and sustaining it, the power of grace. The door to heaven is open. If it were closed this would mean that there were no other powers but those of the Domination system. John insists, the Christian faith believes, that that is not the case.[9]

Revelation is a call to hope grounded on faith, not optimism. It is a call to repentance and action. Action means all the obvious things – recycling, insulating, using cars and aeroplanes less, being responsible about our carbon footprint. As we saw in Chapter 10, it means the struggle for a more just world, which, if it does not begin with the built environment, nevertheless has to be pursued there, for if it is not pursued there it is pursued nowhere. But it also means the realisation of that gracious living which might bring about the moral tipping point towards truly sustainable ways of living. The church, of course, has no monopoly on understandings of grace, or gracious ways of living. Far from it. What it brings to the response to the global emergency, however, is hope in the God who raised Jesus Christ from the dead as the ground of action in the face of imminent danger. As W. H. Auden put it,

> Nothing can save us that is possible:
> We who must die demand a miracle.[10]

Sittler asked whether the affirmation that God is gracious, and that God's creation must be enjoyed and used as gracious gift, has the power to accomplish the radical change in 'the spirit of our minds', the change in our whole lifestyle, that the global emergency requires. Such a change, he noted, requires more than a combination of frightening facts and moral concern. The church betrays the presences and visions by which it lives if it gives up on its account of God's steadily revolutionary activity. 'The community of the people of God, who live by and are held within God's grace, has another and wilder thing to do. They are a people caught and held

---

[9] Wielenga, *Revelation*, p. 34.
[10] W. H. Auden, 'For the Time Being: A Christmas Oratorio', in *The Collected Poetry of W. H. Auden* (New York: Random House, 1945), p. 411.

by a vision of a King, a kingdom, and a consummation – and by the massive contexts of culture, history, nature, as fields of its holy disturbance.'[11] This wilder thing is to live by hope. Luther's *Table Talk* tells us that he was once asked what he would do if he knew the world was going to end the next day. His answer was, 'Plant an apple tree.'[12] This expresses his faith in God's purposes for the creation. Moltmann comments:

In the present situation of our world facile consolation is as fatal as melancholy hopelessness. No one can assure us that the worst will not happen. According to all the laws of experience: it will. We can only trust that even the end of the world hides a new beginning if we trust the God who calls into being the things that are not, and out of death creates new life . . . In view of the deadly dangers threatening the world, Christian remembrance makes ever present the death of Christ in its apocalyptic dimensions, in order to draw forth from his resurrection from the dead hope for 'the life of the world to come', and from his rebirth to eternal life hope for the rebirth of the cosmos . . . Life out of this hope then means already acting here and today in accordance with that world of justice and righteousness and peace, contrary to appearances, and contrary to all historical chances of success.[13]

The God in whom we believe is abroad in the whole universe but does not intervene to stop tragedy. The Triune God calls us, rather, to live by grace. To do that in relation to the world we build for ourselves, in justice and beauty, will be a key factor in whether or not humankind has a future.

---

[11] Sittler, *Evocations of Grace*, p. 186.

[12] We have to ask whether Luther had come across the remark of Johanan ben Zakkai: 'If you have a seedling in your hand, and they say to you, Look, here comes the Messiah, Go out and plant the seedling first and then come out to meet him.' Quoted in C. Rowland, *The Open Heaven* (London: SPCK, 1982), p. 31.

[13] Moltmann, *The Coming of God*, p. 235.

Bibliography

Abbot-Smith, G., *A Manual Greek Lexicon of the New Testament* (Edinburgh: T. & T. Clark, 1936).

Abelard, P., *Petri Abaelardi opera theologica*, ed. E. M. Buytaert, vol. II, Corpus Christianorum, vol. XII (Turnhout, 1969).

Acton, M., *Learning to Look at Modern Art* (London: Routledge 2004).

Adams, J., 'Carmageddon', in Barnett and Scruton (eds.), *Town and Country*, pp. 217–32.

Alberti, L., *The Ten Books of Architecture*, Leonie edn (New York: Dover, 1986).

Alexander, C., *The Luminous Ground* (Berkeley: Centre for Environmental Structure, 2002).

The Phenomenon of Order (Berkeley: Centre for Environmental Structure, 2002).

The Timeless Way of Building (New York: Oxford University Press, 1979).

Alexander, C., with H. Davis, J. Martinez and D. Corner, *The Production of Houses* (New York: Oxford University Press, 1985).

Alexander, C., S. Ishikawa, M. Silverstein, M. Jacobson, I. Fiksdahl-King and S. Angel, *A Pattern Language* (New York: Oxford University Press, 1977).

Alexander, C., H. Neis, A. Anninou and I. King, *A New Theory of Urban Design* (New York: Oxford University Press, 1987).

Andelson, R. V. (ed.), *Commons without Tragedy* (London: Shepheard Walwyn, 1991).

Andruss, V. *et al.*, *Home! A Bioregional Reader* (Philadelphia: New Society 1990).

Aquinas, T., *Summa theologiae*, 60 vols. (London: Blackfriars in association with Eyre and Spottiswoode, 1964–81).

Arendt, H., *The Human Condition* (Chicago University Press, 1958).

Ariès, P., *The Hour of our Death* (New York: Oxford University Press, 1981).

Aristotle, *Complete Works*, ed. J. Barnes (Cambridge University Press, 1984).

Asquith, P. J., and A. Kalland, *Japanese Images of Nature: Cultural Perspectives* (London: Routledge, 1996).

Auden, W. H., *The Collected Poetry of W. H. Auden* (New York: Random House, 1945).

Auerbach, E., *Mimesis* (Princeton University Press, 1974).

Augé, M., *Non Places: Introduction to an Anthropology of Supermodernity* (London: Verso, 1995).

Augustine, *The City of God*, tr. H. Bettenson (Harmondsworth: Penguin, 1972).

Avila, C., *Ownership: Early Christian Teaching* (Maryknoll: Orbis, 1983).

Bachram, H. *et al.*, *Hoodwinked in the Hothouse* (Amsterdam: Transnational Institute, 2005).

Balthasar, H. U. von, *The Theology of Karl Barth* (San Francisco: Ignatius, 1992).

Barman, C., *Early British Railways* (Harmondsworth: Penguin, 1950).

Barnett, A., and R. Scruton (eds.), *Town and Country* (London: Jonathan Cape, 1998).

Barrera, A., *Economic Compulsion and Christian Ethics* (Cambridge University Press, 2005).

Barth, K., *Against the Stream: Shorter Post-War Writings* (London: SCM, 1954).

Church Dogmatics, 13 vols. (Edinburgh: T. & T. Clark, 1956–75).

Evangelical Theology (Edinburgh: T. & T. Clark, 1980).

Bauman, Z., *Globalization: The Human Consequences* (Cambridge: Polity, 1998).

Modernity and Ambivalence (Cambridge: Polity, 1991).

Postmodern Ethics (Oxford: Blackwell, 1993).

Bellah, R., R. Madsen, W. Sullivan, A. Swidler and S. Tipton, *Habits of the Heart: Individualism and Commitment in American Life* (Berkeley: University of California Press, 2008).

Bendixson, T. and John Platt, *Milton Keynes: Image and Reality* (Cambridge: Granta, 1992).

Benevolo, L., *The Origin of Modern Town Planning* (London: Routledge, 1967).

Berry, W., *The Art of the Commonplace* (Washington: Shoemaker and Hoard, 2002).

The Gift of Good Land (Berkeley: Counterpoint, 1981).

Home Economics (New York: North Point, 1987).

Sex, Economy, Freedom and Community (New York: Pantheon, 1992).

The Unsettling of America: Culture and Agriculture (San Francisco: Sierra Club, 1996).

What are People For? (San Francisco: North Point, 1990).

Bird, I., *et al.* (eds.), *Mapping the Futures: Local Cultures, Global Change* (London: Routledge, 1993).

Blake, P., *Form Follows Fiasco* (Boston: Little, Brown & Co., 1974).

Le Corbusier (Harmondsworth: Penguin, 1963).

Mies van der Rohe (Harmondsworth: Penguin, 1963).

Blake, W., *Complete Writings*, ed. G. Keynes (Oxford University Press, 1969).

Boddy, T., 'Underground and Overhead: Building the Analogous City', in Sorkin (ed.), *Variations*, pp. 123–53.

Bookchin, M., *Post-Scarcity Anarchism* (Montreal and Buffalo: Black Rose Books, 1986).

Bové, J., and F. Dufour, *The World is not for Sale* (London: Verso, 2001).

Bowlby, J., *Attachment* (Harmondsworth: Penguin, 1969).

Boyer, C., 'Cities for Sale: Merchandising History at South Street Seaport', in Sorkin (ed.), *Variations*, pp. 181–204.

Branford, V., and P. Geddes, *The Coming Polity* (London: Williams Norgate, 1919).

Braudel, F., *The Structures of Everyday Life* (London: Collins, 1981).
The Wheels of Commerce (London: Collins, 1985).
Brayshay, M. (ed.), 'Post-War Plymouth: Planning and Reconstruction', South West Papers in Geography, University of Exeter, 1983.
Brolin, B. C., *The Failure of Modern Architecture* (New York: Van Nostrand, 1976).
Brown, C. (ed.), *Dictionary of New Testament Theology* (Exeter: Paternoster, 1976).
'Eradicating Hunger', in Brown, Flavin and French (eds.), *State of the World 2001*, pp. 43–62.
The State of the World 1998 (London: Earthscan, 1998).
Brown, L., C. Flavin and H. French (eds.), *State of the World 2001* (London: Earthscan, 2001).
Brownill, S., *Developing London's Docklands: Another Great Planning Disaster?* (London: Chapman, 1990).
Brueggemann, W., *The Land* (Philadelphia: Fortress, 1977).
Buckland, J., *Ploughing up the Farm: Neoliberalism, Modern Technology and the State of the World's Farmers* (London: Zed, 2004).
Bull, H., *The Anarchical Society* (London: Macmillan, 1977).
Burton, T., and L. Matson, 'Urban Footprints: Making Best Use of Urban Land and Resources – A Rural Perspective', in Jenks, Burton and Williams (eds.), *Compact City*, pp. 298–301.
Calvino, I., *Invisible Cities* (London: Vintage, 1997).
Carr, M., *Bioregionalism and Civil Society: Democratic Challenges to Corporate Globalism* (Vancouver: UBCP Press, 2004).
Casey, E., *The Fate of Place: A Philosophical History* (Berkeley: University of California Press, 1998).
Castells, M., *End of Millennium* (Oxford: Blackwell, 1998).
The Power of Identity (Oxford: Blackwell, 1997).
The Rise of the Network Society (Oxford: Blackwell, 1996).
Cherry, G., *Town Planning in Britain since 1900* (Oxford: Blackwell, 1996).
Chrysostom, J., 'Second Homily on the Statues', in P. Schaff (ed.), *Nicene and Post Nicene Fathers*, vol. IX (Grand Rapids: Eerdmans, 1983), pp. 344–54.
Clark, K., *The Gothic Revival* (Harmondsworth: Penguin, 1964).
Clifford, J., 'Travelling Cultures', in Grossberg *et al.* (eds.), *Cultural Studies*, pp. 96–116.
Clifford, S, and A. King, *Local Distinctiveness* (London: Common Ground, 1993).
Coleman, A., *Utopia on Trial: Vision and Reality in Planned Housing* (London: Shipman, 1985).
Commoner, B., *The Closing Circle* (New York: Knopf, 1971).
Crawford, M., 'The World in a Shopping Mall', in Sorkin (ed.), *Variations*, pp. 3–30.
Cresswell, T., *Place: A Short Introduction* (Oxford: Blackwell, 2004).
Critchfield, R., *The Villagers* (New York: Anchor Doubleday, 1994).
Crowe, S., *The Landscape of Roads* (London: Architectural Press, 1960).
Cullingworth, B., and V. Nadin, *Town and Country Planning in the UK*, 13th edn (London: Routledge, 2002).

Daly, H., *Beyond Growth* (Boston: Beacon, 1996).
  'Free Trade: The Perils of Deregulation', in Mander and Goldsmith (eds.), *The Case*, pp. 229–38.
Daly, H., and J. Cobb, *For the Common Good* (London: Green Print, 1990).
Darley, G., *Villages of Vision*, 2nd edn (Nottingham: Five Leaves, 2007).
Davies, J. G., *The Evangelistic Bureaucrat: A Study of a Planning Exercise in Newcastle upon Tyne* (London: Tavistock, 1972).
Davies, W. D., *The Gospel and the Land* (Berkeley: University of California Press, 1974).
Davis, H., *The Culture of Building* (New York: Oxford University Press, 2006).
Davis, H., and C. Alexander, 'Beyond Humanism', *Journal of Architectural Education*, 35/1 (1981), 18–24.
Davis, M., *Planet of Slums* (London: Verso, 2006).
Day, C., *Consensus Design: Socially Inclusive Process* (Oxford: Architectural Press, 2003).
  Places of the Soul (London: Thorsons, 1999).
  Spirit and Place (London: Architectural Press, 2002).
Dodman, D., J. Ayers and S. Huq, 'Building Resilience', in Starke (ed.), *State of the World 2009*, pp. 151–68.
Dunn, J., *Democracy: A History* (New York: Atlantic, 2005).
Edwards, A., *The Design of Suburbia* (London: Pembridge, 1981).
Ellul, J., *The Meaning of the City* (Grand Rapids: Eerdmans, 1970).
Ellwood, W., 'Why are they Dying?', *New Internationalist*, 425 (September 2009), 4–7.
Engelman, R., 'Sealing the Deal to Save the Climate', in Starke (ed.), *State of the World 2009*, pp. 169–88.
Escobar, Arturo, 'Culture Sits in Places: Reflections on Globalism and Subaltern Strategies of Localization', *Political Geography*, 20/2 (2001), 139–74.
Fairlie, S., 'Carbon Colonialism and the Mathematics of Methane', *The Land*, 8 (Winter 2009–10), 13–17.
  Low Impact Development (Charlbury: Jon Carpenter, 1996).
Fathy, H., *Architecture for the Poor* (University of Chicago Press, 1973).
Featherstone, M. (ed.), *Global Culture* (London: Sage, 1990).
Ford, H., *My Life and Work* (London: Heinemann, 1924).
Forester, J., *Planning in the Face of Power* (Berkeley: University of California Press, 1989).
Forrester, D., *Christian Justice and Public Policy* (Cambridge University Press, 1997).
Fox, W. (ed.), *Ethics and Built Environment* (London: Routledge, 2000).
Frameworks for the Future (Rotterdam: National Dubo Centrum, 2000).
Frith, S., 'The Suburban Sensibility in British Rock and Pop', in Silverstone (ed.), *Visions of Suburbia*, pp. 269–78.
Gans, H., *The Levittowners* (London: Allen Lane, 1967).
Gardner, E. C., *Justice and Christian Ethics* (Cambridge University Press, 1995).

Geddes, P., *Cities in Evolution: An Introduction to the Town Planning Movement and to the Study of Civics* (London: Williams and Norgate, 1915).

Giddens, A., *The Politics of Climate Change* (Cambridge: Polity, 2009).

Giedion, S., *Space, Time and Architecture*, 5th edn (Cambridge, Mass.: Harvard University Press, 1974).

Girardet, H., *The Gaia Atlas of Cities*, rev. edn (London: Gaia, 1996).

Glassie, H., *Vernacular Architecture* (Bloomington: Indiana University Press, 2000).

Gorringe, H., *Untouchable Citizens* (New Delhi: Sage, 2005).

Gorringe, T. J., *Harvest: Food, Farming and the Churches* (London: SPCK, 2006).
  Redeeming Time (London: Darton, Longman and Todd, 1986).
  A Theology of the Built Environment (Cambridge University Press, 2002).

Grabow, S., *Christopher Alexander: The Search for a New Paradigm in Architecture* (Stocksfield: Oriel, 1983).

Green, R., 'Not Compact Cities but Sustainable Regions', in Jenks, Burton and Williams (eds.), *Compact City*, pp. 143–54.

Greenhalgh, L., 'Greening the Cities', in Barnett and Scruton (eds.), *Town and Country*, pp. 253–66.

Gross, D., *The Past in Ruins* (Amherst: University of Massachusetts Press, 1992).

Grossberg, D., *et al.* (eds.), *Cultural Studies* (London: Routledge, 1992).

Gruchy, J. de, *Christianity, Art and Transformation: Theological Aesthetics in the Struggle for Justice* (Cambridge University Press, 2001).

Gummer, J., Introduction to *Quality in Town and Country: A Discussion Document* (London: Department of Environment, 1994).

Habraken, N., *Supports: An Alternative to Mass Housing* (London: Architectural Press, 1972).

Haldane, A. R. B., *New Ways through the Glens* (London: Nelson, 1962).

Hall, P., *Cities in Civilization* (London: Weidenfeld and Nicolson, 1998).
  Cities of Tomorrow (Oxford: Blackwell, 1988).
  Urban and Regional Planning (London: Routledge, 1992).

Hamburg, G., 'Russian Political Thought 1700–1917', in Lieven (ed.), *Cambridge History of Russia*, vol. II, pp. 116–44.

Hansen, J., M. Sato, P. Kharecha, G. Russell, D. W. Lea and M. Siddall, 'Climate Change and Trace Gases', *Philosophical Transactions of the Royal Society A*, 365 (2007), 1925–54.

Hansen, M. A., *Polis: An Introduction to the Ancient Greek City State* (Oxford University Press, 2006).

Hardin, G., 'The Tragedy of the Commons', *Science*, 162 (1968), 1243–8.
  'The Tragedy of the "Unmanaged" Commons', in Andelson (ed.), *Commons without Tragedy*, pp. 162–85.

Hardy, D., and C. Ward, *Arcadia for All: The Legacy of a Makeshift Landscape* (London: Mansell, 1984).

Hardy, T., *The Woodlanders* (London: Macmillan, 1906).

Harries, K., *The Ethical Function of Architecture* (Cambridge, Mass.: MIT Press, 1998).

Harrison, S. (ed.), *The Cambridge Companion to Horace* (Cambridge University Press, 2007).

Hartley, J., 'The Sexualization of Suburbia', in Silverstone (ed.), *Visions of Suburbia*, pp. 180–216.

Harvey, A. (ed.), *Theology in the City* (London: SPCK, 1989).

Harvey, D., *The Condition of Postmodernity* (Oxford: Blackwell, 1989).

'From Space to Place and Back Again: Reflections on the Condition of Postmodernity', in Bird *et al.* (eds.), *Mapping the Futures*, pp. 1–29.

Justice, Nature and the Geography of Difference (Oxford: Blackwell, 1996).

Spaces of Hope (Edinburgh University Press, 2000).

Harvey, J., *The Master Builders: Architecture in the Middle Ages* (London: Thames and Hudson, 1971).

Haughton, G., and C. Hunter, *Sustainable Cities* (London: Regional Studies Association, 1994).

Heath, R., *The English Peasant* (London: Fisher Unwin, 1893).

Herman, P., and R. Kuper, *Food for Thought: Towards a Future for Farming* (London: Pluto, 2003).

Hewison, R., *The Heritage Industry: Britain in a Climate of Decline* (London: Methuen, 1987).

Hill, D., *Citizens and Cities* (New York: Harvester Wheatsheaf, 1994).

Hillman, M., 'In Favour of the Compact City', in Jenks, Burton and Williams (eds.), *Compact City*, pp. 36–44.

Hindle, P., *Medieval Roads and Tracks* (Princes Risborough: Shire, 1998).

Hine, J., 'Transport and Social Justice', in Knowles, Shaw and Docherty (eds.), *Transport Geographies*, pp. 49–61.

Hollenbach, D., SJ, *The Common Good and Christian Ethics* (Cambridge University Press, 2002).

Holman, S. R., *The Poor are Dying: Beggars and Bishops in Roman Cappadocia* (Oxford University Press, 2001).

Hook, J., *Siena: A City and its History* (London: Hamish Hamilton, 1979).

Hopkins, R., *The Transition Handbook* (Totnes: Green Books, 2008).

Hoskins, W. G., *Devon* (London: Collins, 1954).

The Making of the English Landscape (Harmondsworth: Penguin, 1955).

Hough, M., *Out of Place: Restoring Identity to the Regional Landscape* (New Haven: Yale University Press, 1990).

House of Commons Environmental Audit Committee, 'Carbon Capture and Storage', Ninth Report of Session 2007–8, HC 654 (London: Stationery Office Ltd, 2008).

Howard, A., *The Soil and Health* (Lexington: University Press of Kentucky, 2006).

Hughes, G., *In Search of a Way* (London: Darton, Longman and Todd, 1986).

Inge, J., *A Christian Theology of Place* (Aldershot: Ashgate, 2003).

Intergovernmental Panel on Climate Change, *Climate Change 2007: Synthesis Report* (Geneva: IPCC, 2007).

Jackson, F., *Sir Raymond Unwin: Architect, Planner and Visionary* (London: Zwemmer, 1985).

Jackson, J.B., *Discovering the Vernacular Landscape* (New Haven: Yale University Press, 1984).
  A Sense of Place, a Sense of Time (New Haven: Yale University Press, 1994).
Jacobs, J., *Cities and the Wealth of Nations* (Harmondsworth: Penguin 1986).
  The Death and Life of Great American Cities (Harmondsworth: Penguin, 1994, 1961).
Jameson, F., *Postmodernism: The Cultural Logic of Late Capitalism* (London: Verso, 1991).
Jencks, C., *The Language of Post-Modern Architecture*, 6th edn (London: Academy, 1991).
Jenks, M., E. Burton and K. Williams (eds.), *The Compact City: A Sustainable Urban Form?* (London: Routledge, 1998).
Judd, D., and T. Swanstrom, *City Politics: Private Power and Public Policy*, 3rd edn (New York: Addison Wesley, 2002).
Kasser, T., 'Shifting Values in Response to Climate Change', in Starke (ed.), *State of the World 2009*, pp. 122–5.
Kaviraj, S., 'Filth and the Public Sphere: Concepts and Practices about Space in Calcutta', *Public Culture*, 10/1 (1997), 83–113.
Kemmis, D., *Community and the Politics of Place* (Norman: University of Oklahoma Press, 1990).
  The Good City and the Good Life (Boston: Houghton Mifflin, 1995).
Kempshall, M. S., *The Common Good in Late Medieval Political Thought* (Oxford University Press, 1999).
Kitchen, T., *Skills for Planning Practice* (Aldershot: Ashgate, 2007).
Kjellberg, S., *Urban Ecotheology* (Utrecht: International Books, 2000).
Klein, N., *The Shock Doctrine* (Harmondsworth: Penguin, 2008).
Kneen, B., *Farmageddon* (Gabriola: New Society, 1999).
  From Land to Mouth (Toronto: NC Press, 1993).
Knowles, R., J. Shaw and I. Docherty (eds.), *Transport Geographies: Mobilities, Flows and Spaces* (London: Wiley Blackwell, 2007).
Koonings, K., and D. Kruijt, epilogue, in Koonings and Kruijt (eds.), *Fractured Cities*, pp. 138–9.
Koonings, K., and D. Kruijt (eds.), *Fractured Cities: Social Exclusion, Urban Violence and Contested Spaces in Latin America* (London: Zed, 2007).
Korten, D., *The Post Corporate World* (West Hartford: Kumarian, 1999).
  When Corporations Rule the World (West Hartford: Kumarian, 1995).
Kostoff, S., *A History of Architecture*, 2nd edn (New York: Oxford University Press, 1995).
Kunstler, J. H., *The Geography of Nowhere* (New York: Simon & Schuster, 1993).
Landry, C., *The Art of City-Making* (London: Earthscan, 2006).
Langdon, P., *A Better Place to Live* (Amherst: University of Massachusetts Press, 1994).
Lawrence, F., *Not on the Label* (Harmondsworth: Penguin, 2004).
Layard, R., *Happiness: Lessons from a New Science* (Harmondsworth: Penguin, 2005).

Leopold, A., *A Sand County Almanac* (New York: Ballantine, 1970).

Lessing, G. E., *Lessing's Theological Writings*, ed. H. Chadwick (London: A. & C. Black, 1956).

Levi, P., *The Drowned and the Saved* (London: Abacus, 1988).

Libeskind, D., *The Jewish Museum in Berlin* (Berlin: Studio Libeskind, H. Bibet and G. & B. Arts International, 1999).

Lieven, D. (ed.), *The Cambridge History of Russia 1689–1917* (Cambridge University Press, 2006).

Light, A., and J. Smith (eds.), *The Production of Public Space* (Lanham: Rowman & Littlefield, 1998).

Lippman, W., *A Preface to Morals* (New York: Macmillan, 1929).

Lloyd, P. C., *Slums of Hope* (Harmondsworth: Penguin, 1979).

Locke, J., *Two Treatises of Government*, ed. P. Laslett (Cambridge University Press, 1960).

Lovejoy, T., 'Climate Change's Pressures on Biodiversity', in Starke (ed.), *State of the World 2009*, pp. 67–70.

Lynas, M., *Six Degrees* (London: Fourth Estate, 2007).

Lynch, K., *City Sense and City Design*, ed. T. Banerjee and M. Southworth (Cambridge, Mass.: MIT Press, 1996).

The Image of the City (Cambridge, Mass.: MIT Press, 1960).

McCamant, K., and C. Durrett, *Cohousing: A Contemporary Approach to Housing Ourselves* (Berkeley: TenSpeed Press, 1994).

McEvoy, A., 'Towards an Interactive Theory of Nature and Culture', *Environmental Review*, 11 (1987), 289–305.

McGinnis, M. V., 'A Rehearsal to Bioregionalism', in McGinnis (ed.), *Bioregionalism*, pp. 1–9.

McGinnis, M. V. (ed.), *Bioregionalism* (London: Routledge, 1999).

McIntosh, A., *Hell and High Water* (Edinburgh: Birlin, 2008).

Soil and Soul: People versus Corporate Power (London: Aurum, 2002).

MacIntyre, A., *After Virtue*, 2nd edn (London: Duckworth, 1985).

MacLaran, A. (ed.), *Making Space: Property Development and Urban Planning* (London: Edwin Arnold, 2003).

MacLaran, A., and D. Laverny-Rafter, 'The Rejuvenation of Downtown Minneapolis: Urban Planning as a Creature of Private-Sector Interests', in MacLaran (ed.), *Making Space*, pp. 95–117.

Madeley, J., *Food for All* (London: Zed, 2002).

Mander, J., and E Goldsmith (eds.), *The Case against the Global Economy* (San Francisco: Sierra Club, 1996).

Massey, D., *For Space* (London: Sage, 2005).

Space, Place and Gender (Cambridge: Polity, 1994).

World City (Cambridge: Polity, 2007).

Mayernik, D., *Timeless Cities: An Architect's Reflections on Renaissance Italy* (Oxford: Westview, 2003).

Meecham, H. G., *The Epistle to Diognetus* (Manchester University Press, 1935).

Migne, J. P. (ed.), *Patrologia graeca*, vol. XLIX (Paris, 1862).

(ed.), *Patrologia latina*, vol. XXXII (Paris, 1844).

Miller, P., and D. McCann (eds.), *In Search of the Common Good* (London: T. & T. Clark, 2005).

Moltmann, J., *The Coming of God* (London: SCM, 1996).

God in Creation (London: SCM, 1985).

Monbiot, G., *Captive State* (London: Macmillan, 2000).

Moran, J., *On Roads: A Hidden History* (London: Profile, 2009).

Muir, E., *Collected Poems* (London: Faber, 1960).

Mumford, L., *The City in History* (Harmondsworth: Penguin, 1991).

Myers, C., *Binding the Strong Man* (Maryknoll: Orbis, 1990).

Newman, P., 'Urban Design, Transportation and Greenhouse', in Samuels and Prasad (eds.), *Global Warming*, pp. 69–84.

Norberg-Schulz, C., *Architecture: Presence, Language, Place* (Milan: Skira, 2000).

Norman, D. (ed.), *Siena, Florence and Padua: Art, Society and Religion 1280–1400*, vol. II (New Haven: Yale University Press, 1995).

Oliver, J., *The Ancient Roads of England* (London: Cassell, 1936).

Oliver, P., 'Ethics and Vernacular Architecture', in Fox (ed.), *Ethics and Built Environment*, pp. 115–26.

Onians, J., *Bearers of Meaning: The Classical Orders in the Middle Ages and the Renaissance* (Cambridge University Press, 1988).

Orlans, H., *Stevenage: A Sociological Study of a New Town* (London: Routledge, 1952).

Orr, D., *The Nature of Design* (Oxford University Press, 2002).

Papanek, V., *The Green Imperative* (London: Thames and Hudson, 1995).

Parekh, B., *Rethinking Multiculturalism: Cultural Diversity and Political Theory* (Basingstoke: Palgrave, 2000).

Parker, B., and R. Unwin, *The Art of Building a Home* (London: Longmans, 1901).

Paton Watson, J., and P. Abercrombie, *Plymouth* (London: Underhill, 1943).

Pearman, J., *Railways and Scenery*, 3 vols. (London: Cassell, 1932).

Pendleton, J., *Our Railways* (London: Cassell, 1894).

Plato, *The Collected Dialogues*, ed. E. Hamilton and H. Cairns (Princeton University Press, 1961).

Potter, S., and I. Bailey, 'Transport and Environment', in Knowles, Shaw and Docherty (eds.), *Transport Geographies*, pp. 29–48.

Pred, A., 'Place as Historically Contingent Process: Structuration and the Time-Geography of Becoming Places', *Annals of the Association of American Geographers*, 74/2 (1984), 279–97.

Pretty, J., *Agri-Culture: Reconnecting People, Land and Nature* (London: Earthscan, 2002).

The Living Land (London: Earthscan, 1998).

Rad, G. von, *The Problem of the Hexateuch and other Essays* (Edinburgh: Oliver & Boyd, 1966).

Rahner, K., *Theological Investigations*, vol. XIV (London: Darton, Longman and Todd, 1976).

Rapoport, A., *House, Form and Culture* (Englewood Cliffs: Prentice Hall, 1969).
    The Meaning of the Built Environment (Tucson: University of Arizona Press, 1990).
Rawls, J., *Political Liberalism* (New York: Columbia University Press, 1993).
Redfield, R., *Peasant Life and Culture* (Chicago University Press, 1965).
Report on the Committee on Land Utilisation in Rural Areas (London: HMSO, 1942).
Robertson Scott, J. W., *England's Green and Pleasant Land* (Harmondsworth: Penguin, 1947).
Robinson, N. (ed.), *Agenda 21 and the UNCED Proceedings* (New York: Ocean, 1993).
Rogers, D., 'Managua', in Koonings and Kruijt (eds.), *Fractured Cities*, pp. 71–85.
Rowland, C., *The Open Heaven* (London: SPCK, 1982).
Rudofsky, B., *Architecture without Architects: A Short Introduction to Non-Pedigreed Architecture* (Albuquerque: University of New Mexico Press, 1964).
Ruskin, J., *The Seven Lamps of Architecture* (New York: Dover, 1989).
    The Stones of Venice, ed. J. G. Links (Cambridge, Mass.: Da Capo, 1960).
Rykwert, J., *On Adam's House in Paradise: The Idea of the Primitive Hut in Architectural History*, 2nd edn (Cambridge, Mass.: MIT Press, 1981).
    The Seduction of Place (Oxford University Press, 2000).
Sale, K., *Dwellers in the Land: The Bioregional Vision* (Athens: University of Georgia Press, 1991).
    Human Scale (New York: Coward, McCann & Geoghegan, 1980).
Samuels, R., and D. Prasad (eds.), *Global Warming and the Built Environment* (London: Spon, 1996).
Sandercock, L., *Cosmopolis II: Mongrel Cities in the 21st Century* (London: Continuum, 2003).
    Towards Cosmopolis (Chichester: John Wiley, 1998).
Sassen, S., *The Global City* (Princeton University Press, 1991).
Satterthwaite, D., and D. Dodman, 'The Role of Cities in Climate Change', in Starke (ed.), *State of the World 2009*, pp. 75–7.
Schaff, P. (ed.), *Nicene and Post-Nicene Fathers* (Grand Rapids: Eerdmans, 1971).
Scherr, S., and S. Sthapit, 'Farming and Land Use to Cool the Planet', in Starke (ed.), *State of the World 2009*, pp. 30–49.
Schlosser, E., *Fast Food Nation* (Harmondsworth: Penguin, 2002).
Scholfield, P. H., *The Theory of Proportion in Architecture* (Cambridge University Press, 1957).
Schumacher, E. F., *Small is Beautiful* (London: Sphere, 1974).
Schweitzer, A., *Civilization and Ethics* (London: A. & C. Black, 1947).
Scott, Lord Justice, *Report of the Committee on Land Utilisation in Rural Areas* (London: HMSO, 1942).
Scott, Geoffrey, *The Architecture of Humanism: A Study in the History of Taste*, 2nd edn (New York: Doubleday, 1956).
Scruton, R., *The Aesthetics of Architecture* (Princeton University Press, 1979).

The Classical Vernacular: Architectural Principles in an Age of Nihilism (London: Carcanet, 1994).

Seabrook, J., *In the Cities of the South* (London: Verso, 1996).

Sennett, R., *The Conscience of the Eye* (New York: Norton, 1990).

The Corrosion of Character (New York: Norton, 1999).

The Fall of Public Man (New York: Knopf, 1974).

The Uses of Disorder (New York: Norton, 1970).

Sharp, T., *Town Planning* (Harmondsworth: Penguin, 1940).

Shepley, C., 'Planning Plymouth's Future', in B. Chalkley, D. Dunkerley and P. Gripalos (eds.), *Plymouth: Maritime City in Transition* (Newton Abbot: David & Charles, 1991), pp. 210–30.

Sherlock, H., 'Repairing our Much Abused Cities', in Jenks, Burton and Williams (eds.), *Compact City*, pp. 289–97.

Shklar, J., *The Faces of Injustice* (New Haven: Yale University Press, 1990).

Shucksmith, M., *Exclusive Countryside? Social Inclusion and Regeneration in Rural Britain* (York: Joseph Rowntree Foundation, 2000).

Silverstone, R. (ed.), *Visions of Suburbia* (London: Routledge, 1997).

Simmie, J. M., *Citizens in Conflict* (London: Hutchinson, 1974).

Simson, O. von, *The Gothic Cathedral: Origins of Gothic Architecture and the Medieval Concept of Order* (Princeton University Press, 1988).

Sitte, C., *The Birth of Modern City Planning*, ed. G. and C. Collins (New York: Dover, 1986).

Sittler, J., *Evocations of Grace* (Grand Rapids: Eerdmans, 2000).

Smith, A. 'Toward a Global Culture?', in Featherstone (ed.), *Global Culture*, pp. 171–91.

Smith, M., J. Whiteleg, and N. Williams, *Greening the Built Environment* (London: Earthscan, 1998).

Sorkin, M. (ed.), *Variations on a Theme Park: The New American City and the End of Public Space* (New York: Hill & Wang, 1992).

Starke, L. (ed.), *State of the World 2009: Confronting Climate Change* (London: Earthscan, 2009).

Stevenson, R. L., *Travels with a Donkey in the Cevennes* (London: Nelson, 1950).

Summerson, J., *The Classical Language of Architecture* (London: Thames and Hudson, 1963).

Georgian Architecture (Harmondsworth: Penguin, 1978).

Georgian London (Harmondsworth: Penguin, 1978).

Heavenly Mansions (New York: Norton, 1963).

Taylor, C., *Roads and Tracks of Britain* (Letchworth: Aldine, 1979).

Tétreault, M. A., 'Formal Politics, Meta Space and the Construction of Civil Life', in A. Light and J. Smith (eds.), *The Production of Public Space* (Lanham: Rowman & Littlefield, 1998), pp. 81–98.

Thayer, R. L., *Life Place: Bioregional Thought and Practice* (Berkeley: University of California Press, 2003).

Thirsk, J., *A History of Alternative Agriculture* (Oxford University Press, 1997).

Thomas, L., and W. Cousins, 'The Compact City: A Successful, Desirable and Achievable Urban Form?', in Jenks, Burton and Williams (eds.), *Compact City*, pp. 53–65.

Thomas, R. S., *Selected Poems 1946–1978* (London: Granada, 1973).

Thucydides, *History of the Peloponnesian War*, tr. R. Crawley (London: Dent & Dutton, 1910).

Tocqueville, A. de, *Democracy in America* (London: Everyman's Library, 1994).

Tomlinson, J., *Cultural Imperialism* (London: Continuum, 1991).

Tönnies, F., *Community and Civil Society*, tr. J. Harris and M. Hollis (Cambridge University Press, 2001).

Torrance, T. F., *Grace in the Apostolic Fathers* (Edinburgh: Oliver and Boyd, 1948).

Trainer, T., *Renewable Energy cannot Sustain a Consumer Society* (Berlin: Springer Verlag, 2007).

Tuan, Y.-F., *Space and Place: The Perspective of Experience* (Minneapolis: University of Minnesota Press, 1977).

Tudge, C., *So shall we Reap* (Harmondsworth: Penguin, 2003).

Turner, J. F. C., *Housing by People: Towards Autonomy in Building Environments* (London: Marion Boyars, 1976).

Turner, J. F. C., and R. Fichter (eds.), *Freedom to Build: Dweller Control of the Housing Process* (London: Macmillan, 1972).

UN Habitat, *The Challenge of Slums: Global Report on Human Settlements 2003* (London: Earthscan, 2003).

'Co-operation in Building', in Parker and Unwin, *Art of Building*, pp. 91–108.

Town Planning in Practice: An Introduction to the Art of Designing Cities and Suburbs, 2nd edn (London: Fisher Unwin, 1911).

Vale, R. and B., *Time to Eat the Dog? The Real Guide to Sustainable Living* (London: Thames and Hudson, 2009).

Vance, J. E. Jr, *The Continuing City* (Baltimore: Johns Hopkins University Press, 1990).

Veerkamp, T. *Autonomie & Egalität: Ökonomie, Politik, Ideologie in der Schrift* (Berlin: Alektor, 1993).

Venkateswaran, S. V., *Indian Culture through the Ages* (London: Longmans, 1943).

Venturi, R., *Complexity and Contradiction in Architecture* (New York: Museum of Modern Art, 1966).

Verma, G., *Slumming India: A Chronicle of Slums and their Saviours* (New Delhi: Penguin India, 2002).

Vitruvius, *The Ten Books of Architecture*, tr. M. Morgan (New York: Dover, 1960).

Wackernagel, M., and W. Rees, *Our Ecological Footprint* (Gabriola Island: New Society, 1996).

Wagner, O., *Modern Architecture* (Santa Monica: Getty Centre, 1988).

Waley, D., *Siena and the Sienese in the Thirteenth Century* (Cambridge University Press, 1991).

Walker, B., 'Another Kind of Science: Christopher Alexander on Democratic Theory and the Built Environment', *Canadian Journal of Political Science*, 36/5 (December 2003), 1053–72.

Walker, D., *The Architecture and Planning of Milton Keynes* (London: Architectural Press, 1982).

Waller, P. J., *Town, City and Nation: England 1850–1914* (Oxford University Press, 1983).

Wallin, L., 'The Stranger on the Green', in Sorkin (ed.), *Variations*, pp. 99–114.

Walter, E. V., *Placeways: A Theory of the Human Environment* (Chapel Hill: University of North Carolina Press, 1988).

Warburton, D., *Reinventing Planning* (London: TCPA, 1999).

Ward, C., *Cotters and Squatters* (Nottingham: Five Leaves, 2002).
  Talking Houses (London: Freedom Press, 1990).
  Talking to Architects (London: Freedom, 1996).
  When we Build Again (London: Pluto, 1985).

Wates, N., and C. Knevitt, *Community Architecture* (Harmondsworth: Penguin, 1987).

Watkin, D., *Morality and Architecture Revisited* (University of Chicago Press, 2001).

Webb, S. and B., *The King's Highway* (London: Longman, 1913).

Weizsacker, E. von, A. Lovins and L. Lovins, *Factor Four* (London: Earthscan, 1996).

Westermann, C., *Genesis 1–11* (London: SPCK, 1984).

Westfall, C., and J. van Pelt, *Architectural Principles in an Age of Historicism* (New Haven: Yale University Press, 1991).

White, L., 'The Historical Roots of our Ecological Crisis', *Science*, 155/3767 (March 1967), 1203–7.

White, M. and L., *The Intellectual versus the City: From Thomas Jefferson to Frank Lloyd Wright* (Oxford University Press, 1977).

Wielenga, B., *It's a Long Road to Freedom* (Madurai: TTS Press, 1981).
  Revelation to John: Tuning into Songs of Moses and the Lamb (New Delhi: ISPCK, 2009).

Williams, D., *Sustainable Design: Ecology, Architecture and Planning* (Hoboken: Wiley, 2007).

Williams, N. P., *The Grace of God* (London: Hodder and Stoughton, 1930).

Wilmer, H., 'Images of the City and the Shaping of Humanity', in Harvey (ed.), *Theology in the City*, pp. 32–46.

Wink, W., *Engaging the Powers* (Minneapolis: Fortress, 1992).

Winstanley, G., *The Works of Gerrard Winstanley*, ed. G. Sabine (New York: Cornell University Press, 1941).

Wittkower, R., *Architectural Principles in the Age of Humanism* (London: Tiranti, 1967).

Wolterstorff, N., *Art in Action* (Carlisle: Solway, 1997).

Wood, J., *The Origin of Building or the Plagiarism of the Heathen Detected* (Bath, 1741).

Worpole, K., 'In the Midst of Life', in Barnett and Scruton (eds.), *Town and Country*, pp. 304–16.

Wotton, H., *The Elements of Architecture* (London, 1643).

Young, I. M., *Justice and the Politics of Difference* (Princeton University Press, 1990).

Zepp, I., Jr, *The New Religious Image of Urban America: The Shopping Mall as Ceremonial Centre* (Niwot: University Press of Colorado, 1997).

Index